CW01475653

Special Edition Using XML Schema

David Gulbransen

que®

201 W. 103rd Street
Indianapolis, Indiana 46290

SPECIAL EDITION USING XML SCHEMA

Copyright © 2002 by Que

International Standard Book Number: 0-7897-2607-6

Library of Congress Catalog Card Number: 200136726072

Printed in the United States of America

First Printing: November 2001

04   03   02   01   4   3   2   1

Trademarks

Warning and Disclaimer

Associate Publisher
Dean Miller

Acquisitions Editor
Todd Green

Development Editor
Sean Dixon

Managing Editor
Thomas F. Hayes

Senior Editor
Susan Ross Moore

Production Editor
Benjamin Berg

Indexer
Sharon Shock

Proofreader
Bob LaRoche

Technical Editors
Robert Brunner
K. Ari Krupnikov

Team Coordinator
Cindy Teeters

Media Developer
Michael Hunter

Interior Designer
Ruth Harvey

Cover Designers
Dan Armstrong
Ruth Harvey

Page Layout
Rebecca Harmon

CONTENTS

ABOUT THE AUTHOR

David Gulbransen has been employed as an information systems professional for more than eight years. He began his career with the Indiana University Departmental Support Lab as an analyst/manager, overseeing a consulting group responsible for advising university departments on technology deployment. After an appointment as the computing support specialist for the School of Fine Arts, David left for a position as the manager of information systems at Dimension X, a Java tools development company. While there, he grew the information systems environment from a small Unix-based shop to a shared Unix/NT environment serving customers as diverse as Fox Television, MCA Records, Intel, and Sun Microsystems. Upon the purchase of Dimension X in 1997 by Microsoft, David co-founded Vervet Logic, a software development company developing XML and Web tools for new media development. Some of his other titles include *Creating Web Applets with Java*, *The Netscape Server Survival Guide*, *Special Edition Using Dynamic HTML*, and *The Complete Idiot's Guide to XML*. David holds a B.A. in computer science and theatre from Indiana University.

DEDICATION

To my friends and family, without whom titles such as this would simply not be possible.

ACKNOWLEDGMENTS

I'd like to thank Todd Green, Sean Dixon, Robert Brunner, Ari Krupnikov, Ben Berg, Susan Moore, and all the other fine people at Que who work so hard to make each title the best it can be! Also thanks to James Clark, Makoto Murata, Robin Cover, Rick Jelliffe, Henry S. Thompson, Simon St. Laurent, Kendall Clark Grant, Roger Costello, David Beech, Murray Maloney, Noah Mendelsohn, Paul V. Biron, Ashok Malhotra, David Fallside, Tim Bray, C.M. Sperberg-McQueen, Jean Paoli, Eve Maler, and countless others whose work in the development of XML and XML Schema has made this book and other really nifty stuff possible. Finally, I'd like to thank my family (Mary, Matt, David, and Anne) and friends (Kim, Dusty, Ken, Stef, Mikey, Kate, Aubrey, Zack, and countless others!) for putting up with my over-enthusiastic efforts to test explanations out on them, and for riding out tight deadlines. And of course, many thanks to the staff at Vervet Logic for their continued support, as well as Ken Rawlings, for coming to me one day so many years ago with this then-unknown technology called XML.

INTRODUCTION

The Extensible Markup Language is one of the most controversial technologies to come into vogue in recent years. Starting with humble roots with the desire to create a simple subset of SGML, XML burst onto the scene to a fantastic fanfare from developers and hype from the press. As more people have started to adopt XML, more features have been added to address practical implementations, and as a result, the complete families that make up XML today are far more complicated than SGML!

XML is no longer simply one Recommendation from the W3C. Instead, XML is really a collection of technologies, including XML Namespaces, XSL and XSLT, XPath, XPointer, XML Base, XML Encryption, XML Query, XML Signature... and of course, XML Schema.

The XML Schema Recommendation itself has been riddled with controversy. Political in-fighting with regard to features, backward compatibility, and complexity have led to many heated debates, and more than a few suggested alternative technologies (such as RELAX NG and Schematron).

Most users will never know the painstaking give and take that goes into the development of a set of standards such as the XML Recommendations, but they will certainly know the results, and that is the goal of this title: to familiarize you with the contents of the XML Schema Recommendation, so that you can put it to practical use in your XML development projects.

WHO SHOULD BUY THIS BOOK

This book is designed for readers who already have an understanding of well-formed XML. Web developers, application developers, database administrators, project managers, IT personnel, and other technical professionals who have an interest in expanding their XML authoring skills should also consider this title. Extensive experience working with DTDs is not required, but the reader will gain more from this title if they have an understanding of valid XML, or are at least familiar with the concept of valid XML.

Finally, some of the subject matter presented in this title relies on related subjects, such as regular expressions. Where appropriate, we have tried to provide basic information to readers on these related subjects, and point to outside resources for expanding your knowledge of those topics. The ideal reader of this book should be comfortable using the Web as a research tool, and be unafraid to consult those outside sources when necessary. This title is best utilized by an intermediate or advanced technical reader.

How This Book Is Organized

In Part I, we will take a look at the background of XML Schema and at some of the ways in which XML Schema relate to other schema mechanisms, such as DTDs. The relationship between XML Schema and DTDs is important, because support for DTDs will always be necessary on some level to support legacy applications.

In Part II, we will take a look at the basic syntax and structure of XML Schema. We'll examine XML Schema components, and get you started working with elements and attributes. By the end of Part II you will be prepared to write your own XML Schema.

With the basics of XML Schema solid, we then move on to Part III, where we will take a look at datatypes. We will examine what datatypes are and how they are used in XML. We'll also look at the primitive datatypes which are included in the XML Schema Recommendation, as well as talk about the definition and derivation of your own datatypes. And we'll round it off with another step-by-step example of using datatypes in a fully functional XML Schema.

Finally, in Part IV, we will turn our attention to some advanced XML Schema topics. We will look at project planning and development for authoring Schema, so that you know how to go about planning your own Schema development. We'll look at a case study for building a Human Resources Schema from start to finish. Finally, we'll end your Schema education by discussing some of the developments in "best practices" for XML Schema, and also take a look at some alternatives and the future direction of XML Schema.

Throughout this title, you will see an emphasis on planning, which is no accident. The key to any successful XML-based project is planning. With the right map in front of you, XML can take you anywhere. And without it, XML can be a confusing mess of twists and turns.

We hope that you will find this title as enjoyable as structured information can be, and that you will begin to think of your own innovative and creative ways to exploit the power of XML Schema in your projects. So now, let's get started with your XML Schema education.

Conventions Used in This Book

This book uses various stylistic and typographic conventions to make it easier to use:

Convention	Meaning
Italic	New terms and phrases when initially defined
`Monospace`	Parts of code, Web addresses, and filenames
`Bold Monospace`	Information that you type
➡	Indicates the continuation of a long code line from the previous line

Note

When you see a note in this book, it indicates additional information that can help you better understand a topic or avoid problems related to the subject at hand.

Tip

Tips introduce techniques applied by experienced developers to simplify a task or to produce a better design. The goal of a tip is to help you apply standard practices that lead to robust and maintainable applications.

Caution

Cautions warn you of hazardous procedures (for example, actions that have the potential to compromise the security of a system).

Cross-references are used throughout the book to help you quickly access related information in other chapters.

See "Representing and Modeling Data," **p. 231**

At the end of each chapter, you will also find an "In the Real World" section, where we discuss issues surrounding the materials presented in the chapter as they may occur in actual XML Schema authoring practice. This is where we raise issues that might not have a clear-cut, technical answer, or suggest real-world, quick-and-dirty workarounds that are not technically the best practices, but which in reality you are likely to encounter as you work with XML Schema.

XML Schema Basics

CHAPTER 1

AN OVERVIEW OF XML SCHEMA

In this chapter

THE POLITICS OF XML

XML was originally derived from another meta-language for developing structured markup, the Standard Generalized Markup Language (SGML). SGML is a powerful technology that allows users to engage in very complex descriptions of documents and data. SGML allowed the creation of customized markup languages, such as HTML, which allow users to use a common markup language for various applications, such as Web display with HTML. SGML is powerful and flexible, but it is also intimidating. Many people who could have benefited from SGML were afraid of getting lost in the complexities of the technology and so were reluctant to use it.

This gave rise to XML. XML was designed to take some of the power of SGML but make it simpler and easier to use. The goal of the original working group was "80/20", that is, to get 80% of the functionality of SGML with only 20% of the complexity. With the XML 1.0 Recommendation, it seemed that XML would achieve the 80/20 goal, but then a confusing array of related technologies entered the picture: XML Namespaces, XSL, XSLT, XPath, XPointer, XQuery, and eventually XML Schema.

XML is growing more and more complex everyday. Many XML experts lament the situation and view the current set of XML-related standards as growing chaotically out of control. One expert lamented, "As if Internet time weren't fast enough, now we seem to have XML time!" The result is that recommendations coming from the W3C are seemingly increasing in complexity, and decreasing in the time spent contemplating them.

Many of the recommendations are mired in controversy, with the XML community divided into two camps: those who want recommendations that include every possible usage of the language, and those who are still dedicated to the 80/20 philosophy. XML Schema are certainly mired in the simplicity versus comprehensiveness debate as well.

The controversy surrounding XML Schema has followed the technology around from conference to conference, and even resulted in the development of competing technologies such as RELAX (REgular LAnguage for Xml) and TREX (Tree Regular Expressions for XML). These technologies are gaining a growing following, even though they are not specifications which originate from or are even being considered by the W3C.

XML Schema are a very useful technology, but how and why you might choose to use XML Schema varies widely.

No one schema mechanism suits all applications of XML. It is virtually impossible to imagine one technology that addresses all of the potential uses for XML.

Such is the case with XML Schema. Some of you will delve into XML Schema only to find that you barely need to scratch the surface in order to accomplish your needs. Others will read this entire book only to find that Schema simply don't do everything you need. Others may find that an alternative technology, such as RELAX NG or Schematron or even the "older" Document Type Definitions (DTDs), is better at solving your particular problems.

Note

The controversy over which features to include in XML Schema and the level of complexity gave birth to several suggested alternatives, including RELAX, TREX, Schematron, and so on. Already, RELAX and TREX have been combined into RELAX NG, and as time passes there will certainly be more shakeouts in the alternative schema world. We will discuss alternatives to the XML Schema Recommendation more in Chapter 18, and in the Appendixes.

That's why this book sets out to accomplish two goals: not only to explain to you the syntax and language of XML Schema, but also to educate you about the *why* of XML Schema. It is as important, if not more important, to know when you need to use a Schema as it is to know how.

By working your way through the sections of this book, you'll get a solid understanding of what schema are, why you would want to use them, and finally, how you would write a schema in the XML Schema language.

The first step is to look at what brought the XML Schema Recommendation into being in the first place and understand why it is such a political beast.

A SCHEMA IS NOT NECESSARILY AN XML SCHEMA

Semantically, a *schema* is a diagrammatic presentation, a structured framework, or a plan. Conceptually, you can think of a schema as being a set of rules used to define the structure of data, but that's not the most accurate definition. Strictly speaking a set of rules would provide a very granular level of control that can be quite difficult to achieve.

The best way to understand what a schema is is to think of it like grammar. A schema is a set of requirements that need to be met in order for a document or set of data, which is all a document really is, to be a valid expression within the context of that grammar.

For example, take a look at the English language. A formal sentence in English needs to contain a subject and a verb. You can think of that basic constraint on a sentence (that it must contain a subject and a verb) as a schema. If you were to write that as a rule, you could say:

A formal English sentence must contain a subject and a verb.

Now, working within that structure, you can have a sentence as simple as "I am," which contains only two words—"I" being the subject, and "am" being the verb. But you will notice that our grammar rule doesn't specify that a sentence can't contain other words, such as adjectives and adverbs. So we could write "I am tired," or "I am sleeping soundly," and those would both be valid formal sentences because they still contain a subject and a verb.

Looking at this model, it's easy to see how grammar can become complex very quickly. For example, what if you wanted to specify that a sentence could have more than one subject? What if you wanted to specify the use of direct objects or indirect objects? You could quickly and easily outgrow your simple grammar.

That's what schema design is all about: designing the best grammar to describe your document or data. It is really an art more than a science, much like computer programming. And it is an area that inspires debate. There are camps that believe in the grammar model, and there are camps that believe in a rules-based model. A grammar model lends itself to more flexibility, in both design and interpretation, while a strict, rules-based system offers more precision, and might be easier to implement.

Grammars express structure while still allowing for a flexible data model. However, strict rules can have valid applications as well. When you need generic guidelines for forming sentences, a grammar works great. But what if you wanted to say that any time the subject of a sentence was "Steve" then the verb had to be "went"? That would be best accomplished with a rule. (Not "Steve drove to the store" but "Steve went to the store.") Now, if the subject were "Mary", we could still say "Mary drove to the store," because that doesn't violate the rule. The level of granularity is specific enough that a loosely formed grammar would not be as restrictive as a rules-based system would be.

These are the types of issues that surround the world of XML and the debate around XML Schema. As we delve into the world of schema, and as you begin to write your own, you will need to address these issues in order to get the most out of XML. XML Schema do provide a mechanism for defining grammars, and some mechanisms for rules as well. But if strict rules are what you are after, XML Schema might get you into some tricky situations.

How Schema Relate to Document Type Definitions

In order to take advantage of XML Schema, you should already be familiar with the basics of XML. You should know about elements and attributes, and you should be able to write your own well-formed XML documents.

You may or may not already be familiar with the concept of validation. XML documents can be validated using a Document Type Definition, or DTD. In fact, DTDs are actually a type of schema.

A DTD is not actually a separate document, even though most people use a DTD as an external subset. To the XML parser, however, the DTD is still part of the XML document, specifically the part that allows you to specify the structure of the document. Within the DTD you can define your elements, the attributes for those elements, and other facets of your XML document, such as how many times an element can occur.

Document Type Definitions are a holdover from the days of SGML. However, DTDs when used with XML are more limited than what can be accomplished using DTDs with SGML. DTDs basically provide a mechanism for specifying elements, attributes, entities, and notations. Now, that does not mean that DTDs are not useful. In fact, there are many applications of XML where DTDs are more than powerful enough.

Using DTDs as "Schema"

Take a look at a very basic XML document. The following is a very simple contact record:

```
<contact>
 <name>David Gulbransen</name>
 <phone>812-856-5270</phone>
</contact>
```

There are only three elements, with no attributes. The DTD for this document would be very simple as well:

```
<!ELEMENT contact (name, phone)>
<!ELEMENT name (#PCDATA)>
<!ELEMENT phone (#PCDATA)>
```

That's all there is to it. The element declaration defines the contact element, specifies that a contact has a name child and a phone child, and further specifies that those name and phone elements contain text. (The text is represented by the #PCDATA keyword, which stands for parsed character data.)

This is a schema. The DTD maps out the structure of the document. The order of the name and phone elements is specified in the content model of the contact element. Similarly, you can specify that each contact has one name and one phone. You could change the definition to

```
<!ELEMENT contact (name*, phone*)>
```

Now there could be any number of names and phone numbers for each contact. However, if you wanted to start building dependencies, such as requiring that each name have a minimum of 3 phone elements, but a maximum of 7, you can't really do it. That's one of the limitations of DTDs.

Another limitation of DTDs is that you cannot specify that an element or attribute must contain a specific *kind* of data. Take a look at another example. The following is a price tag XML record:

```
<tag>
 <sku>9983022</sku>
 <price>19.95</price>
 <department>Clothing</department>
</tag>
```

Here you have three elements that contain CDATA, or character data (the tag element contains the other elements). The sku is an inventory number, and will always contain exactly seven digits. The price is always a decimal, and the department is always a text location.

A DTD allows us to define those elements, but it doesn't give us any control over the type of content, or enable us to specify a datatype. In fact, we can't even require that a CDATA element hold a value. We cannot use a DTD to specify that the sku is always an integer, or that the price, being a currency value, should always have two decimal places.

SCHEMA ARE DESIGNED TO BE MORE FLEXIBLE THAN DTDS

The lack of flexibility to model complex data and relationships gave rise to the XML Schema working group.

The W3C and its members recognized that as XML becomes more pervasive, more complex schema would also become necessary.

THE EVOLUTION OF XML SCHEMA

One of the precursors to XML Schema at the W3C was a proposal called "Datatypes for DTDs." This W3C Note, published in January 2000, recognized not only the need for datatyping, which would be introduced in XML Schema, but also the need for users of XML and DTDs to transition their documents to XML Schema.

Schema have been on the agenda at the W3C for a long time. Proposals such as "Document Content Description (DCD)" and "XML Data" date as far back as 1998. These were early-stage proposals for mechanisms designed to replace the DTD. In 1999 the W3C published the Note "XML Schema Requirements." This Note outlined the direction that XML was taking, even though the 1.0 XML Recommendation was still taking hold. Schema are not new; they have been a long time coming. They are related (in theory) to the way that people use XML.

What can XML be used for? There is no set answer to that question. You can use XML for documents, such as marking up entries in an encyclopedia. XML can be used to organize data, such as parts lists in a manufacturing facility. And XML can be used for interprocess communication, such as establishing a common messaging format between two chat applications. XML is flexible, and the basic idea of XML and structured data is simple. Therein lies the expressive power of XML.

However, as you have seen in just a few simple, small examples, there are many XML applications for which a straightforward, well-formed XML document might not be sophisticated enough. As XML moves into other areas of computing and data management, the need to map XML to database applications and complex record sets means that XML grammars will need to mature.

Note   Remember that "well-formed" describes XML instance documents that conform to all of the Well-Formedness constraints in the W3C XML 1.0 Recommendation. "Valid" XML consists of well-formed XML which also meets the constraints contained in a Document Type Definition.

Just as flat-file databases have valid applications, well-formed XML has applications. But just as databases have matured from flat-files and indexes into complex object stores and relational databases, so too must XML mature.

THE NEED FOR DATATYPES IN XML

Datatypes are pervasive in computing applications. From programming languages to databases, it is often useful to assign a "type" to a chunk of data, so that you can then use that data appropriately, and transform it if necessary. For example, look at the following pieces of information:

5

3.14

John Doe

010010010001001011000101

The first, "5", is an integer. The value of Pi is a decimal. "John Doe" is a string. The last is a binary sequence. The uses for each of these types of data are almost limitless. But when working with data, you often want, and just as often *need*, to treat different types of data differently.

For example, you can multiply 5 × 5 to get a result of 25. But you can't multiply "John Doe" × "John Doe". It doesn't really make any sense to try.

However, with XML and DTDs, there is no mechanism to let applications using the XML data know that one element contains a number, and another element contains a string. In well-formed XML, and even valid XML with a DTD, all information is text. All information is treated as a string.

Obviously, the inability to specify what type of data is contained in elements creates a problem for mathematical and scientific data. But it goes beyond that. It also creates a problem for financial data. And it creates a burden for applications processing XML documents. Because no datatype is associated with XML data, the application has the added burden of trying to determine the datatype for any given content, and how that content may then be used or altered.

Let's look at another example. If we were using a DTD to define an element called <amount>, which was used for currency exchange, we might have a document which contained the following:

```
<amount>100</amount>
<amount>+100</amount>
<amount>100.00</amount>
```

With a DTD, the value for each of the <amount> elements is different, because the content is treated as three different strings. However, if we were using a schema and datatypes, we could declare the datatype for the <amount> element to be a decimal, which would mean that all three <amount> element instances would have the *same* value, only with a slightly different lexical representation. This type of application highlights one of the key differences between DTDs and schema, and shows how effective datatypes can be.

ADVANTAGES OF SCHEMA

XML Schema offer an alternative to describing an XML grammar using DTDs. They do not "replace" DTDs, nor do XML Schema necessarily make DTDs obsolete. DTDs are simple, and they are an established technology. There are times when in the interest of expedience and compatibility, it would make sense to use a DTD.

One way to look at this might be to think of DTDs as a station wagon, and XML Schema as a semi-truck. Both can haul payloads, and if you need to move something small in a hurry, a station wagon does the trick. But if you have a really large moving project, a semi might save you a lot of trouble.

From the XML Schema Requirements Note (http://www.w3.org/TR/NOTE-xml-schema-req) published by the W3C, the goals of the XML Schema Recommendation state that XML Schema should be

- "More expressive than XML DTDs"—Because of some of the limitations of DTDs, such as the lack of datatypes, one design goal was to account for some of the shortcomings of DTDs and add functionality.

- "Expressed in XML"—XML Schema were designed to be expressed using XML syntax. This aids developers in designing and implementing XML Schema–compliant applications.

- "Self-describing"—XML Schema are self-contained, and the structure of the schema also maps to the structure of the XML document it is defining.

- "Usable by a wide variety of applications that employ XML"—XML Schema were designed to be as compatible as possible with existing XML applications.

- "Straightforwardly usable on the Internet"—As with XML, XML Schema are designed with the idea that they are primarily for use in conjunction with Web applications.

- "Optimized for interoperability"—Schema are designed to work well with existing XML implementations, and include mechanisms for including and importing schema into each other.

- "Simple enough to implement with modest design and runtime resources"—XML Schema were to be designed with a straightforward implementation and avoid overly complex syntaxes and features.

- "Coordinated with relevant W3C specs (XML Information Set, Links, Namespaces, Pointers, Style and Syntax, as well as DOM, HTML, and RDF Schema)"—Because XML is really branching from the XML 1.0 Recommendation into a technology with many interrelated Recommendations, XML Schema are designed to work with these other XML-related technologies, such as XML Namespaces.

SCHEMA GO BEYOND DTDs

A Document Type Definition is a great way to express an XML grammar. However, there are some limitations to what you can achieve with a DTD. DTDs only allow limited inheritance or scoping. And DTDs don't allow for datatyping. These are features which can be very useful in XML design, and thus XML Schema are designed to include these types of functionality.

SCHEMA ARE XML

One of the biggest advantages of working with XML Schema is that XML Schema are actually XML documents themselves. Unlike DTDs, XML Schema follow the structure of a well-formed XML document.

This is a very simple XML Schema:

```
<?xml version="1.0" encoding="utf-8" ?>
<xs:schema xmlns:xs="http://www.w3.org/2000/10/XMLSchema">
<xs:element name="Name" type="xs:string"/>
</xs:schema>
```

This Schema defines an element called `"Name"` that is a string. That's all it does, which isn't very useful in itself.

However, take a closer look at the Schema. Notice that it starts with an XML declaration:

```
<?xml version="1.0" encoding="utf-8" ?>
```

This same declaration starts off any XML document. It lets an application know that the document is an XML document, that it is based on the 1.0 XML Recommendation, and that it uses the UTF-8 character encoding set. This declaration should already be familiar to you from well-formed XML documents. It is used with XML Schema because XML Schema themselves are well-formed XML documents.

This is a very important feature of XML Schema, because it allows any application that is already XML-aware to process XML Schema. Not every application might be able to completely implement the Schema's functionality, but this declaration does allow the same parser to parse both Schema and other XML documents. Unlike DTDs, which have their own complicated syntax, XML Schema are based on well-formed XML, and make extensive use of namespaces in order to define elements, attributes, datatypes, and so on.

If you look at the next line in the sample Schema, you see that it is a namespace declaration:

```
<xs:schema xmlns:xs="http://www.w3.org/2000/10/XMLSchema">
```

This defines the `xs` namespace, and points back to the XML Schema spec at the W3C. This is also important, as it provides a mechanism for scoping and versioning, which we will discuss later, in Chapter 12, "Representing and Modeling Data."

Following the namespace declaration is the meat of the Schema, the actual element declaration:

```
<xs:element name="Name" type="xs:string"/>
```

The declaration makes use of the xs namespace. It uses attributes to provide information about the element you are defining. Here you define an element called "Name". The example goes on to specify that Name is a string. The type attribute is a critical component of XML Schema, as it is what allows you to do datatyping. We'll discuss datatypes in more detail starting in Chapter 9, "Introducing Datatypes."

SCHEMA ARE FAR REACHING

Because XML Schema are written using XML, applications that already use XML can adopt Schema quickly and easily. This helps Schema meet the requirements of the Working Group that Schema be "usable by a wide variety of applications that employ XML; and straightfor-wardly usable on the Internet." Because XML is text-based, it is easily transferable via common Internet file transfer methods, such as FTP and HTTP. This means that accessing XML files, and therefore XML Schema, is as simple as e-mailing an attachment or visiting a Web page.

Schema are "optimized for interoperability" in this way because they are self-describing doc-uments. By employing XML as the language of Schema (unlike DTDs which have their own complex syntax), Schema are already optimized to work with other XML-based applications.

SCHEMA ARE SIMPLE AND POWERFUL

Whenever people talk about XML anymore, they invariably no longer mean just the "Extensible Markup Language" as defined in the XML 1.0 Recommendation, even though that is *technically* all XML is. Practically speaking, you simply *have* to use the other XML related technologies, such as Namespaces, Schema, and XSL to do *virtually any* kind of practical XML development. These technologies, such as XML (as defined in the 1.0 Recommendation), XSL, and namespaces, all work together to provide structured data solutions that have a high degree of human-readability and portability. That is one of the goals of XML.

Schema also follow that goal, and are interdependent on other XML technologies as well. You've already seen a very simple Schema and how it makes use of the XML Namespaces Recommendation. This interdependence of XML technologies on each other helps build a very robust set of solutions from what individually are very simple technologies. That is "XML" today. XML is no longer simply the 1.0 Recommendation. Today it is a collection of Recommendations, including XML Namespaces, XSL and XSLT, and XML Schema.

SCHEMA ALLOW DATA TYPING

That XML Schema are written in XML is significant, but the main reason people are look-ing to XML Schema is for datatyping.

I have already explained how datatypes are useful, so I won't belabor that point now. I cover this in much greater detail as you continue into more advanced schema authoring, such as in Chapter 13, "Example Schema: Customer Invoice."

At the same time, it is important to note that this is a feature that differentiates Schema from DTDs, and it is also one of the significant advancements in Schema.

WHY THE SCHEMA RECOMMENDATION HAS TWO PARTS

The XML Schema Recommendation itself is actually written in two parts: Structures and Datatypes. Each part covers a specific area of implementing XML Schema. The Recommendation is not easy for novices to read. By dividing the Recommendation into two parts, the first part covering structures and the second datatypes, everyone who wants to understand Schema but who has no use for datatypes can ignore the second part of the Recommendation.

THE STRUCTURE OF SCHEMA

Part One deals with the structures of Schema. This section of the Recommendation really delivers all of the functionality that you would find in Document Type Definitions, with some added improvements. For many applications of XML, Part One of the Recommendation is all you will need to create valid XML with the same functionality provided by DTDs, especially if you are currently working with DTDs and find that they are meeting 90%–95% of your needs.

DATATYPES

Part Two of the XML Schema Recommendation, which concerns itself with datatypes in XML, really goes a level beyond what is currently possible with DTDs. Part Two provides the mechanisms for a whole new level of complexity with XML.

If you have never been exposed to datatypes before, either through programming languages or databases, then this will be the more difficult of the two parts for you to learn. But even if you haven't been exposed to datatypes before, it won't take long for you to realize their power and potential.

If you have been exposed to datatypes, then this is a section of critical value, as using typed data greatly increases the ways in which you can use XML with your current data sets, be that application data (such as communications between two applications) or data extracted from databases. Datatypes bring a previously unknown sophistication to designing and implementing XML-based solutions.

OVERVIEW OF PART ONE: STRUCTURES

In the XML Schema Requirement Note, there are several stated goals for the Structures Part of the Schema Recommendation. These state that the Structures should provide

- "Mechanisms for constraining document structure (namespaces, elements, attributes) and content (datatypes, entities, notations)"—These are the same types of mechanisms provided by DTDs. They allow you to declare elements, attributes, and so on. But with Schema, these structures also allow you to define simple and complex datatypes.

- "Mechanisms to enable inheritance for element, attribute, and datatype definitions"—This refers to the ability to define characteristics for an attribute or datatype, which are then easily passed on to other declarations.

- "Mechanism for URI reference to standard semantic understanding of a construct"—This refers to including namespace constraints on various declarations.

- "Mechanism for embedded documentation"—This serves as a means of commenting, but with some extensions which might allow the automation of creating documentation.

- "Mechanism for application-specific constraints and descriptions"—Because Schema can never be all-inclusive, there needs to be a mechanism for allowing Schema (and instance document) authors to directly pass information to a processing application.

- "Mechanisms for addressing the evolution of schemata"—Once a Schema is written, it will often need to be revised at a later date. Addressing the revisions of Schema is important to their practical use.

- "Mechanisms to enable integration of structural schema with primitive data types"—Datatypes are an important new feature of XML Schema, which must be easily integrated with declarations for elements, attributes, and so on.

These are lofty goals and the subject of much political debate in the standards adoption process. However, the Schema Working Group has operated with these goals in mind. So let's take a closer look at what these goals mean in practical terms.

CONSTRAINING DOCUMENT STRUCTURE AND CONTENT

What makes a schema (in the generic sense) most useful is the ability to restrict how data is stored in a document. For example, in the contact example, you want to make sure that your contacts have a name and a phone number. You could just use a well-formed XML document and tell whoever is writing the documents that they *must* include both a name and a phone number for each contact record. If you're lucky, they will. But with multiple people entering data, the possibility of the introduction of errors is real. However, we could use a schema (such as a DTD or XML Schema) to enforce our wishes.

This is what "constraining document structure and content" refers to: establishing a set of guidelines or rules that a document must adhere to in order to be considered a valid document. That is the difference between well-formed and valid XML, and providing a mechanism for specifying those constraints is one of the goals of XML Schema.

ENABLING INHERITANCE

Anyone who has worked with large sets of data knows that most information is repeated. For example, think about when you order something from an online store. You need to enter a billing address and a shipping address, and more often than not, those addresses are the same.

The same thing holds true when you are developing a structured document; often there are constraints or features that you want to apply not only to one element, but also to any other similar elements.

Allowing the properties of one element (or other features as well) to be passed along to other elements is called inheritance. Just like two blue-eyed parents will likely pass along blue eyes to their children, XML Schema provide a mechanism for passing along traits from one element to another inside the Schema.

So, you might have a datatype called address which defines that an address has street information, city, state, and a ZIP code. Now you could create both billing address and shipping address elements, based on the generic address type, and they would inherit the properties of that type.

URI REFERENCES TO SEMANTIC UNDERSTANDING OF A CONSTRUCT

What's in a name? In the world of structured data, quite a lot! For example, what if you have three different organizations, all using an element they call Name—however, Organization #1 uses the format "First_Name Last_Name", Organization #2 uses the format "Last_Name, First_Name", and Organization #3 uses "First_Name Middle_Initial Last_Name"? Here are three completely valid, yet completely different formats for specifying a person's name. If the goal of XML is to allow the exchange of data, that goal cannot be achieved unless you can agree on common formats.

The answer to this problem lies in URI references to constructs. To put it more simply, you point to a standard definition somewhere on the Internet. So, if you are constructing a document and using a definition for a Name element, you can make that definition freely available, via a URI (such as a Web site address), and that way anyone exchanging data with your organization can also access that definition for their records. This keeps everyone using the same definitions for their data, so you can stay on track when you are processing that data in your applications.

EMBEDDING DOCUMENTATION

One of the most frustrating things that can happen for developers is to be staring at a piece of code someone else has written, and to be unable to figure out *why* someone performed a task in a certain way. You have no idea why they chose a certain API or method for the program, and changing it might have dramatic effects down the line.

The only thing more frustrating is to look at something *you* have written, only to have forgotten why you did something a certain way! This happens more than you might suspect in the development world. As people are shuffled from project to project, your mind archives non-essential knowledge, and sometimes accessing that information proves difficult.

That is why the ability to document your code is so essential, and the same holds true for Schema. Annotations to the Schema can be critical for communicating your schema design to other users, and maybe even yourself someday.

In order to provide a level of documentation which goes beyond that of ordinary comments, XML Schema provide a special mechanism called annotations which allows for more robust commenting than standard XML comments. We'll talk more about annotations and their uses in Chapter 12.

APPLICATION-SPECIFIC CONSTRAINTS AND DESCRIPTIONS

The idea of generic schema that are readable by all applications that process XML is a noble goal. However, as anyone who has developed any systems knows, there are often proprietary or internal requirements for systems, or added functionality that is critical for an application internally but of little use to other users.

Just as XML provides mechanisms for passing along information to applications in the form of notations and processing instructions, so too do XML Schema provide such mechanisms. That is part of the key to the extensibility that makes the XML family such a robust set of technologies.

ADDRESSING THE EVOLUTION OF SCHEMATA

The document that never evolves is a rare document. Even the Constitution of the United States is a living document which can be amended. In the world of corporations, user data, and Internet Time, document content can change at a frightening speed, and with those changes come changes in structure. So Schema are not something you design once and then never revisit. They are evolving documents, and changes are often necessitated by changes in the marketplace and changes in your data.

So what happens when you need to change a Schema? You need to have some mechanism for keeping your data intact, and you need some way of tracking the version of your Schema. Keeping track of evolving Schema is one component of this requirement.

Another component of this requirement is building in the mechanisms to allow Schema to grow and become more complex as your data needs become more complex. This issue is addressed though the flexibility of Schema: their recursive nature, the ability to inherit properties, and the ability to derive new datatypes from primitive atomic datatypes (which are the basic datatypes already built in to the Schema Recommendation).

INTEGRATING STRUCTURAL SCHEMA WITH PRIMITIVE DATATYPES

The final stated goal of the Structures portion of the Recommendation is to integrate structural schema with datatypes. This is an important goal, because you will recall that previous structural schema (namely DTDs) do not incorporate datatypes at all. Schema need to have some way to integrate the new datatype components, while still maintaining the structural goals that are taken from legacy schema.

Fortunately, the XML Schema Recommendation does this quite well, and integrating primitive datatypes into your Schema is not a difficult task. We address the issues of datatypes more completely in Part III: "XML Schema Datatypes." In Chapter 10, "Primitive Datatypes," we will look closely at the primitive datatypes, and in Chapter 11, "Derived Datatypes," we will take a look at derived datatypes.

OVERVIEW OF PART TWO: DATATYPES

Part Two of the XML Schema Recommendation addresses datatypes. Datatyping is defining the type of data that is contained in an XML element, attribute, and so on. You've already seen (in the extremely simple example earlier in the chapter) how datatypes can be useful, and if you are working with XML in an application context, chances are you've already encountered a situation where the investment in datatypes and schema would pay off for your project.

Datatypes provide us with information about the data we are storing and manipulating. Because XML is a technology that is designed to work with programming languages and with databases, providing information about the type of data can greatly aid development. That's why we need datatypes in XML.

The following are the stated design goals for datatypes and XML Schema:

- "Provide for primitive data typing, including byte, date, integer, sequence, SQL, and Java primitive data types."
- "Define a type system that is adequate for importing to and exporting from database systems (for example, relational, object, and OLAP systems)."
- "Distinguish requirements relating to lexical data representation versus those governing an underlying information set."
- "Allow creation of user-defined datatypes, such as datatypes derived from existing datatypes, that might constrain certain of its properties (for example, range, precision, length, and mask)."

Now, there are fewer goals for datatypes and Schema than there were for structures, but it's also easy to see that these goals are a little more complicated as well!

PROVIDE FOR PRIMITIVE DATATYPING

Imagine that we were builders, and we were constructing a building out of stone, bricks, and so on. While our type of material might be a "block", you could break those blocks up into some categories. For example, one type of building blocks would be `bricks` and another type might be `cinder block`. Those basic forms are *primitive* types. That is, they are the most basic type of blocks you can get, and still have them be "blocks". That is what a primitive datatype is: the most basic form of a datatype.

Using those types (`brick` or `cinder block`) you could then construct new formations, such as `wall` or `chimney`. A `wall` isn't a primitive type, because you could actually build a `wall` using one type of the primitive datatypes you have already defined.

Each of the blocks works as a basic form, which can then be used as the foundation for new forms. The same holds true for primitive datatypes: They each work as a basic form—for example, a string—which might be part of a larger form, such as an address. Primitive types include things like `strings` or `Date` or `binary`. These are types that are defined at a very basic level within the XML Schema Recommendation.

The reason that these primitive types are defined is to ensure that everyone is using the same basic building blocks to build their own, more complex structures. Primitive datatypes are built in to the XML Schema Recommendation, as defined by the Recommendation's authors. That helps ensure compatibility with other XML applications. And that means that when you or anyone else uses the primitive datatypes as the basis for new types, everyone is starting on the same page.

Additionally, datatypes are nothing new. They have been around in programming languages and databases for a very long time. Therefore, there are some primitive datatypes (such as `Boolean`, `string`, and so on) which are widely accepted as primitive types. Including them in the XML Schema Recommendation so that users can use them in conjunction with other applications makes good sense, and they serve as the building blocks for more complex derived datatypes as well.

DEFINE A TYPE SYSTEM THAT IS ADEQUATE FOR IMPORT/EXPORT

Because datatypes are not new, it is important that XML Schema have some level of interoperability with existing technologies. Providing mechanisms for importing and exporting data is important as XML moves into more complex data applications.

Databases are commonplace in modern technology, and it is important to keep that in mind when working with XML technology. The best XML solution isn't worth much if it is incompatible with your current data delivery and storage mechanisms.

LEXICAL DATA REPRESENTATION VERSUS THE UNDERLYING INFORMATION SET

XML Schema provide a means of separating the lexical meaning from the grammatical meaning of the information in an XML instance document.

For example, take the word "sing." You can say "The birds sing," "I heard him sing," or "We are going to sing the National Anthem." In all of these sentences, the lexical meaning of the base word "sing" does not change. They all refer to a musical sound being made by the vocal system. However, in each of these sentences, the grammatical meaning of "to sing" changes. It can mean "currently singing," "previously having sung a song," or "going to sing in the future." That is the grammatical meaning.

Lexical representations are important in XML Schema, particularly when it comes to representing data. For example, the number "one hundred" can either be represented as 100 or 1.0E2. Both are valid lexical representations of the number, but depending on the datatype you are using, there is a correct and incorrect way to represent that data.

As you can see, this leads to a great deal of complexity when it comes to representing your own data and abstracting the data's representation in the Schema. That's why a lot of thought and effort has gone into the design of XML Schema and datatypes, and why there is no way to please everyone when making such difficult choices.

ALLOW CREATION OF USER-DEFINED DATATYPES

As was mentioned earlier in this chapter, the primitive datatypes are often enough to perform necessary tasks. However, you might have the need to develop a more complex datatype which is specific to your application.

For that, it is important that XML Schema provide a mechanism that allows you to use those primitive datatypes as a base and create your own datatypes. And the Schema delivers: It is possible to create your own user-derived datatypes using XML Schema.

For example, you could use the primitive datatype of `decimal` as the basis for a new datatype called `currency` in which you limit the decimal places to 2, so that your currency values would always be written as 1.00, or 2.99, and so forth.

DATATYPES IN PART TWO

The datatypes supported in Part Two of the XML Schema Recommendation consist of a number of built-in datatypes that will allow users to incorporate datatypes into their Schema right away. Some of these datatypes include `string`, `boolean`, `float`, `double`, `decimal`, `timeDuration`, `ID`, `IDREF`, and `ENTITY`. These are the basic datatypes that can then be used to build other datatypes.

There are also a number of derived datatypes included in the Recommendation. These derived datatypes are built on top of the primitive datatypes, but are felt to be common enough that they were included in the Recommendation. These include `CDATA`, `token`, `IDREFS`, `ENTITIES`, `Name`, `NOTATION`, `integer`, `time`, `date`, `month`, and `year`.

The Recommendation also sets out how to define the user-derived datatypes we mentioned earlier.

CONCLUSION

From the inception of XML at the W3C, there has always been the goal of finding a better way to represent XML grammars. The natural choice for the first incarnation of XML was the Document Type Definition. It was a logical choice, given that XML was based on SGML. And DTDs have served XML well, and will continue to do so in the future.

However, beginning with proposals such as Document Content Descriptions (DCDs), XML Data, and Datatypes for DTDs, there has been steady progress toward defining a better schema mechanism for XML.

Now, with the two-part XML Schema Recommendation, that method is here. With Part One: Structures embracing and extending the features of DTDs, and with Part Two: Datatypes taking XML Schema to the next level, the Recommendation offers a great deal of flexibility for XML. The Recommendation has not come easily. The data requirements of users vary incredibly, and the adoption of a standard has been surrounded by political fighting.

Now that you have an overview of what lies ahead, it's time to get started with an actual XML Schema. So read on as we look at the structure of an XML Schema and how it is constructed.

IN THE REAL WORLD

You are likely to encounter more than one type of grammar when dealing with complicated projects. Although many in the trade press might have you believe that XML Schema will totally replace DTDs, the truth is that DTDs are here to stay. Many organizations have a long-term investment in DTDs, as holdovers from the days of SGML and the early days of XML. And because XML Schema are a relatively new technology, the software to support Schema is not readily available yet. For many projects, utilizing Schema isn't even an option.

However, this doesn't mean that XML Schema are useless. On the contrary, many XML authors are confused by the syntax of DTDs, and XML Schema are easier for humans to read. Along those lines, XML Schema also offer more flexibility than DTDs, and the Recommendation was created specifically to deal with the shortcomings of DTDs.

The most common feature of Schema you are likely to see exploited immediately is the capability to specify datatypes for elements and attributes. This functionality greatly enhances the ability of database vendors to make their databases more XML-friendly. Given the importance that databases play in nearly any kind of Information Systems project, that is probably the single best motivating factor for learning to use XML Schema.

CHAPTER 2

SCHEMA STRUCTURE

In this chapter

SCHEMA ARE XML

The most obvious difference between a Document Type Definition and an XML Schema is the syntax. A quick look at even the most basic schema reveals some interesting features:

```
<?xml version="1.0" encoding="UTF-8" ?>
<schema xmlns="http://www.w3.org/2001/XMLSchema">
        <element name="myElement" type="string"/>
</schema>
```

The first thing you may notice is that the Schema starts with an XML declaration. That's because a Schema is an XML document. XML Schema must be well-formed XML.

The second thing you will notice is that the Schema contains a namespace declaration, used to specify the namespace for the elements in our XML Schema. This is particularly important, because we are not simply using arbitrary elements and attributes inside the Schema: We are using the elements and attributes defined by the W3C. So namespaces play a critical role in XML Schema. We'll discuss namespaces more later.

> **Note**
>
> Because the use of namespace prefixes such as "xs" within an XML Schema tends to decrease reability, we will leave the prefixes off of the individual code snippets we show throughout the chapters. Keep in mind that this is okay, because in an actual Schema, we can set the default namespace and write that way as well. We will discuss using namespaces in more detail later, but for now, we will concentrate on learning the XML Schema syntax without the burden of namespace prefixes.

UNLIKE DTDS, SCHEMA USE AN XML SYNTAX FOR DEFINITIONS

If you have worked with Document Type Definitions before, then you might have expected to see something like this in an XML Schema:

```
<!ELEMENT title (#PCDATA)>
```

That is the syntax used in DTDs for element declarations. !ELEMENT represents an element declaration, followed by the name of the element (in this case, title), and then finally the content model for the element is specified in the parentheses (#PCDATA).

The content model in this element declaration is very straightforward; it is simply parsed character data, or PCDATA. Essentially, the content of the title element will simply be a text string.

> **Note**
>
> PCDATA sections are strings of text; however, this should not be confused with the string datatype, which is discussed later. Also, keep in mind that PCDATA means "Parsed Character Data"; a PCDATA section may not include symbols such as < or >, which might be mistaken for markup tags.

But in the XML Schema, our `title` element is declared with the following:

```
<element name="title" type="string"/>
```

Here, the element declaration is an element itself. We have an element called `element` which has a couple attributes that are used to define the characteristics of the new element that we are creating.

So, we can establish the name of our new element using the `name` attribute, and we can establish what type of element it is by using the `type` attribute.

The `type` attribute is something that is actually new to XML Schema. In our DTD element declaration, you will recall that we had no type for the element, rather we defined a content model, that is, we defined a model for the type of content, either text or other elements, contained in the parent element. It is possible to define content models for elements in XML Schema; however, XML Schema also have two different content models, `simpleType` and `complexType`. Because our `title` element is going to contain only text, it is a `simpleType` element, and we don't have to worry about the content model. Instead, we can use the `string` datatype to specify that our `title` element is going to hold a value in the form of a text string.

The important feature to note here isn't the content model options (we discuss those in great detail in later chapters). Rather, it is important to note that we are defining XML elements and attributes *using* XML elements and attributes. XML Schema are highly recursive in nature; they use XML to define XML.

SCHEMA CAN BE PROCESSED BY XML-AWARE APPLICATIONS

The advantage of using XML to define XML Schema is that it makes them more accessible to applications that are currently using XML parsers. Although you would need to extend the application to apply validation via an XML Schema, the Schema itself can still be easily read by any XML-enabled application.

Give it a try! You should be able to load the simple Schema shown earlier in this chapter in any application that supports XML, such as Internet Explorer.

THE <schema> ELEMENT

After the XML declaration, the root element of the document is the <schema> element. This is the root element that serves as the parent for all the other element declarations, attribute declarations, and so on inside your XML Schema.

Note

You should always use the <schema> element as the root element in your XML Schema documents, for the sake of good style, even though there is technically no requirement to do so in the XML Schema Recommendation.

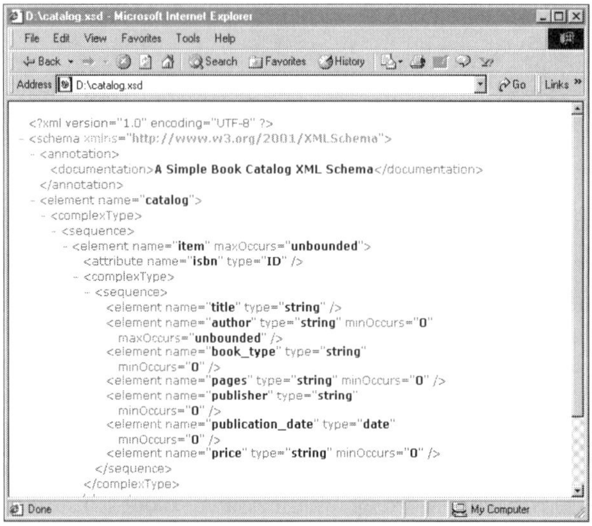

Figure 2.1
An XML Schema
displayed in Internet
Explorer.

The `<schema>` element itself has several attributes that can be used in conjunction with the element to specify information about the Schema. The meaning of these attributes will become more clear after you understand how namespaces work. (Namespaces are discussed in detail in the following section.) These attributes include

■ `attributeFormDefault`

This attribute allows you to specify a default value for the attribute form in the Schema using an attribute declaration. You can specify if the form should be qualified or unqualified by default. The qualified form of an attribute refers to the namespace status of the attribute, whether it is a namespace qualified attribute (meaning that it belongs to a specific namespace with the namespace prefix) or namespace unqualified. The default value for `attributeFormDefault` is unqualified.

■ `blockDefault`

The `blockDefault` attribute allows you to specify a default value for the `block` attribute which may be used with element or attribute declarations. The `block` attribute may have a value of `#all`, `substitution`, `extension`, `restriction`, `list`, or `union`. These values are used in conjunction with defining derived datatypes, which we will cover later in Part III, "XML Schema Datatypes," dealing with datatypes.

■ `finalDefault`

The `finalDefault` attribute allows you to specify a default value for the `final` attribute which may be used with element or attribute declarations. The `final` attribute may have a value of `#all`, `extension`, or `restriction`. These values are used in conjunction with defining derived datatypes, which we will cover in later sections of this text.

■ `elementFormDefault`

This attribute allows you to specify a default value for the element `form` in the schema with an element declaration. You can specify if `form` should be qualified or unqualified by default.

The qualified form refers to the namespace status of the element, if it is a namespace qualified element or unqualified. The default value for `elementFormDefault` is unqualified.

- `id`

  The `id` attribute is defined by the XML Schema Recommendation to be a special datatype of "ID". This attribute is simply provided as a convenience for users of Schema to be able to set an ID for their own Schema.

- `targetNamespace`

  The `targetNamespace` attribute allows you to specify a target namespace, or the namespace which is associated with the element and attribute declarations in your Schema. There is no value for this by default, and you can also use a null string as the value.

- `version`

  The `version` attribute, like the `id` attribute, is not semantically defined in the Schema Recommendation. It's a convenient method for keeping track of the version number on Schema you create, but nothing more.

- `xml:lang`

  This attribute is actually in the XML namespace, and corresponds to the language code for the document. For example, `"en"` for English, and `"en-GB"` for British English.

There is another attribute which can be used with the `<schema>` element that is far more common than any of those mentioned previously. It will be very rare that you see a Schema without it. In fact, best practices dictate that you should always use it: `xmlns`. This is the attribute you use to define the namespace of the Schema. Namespaces play a vital role in schema and their usage, so let's take a look at how Schema and namespaces interact.

USING NAMESPACES IN SCHEMA

Namespaces play a critical role with XML Schema, so it is important to understand how namespaces are used, and why they are valuable.

An XML namespace according to the W3C "Namespaces in XML" Recommendation is a "collection of names, identified by a URI reference, which are used in XML documents as element types and attribute names." What does that mean, practically speaking? Well, let's look at an example.

> **Note**
>
> If you are already familiar with namespaces, and have used them before or seen them used before, then this section will serve as a refresher for XML namespaces. However, if you are not at all familiar with namespaces, it would be a good idea to take a look at the XML Namespaces Recommendation located at `http://www.w3.org/TR/1999/REC-xml-names-19990114/` right now. Otherwise, you are in for a major headache. This chapter describes how namespaces work in some detail, but you should be familiar first with how the Recommendation defines namespaces.

The author and publisher of this book are based in the United States, where we happen to record dates "Month Day Year"—for example, "May 10 2002". However, in many locations around the world, the convention for dates is "Day Month Year" or "10 May 2002".

When we are writing the dates out in a long form, that isn't much of a problem. However, what happens when we use a shorthand, such as "5/10/02"? In the U.S. that is clearly May 10, 2002. But elsewhere in the world it could easily be read as October 5, 2002. So what happens if we define a date element in XML? How do we keep track of which format is used? How do we let others know which format we have chosen for our documents? One way is through namespaces.

BRIEF OVERVIEW OF NAMESPACES

You can put an identifier on your documents which uniquely identifies elements as belonging to a specific namespace. This is very useful for keeping tags that belong in one set of information distinct, and yet still using another set of tags which might have identical names. Let's take a look:

```
<?xml version="1.0" encoding="UTF-8" ?>
<card xmlns="http://www.myserver.com/myNamespace">
<title>Mr.</title>
<name>David Gulbransen</name>
</card>
```

This example uses the xmlns attribute to define a namespace for the card element. Any of the child elements contained in the card element will be a part of the same namespace, until another namespace is defined with another xmlns attribute. You can also define a prefix to be used to specify qualified names, which means that they use the prefix to identify them as part of that namespace:

```
<?xml version="1.0" encoding="UTF-8" ?>
<mySpace:card xmlns:mySpace="http://www.myserver.com/myNamespace">
<mySpace:title>Mr.</mySpace:title>
<mySpace:name>David Gulbransen</mySpace:name>
</mySpace:card>
```

This example defines the same namespace as the previous example, but it associates the prefix mySpace with it. That means in order to specify that an element is part of that namespace, you need to add the prefix to the element, in the form <mySpace:tagname>, creating a qualified name.

Using the prefixes can be very useful for mixing namespaces within a document. For example, if we wanted to use standard HTML tags within an XML document, we could use a namespace:

```
<?xml version="1.0" encoding="UTF-8" ?>
<mySpace:card xmlns:mySpace="http://www.myserver.com/myNamespace">
<html:html xmlns:html="http://www.w3.org/TR/REC-html40">
<html:b>
<mySpace:title>Mr.</mySpace:title>
<mySpace:name>David Gulbransen</mySpace:name>
```

```
</html:b>
</html:html>
</mySpace:card>
```

In this example, we've used both our defined namespace and the HTML namespace. As you can see, mixing namespaces adds a little clutter to the code; however, it is also a very convenient way to use tags from different namespaces in the same document. That's a small part of what makes XML so extensible.

PART

I

CH

2

What's in a Name? Nothing.

There is currently some debate about what the URI used with the `xmlns` attribute should mean. Should that URI point to a resource descriptor of some sort? Many people assume that because the URI often takes the form of a URL, the URI should actually resolve to some location on the Web which contains a Schema or some other type of description related to the namespace.

However, the W3C had no such goal in mind when it published the Namespaces recommendation. The URI doesn't have to point to anything at all. It simply functions as a unique identifier and as a way of grouping the "names" in a namespace together. That leaves many people a little confused, because it *appears* as though a namespace URI should be a valid URL.

Many people thought that the issue would be addressed by the XML Packaging Working Group, which was supposed to be working on methods for packaging all the various XML-related technologies that are being developed. However, the W3C has disbanded the Packaging Working Group, and it is no more. Practically speaking, that means when you see a namespace attribute, such as `xmlns="http://www.myserver.com/myNamespace"`, you should not assume that *anything* resides at that server address.

HOW NAMESPACES ARE USED TO DEFINE ASPECTS OF SCHEMA

When XML Schema are read by an XML processor, there needs to be a mechanism that lets the processor know that the tags that make up the Schema are part of the XML Schema Recommendation, and therefore not part of the document itself. The mechanism for defining which specific tags belong to which set of information is XML namespaces, and namespaces play a very important role in the authoring of XML Schema.

Namespaces are the mechanism designed to help define a unique identifier for markup tags. That is why Schema use the Namespaces recommendation to define a Schema namespace:

```
<schema xmlns="http://www.w3.org/2001/XMLSchema">
```

As we saw in the earlier example, every XML Schema should include a namespace declaration such as this one. Keep in mind that Schema are still new. You might see variations of this namespace in different documents, depending on whether those schema were written based on a working draft, the release candidate, or the final Schema Recommendation.

Using the namespace in a schema can be done in one of two ways. The first is by simply declaring a default namespace (the namespace which elements and attributes are assumed to be members of) for the entire document, as we did previously:

```
<?xml version="1.0" encoding="UTF-8" ?>
<schema xmlns="http://www.w3.org/2001/XMLSchema">
        <element name="myElement" type="string"/>
</schema>
```

This does the trick: There is a namespace associated with the Schema so that our Schema elements are properly attributed to the XML Schema namespace. However, every Schema really makes use of two namespaces, the XML Schema namespace and the targetNamespace for the elements the Schema is describing.

In the preceding example, we have used only one namespace, the XML Schema namespace. There is no namespace associated with elements we are going to use the Schema to define. This will actually work fine for simple Schema and simple XML documents, if you are not concerned with your XML documents having a separate namespace for the elements you are describing with the Schema. However, in practice, because you are defining elements that will be used in a particular namespace, you should use the targetNamespace attribute:

```
<?xml version="1.0" encoding="UTF-8" ?>
<schema xmlns="http://www.w3.org/2001/XMLSchema"
        targetNamespace="http://www.myserver.com/MyNamespace">
<element name="myElement" type="string"/>
</schema>
```

Now we have defined the default namespace for the document to be the XML Schema namespace, but we have also provided a targetNamespace, which is the namespace that contains the elements/attributes we will describe with our Schema.

For example, it might be a good idea to use a prefix with the namespace for Schema, which would allow you to use other schema alternatives for validation, and helps if you are importing other Schema to combine the two Schema into one information set. If we apply the namespace conventions to the Schema, using a prefix, that gives us something like this:

```
<?xml version="1.0" encoding="UTF-8" ?>
<xs:schema xmlns:xs="http://www.w3.org/2001/XMLSchema">
<xs:element name="myElement" type="string"/>
</xs:schema>
```

The only real difference between the two Schema examples in this section is that one uses the xs prefix to denote that elements are members of the Schema namespace, while the other declares a default namespace for the entire document. Either way is correct, and each way has some benefits. Declaring a default namespace certainly makes the document easier to read, and saves some typing. But using the xs prefix allows us to build some complex Schema by importing and using other Schema, as we will see in later examples.

Note

You may see both xsd and xs used as a namespace prefix in XML Schema. Both will work just fine, as long as you are consistent within the document. However, because the XML Schema Recommendation uses xs, that is the convention we will follow in this text.

It is also possible to import or include a Schema inside another Schema. However, when doing that, it is easy to run into conflicts between various declarations. That is why using namespaces can be important.

Let's look at an example. Let's say we are going to write a Schema to describe a corporate memo. We want the elements we define to be a part of our company namespace: `http://www.mycompany.com/memo/`.

We'll make this Schema very simple. The memo document will have four elements: `to`, `from`, `date`, and `memo_text`. So the first thing we do is declare the XML document:

```
<?xml version="1.0" encoding="UTF-8" ?>
```

Next, we can add the root `<schema>` element and the namespace attributes:

```
<xs:schema xmlns:xs="http://www.w3.org/2001/XMLSchema"
        targetNamespace="http://www.mycompany.com/memo/"
        xmlns="http://www.mycompany.com/memo/">
```

We have defined both a `targetNamespace` and the default namespace (by using the `xmlns` attribute with no qualifying prefix) as our company `memo` namespace. That means we can go ahead and declare our elements in the Schema as follows:

```
 <xs:element name="memo">
  <xs:complexType>
   <xs:sequence>
      <xs:element name="to" type="xs:string"/>
      <xs:element name="from" type="xs:string"/>
      <xs:element name="date" type="xs:string"/>
      <xs:element name="memo_text" type="xs:string"/>
   </xs:sequence>
  </xs:complexType>
  </xs:element>
</xs:schema>
```

Now, you will notice that all of the markup related to the Schema uses the `xs` prefix. However, we don't need to use the prefix with the element names defined with the `name` attribute, because those are by default in our `memo` namespace. But you should note that all of the type attributes do have the `xs` prefix because those values belong to the XML Schema namespace. The final code for this Schema is shown in Listing 2.1.

LISTING 2.1 A SIMPLE XML SCHEMA THAT MAKES USE OF THE XML SCHEMA NAMESPACE AND THE `targetNamespace` ATTRIBUTE

```
<?xml version="1.0" encoding="UTF-8" ?>
<xs:schema xmlns:xs="http://www.w3.org/2001/XMLSchema"
targetNamespace="http://www.mycompany.com/memo/"
xmlns="http://www.mycompany.com/memo/">
 <xs:element name="memo">
  <xs:complexType>
   <xs:sequence>
      <xs:element name="to" type="xs:string"/>
      <xs:element name="from" type="xs:string"/>
```

LISTING 2.1   CONTINUED

```
            <xs:element name="date" type="xs:string"/>
            <xs:element name="memo_text" type="xs:string"/>
     </xs:sequence>
    </xs:complexType>
    </xs:element>
</xs:schema>
```

That covers the basics of using namespaces with Schema. We will cover more advanced uses of namespaces in conjunction with Schema in later chapters.

XSI

Another very important way in which namespaces are used in conjunction with XML Schema is through the XML Instance namespace.

There are a number of elements described by the XML Schema: Structures recommendation which are designed to link with a Schema to a specific XML instance document. Those elements have actually been given their own namespace:

```
http://www.w3.org/2001/XMLSchema-instance
```

The XML Instance namespace is a very important one, even though it does not contain many elements. It is so important because it is how you associate an XML Schema with a document.

Let's take a look at a very simple Schema and an XML document. This will simply be a document for storing a person's name and telephone number. Our schema might look something like the one shown in Listing 2.2.

> **Note**
>
> There is no right or wrong way to write a Schema. I could ask five authors to write a sentence about a man walking a dog, and I would get five sentences, each structured differently. It is the same with code; I could give an instance example to five schema authors and get five different-looking Schema in return. There can be several "right" Schema for any given instance.

LISTING 2.2   A VERY SIMPLE XML SCHEMA FOR CONTACT INFORMATION

```
<?xml version="1.0" encoding="UTF-8" ?>
<xs:schema xmlns:xs="http://www.w3.org/2001/XMLSchema">

  <xs:element name="contact">
   <xs:complexType>
    <xs:sequence>
        <xs:element name="name" type="string"/>
        <xs:element name="phone" type="string"/>
     </xs:sequence>
    </xs:complexType>
   </xs:element>
</xs:schema>
```

This Schema would define a document with a `contact` root element, which would contain two child elements, `name` and `phone`, each of which may contain a string. A valid XML document for this Schema might look something like this:

```
<?xml version="1.0" encoding="UTF-8" ?>
<contact>
<name>David Gulbransen</name>
<phone>812-555-1212</phone>
</contact>
```

But how do we know that this is a valid XML document? How does an application parsing this document know that we have even defined a Schema for the document, let alone know where that Schema is? If we were using a DTD with the document, we would use the DOC-TYPE declaration to point a parser to the DTD file that described this document. But since we are using an XML Schema, we will use an XML instance element.

PART

I

CH

2

Note

> The XML Instance namespace is commonly associated with the `xsi` prefix. Because it is a namespace, you could actually use any prefix you wanted to, so long as you were consistent, and as long as it didn't clash with another namespace prefix. However, because the XML Schema Recommendation uses the `xsi` convention, it probably is a good idea to stick to that unless you have a compelling reason not to.

There are four attributes defined in the XML Schema: Structures Recommendation for the XML Instance namespace which are particularly important to using Schema with your XML documents:

- `xsi:type`
- `xsi:nil`
- `xsi:schemaLocation`
- `xsi:noNamespaceSchemaLocation`

In order to use any of these attribute types with your XML documents, you must first define the `xsi` namespace, using the following:

```
xmlns:xsi="http://www.w3.org/2001/XMLSchema-instance"
```

Once that has been defined, you may use the XML instance attributes in the following manner:

- `xsi:type`

  The XML instance `type` attribute is a way for you to explicitly assert a type for the instance of a particular element. For example, let's say that your Schema had an element called `phone` for storing a phone number. You might also have defined several derived datatypes for the phone element, such as `USPhone`, `UKPhone`, and so on, to allow for international phone number formats. If you then use the `<phone>` element in your document, you could use the `xsi:type` attribute to assert a specific type, for example `<phone xsi:type="USPhone">`.

- `xsi:nil`

  The XML instance `nil` attribute is used to denote that an element may still be considered valid with empty content, even if the element is supposed to have content (be it a string or other child elements) according to the Schema. Valid values for the attribute are `true` and `false`. If you have an element which is supposed to have content but does not for some reason, such as an item that normally has an SKU number but is temporarily out of stock, you can set `xsi:nil` equal to `true` and then the element could be empty even though it is normally supposed to contain a value. Another example of empty content would be a form on the World Wide Web, in which a user failed to enter all of the fields. For example, a user without a fax might leave the fax number field blank, even though one was required.

Note

One of the primary reasons the `nil` attribute was added was to aid the implementation of XML with database applications. It allows vendors to model SQL NULL as a specific representation of empty content, which is not the same as an empty string.

- `xsi:schemaLocation`

  The XML instance `schemaLocation` attribute is used to specify the location of an XML Schema associated with an XML document. The attribute value is a pair of URIs, the first of which is the `targetNamespace` for the XML Schema, and the second is the URI that points to the location of the Schema.

- `xsi:noNamespaceSchemaLocation`

  The XML instance `noNamespaceSchemaLocation` attribute is very similar to the `schemaLocation` attribute, in that it allows you to specify the location of a Schema for use with your document. However, since a Schema is not required to have a `targetNamespace`, this attribute can be used for Schema that do not have a namespace.

That covers the XML instance attributes that you will use with your XML Schema. Let's take a look at using the XML instance attributes to link an XML Schema to an XML document.

Say that we save the XML Schema in Listing 2.2 out to a file called `contact.xsd` on a server, located at `www.mycompany.com`. If we then wanted to create a document based on that Schema, it would look something like this:

```
<?xml version="1.0" encoding="UTF-8" ?>
<contact xmlns="http://www.mycompany.com/contact"
         xmlns:xsi="http://www.w3.org/2001/XMLSchema-instance"
         xsi:schemaLocation="http://www.mycompany.com/contact
                             http://www.mycompany.com/contact.xsd">
<name>David Gulbransen</name>
<phone>812-555-1212</phone>
</contact>
```

The key to using the Schema lies in the attributes we have used with the `<contact>` element. The first attribute

```
xmlns="http://www.mycompany.com/contact"
```

is used to declare the namespace for the document. That will usually be the same as the `targetNamespace` of the Schema, but isn't necessarily, for example, if you have a document using multiple namespaces. Next, we have the `xsi` namespace:

```
xmlns:xsi="http://www.w3.org/2001/XMLSchema-instance"
```

This defines the `xsi` prefix for use with the XML Instance namespace, which will allow us to use those attributes associated with the namespace. Finally, we have

```
xsi:schemaLocation="http://www.mycompany.com/contact
                    http://www.mycompany.com/contact.xsd">
```

The `xsi:schemaLocation` attribute here has two values. The first value is the default or `targetNamespace` of the XML Schema we are pointing to. The second value is the actual location of the `.xsd` file which defines the Schema. This will let any XML Parser processing the document know

- The `targetNamespace` of the document and the Schema
- The location of the Schema on a server

COMPARING A DTD AND AN XML SCHEMA

So now that you have seen how a Schema is structured, and understand some of the basics of using XML Schema with namespaces and your documents, let's take a look at XML Schema in relation to the old XML standby, the Document Type Definition.

Don't worry too much about the specifics of the XML Schema syntax here. We will cover element declarations in greater detail in Chapter 5, "Element Declarations," and attribute declarations in Chapter 6, "Attributes." For now, just look at the document as a whole, and let the obvious differences in format sink in.

Let's take a look at an example, a very simple book catalog. We'll start with a `<catalog>` root element. That root element will contain `<item>` elements.

To uniquely identify each item, we will use the International Standard Book Number (ISBN) as an attribute. Each `<item>` will then contain a number of elements to describe the item:

- `item`

   This is the parent element for each item in the catalog. It contains only other elements, and it has one attribute, `isbn`.

- `title`

   The element for the book's title. Each item may only contain one title. The element has no attributes.

- author

  The element for the author's name. Each item may contain multiple <author> elements. The element has no attributes.

- book_type

  The element for the item's book type, such as softcover or hardcover. Each item will either have one or zero book_type elements.

- pages

  The number of pages in the book. The element will occur either once or not at all.

- publisher

  The publisher of the book. This element will occur either once or not at all.

- publication_date

  The publication date of the book. This element will occur once or not at all.

- price

  The price of the book. This element will occur once or not at all.

So, based on these elements, we can build the XML document shown in Listing 2.3.

LISTING 2.3   A SAMPLE XML DOCUMENT FOR A BOOK CATALOG, catalog.xml

```
<?xml version="1.0" encoding="UTF-8" ?>

<catalog>
 <item isbn="0789726076">
  <title>Special Edition: Using XML Schema</title>
  <author>David Gulbransen</author>
  <book_type>Paperback</book_type>
  <pages>450</pages>
  <publisher>Que</publisher>
  <publication_date>September 2001</publication_date>
  <price>49.95</price>
 </item>

 <item isbn="0735710201">
  <title>Inside XML</title>
  <author>Steven Holzner</author>
  <book_type>Paperback</book_type>
  <pages>450</pages>
  <publisher>New Riders</publisher>
  <publication_date>November 2000</publication_date>
  <price>49.99</price>
 </item>
</catalog>
```

THE DTD

We can use the XML document in Listing 2.3 as is. There is no requirement that we use a schema of any kind. As it stands, the document is well-formed XML and we could stop there. However, if we want to validate the document, we need a schema to validate the document against. Traditionally, this would be a Document Type Definition (DTD).

Now, if we develop a DTD to describe the document, it will look like the DTD in Listing 2.4.

LISTING 2.4   A SIMPLE CATALOG DTD WHICH DESCRIBES THE catalog.xml EXAMPLE

```
<!-- Simple Book Catalog DTD -->

<!ELEMENT catalog (item)* >

<!ELEMENT item (title, author+, book_type?, pages?, publisher?, publication_
➥date?, price? )>

<!ELEMENT title (#PCDATA)>
<!ELEMENT book_type (#PCDATA)>
<!ELEMENT pages (#PCDATA)>
<!ELEMENT publisher (#PCDATA)>
<!ELEMENT publication_date (#PCDATA)>
<!ELEMENT price (#PCDATA)>

<!ATTLIST item
    isbn    ID    #REQUIRED>
```

There are a number of element declarations, which take the form

```
<!ELEMENT name (content model)>
```

For example, the element declaration for the <item> element looks like this:

```
<!ELEMENT item (title, author+, book_type?, pages?, publisher?, publication_
➥date?, price? )>
```

You will note that the elements that are declared in the content model are followed by symbols such as + and ?. These are used to specify the number of times an element may occur:

*	Zero or more occurrences
+	One or more occurrences
?	Zero or One occurrences

So, for example, author+ means that the author element must occur at least once, but it may occur many times. The price? declaration means that the price element does not have to be used, but if it is used, it may only be used once.

THE XML SCHEMA

Just as we can use a DTD to validate the XML document, we can also use an XML Schema. To do this, we start off with the XML declaration, and the schema element:

```
<?xml version="1.0" encoding="UTF-8" ?>
<schema xmlns="http://www.w3.org/2001/XMLSchema">
```

Next, we can define our root element <catalog>. We know that the catalog element will contain other elements, so it is defined like this:

```
<element name="catalog">
  <complexType>
   <sequence>
    <!-- Element content -->
   </sequence>
  </complexType>
</element>
```

Because we are using a technique called the "Russian Doll" model for building this Schema. The Russian Doll method is a style of authoring Schema where the structure of the Schema self-describes the structure of the document; the element declarations are nested within each other, unlike the DTD model which specifies the content model separately.

Note

> The Russian Doll method is only one method for structuring an XML Schema. There are many others, with clever names like "Salami Slice" and "Venetian Blind". We will cover other methods for structuring Schema in Chapter 17, "Schema Best Practices."

Next we define the <item> element and its attribute isbn. Because the item is contained in the catalog element, we nest it:

```
<element name="catalog">
 <complexType>
  <sequence>
   <element name="item" maxOccurs="unbounded">
    <attribute name="isbn" type="ID"/>
    <complexType>
     <sequence></sequence>
    </complexType>
   </element>
  </sequence>
 </complexType>
</element>
```

You may also notice that in the <element> tag used to define the <item> element, there is an attribute called maxOccurs. These types of attributes take the place of the *, +, and ? symbols used in DTDs, but go one step further allowing you to specify a specific number of occurrences.

Now we can add the simple element declarations for the remaining elements:

```
<element name="title" type="string"/>
<element name="author" type="string" minOccurs="0" maxOccurs="unbounded"/>
<element name="book_type" type="string" minOccurs="0"/>
<element name="pages" type="string" minOccurs="0"/>
<element name="publisher" type="string" minOccurs="0"/>
<element name="publication_date" type="date" minOccurs="0"/>
<element name="price" type="string" minOccurs="0"/>
```

You will also notice that these element declarations have `type` attributes. The `type` attribute is used to define a datatype for the element, which is something not possible in the DTD. We will cover datatypes extensively in Part III.

Now, if we bring all the pieces together, the result is the Schema shown in Listing 2.5.

PART

I

CH

2

LISTING 2.5 THE `catalog.xsd` XML SCHEMA FOR THE `catalog.xml` FILE EXAMPLE

```
<?xml version="1.0" encoding="UTF-8" ?>
<schema xmlns="http://www.w3.org/2001/XMLSchema">

 <element name="catalog">
  <complexType>
   <sequence>
    <element name="item" maxOccurs="unbounded">
     <attribute name="isbn" type="ID"/>
     <complexType>
      <sequence>
       <element name="title" type="string"/>
       <element name="author" type="string" minOccurs="0" maxOccurs="unbounded"/>
       <element name="book_type" type="string" minOccurs="0"/>
       <element name="pages" type="string" minOccurs="0"/>
       <element name="publisher" type="string" minOccurs="0"/>
       <element name="publication_date" type="date" minOccurs="0"/>
       <element name="price" type="string" minOccurs="0"/>
      </sequence>
     </complexType>
    </element>
   </sequence>
  </complexType>
 </element>

</schema>
```

Looking at the finished Schema, you can see quite easily how it differs from a Document Type Definition. The important thing to notice is that the content model is described by the entire Schema, not just a few element declarations. And it's easy to see that the syntax for Schema is XML-based, unlike the DTD.

The Schema still needs to be associated with an instance document to be of much use. So, if we want to associate the XML Schema with our XML document, we need to add the appropriate namespaces:

```
<catalog xmlns:xsi="http://www.w3.org/2001/XMLSchema-instance"
         xsi:noNamespaceSchemaLocation="catalog.xsd">
```

Because we did not define a `targetNamespace` for our Schema, we can use the `noNamespaceSchemaLocation` tag to locate our Schema. The final code for the XML document is shown in Listing 2.6.

LISTING 2.6 THE `catalog.xml` FILE WITH THE XML INSTANCE NAMESPACE AND SCHEMA LOCATION

```xml
<?xml version="1.0" encoding="UTF-8" ?>

<catalog xmlns:xsi="http://www.w3.org/2001/XMLSchema-instance"
         xsi:noNamespaceSchemaLocation="catalog.xsd">

 <item isbn="0789726076">
  <title>Special Edition: Using XML Schema</title>
  <author>David Gulbransen</author>
  <book_type>Paperback</book_type>
  <pages>450</pages>
  <publisher>Que</publisher>
  <publication_date>September 2001</publication_date>
  <price>49.95</price>
 </item>

 <item isbn="0735710201">
  <title>Inside XML</title>
  <author>Steven Holzner</author>
  <book_type>Paperback</book_type>
  <pages>450</pages>
  <publisher>New Riders</publisher>
  <publication_date>November 2000</publication_date>
  <price>49.99</price>
 </item>
</catalog>
```

CONCLUSION

XML Schema follow the structure of a well-formed XML document. With a `<schema>` element as the root-element, they also contain `<element>` and `<attribute>` declarations that are used to define the elements and attributes for your XML documents. XML namespaces play an important role in XML Schema. Because XML Schema are XML documents, it is necessary to define the XML Schema namespace in order to use Schema properly. In addition, the XML Instance namespace is what is used to link XML Schema to XML documents.

Now that you have a basic understanding of the structure of Schema, we're going to round out the introduction to Schema by showing you some methods and resources for converting existing DTDs into XML Schema.

In the Real World

Practically speaking, there isn't much reason you would ever need to translate a DTD into an XML Schema, *unless* you needed to add features to your grammar that aren't possible with DTDs. If you have a DTD that meets all of your requirements, you can rest assured that applications will support DTDs for a very long time and simply keep your DTDs. However, if you compromised in the development of your DTD, or you have an SGML-based DTD that wouldn't translate properly to XML, these are prime candidates for conversion.

This chapter also dealt extensively with namespaces and the importance of relating namespaces to XML Schema. In many projects you can get by with simply declaring the default namespace for your Schema to be the same as the `targetNamespace`, and then using the `xs` prefix for Schema elements.

However, understanding how you are actually applying the namespaces is a good idea, and because so many other XML-related Recommendations use namespaces, familiarizing yourself with the Namespaces Recommendation is a very good idea.

PART

I

CH

2

CHAPTER 3

CONVERTING A DTD INTO A SCHEMA

In this chapter

THE LEGACY OF DOCUMENT TYPE DEFINITIONS

There are still many organizations using SGML. Even though XML is widely available, and the Recommendation has been around a few years, there are still valid reasons to use SGML. There are still organizations using DTDs, and there probably always will be. While DTDs might not offer all of the functionality of XML Schema, they do offer some compatibility with SGML, and the fact is that for some applications they provide enough functionality that converting from DTDs to XML Schema might not really be necessary.

Of course, there are some times when DTDs don't offer the functionality you need for your XML documents. And there are also some reasons you might want to convert an existing DTD into an XML Schema. For example, you might want to convert to an XML Schema for some of the following reasons:

- To ensure compatibility with new XML products
- To make use of datatypes
- To create more complex constraints on the validity of documents

All of these are valid reasons for converting from a DTD to an XML Schema.

So in this chapter we will discuss the differences between DTDs and Schema. It really is important that you have a good handle on these differences: Knowing them can save you a lot of effort if, in fact, the DTD you already have really suits your needs. Additionally, if you already have a DTD that is in need of conversion, it's a good idea to know how functionality translates, but even more importantly, how you can add new functionality once you have converted the DTD into an XML Schema.

DIFFERENCES BETWEEN DTDS AND SCHEMA

The critical difference between DTDs and XML Schema is that XML Schema utilize an XML-based syntax, whereas DTDs have a unique syntax held over from SGML DTDs. Although DTDs are often criticized because of this need to learn a new syntax, the syntax itself is quite terse. The opposite is true for XML Schema, which are verbose, but also make use of tags and XML so that authors of XML should find the syntax of XML Schema less intimidating.

The goal of DTDs was to retain a level of compatibility with SGML for applications that might want to convert SGML DTDs into XML DTDs. However, in keeping with one of the goals of XML, "terseness in XML markup is of minimal importance," there is no real concern with keeping the syntax brief.

PART

I

CH

3

Tip

The documentation provided by the W3C related to the Working Groups and Recommendations can be extremely useful in understanding the design philosophy and goals of a technology. If you are considering development work with a new technology, you should consult the W3C documentation to learn about the appropriate uses for the technology and to keep up with changes in a working draft or updates to a published Recommendation.

However, you might care if you are dealing with a complex Schema. Schema can become long rather quickly. In general, DTDs tend to be shorter, since the syntax is more compact—not necessarily any less convoluted, but usually shorter.

So what are some of the other differences which might be especially important when we are converting a DTD? Let's take a look.

TYPING

The most significant difference between DTDs and XML Schema is the capability to create and use datatypes in Schema in conjunction with element and attribute declarations. In fact, it's such an important difference that one half of the XML Schema Recommendation is devoted to datatyping and XML Schema. We cover datatypes in detail in Part III of this book, "XML Schema Datatypes."

It's very easy to see how datatypes can be useful in Schema design. Take, for example, a ZIP code element. Using a DTD, we would only be able to specify that a `<zip>` element was text. That would mean that someone could enter **W321GWG@(!#@** as a ZIP code, and it would still be considered valid. However, if we are following the U.S. ZIP Code format, this is obviously not valid. Using XML Schema, we could actually create a datatype for ZIP codes using regular expressions (simply a pattern that matches a specific set of strings) that would limit the `zip` element to the standard 5-digit ZIP code. We could also create a datatype to deal with ZIP+4 if we wanted. For example:

```
<xs:simpleType name="zip">
 <xs:restriction base="xs:string">
  <xs:pattern value="[0-9]{5}(\-)?([0-9]{4})?"/>
 </xs:restriction>
</xs:simpleType>
```

makes use of a regular expression (in the pattern value) to see if the string matches the ZIP+4 format. We'll talk more about both datatypes and regular expressions in Chapter 12, "Representing and Modeling Data."

The ability to get that specific with the datatypes of the content for our elements and attributes is a very powerful aspect of XML Schema.

OCCURRENCE CONSTRAINTS

Another area where DTDs and Schema differ significantly is with occurrence constraints. If you recall from our previous examples in Chapter 2, "Schema Structure" (or your own work with DTDs), there are three symbols that you can use to limit the number of occurrences of an element: *, + and ?.

The * allows you to specify that an element may occur any number of times, the + signifies that an element may occur one or more times, and ? limits the element occurrence to zero or one. So, let's say we have an element called carton, which can contain egg elements. Table 3.1 shows how we might use the DTD occurrence operators to limit the number of times the elements may appear in an XML document.

TABLE 3.1   LIMITING ELEMENT OCCURRENCES IN A DTD

DTD Syntax	Meaning
`<!ELEMENT carton (egg*)>`	carton could contain any number of eggs.
`<!ELEMENT carton (egg+)>`	carton must contain at least one egg, but there is no limit to the maximum number of eggs.
`<!ELEMENT carton (egg?)>`	carton does not have to contain any eggs, but may contain one.
`<!ELEMENT carton (egg)>`	carton may contain one, and only one egg.

As you can see, these options are a little limited. For example, how often do you buy a carton of one egg? And are you aware of any cartons that can hold an infinite number of eggs? What if you wanted to define a carton that could hold exactly a half-dozen eggs? You could do that; the declaration would look like this:

```
<!ELEMENT carton (egg, egg, egg, egg, egg, egg)>
```

What if you wanted to be more flexible, and say that carton had a minimum of a half-dozen eggs, but it could store up to a dozen? That could be done in a DTD too, but it's ugly looking:

```
<!ELEMENT carton (egg, egg, egg, egg, egg, egg, egg?, egg?, egg?, egg?, egg?, egg?)>
```

That declaration specifies that there are six egg elements which occur once and only once, and then six more egg elements which may occur once, but don't have to. The result is that we must have 6 egg elements in our carton but we can have up to 12.

As you can see, the definitions for accomplishing this level of granularity are really ugly. Schema allow a much cleaner mechanism for occurrence restraints, the minOccurs and maxOccurs attributes, which allow you to specify the minimum and maximum number of occurrences of an element:

```
<xs:element name="carton">
   <xs:complexType>
```

```
    <xs:sequence>
        <xs:element name="egg" type="xs:string"
                    minOccurs="6" maxOccurs="12" />
    </xs:sequence>
  </xs:complexType>
</xs:element>
```

This is a much cleaner mechanism for defining elements which have specific occurrence constraints. If you need this type of control over the elements in your schema, DTDs fall short. This is the up side of verbosity in XML Schema: The added descriptiveness allows Schema to be more human-readable.

ENUMERATIONS

An *enumeration* is simply a list of values. Surfing the Web, you encounter enumerations every time you come across a pull-down menu: The menu presents you with a predefined list of choices. Those choices, or enumerations, can be defined in a DTD for a list of attributes.

So, let's say we had a `<shirt>` element, and we wanted to be able to define a `size` attribute for the `shirt`, which allowed users to choose a size: `small`, `medium`, or `large`. Our DTD would look like this:

```
<!ELEMENT item (shirt)>
<!ELEMENT     shirt (#PCDATA)>
<!ATTLIST     shirt
              size_value (small | medium | large)>
```

PART

I

CH

3

That would allow us to create an XML document that looked like this:

```
<item>
<shirt size="medium">Cotton</shirt>
</item>
```

We can also use a Schema to describe the same thing, an attribute called `size` that is an enumeration:

```
<xs:simpleType name="size_value">
   <xs:restriction base="xs:string">
      <xs:enumeration value="small"/>
      <xs:enumeration value="medium"/>
      <xs:enumeration value="large"/>
   </xs:restriction>
</xs:simpleType>
<xs:element name="shirt" type="xs:string">
   <xs:attribute name="size" type="size_value"/>
</xs:element>
```

But what if we wanted `size` to be an element? We can't do that with a DTD. DTDs do not provide for enumerations in an element's text content. However, because of datatypes with Schema, when we declared the enumeration in the preceding example, we actually created a `simpleType` called `size_values` which we can now use with an element:

```
<xs:element name="size" type="size_value">
```

That would allow us to use the following XML:

```
<item>
<shirt>
<size>medium</size>
</shirt>
</item>
```

This kind of flexibility is directly related to datatypes, but it is still one way in which XML Schema can be more flexible than DTDs.

WHEN YOU SHOULD USE A DTD

Just because the W3C built it does not mean you have to use it. There are times when it will be perfectly reasonable to stick with the DTD you are currently using. Obviously, if your DTD is functional and you don't have any need to extend it, then chances are you might be better off leaving well enough alone. But let's say that you are developing a schema from scratch. When should you use a DTD instead of an XML Schema? Here are a few examples.

WHEN BREVITY MATTERS

We mentioned before that DTDs tend to be more concise than XML Schema. XML in general is not designed for brevity; it is a verbose language, which is part of what helps make it more human-readable. So, if brevity is important, you might want to see if you can accomplish your goals with a DTD instead of a Schema. Need proof? Take a look at an example of a DTD and a Schema, side-by-side, which both define the same thing, a schema for a TV Listing.

The XML Document we are defining the schema for looks like this:

```
<listing>
<show>
<title>Frontline</title>
<cast>NA</cast>
<rating>TV-PG</rating>
<description>A PBS news/documentary</description>
<date>April 1, 2004</date>
<time>10pm EST</time>
</show>
</listing>
```

This is a very simple XML document. The root element is the <listing> element, which can contain multiple <show> elements, and the show must contain one each of the title, cast, rating, description, date, and time elements. Here is the DTD which would describe our TV Listing document:

```
<!ELEMENT listing (show*)>
<!ELEMENT show (title, cast, rating, description, date, time)>
<!ELEMENT title (#PCDATA)>
<!ELEMENT cast (#PCDATA)>
<!ELEMENT rating (#PCDATA)>
<!ELEMENT description (#PCDATA)>
<!ELEMENT date (#PCDATA)>
<!ELEMENT time (#PCDATA)>
```

Because this example does not make use of any complex content models or even attributes, this is as straightforward as DTDs get. Let's take a look at the Schema that describes the exact same document:

```
<?xml version="1.0" encoding="UTF-8" ?>
<schema xmlns="http://www.w3.org/2001/XMLSchema">

<element name="listing">
 <complexType>
  <sequence>
   <element name="show" maxOccurs="unbounded">
    <complexType>
     <sequence>
      <element name="title" type="string"/>
      <element name="cast" type="string"/>
      <element name="rating" type="string"/>
      <element name="description" type="string"/>
      <element name="date" type="string"/>
      <element name="time" type="string"/>
     </sequence>
    </complexType>
   </element>
  </sequence>
 </complexType>
</element>

</schema>
```

The Schema takes 22 lines of code to accomplish what the DTD accomplishes in 8 lines. Just comparing the two examples side-by-side shows that Schema are verbose, so if brevity is important to your needs, consider a DTD.

WHEN YOU WANT USERS TO BE ABLE TO OVERRIDE DEFINITIONS EASILY

XML Schema use namespaces. In the previous chapter you saw how XML Schema use namespaces. Schema have one namespace declared for the Schema elements themselves (such as <element>) and another targetNamespace declared for the elements you are defining. With all of these namespaces floating about, it is easy to confuse them, or to create a *namespace collision*: a situation where there are conflicting references to a namespace. Practically speaking, that means that redefining elements using Schema can be complicated.

When would you want to redefine an element? Well, for example, if we defined an address element in an XML Schema, a user in the U.S. might want to redefine the element to conform to the U.S. address format, which includes a ZIP code:

John Doe

1023 Easy Street

New York, NY 10002

PART

I

CH

3

while a user in the U.K. won't use ZIP codes, but instead would use postal codes:

John Doe

2312 Kingsbury Way

Southhampton

Lincolnshire

3SW 1N2

With DTDs, redefining or overriding declarations can be pretty easy. It can be done within an external DTD using parameter entities, or it can be done in an internal DTD, contained within the DOCTYPE literal in an XML document. For example, the DOCTYPE declaration used to link an XML document to the DTD can also contain element declarations, attribute declarations, and so on, internally as well. If those internal DTD declarations are in conflict with the declarations in the external DTD, then the internal declarations are used.

Having both an internal DTD (contained in the XML document) and an external DTD (referenced in the document) makes it very easy to manipulate the DTD by extending or overriding the declarations. Of course, XML Schema have methods to import or include other XML Schema; however, doing so is not necessarily trivial, and in fact can be quite complex because of namespace issues that might arise from having two elements with the same name, and keeping track of the various namespaces elements belong to. So if you are using a base schema, but have the need to easily override or extend that schema, a DTD might be a better choice than XML Schema.

WHEN YOU HAVE MOSTLY TEXT DOCUMENTS

Everyone talks about the power of XML Schema, especially the power of datatypes. And it is true that datatypes offer a high degree of flexibility and power that was not possible before with DTDs. But not everyone needs that kind of flexibility and power. What if your needs center around large-scale documents which are mostly (if not entirely) text?

Some examples might include manuals, documentation, encyclopedias, and dictionaries. While these might have some elements used for indexing and cross-referencing, the majority of the elements might simply contain large blocks of text.

That's a perfect example of the type of document which might not benefit from an XML Schema. In fact, those types of documents might even benefit from DTD usage, since there are fewer differences between an XML and SGML DTD, and many document solutions were originally built around SGML, making it faster and easier to port an SGML DTD into and XML DTD than into an XML Schema.

If your uses for XML are mostly large blocks of text, then you might want to just stick with DTDs. Unless there is a compelling Schema feature which is essential to your document needs, chances are a DTD will satisfy your schema requirements adequately, and quite possibly more efficiently.

IF YOUR TOOLS DON'T SUPPORT SCHEMA

You spend six months researching, designing, and writing the perfect XML Schema. It is a thing of beauty, designed to anticipate your every data need. It is compatible with your database Schema and it describes your XML document perfectly. It allows you to do things you could have never done with a DTD, and even though you don't need that functionality now, your foresight will pay off tenfold in the future. You are proud of your work.

And then you discover from your Web department that the parser it has chosen to use for implementing XML in conjunction with your Web site doesn't support XML Schema.

XML Schema are a fairly new technology. If the tools you rely upon everyday in order to be productive don't support XML Schema, then you might just have to stick to DTDs for a while. That doesn't mean you can't think about XML Schema, or learn how you might use them in the future. But in the meantime, if your software doesn't support XML Schema, it won't do you much good to use them.

A SIMPLE AIRLINE TICKET ITINERARY DTD

In this section, let's take a look at building a simple DTD, so that we have a solid understanding of the DTD's structure and the process of converting the DTD into an XML Schema. Because we have not dealt extensively with the mechanics of Schema yet, we will keep this example very straightforward and simple. But it's still a good idea to cover this kind of information now, so that you have these types of applications in mind going forward, as we learn about the finer details of XML Schema.

For this example, we are going to build a DTD that could be used to describe an airline ticket itinerary. This would include information about the flight and airline, including departure times, arrival times, seating information, flight duration, and so on. Of course, if we were actually building an application for the travel industry, this type of schema could be very complex, but for our application, we will limit the data to the basics, so it should be easy to follow.

DESIGN GOALS FOR A TICKET ITINERARY XML DOCUMENT

What kind of information needs to be contained in our ticket itinerary document? Well, let's start off by making our root element `<itinerary>`, and then creating a child element called `<ticket>` that contains the actual ticket information.

Within that ticket, we will need information about the airline, the flight number, departing information, arrival information, and some details about the flight.

So, let's create some elements for that information, say `<airline>`, `<flight>`, `<departing>`, and `<arriving>`, to deal with the details. It's also pretty common to have information about the seating arrangements, and some details like the mileage and duration of the flight.

Of course, there are more details that we need in the document. For example, we need the date and time of the departure and arrival. It would probably also be a good idea to include information about the gate and airport of the flights, since many areas have more than one airport.

We could also include some information about the seating arrangements for the flight, as that can also be known in advance. For this type of information, we'll use attributes. Is it better to use attributes for this information? Maybe, maybe not. There are no hard, fast rules for designing this kind of information. However, for detail-oriented information like this which describes an element (like an adjective describes a noun), attributes are certainly appropriate.

So, let's take a look at the elements we have for our document so far. The elements (and the attributes) are summarized in Table 3.2.

TABLE 3.2 AN OVERVIEW OF THE TICKET ITINERARY ELEMENTS

Element	Attributes	Description
itinerary	None	The document root element. Parent to the `<ticket>` child element.
ticket	None	The `ticket` serves as the parent element for all of the children containing information about the airline ticket.
airline	None	The name of the airline.
flight	None	The flight number for the ticket.
departing	date, time, airport, gate	An element for the departing information about the flight, with attributes for the details.
arriving	date, time, airport, gate	An element for the arriving information about the flight, with attributes for the details.
miles	None	The total mileage of the flight.
seating	class, seat	The seating assignment for the flight.
duration	None	The duration of the flight in hours and minutes.

Those elements will make up the bulk of our document. And the remaining information will be stored in attributes, as outlined in Table 3.3.

TABLE 3.3 AN OVERVIEW OF THE ATTRIBUTES FOR THE TICKET ITINERARY ELEMENTS

Attribute	Description
date	An attribute describing the day, month, and year.
time	The time of the flight.
airport	The three-letter airport code.
gate	The boarding gate of the flight.

TABLE 3.3   CONTINUED

Attribute	Description
class	The seating class.
seat	The seat number assignment.

Now that you have an outline, build an XML document which uses the elements and attributes outlined in Tables 3.2 and 3.3. It would look something like Listing 3.1

LISTING 3.1   THE XML DOCUMENT FOR AN AIRLINE TICKET ITINERARY

```
<?xml version="1.0" encoding="UTF-8" ?>
<itinerary>
  <ticket>
    <airline>American</airline>
    <flight>4090</flight>
    <departing date="10-Apr-01" time="6:45AM" airport="IND" gate="A20" />
    <arriving date="10-Apr-01" time="7:52AM" airport="ORD" gate="B64" />
    <miles>168</miles>
    <seating class="Coach" seat="D3"/>
    <duration>1hr 7mn</duration>
  </ticket>
</itinerary>
```

DESCRIBING THE TICKET ITINERARY XML DOCUMENT IN A DTD

Okay, now that we have an outline of the elements and attributes for our document, and we have an idea of what we want our final document to look like, let's take a look at the DTD.

The first thing we need to do is define the root <itinerary> element, which will contain the <ticket> element. We can do that with a simple element declaration:

```
<!ELEMENT itinerary (ticket*)>
```

The * following the ticket element simply indicates that the itinerary may contain more than one ticket. Next, we need to declare the ticket element, and specify the content model:

```
<!ELEMENT ticket (airline, flight, departing, arriving, miles, seating, duration)>
```

Here, the ticket element contains a number of elements which will hold the data about the ticket. Note that none of the *, +, or ? symbols were used, which indicates that each of these elements will be used exactly once per ticket element.

Now we can move on to declaring our other elements. These elements are very straightforward. Since they will all simply contain text, we can use a very simple element declaration:

```
<!ELEMENT airline (#PCDATA)>
```

For the elements such as departing which will not have any content, but instead use attributes, we could use the EMPTY keyword in place of #PCDATA. However, in order to keep this

DTD (and the later conversion to a Schema) as simple as possible, we'll just leave them as #PCDATA. That gives us the following as the rest of our element declarations:

```
<!ELEMENT flight (#PCDATA)>
<!ELEMENT departing (#PCDATA)>
<!ELEMENT arriving (#PCDATA)>
<!ELEMENT seating (#PCDATA)>
<!ELEMENT miles (#PCDATA)>
<!ELEMENT duration (#PCDATA)>
```

We now have all of our elements defined. Next, we need to declare our attributes. This is done with the ATTLIST declaration:

```
<!ATTLIST departing
        date        CDATA   #REQUIRED
        time        CDATA   #REQUIRED
        airport     CDATA   #REQUIRED
        gate        CDATA   #IMPLIED>
```

The ATTLIST declaration allows us to specify the element we are declaring attributes for, and then list the attributes, followed by the value type (CDATA) and then by a keyword which indicates whether an attribute is #REQUIRED or #IMPLIED. Of course, required attributes must be used, while implied attributes are optional. Our ATTLIST declaration for the arriving element is the same as our declaration for the departing element, since they have the same attributes:

```
<!ATTLIST arriving
        date      CDATA     #REQUIRED
        time      CDATA     #REQUIRED
        airport   CDATA     #REQUIRED
        gate      CDATA     #IMPLIED>
```

Finally, we declare the attributes for our seating element:

```
<!ATTLIST seating
        class     CDATA     #REQUIRED
        seat      CDATA     #IMPLIED>
```

Now all of the pieces for our DTD are done, and if we pull them all together, we get the final code for the Airline Ticket Itinerary as shown in Listing 3.2.

LISTING 3.2 THE DTD DESCRIBING AN AIRLINE TICKET ITINERARY

```
<!-- A Simple Airline Ticket Itinerary DTD -->

<!ELEMENT itinerary (ticket*)>

<!ELEMENT ticket (airline, flight, departing, arriving, miles, seating,
➥duration)>

<!ELEMENT airline (#PCDATA)>

<!ELEMENT flight (#PCDATA)>

<!ELEMENT departing (#PCDATA)>
<!ATTLIST departing
```

LISTING 3.2   CONTINUED

```
        date     CDATA    #REQUIRED
        time     CDATA    #REQUIRED
        airport  CDATA    #REQUIRED
        gate     CDATA    #IMPLIED>

<!ELEMENT arriving (#PCDATA)>
<!ATTLIST arriving
        date     CDATA    #REQUIRED
        time     CDATA    #REQUIRED
        airport  CDATA    #REQUIRED
        gate     CDATA    #IMPLIED>

<!ELEMENT miles (#PCDATA)>

<!ELEMENT seating (#PCDATA)>
<!ATTLIST seating
        class    CDATA    #REQUIRED
        seat     CDATA    #IMPLIED>

<!ELEMENT duration (#PCDATA)>
```

CONVERTING THE DTD TO A SCHEMA

Now that we have a finished DTD, you could associate that DTD with the XML document and start writing valid XML. But of course, that isn't what you want to do. What you really want is to be able to use an XML Schema. So now let's take a look at converting the DTD into an XML Schema by walking through it step by step.

CONVERTING THE DTD STEP BY STEP

The first order of business, now that we are building an XML Schema, is to start out with the XML declaration and set up the Schema namespace:

```
<?xml version="1.0" encoding="UTF-8" ?>
<schema xmlns="http://www.w3.org/2001/XMLSchema">

    Schema content...

</schema>
```

Note

In the following section, we are going to take the element and attribute declarations slightly out of context (by not showing the examples nested in the element content of their parent elements). That is because when we build the final Schema, those declarations are going to be nested within each other, and that might make them more difficult to read. We will bring them all together at the end of the section, but in the meantime, keep in mind that these will later be nested.

Now that we have our schema element set up, we have to declare the root element for our XML document, <itinerary>. This is accomplished using the <element> tag and the name attribute:

```
<element name="itinerary"></element>
```

That's all there is to it; however, in this case, it's not quite that simple. Because the <itinerary> element is going to contain other elements, we need to create the tags which will allow us to include other elements inside an <itinerary> element. The result looks like this:

```
<element name="itinerary">
  <complexType>
  <sequence>
  this is where the ticket element will nest
  </sequence>
  </complexType>
</element>
```

You can see that we've added two tags, <complexType> and <sequence>. Those are tags that establish that the <itinerary> element is a complexType element, and that it will contain a sequence of other elements, which we will then specify by nesting their declarations between the two <sequence> tags.

Note

This is the Russian Doll method first introduced in Chapter 2. Chapter 17, "XML Schema Best Practices," discusses Russian Doll in greater detail.

This is often the simplest method of authoring an XML Schema because it describes the content model simultaneously with the element declarations. However, in DTDs, content model declarations are separate from the declarations of elements contained in them. A content model in DTD is always exactly one level deep, which is the exact opposite of a Russian Doll, which contains all levels of a content model in one place. There are other methods for structuring your Schema, and we will discuss them in greater detail in Chapter 17.

With the <itinerary> element declared, now we can move on to declaring our <ticket> element, which is going to follow the same structure, right down to the <complexType> and <sequence> tags, because it too will contain other elements:

```
<element name="ticket" maxOccurs="unbounded">
  <complexType>
  <sequence>
  this is where the other elements will nest
  </sequence>
  </complexType>
</element>
```

The only difference, aside from the name, is that the <ticket> declaration also makes use of the maxOccurs="unbounded" attribute. This is an attribute that allows us to specify that there may be any number of <ticket> elements inside an <itinerary>, which is similar to using the * symbol in a DTD. Now that the <ticket> element is defined, we can move on to the next element in our DTD.

The next element is the `<airline>` element, which only has text as the content, and is therefore a simple type:

```
<element name="airline" type="string"/>
```

Here, we make use of only the `type` attribute to specify that the element is a string. In fact, we can define our `<flight>`, `<miles>`, and `<duration>` elements in the same way, since they don't have any complex content either, nor any attributes:

```
<element name="flight" type="string"/>
<element name="miles" type="string"/>
<element name="duration" type="string"/>
```

With those elements out of the way, we only have three elements remaining to define: `<departing>`, `<arriving>`, and `<seating>`. As you can imagine, the syntax for declaring our `<departing>` and `<arriving>` elements is nearly identical, save the value of the `name`. They will both look like this:

```
<element name="departing">
  <complexType>
  </complexType>
</element>
```

Now, this is not yet complete, because these elements do have attributes. The attributes are declared using an `<attribute>` element, along with attributes that specify the `name` of the attribute, the `type` of the attribute, and the use of the attribute. So for the `<departing>` and `<arriving>` elements, our attribute elements will look like this:

```
    <attribute name="date" type="string" use="required"/>
    <attribute name="time" type="string" use="required"/>
    <attribute name="airport" type="string" use="required"/>
    <attribute name="gate" type="string" use="optional"/>
```

Each of the attributes is given a unique name. All of the attributes share the same type, `"string"`, since they are all going to contain text as their values. Note, however, that similar to the `#REQUIRED` and `#IMPLIED` keywords in the DTD, we can use the use attribute in the Schema with `"required"` or `"optional"` to specify whether an attribute must be used.

Now, if we bring the attribute and element declarations together, we end up with this:

```
<element name="arriving">
  <complexType>
    <attribute name="date" type="string" use="required"/>
    <attribute name="time" type="string" use="required"/>
    <attribute name="airport" type="string" use="required"/>
    <attribute name="gate" type="string" use="optional"/>
  </complexType>
</element>
```

Now, we only have one remaining element to declare, `<seating>`, which also has attributes. Following the examples above, we use the `<element>` tag to declare the element, and then we nest the `<attribute>` tags accordingly, and end up with

```
<element name="seating">
  <complexType>
    <attribute name="class" type="string" use="required"/>
```

```
        <attribute name="seat" type="string" use="optional"/>
    </complexType>
</element>
```

That's it. If we wanted to, we could pull this all together now and we would have a finished XML Schema. But why don't we pause for a moment and see if there is anything we can do to make use of the expanded capabilities of XML Schema?

EXTENDING THE DTD

As it so happens, we can do something to improve upon our base converted Schema that is not complicated, but would still make an improvement.

Remember the <arriving> and <departing> elements? They both feature date and time attributes that store information about the flight. As it so happens, the XML Schema Recommendation has both a date and a time datatype that we could use in our Schema, to reflect the content of those elements.

The date and time datatypes make use of the ISO 8601 standard for the format, so if we use them, our date will need to be in the form

YYYY-MM-DD

And our time will be in the form

HH:MM:SS-HH:MM

where the second set of hours and minutes is the deviation from Universal Coordinated Time. So, for example, if we wanted to say 1:30 p.m. EST, we would use:

13:30:00-05:00

Now, even though this places some restrictions on the format for our data, it also helps ensure that our data will work well with other applications, and makes it easier in the long run for us to work with that data. So to update our Schema, we would need to change the attribute declarations for date and time as follows:

```
<attribute name="date" type="date" use="required"/>
<attribute name="time" type="time" use="required"/>
```

Now we're ready to bring it all together.

THE FINISHED SCHEMA

As mentioned before, the XML Schema describes the XML document structure by nesting all of the declarations for elements and attributes, so we now need to bring together all of our previous declarations into one document.

The overall structure looks like this:

```
schema:
  itinerary_declaration:
    ticket_declaration:
```

```
-airline_declaration
-flight_declaration
-departing_declaration
  (attributes)
-arriving_declaration
  (attributes)
-seating_declaration
  (attributes)
-miles_declaration
-duration_declaration
```

That is the basic outline of how everything nests together. If we go through that list, replacing the placeholders with the actual declarations, we end up with the final XML Schema, as shown in Listing 3.3.

LISTING 3.3   THE XML SCHEMA FOR THE AIRLINE TICKET ITINERARY

```xml
<?xml version="1.0" encoding="UTF-8" ?>
<schema xmlns="http://www.w3.org/2001/XMLSchema">

 <annotation>
  <documentation>A Simple Airline Ticket Itinerary XML Schema</documentation>
 </annotation>

 <element name="itinerary">
  <complexType>
   <sequence>
    <element name="ticket" maxOccurs="unbounded">
     <complexType>
      <sequence>
        <element name="airline" type="string"/>
        <element name="flight" type="string"/>
        <element name="departing">
         <complexType>
          <attribute name="date" type="date" use="required"/>
          <attribute name="time" type="time" use="required"/>
          <attribute name="airport" type="string" use="required"/>
          <attribute name="gate" type="string" use="optional"/>
         </complexType>
        </element>
        <element name="arriving">
         <complexType>
          <attribute name="date" type="date" use="required"/>
          <attribute name="time" type="time" use="required"/>
          <attribute name="airport" type="string" use="required"/>
          <attribute name="gate" type="string" use="optional"/>
         </complexType>
        </element>
        <element name="seating">
         <complexType>
          <attribute name="class" type="string" use="required"/>
          <attribute name="seat" type="string" use="optional"/>
         </complexType>
        </element>
       <element name="miles" type="string"/>
       <element name="duration" type="string"/>
```

PART

I

CH

3

LISTING 3.3   CONTINUED

```
        </sequence>
       </complexType>
      </element>
     </sequence>
    </complexType>
  </element>

</schema>
```

Now, based on that XML Schema we can produce a final XML document, which looks like Listing 3.4.

LISTING 3.4   THE XML DOCUMENT FOR THE AIRLINE TICKET ITINERARY, INCLUDING THE XML INSTANCE TAGS LINKING IT TO THE XML SCHEMA

```
<?xml version="1.0" encoding="UTF-8" ?>

<itinerary xmlns:xsi="http://www.w3.org/2001/XMLSchema-instance"
      xsi:noNamespaceSchemaLocation="itinerary.xsd">
  <ticket>
    <airline>American</airline>
    <flight>4090</flight>
    <departing date="2001-04-01" time="06:45:00-05:00" airport="IND" gate="A20" />
    <arriving date="2001-04-01" time="07:52:00-05:00" airport="ORD" gate="B64" />
    <seating class="Coach" seat="D3"/>
    <miles>168</miles>
    <duration>1hr 7mn</duration>
  </ticket>
</itinerary>
```

RESOURCES FOR CONVERTING DTDs

Converting a DTD to an XML Schema by hand is still the best way to ensure that the new Schema you end up with most accurately fits your demands. It is also the best way to consider new features that moving to an XML Schema might allow you to implement. As you work your way through conversion, you can add features such as datatypes to make your XML Schema more robust, allowing you to place very specific constraints on the element or attribute content in an XML document.

However, sometimes it is handy just to have an automated conversion process, or to use an automated process to perform the base conversion so that you can then go in and add new features and clean up the converted Schema. As more software becomes XML Schema–aware, automated conversions will become easier. However, in the meantime, here are some resources for automatic conversion between DTDs and XML Schema.

DTD2Schema

The DTD2Schema project is a Perl script that automates the conversion of DTDs into XML Schema. The project is located at

```
http://www.w3.org/2000/04/schema_hack/
```

The site features an explanation of how the Perl script performs the conversion. Because the script is written in Perl, it has the flexibility of running under Windows, Unix, or any system that has a Perl implementation available. Figure 3.1 shows the DTD2Schema Web site with information about the script.

Figure 3.1
A Perl script resource for converting DTDs into XML Schema.

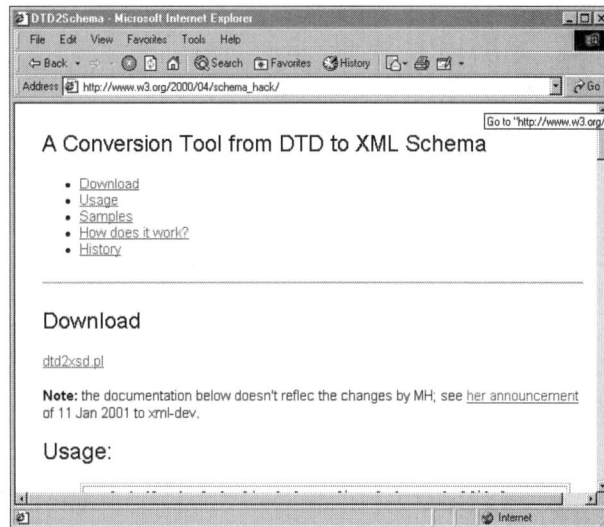

PART

I

CH

3

If you are familiar with Perl, this script can be a good resource. It allows users to automate the conversion of DTDs into Schema, which can be nice if you are converting a large number of DTDs. Of course, as with any conversion process, it isn't perfect, but it can serve as a good starting point for converting your DTDs.

XML Authority

For those users who are not familiar with Perl, or who are more comfortable using a GUI application for conversion, there is XML Authority, from TIBCO Extensibility. XML Authority is an application for schema design that actually converts between many different types of schema, not just DTDs and XML Schema.

A trial version of the application can be downloaded from its Web site at

```
http://www.extensibility.com/tibco/solutions/xml_authority/index.htm
```

The application, shown in Figure 3.2, allows you to open a DTD and then export the file to an XML Schema.

Figure 3.2
XML Authority from
TIBCO Extensibility
converts DTDs into
Schema and other for-
mats.

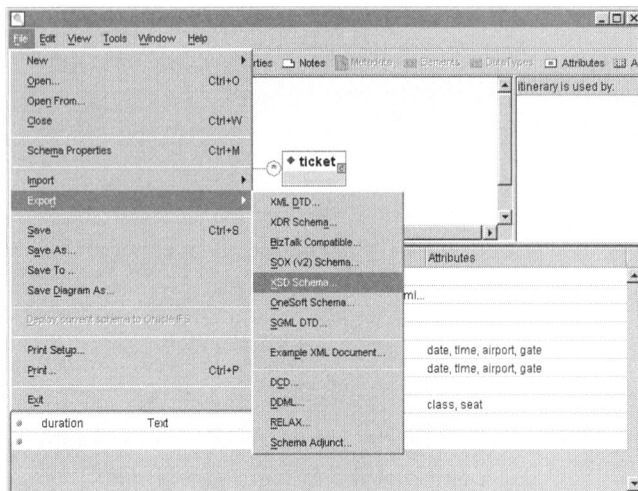

Again, although the conversion might not be perfect, it is a good starting place for converting DTDs into XML Schema. And one advantage of using an application like XML
Authority is that once you have converted the file, you can then continue to use the application for customization of the XML Schemaschema as well.

CONCLUSIONS

There are a number of differences between DTDs and Schema. The most superficial, but
still significant, difference is that DTDs use their own syntax, while XML Schema are well-
formed, valid XML documents. Some other differences include Schema' capability to use
datatyping, their capability to enumerate elements as well as attributes, and their flexibility
when implementing occurrence constraints.

It is, however, possible to convert a DTD into an XML Schema, either by stepping through
the document, declaration by declaration, and adding Schema improvements when desir-
able, or by using an automated conversion mechanism, such as a script or application. Either
way, converting a DTD into a Schema creates a good base, which can then be extended to
offer more flexibility than previously possible.

IN THE REAL WORLD

It is highly unlikely that you will ever need to convert a DTD into a Schema step by step.
But as an exercise, this is a good technique for illustrating the similarities and differences
between Document Type Definitions and XML Schema.

However, because there will continue to be widespread support for DTDs, conversion is
usually not necessary. When conversion is necessary, the odds are also quite high that you
will be able to employ an automated tool, such as is available from TIBCO Extensibility at

```
http://apps.xmlschema.com/log_on_page.asp
```

Although the tools currently supporting XML Schema are not perfect (many are still based on the Working Draft), as these tools are updated to reflect the changes in the Recommendation they will be the best route for updating your DTDs to XML Schema. After you have the base DTD converted into an XML Schema automatically, with a proper knowledge of Schema syntax you can easily go into the converted Schema and fix any existing errors by hand.

PART

I

CH

3

PART

II

XML Schema Structures

CHAPTER 4

THE COMPONENTS OF XML SCHEMA

In this chapter

INTRODUCING COMPONENTS

The structures that make up an XML Schema are called *components*, and every XML Schema is essentially a set of components which outline the constraints placed on the content of an XML document. Documents which contain XML elements and attributes are XML instance documents, and Schema can constrain those instances.

The structures used to constrain those XML instances in documents are components, and in this chapter we are going to provide you with an overview of the concepts and functionality of Schema components.

A component of an XML Schema is any of the structures that can be used to describe the information set of an XML document. So any of the structures of a schema that are used to define or describe the properties of an XML instance document can be seen as a component. Specifically, the XML Schema: Structures Recommendation defines the following components:

- Element declarations
- Particles
- Complex Type Definitions
- Complex Type Definitions with `simpleContent`
- Attribute declarations
- Attribute groups

There are other components, such as notations, that later chapters will cover in detail; however, we will concentrate now on how the basics of components apply to elements and attributes, as those basic principles will then carry over to other Schema components.

The XML Schema itself breaks components up into three groups. The first group is called *Primary* components, and consists of

- Simple type definitions
- Complex type definitions
- Element declarations
- Attribute declarations

In the Primary components group, both element and attribute declarations must have names, although type definitions do not necessarily have to have names. For example, if they are deriving a type for a single element, then they are a child of that element, and therefore, they don't need a name.

The Primary components are the major structures used to declare and define grammars for your XML instance documents. Simple and complex type definitions can be used to define your own datatypes within a document that you can then apply to element and attribute declarations. Element and attribute declarations, of course, are used to define the element types and attribute types that are considered valid in your XML instance documents.

Components in the next group, *Secondary* components, must all have names:

- Attribute group definitions
- Identity-constraint definitions
- Model group definitions
- Notation declarations

Attribute group definitions are a mechanism for defining a commonly used group of attributes, so that they can be easily applied to many different elements. Attribute groups function similarly to parameter entities in DTDs.

Identity-constraint components are used to place restrictions for uniqueness or references for other components. For example, you can use the unique identity constraint to specify that the content of a component has to be unique. These components are quite useful for modeling data similarly to how you would model data for database applications.

Model group definitions are a mechanism for defining a content model, which can then be used with type definitions. They function similarly to parameter entities in DTDs.

Notations are included as a mechanism for working with certain types of data, such as images, which cannot be natively included in XML documents. Notations are provided primarily for backward compatibility with the XML 1.0 Recommendation.

Finally, there are a number of components referred to as *Helper* components:

- Annotations
- Model groups
- Particles
- Wildcards
- Attribute uses

These components are not used independently, but rather as auxiliary components which contribute to the other major components.

Annotations are used to provide documentation within the Schema itself, similar to comments but much more flexible, including a mechanism that can replace Processing Instructions from the XML 1.0 Recommendation.

Model groups, particles, wildcards, and attribute uses are all components which do not appear on their own in Schema, rather in conjunction with other components in order to flesh out their definitions. We'll look at them in context as we examine components.

One thing all of these components have in common is that they use properties which constrain their functionality and in turn influence the structure of an XML instance document.

PART

II

CH

4

PROPERTIES

Every XML component has a number of properties associated with it which can be manipulated to place constraints on the values of XML instances. For example, if you create an XML element called <state>, you can manipulate the properties of the `element` declaration in order to specify that the value of the <state> element must be a valid two-character state abbreviation. This is just one way in which properties can be manipulated in a Schema, and in turn influence the information set of your instance document.

> **Note**
>
> In order to create a common language that can be used to describe XML documents, the W3C published the XML Information Set recommendation, which can be found at
>
> `http://www.w3.org/TR/xml-infoset/`
>
> This recommendation specifies an abstract dataset for XML documents called the *information set*, which contains "information items" and can be thought of as functioning like trees and nodes in other programming applications. Each item in the information set has properties that can be manipulated, as well as constraints for well-formedness.

Many components, such as an `element` declaration, are defined through their relationships with other components and may have other components as their content. For example, if you are declaring a parent element and its children, the parent `element` declaration will contain the children's `element` declarations. These relationships between components depend on the properties that restrict their usage in order to build content models for your XML instance documents.

HANDLING NAMES WITH SCHEMA

In general, Schema rely on two types of names, and it is important that you are familiar with naming conventions in XML.

The first thing you should keep in mind is that XML names are case sensitive. Therefore, there is a difference between NAME and name and NaMe. Some other general rules that apply to names in XML follow:

- Names must begin with a letter.
- Names may contain numbers, but may not begin with them.
- Names may contain underscores "_", hyphens "-", periods ".", and colons ":", but may not begin with any of those symbols.
- Colons are reserved as namespace characters.
- Names may not begin with any case-combination of the letters "xml".

Names that conform to these rules but which are not formally part of a namespace are referred to as *NCNames*.

Note An NCName is a "Non-Colon Name" and is used to refer to names that do not have a qualifying namespace prefix. While it is legal to use colons in your names, to do so is considered poor form as it causes confusion with namespace qualified names. Therefore, the only time you should use colons is when appending a namespace prefix to your tags.

Note A namespace qualified name is a name that is associated with a namespace by using the `xmlns` attribute to declare a namespace and specify a namespace prefix. The element name then uses the prefix before the name, with a colon ":" to delineate between the prefix and the name. For example

```
<prefix:myelement/>
```

The Schema: Structures Recommendation also makes use of namespace-qualified names, or Qnames, which take the form of any formally qualified name:

```
MyNamespace:element_name
myNspace:myElement
```

Qualified names make use of the *prefix:name* syntax to identify a component or value as being a part of a specific namespace.

Keep those naming rules in mind; they will come up when dealing with various components and their properties as you delve deeper into XML Schema.

GENERAL CONSTRAINTS AND VALIDATION RULES

During the validation process, an XML Schema is parsed as an XML document. Declaration components are associated with instances by their qualified names, and then the information set of the instance document is validated against the declaration. For example, when you want to specify a tag such as `<item>` you would use a *declaration*.

Definitions, however, are used to define the internal schema components themselves. They can usually make use of NCNames, and are used to describe the components within the Schema itself. For example, if you wanted to create your own datatype, which could later be applied to an `<item>` element, you would use a *definition*. Elements and attributes are declared, and types are defined.

TYPE DEFINITIONS

The first type of component we will take a look at is the *type definition*. There are two types of type definition components: *simple* and *complex*. These components can be used to define datatypes which may either act as global type definitions or be applied to other components, such as element declarations and attribute declarations.

PART

II

CH

4

At the top of the type definition hierarchy is the *ur-type definition*, the root type definition from which all other types are derived. This ur-type definition has the name `anyType`, which can be used to provide a very generic type which essentially allows any type of data content.

By definition, according to the XML Recommendation, all types are derived from the `anyType` type, which is the father of all types. Therefore, all type definitions take the form of an extension or restriction of a given type.

Note

The XML Schema: Datastructures Recommendation does include a number of built-in datatypes which can be treated, practically speaking, as elemental types. However, while you don't need to worry about it too much in practice, all of the built-in types are still descendents of `anyType`. This is similar to the Java Object Class hierarchy, in which all classes derive from Object, even if they seem to be primitives. We will discuss datatypes and their derivation and relationships in greater detail in Part III, "XML Schema Datatypes."

When you are constructing a datatype, the type you use as the basis for your new type definition is referred to as the base type. All type definitions make reference to the base type they are restricting or extending.

When we talk about a restriction, we are talking about a new type definition that makes use of a base type but then places restrictions on the properties of that type. For example, let's say we had a type we called `name` and we based that type on the `string` type. If we were creating our `name` type as a restriction, we could do something like limit the number of characters to 25. Our new type, then, would be a restriction of the `string` type, because although our `name` is based on `string`, we have limited the number of characters which can be used in our new type.

Similarly, we can start with a base type, and then extend the properties of the type, creating a new type definition which is an extension.

SIMPLE TYPES

Simple type definitions are always restrictions. The primitive datatypes that are built into XML Schema are actually a restriction of the ur-type called `anySimpleType`.

A user-defined simple type must be a restriction of one of the primitive simple types or another user-derived simple type. Simple types are always restrictions because to extend a simple type would make it a complex type!

For example, if you wanted to create a type for passwords that is a string, but limited in length to a minimum of 6 characters, and a maximum of 8 characters, we can use a `simpleType` definition:

```
<simpleType name="password">
 <restriction base="xs:string">
  <minLength value="6"/>
```

```
    <maxLength value="8"/>
   </restriction>
</simpleType>
```

This simple type can then be applied to an element declaration:

```
<element name="passwd" type="password"/>
```

`simpleType` definitions can be defined anywhere in the Schema, and named, as in our example above, or they can be included directly in the declaration of an element. For example, if we wanted to define a type for a question as a string with either `"true"` or `"false"` as acceptable values, we could use

```
<element name="answer">
 <simpleType>
  <restriction base="xs:string">
   <enumeration value="true"/>
   <enumeration value="false"/>
  </restriction>
 </simpleType>
</element>
```

There are times, however, when you might want to expand on the capabilities of a built-in type, in which case you will need to utilize a `complexType` definition.

COMPLEX TYPES

Complex types can be either restrictions or extensions. A complex type can take one of the following forms:

- A restriction of the ur-type `anyType`
- A restriction of some other complex type
- An extension of a simple type
- An extension of another complex type

When a complex type is defined as an extension, the new properties are simply appended to the existing type. Complex types can be declared globally or locally. We will cover complex types in greater detail when we discuss datatypes in Part III.

RESTRICTIONS AND EXTENSIONS

Let's take a look at the syntax that we use to create restrictions and extensions. Both are represented by Schema elements: `<restriction>` and `<extension>`.

`<restriction>`

Restrictions begin with the `<restriction>` element, which has two attributes: `base` and `id`. The `base` attribute accepts a qualified name (QName) which represents the base type definition which is being restricted. The `id` attribute is an ID type, which serves as a unique identifier for the restriction.

PART

II

CH

4

The content of a restriction may consist of several different components, including

- minExclusive
- minInclusive
- maxExclusive
- maxInclusive
- totalDigits
- fractionDigits
- length
- minLength
- maxLength
- enumeration
- whiteSpace
- pattern

All of these attributes accept values that place limits on the values of the new derived type. Restrictions may also contain annotations, attributes, `attributeGroup`, or `anyAttribute`. Restrictions are really an essential part of datatypes, so we won't go into great detail about them here. We will look into using restrictions in greater detail in Part III.

<extension>

Extensions are similar to restrictions, in that they have a `base` attribute and an `id` attribute, both of which are used in the same manner as they are with restrictions. The `base` attribute specifies the base type for the extension, and the `id` serves as a unique ID.

Extensions do not make extensive use of attributes; however, they accept annotations, attributes, `attributeGroup`, and `anyAttribute` as content. This allows you to extend the content of a type, creating a new extension type. Once again, we will cover these techniques in more detail when we examine datatypes in Part III.

ELEMENT SCHEMA COMPONENTS

The element declarations in Schema are used to declare an element type for use in an XML instance document. The basis of the element declaration is the `<element>` component, which serves as the base for declarations. Through attributes, the `element` declaration can be constrained in terms of usage and content. Additionally, the `element` declaration can make use of `simpleType` and `complexType` as well as `simpleContent` and `complexContent` to specify details about the content model for the element being declared.

ELEMENT DECLARATION SCHEMA COMPONENT

The element declaration Schema component takes the form of `<element>` within a Schema, and it exhibits a number of properties that can be constrained. Most of these properties are expressed through attributes that are used with the `element` declaration, but some, such as scope, are expressed through other means, such as the element declaration's placement within the Schema document.

Here are the properties of the `element` declaration component:

- name—The name property is used to specify the name of the element declaration. It takes the form of an NCName.

- target namespace—The target namespace is the namespace for the element which is being specified. Values for target namespaces are not required.

- type definition—The type being referenced for the element being declared. The value can be either a built-in or a user-derived datatype.

- scope—Either a locally scoped element or a globally scoped element.

- value constraint—Either `"default"` or `"fixed"`, allowing the specification of a default value or fixed value for the element content.

- nillable—A value of true or false denoting if the element may be set to `nil` using the `xsi:nil` attribute. Added to allow the modeling of SQL NULLs.

- identity-constraint definitions—Specify constraints on the identity of the element. The sub-properties include `name`, target namespace, identity-constraint category, selector, fields, referenced key, annotation.

- substitution group affiliations—An association of the element with a substitution group (a group of elements which are interchangeable with one another).

- disallowed substitutions—Places restrictions on whether the element may be a member of a substitution group.

- abstract—Specifies whether the element is an abstract element. Abstract elements may not be used in XML instance documents.

- annotation—An annotation for the declaration, which does not affect validation.

Names for elements need to conform to the standards for XML names, but they do not necessarily need to be qualified names.

PART

II

CH

4

The scope of an element declaration is determined by `element` declaration's location within the `<schema>`. For example, if the element declaration is nested within another element declaration, then the scope of the nested element is local:

```
<schema>

<element name="contact">
  <complexType>
    <element name="phone" type="xs:string"/>
  </complexType>
</element>

</schema>
```

In this example, the `<contact>` element would be considered a globally scoped element, because it is not nested within another component. The `<phone>` element however is locally scoped, because it is nested within the element declaration for the `contact` element. Because the `<phone>` element is locally scoped, it is only available to the `<contact>` element. However, because the `contact` element is globally scoped, it is available to any other element within the Schema. Having the element globally declared is important if you want to be able to reference the element as a base type, or if you want to be able to create a substitution group for the element.

Value constraints allow you to control the specific value of element contents within an XML instance document. For example, value constraints allow you to specify a default value for an element, providing a failsafe should an XML author neglect to provide content for an element. Also, you can require that the author use a specific value for an element by using the "fixed" value constraint, which allows you to make certain that the element is always present with a specific value. This can be used to aid automatic processing, or to ensure that an element, such as a legal notice, is always included in the proper form with the proper content.

The nillable and abstract properties allow you to control the usage of elements in the XML instance document. If an element is declared as nillable, then that means the element may be set to be a nil (or NULL) value using the `xsi:nil` attribute. This is not the same as having simply an empty string, for an empty string is a specific type of data, a string of zero length. A nil or null has no implications on the type of data; it is simply empty in the abstract sense. Declaring an abstract element means that the element may not be used in an XML instance document at all. An abstract element might be declared just to provide a `complexType` to be used as a base for other types within a Schema.

SUBSTITUTION GROUPS

One of the features of Schema you can take advantage of with a globally scoped element is the substitution group. A substitution group allows you to declare a *head element* which is the main element referenced in the Schema and content model, and is expected to be used in the XML instance document. With the head element in place, you can then declare other elements in the same substitution group which allows those elements to be used in place of the other substitution group member elements within the XML instance document.

For example, we could declare an element called <color> as our head element, and then we could declare a number of other elements, such as <red>, <blue>, and <green>, as members of the same substitution group. Then, in an XML document, anywhere we would be expected to use the <color> element, we could also use <red>, <blue>, or <green> instead.

Substitution groups add a great deal of flexibility to a document, and we'll talk about them more in Chapter 5, "Element Declarations."

COMPLEX TYPE DEFINITIONS

Type definitions differ from declarations in that they do not declare a component for use in an XML instance document, but rather they provide a link between a set of constraints and a component declaration. What that means is that when you define a type, simple or complex, what you are really doing is defining the constraints that will be applied to an element or attribute in an XML document.

> **Note**
>
> Attributes cannot actually be complex types; they may only be simple types. However, attributes may be used inside complex type definitions.

PART

II

CH

4

There are a number of properties which apply to complex types, regardless of the content of the type definition itself. Those properties include

- name—The name property is used to specify the name of the complex type. It takes the form of an NCName.

- target namespace—The target namespace is the namespace for the type which is being specified. Values for target namespaces are not required.

- base type definition—The base type which serves as the basis for the complex type restriction or extension.

- derivation method—Either a restriction or an extension.

- final—Determines whether the type is limited from being further extended or restricted.

- abstract—A Boolean value of true or false, specifying whether the complex type is an abstraction.

- attribute uses—A set of attribute uses, such as optional or required.

- attribute wildcard—Used for inclusion of wildcards which instruct the processor to skip or include an attribute.

- content type—A specification of the content type, such as "empty", "mixed", or "element-only".

- prohibited substitutions—Used to prohibit either restriction or extension of the complex type.

- annotation—An annotation for the definition.

However, complex type definitions may have two different types of content: simple content or complex content.

COMPLEX TYPE DEFINITION WITH SIMPLE CONTENT

Complex type definitions may contain simpleContent, or content that is simply text character data. If the complexType contains simpleContent, then you may also need to consider the property requirements of simpleContent as well. simpleContent is discussed in more detail in Chapter 5, in the "simpleContent" section.

A <simpleContent> element may itself only contain extensions and restrictions. An <extension> allows you to extend the simpleContent type in order to construct the complexType definition in a Schema. A <restriction> allows you to restrict the simpleContent.

Here is an example of a complexType definition with simple content:

```
<complexType name="item">
  <simpleContent>
    <extension base="string">
     <attribute name="quantity" type="xs:integer"/>
    </extension>
  </simpleContent>
</complexType>
```

This example creates a new complex type for an inventory item. You want the item to have an attribute called quantity that will always be associated with the type for the quantity of the item in stock. By using the <simpleContent> element and an extension, you can create the new complexType based on the string type built in to Schema.

We could do the same thing with an extension. Just remember that <simpleContent> must have either a <restriction> or an <extension> as its content.

When used with a <simpleContent> element, a <restriction> has the following content options:

- annotation—An annotation element.
- simpleType—A simpleType definition, which may be based on a built-in type, or a <restriction> of another simpleType.
- minExclusive—Accepts an integer value indicating the minimum value of integer content, exclusive.
- minInclusive—Accepts an integer value indicating the minimum value of integer content, inclusive.
- maxExclusive—Accepts an integer value indicating the maximum value of integer content, exclusive.
- maxInclusive—Accepts an integer value indicating the maximum value of integer content, inclusive.
- totalDigits—The total number of digits (expressed as an integer) that may occur in the content.

- `fractionDigits`—The number of decimal places which may be used with a value.
- `length`—An integer value limiting the number of characters in a string.
- `minLength`—The minimum number of characters for a string value.
- `maxLength`—The maximum number of characters for a string value.
- `enumeration`—A list of choices which may be used for the value of a component.
- `whiteSpace`—Accepts a value on how whitespace is to be treated within the content: may be preserved, replaced, or collapsed.
- `pattern`—Accepts a regular expression as the value, which allows for complex pattern matching.
- `attribute`—An attribute declaration.
- `attributeGroup`—An `attributeGroup` declaration.
- `anyAttribute`—A wildcard allowing the specification of any attribute from a given namespace.

When used with a `<simpleContent>` element, an `<extension>` has the following content options:

- `annotation`—An annotation for the component.
- `attribute`—An attribute declaration.
- `attributeGroup`—An `attributeGroup` declaration.
- `anyAttribute`—A wildcard allowing the specification of any attribute from a given namespace.

Keep in mind that the acceptable values for both `<restriction>` and `<extension>` change depending on whether they are used with `<simpleContent>` or `<complexContent>`.

COMPLEX TYPE DEFINITION WITH COMPLEX CONTENT

Complex type definitions may also include `complexContent`. `complexContent` in this case must be a restriction or extension of a previous type. This is a useful construct for deriving datatypes, and we will touch on it briefly in this chapter and in Chapter 5; however, we will deal with complex types more extensively in Part III.

It's easy to confuse `complexType` and `complexContent`, because they are so similar both in structure and syntax, but remember that `complexContent` will always be a child element of a `complexType`. Another important thing to remember is that although `complexContent` also makes use of `<restriction>` and `<extension>`, when those elements are used in `complexType`, they have different properties.

When used with a `<complexType>` element, a `<restriction>` and `<extension>` each have the following content options:

- `annotation`
- `group`

- `all`
- `choice`
- `sequence`
- `attribute`
- `attributeGroup`
- `anyAttribute`

These options are related to model groups, which we will be discussing more in Chapter 7, "Model Groups."

ATTRIBUTE SCHEMA COMPONENTS

Attribute declarations can be scoped either locally or globally, and, according to the XML Schema Recommendation, are "an association between a name and a simple type definition, together with occurrence information and (optionally) a default value."

What that means is that every attribute has a name, and that name is associated with a simple type. The name is used to identify the attribute, which can be applied to element declarations. Attribute declarations also contain information about when an attribute occurs, for example, whether it is required or optional. Default values can also be declared for attributes or enumerations.

ATTRIBUTE DECLARATION SCHEMA COMPONENT

The attribute declaration schema component is the component used to declare attributes which are associated with elements in an XML instance document. The declaration makes use of the `<attribute>` element, in conjunction with the following properties:

- name—The name property is used to specify the name of the attribute. It takes the form of an NCName.

- target namespace—The target namespace is the namespace for which the attribute is being specified. Values for target namespaces are not required.

- type definition—The type definition is a simple type definition which denotes the datatype for the attribute value.

- scope—The scope of the attribute declaration. Either local to the complex type or global for the entire Schema.

- value constraint—Either "default" to declare a default value for the attribute, or "fixed" to declare a fixed value for the attribute.

- annotation—An annotation for the declaration.

Many of the properties for an attribute declaration will look familiar to you; properties such as name and scope are similar to the properties applied to element declarations. The one property that is significantly different is type definition. Attributes cannot be complex types; they must be simple types. Therefore, the type for your attributes must be either one of the built-in simple types, or a restriction of a built-in or derived simple type.

"ATTRIBUTE USE" SCHEMA COMPONENT

The attribute use schema component exhibits the properties that control when an attribute may be used. The properties associated with the attribute use schema component are

- required—This property defines whether the attribute is required or optional.
- attribute declaration—This property links the use schema component to an attribute declaration.
- value constraint—A constraint on the attribute value, either a default value or a fixed value which may not be changed.

These attributes allow you to control whether an attribute is required or optional, and also allow you to declare default values for attributes. Attributes may also have fixed values, to ensure that the author of an instance document cannot change the value of the attribute.

ATTRIBUTE GROUP DEFINITION SCHEMA COMPONENT

The final attribute component is the attribute group definition component. This component can be used to group attributes together so that they may easily be linked to a specific element declaration. Attribute groups exhibit the following properties:

- name—The name property is used to specify the name of the attribute group. It takes the form of an NCName.
- target namespace—The target namespace is the namespace for which the attribute group is being specified. Values for target namespaces are not required.
- attribute uses—The set of attribute uses, such as default or fixed values.
- attribute wildcard—This property provides for use of a wildcard with the attribute group. Wildcards allow for flexibility in processing the Schema and instance documents.
- annotation—an annotation for the declaration.

Attribute groups are a good way to organize attributes and make your Schema more readable, and are functionally very similar to parameter entities in DTDs. They are also a convenient way to create a group of attributes which could be applied to multiple elements.

PART

II

CH

4

NOTATIONS

The notation component is included in XML Schema as an implementation of Notations from the XML 1.0 Recommendation. Notations are used to create a means for identifying data that you might want to reference from within an XML file, such as the binary data in a .gif or .jpeg, since these types of binary data cannot be included in the document directly.

The notation component exhibits the following properties:

- name—The name property is used to specify the name of the notation. It takes the form of an NCName.

- target namespace—The target namespace is the namespace for the type which is being specified. Values for target namespaces are not required.

- system identifier—A URI reference for the notation. Optional if a public identifier has been specified.

- public identifier—An XML Public Identifier, optional if a system identifier has been specified.

- annotation—An annotation for the notation declaration.

Functionally, notations in Schema are no different than notations as specified in DTDs. However, you can declare notations for use in an XML instance document, but you may not use notations in an XML Schema document itself, since the notation would have no meaning to the schema processor.

We will cover notations in greater detail in Chapter 7 in the "Notations" section.

PARTICLES, MODEL GROUPS, AND ANNOTATIONS

Particles are very granular Schema components that can be used to construct other Schema components. Model groups represent groupings of Schema components which can be used to construct complicated content models within a Schema, and are a powerful feature.

Annotations are a Schema component which can be used to document the features and structures of a Schema, similar to comments. Annotations do differ from comments in some ways though, such as their extensibility and their syntax.

We will cover particles, model groups, and annotations more extensively in their own sections in Chapter 7, "Model Groups."

CONCLUSIONS

XML Schema are constructed using components, and each XML Schema component has a set of properties which can be manipulated to define how the component influences XML instances. Many components have similar properties, but those properties can affect different components in different ways.

Components can be roughly divided into definitions and declarations. Most definitions are used to define components which act on other components in the Schema, and declarations are generally used to specify components which act on XML instance documents.

In the next few chapters we will take a look at two of the most important types of declarations: elements and attributes. With element declarations and attribute declarations out of the way, we will take a look at some of the other components, such as model groups, and take a look at how to build a Schema from the ground up making use of all the Schema components at your disposal.

IN THE REAL WORLD

The most important components that you will work with in your XML Schema will be element and attribute declarations. You will use them to declare the elements and attributes that appear in your final XML documents, and therefore you will need to be very familiar with their usage in order to create useful Schema.

The second most important components are the simple and complex type definitions, because these will allow you to create your own datatypes, which you can use in conjunction with element and attribute declarations. Additionally, they allow you to define types that you or other developers can reuse, and therefore they are almost as important as the element and attribute declarations themselves.

One thing to keep in mind about properties in XML is that they are *abstract*, that is, the properties that we have discussed in this chapter are not necessarily linked directly to a keyword in the syntax of Schema. If you are coming from a programming background, such as Java, you might find this a little confusing at first, but just remember that a property in the context of XML Schema is just an abstract property of a Schema component, just as the number of tires on a vehicle is a property you might use when describing a car.

It is important that you be familiar with components and their properties; however, you will be getting into much more specific syntaxes as you continue on with element declarations and attribute declarations.

ELEMENT DECLARATIONS

In this chapter

THE IMPORTANCE OF ELEMENTS

Elements are an essential part of any XML document, so much so that all XML documents even start off with a root element which is the parent element of all the document's content. In well-formed XML, elements must have matching start and end tags, and must have a valid name. Because well-formed XML does not provide for any kind of element declarations, it is not possible to limit or place any restrictions on the content of elements using only well-formed XML. That is why DTDs have been used with XML documents to provide for *validated* XML, in which a schema (such as a DTD or an XML Schema) is used to define a number of validity constraints for a document.

The XML Schema Recommendation, Part One: Structures, provides for three specific types of declarations: elements, attributes, and notations. In this chapter we are going to deal with elements. We will look at how elements are declared using the Schema syntax, and what constraints can be applied to the element declaration which will influence the usage and content model of the element.

DEFINING ELEMENTS WITH SCHEMA

In previous chapters we have declaration component> declaration> already taken a look at some basic Schema, and you have seen the `<element>` tag used already. That `<element>` tag is really an instance of the element declaration component in the XML Schema namespace.

As we've seen in some previous examples, the syntax for element declarations in a DTD is

```
<!ELEMENT name (content model)>
```

The syntax for XML Schema is different:

```
<element name="MyElement" type="string"/>
```

The `<element>` tag denotes an element type declaration component, and the properties and constraints for the element are expressed using a number of attributes.

The content model for elements using XML Schema is more complicated: Elements can be simple types or complex types. Unlike the limitations of element declarations in DTDs, this allows for some very robust expression of content models using XML Schema, which we will see later in this chapter.

The XML Schema: Structures Recommendation states that element declarations provide

- Local validation of element information item values using a type definition.
- Default or fixed values for an element information item (the ability to control the element content).
- Uniqueness and reference constraint relationships among the values of related elements and attributes.
- The capability to control how element substitution groups may be used.

What does all that mean in terms of practical schema authoring?

Schema provide a grammar describing a document's structure, which XML processors may then use for validating the content of elements in your XML documents based on type definitions; for example, if you wanted to create an element called <date>, when declaring the element you could define it as a date type, which could then be validated to determine if the element content was an actual date.

The element declaration component also allows you to specify the default values or fixed values for the content of your elements, depending on the content model. Using default values can help streamline the authoring of instance documents, and fixed elements can be useful for managing content as well, allowing you to define elements that must always have specific content whenever they are used.

Managing relationships between related elements and their values is also a function of the element declaration. Establishing relationships between similar or related elements (such as <city>, <state>, and <zip> elements in an <address>) is another function of element declarations.

And finally, XML Schema provide a powerful new mechanism called *element substitution groups* which allows one element to be substituted for another. We'll examine substitution groups in greater detail later in the chapter.

All of these aspects of elements make the <element> declaration component a central part of XML Schema. So now let's examine the <element> declaration in greater detail.

<element> PROPERTIES

As mentioned in Chapter 4, "Component Details," in the section "Introducing Components," when discussing a Schema component, such as the <element> declaration, the component can be described in terms of properties which can in turn be restricted by a range of potential values.

PART

II

CH

5

Caution

In the discussion of the features linked to a specific component in XML Schema, such as an element declaration, those features are referred to as "properties," which are not always the exact syntax for specifying those properties. Unlike some other languages, such as Java, the properties expressed here are abstract properties of the component, not meant to necessarily translate directly into the syntax for manipulating them in XML Schema.

The <element> declaration component has a number of properties which contribute to the final formation of an XML element, which include

- name
- target namespace
- scope
- value constraint
- nillable
- identity-constraint definitions
- substitution group exclusions
- disallowed substitutions
- abstract
- annotation

Let's take a closer look at these properties and how they influence the `<element>` component.

NAME

The name property refers to the name of the element, which is the NCName from the Namespaces Recommendation (an XML name without the colon and the prefix). The XML 1.0 well-formedness constraints dictate that a name

- Must begin with a letter
- May not begin with the letters "xml" in any combination of lower- or uppercase, such as "XmL" or "xmL"
- Should not contain colons (the colon ":" is a special character for namespaces)
- May not contain spaces
- May use the underscore character "_"

Those guidelines for naming must always be followed. Keep in mind that XML is case sensitive as well.

TARGET NAMESPACE

The target namespace property refers to the namespace of the element information set of the document that you will be validating with the Schema. If you specify a target namespace, the element declared will be considered a part of that namespace, and validated accordingly as a namespace-qualified element. If you do not specify a target namespace, then the element will be evaluated as an unqualified element.

In practice, you generally won't need to specify the target namespace if you are developing a Schema for one namespace. If that's the case, you can specify a default target namespace so that you won't have to do this on an element-by-element basis (for an example, see Chapter 8, "Example Schema: A Contact Schema," Listing 8.1). However, if you are mixing and matching namespaces within a Schema, this is the property you would use for multiple namespaces.

SCOPE

The scope property of an element declaration allows you to make the element available either to the entire Schema or to a limited set of other elements. For example, if you have an element like <name> that you want to use many times in your Schema, you can declare it with a global scope, and it can then be used anywhere within the Schema. However, if you have something such as <part_number>, you might want to limit the scope of the element to a specific element, such as <item>.

Another example where scope might come in handy would be with establishing relationships between elements. For example, if you wanted to create a <name> element that had two child elements, <first> and <last>, you would probably not want to scope the <first> and <last> elements globally, since they would only be used in the local <name> context.

Scoping is accomplished through a variety of mechanisms, such as limiting the substitution groups for an element, but mostly scoping is accomplished through the structure of the Schema itself. For example, elements can be declared anywhere inside the <schema> element and when they are declared as direct children of the <schema> element they have a global scope. However, elements can also be declared inside <group> or <complexType> elements. When an element is declared inside a complex type or element group, its scope is local; that is, the element is not available throughout the Schema, only inside the <group> or <complexType> element in which it was declared.

VALUE CONSTRAINT

The value constraint property of the element declaration allows you to specify whether an element has a default value or fixed value. This can be a very useful tool for specifying the content of XML documents based on your Schema.

For example, if you had an element such as <publisher> and you wanted authors to be able to specify a new value, but you wanted it to default to "Computer Books USA" if they did not specify a value, then you could use a value constraint for the default value of the element to accomplish this.

Similarly, if you wanted the value of <publisher> to always be "Computer Books USA", then you could do that by specifying a fixed value for the element. That would mean that the person authoring an XML document based on your Schema would need to use the <publisher> element, and that its value would always be the same:

```
<element name="publisher" fixed="Computer Books USA"/>
```

This is a useful technique for specifying the content of elements which you always want to appear in an XML instance document, and always with the same information, such as legal notices, copyrights, and so on.

NILLABLE

With DTDs it is possible to declare that an element is to be EMPTY, that is, that the element is forbidden from having any content. This allows you to make use of an element simply by having it present in the document, since an empty element is an element which still appears in the document, but does not have any content.

The nillable property is actually a part of the XML Instance Namespace (xsi:nil) which allows you to specify whether an element's content is "nil". Making use of this property allows you to create elements which are not just empty, as in a string with zero length, but that have no value whatsoever, comparable to a SQL NULL.

IDENTITY-CONSTRAINT DEFINITIONS

As with XML and DTDs, "identity" properties refer to providing a unique ID for an element, so that multiple occurrences of the same element may be differentiated from one another. Identity-constraint properties refer to this ability to create uniqueness for an element.

As a property, identity-constraint definitions go beyond simple ID tags, allowing you to specify properties such as a unique element, or limit the relationships between elements and attributes.

SUBSTITUTION GROUP EXCLUSIONS

Substitution groups are a powerful feature of XML Schema. Substitution groups allow you to specify a group of elements which may be used in place of another element within an instance document. So, for example, if we had an <address> element functioning as our "head" element, we could specify a substitution group that included <USaddress> and <UKaddress> as members of the substitution group. Then, when we are authoring documents, anytime we might have an <address> element, we could legally substitute a <USaddress> element for it.

The substitute group exclusions property allows you to specify elements that may not be a part of a substitution group, or to limit the way in which an element may function within a substitution group. For example, if you created a phone number type for phone numbers based on the U.S. 10-digit phone number, and you always wanted that format used, you could prohibit a substitution group from being created for that type, thus ensuring that your phone number type would always be used.

DISALLOWED SUBSTITUTIONS

This property is very similar to substitution group exclusions, but rather than restricting whether the declared element can be a part of a substitution group, it specifies which elements may not be substituted in its place.

For example, if we disallowed <USaddress> as a substitution for <address> then authors could not make that substitution in their XML documents.

We will talk more about substitutions and substitution groups later on in the chapter in the "Substitution Groups" section.

ABSTRACT

The abstract property can be used to declare an element that is an abstract type, that is, a type which may not be used in an instance document. While it might not seem obvious why you would want to declare an element that could not be used in a document, when you consider substitution groups, it makes more sense.

For example, we could declare our <address> element as an abstract type, with our <USaddress> and <UKaddress> substitutions. That means anywhere in the Schema that we specify an <address> element, authors of an instance document would need to choose between <USaddress> and <UKaddress>. This provides a pretty powerful mechanism for structuring a document while still providing extensible choices for the XML authors creating instance documents based on your Schema.

ANNOTATION

Annotations are simply comments, but they do offer a little more flexibility. Annotations don't use a special syntax like comments do, but instead make use of an <annotation> element.

Annotations also allow for a greater degree of flexibility than comments, allowing you to provide annotation information, such as <documentation> or <appinfo>, to differentiate between documentation notes and information for applications using your XML documents.

> **Note**
>
> Annotations are a very nice feature of XML Schema, with <documentation> functioning as a replacement for comments, and with <appinfo> functioning as a replacement for Processing Instructions. Another plus of <appinfo> is that unlike PIs in a DTD, <appinfo> can contain structured markup (such as a Schematron Schema) to extend the functionality of your Schema even further.

CONSTRAINING ELEMENTS WITH ATTRIBUTES

All of the properties we discussed in the last section are just that: properties. They are not the actual markup that you would use in your element declarations; rather, they are the abstractions of the properties that you are manipulating when you are writing the element declaration.

In this section, let's take a look at the actual syntax that you would use in an XML Schema to manipulate those properties.

VALID <element> ATTRIBUTES

Now, we already know that the element declaration in an XML Schema takes the form of the <element> tag. That tag forms the start of any element declaration in your Schema. But how do we manipulate the properties we discussed in the previous section? Attributes.

The `<element>` declaration can accept a number of attributes, each one designed to manipulate one or more of these properties. The attributes that can be used with an `<element>` declaration include

- `abstract`
- `block`
- `default`
- `final`
- `form`
- `id`
- `maxOccurs`
- `minOccurs`
- `name`
- `nillable`
- `ref`
- `substitutionGroup`
- `type`

So now let's take a look at each of these attributes and the possible values for each one, so we can see how element declarations are structured.

name

The `name` attribute is used to specify the name for each instance of the element in an XML instance document. For example, if we have

```
<element name="address"/>
```

this would declare an element called `<address>` which we could use in an XML document.

Keep in mind also that XML is case sensitive, so "ADDRESS" and "address" are not the same name, and the name must conform to the XML naming standards.

abstract

The `abstract` attribute is a Boolean, which accepts a value of `true` or `false`. The default value for the attribute is `false`.

As mentioned in the section "`<element>` Properties," earlier in this chapter, this attribute is used to specify that an element is an abstract type, which means that the element cannot be used in an XML instance document. So, if we were declaring our `address` element as an abstract type

```
<element name="address" abstract="true"/>
```

this would specify an `<address>` element which was a valid element, but could not appear in an XML document. In order to make use of this element, we would have to use it as the head element for a substitution group.

block

Substitution groups and derived element types create a great deal of flexibility in XML Schema. Using an abstract element type, you can build new element types based on that element. For example, you can create an `extension` which uses the abstract element as a basis, and then adds features to the new extended element. Or you can create a `restriction` which takes a previous abstract element and removes features to create a new restricted element.

There are times, however, when you might want to limit the usage of "extension" or "restriction" elements, when preserving the features of an element might be critical. For example, if we created an `<item>` element which contained `<part>` and `<sku>` elements, we might not want to allow anyone to create a restriction based on the `<item>` element, because then they could change the requirements for our `<part>` and `<sku>` elements. One way we could limit that type of re-use of the element is to use the `block` attribute.

The `block` attribute accepts an `#all` value, which blocks all manipulation of the element, or a combination of any or all of the following values:

- `substitution`—Blocks the element from being used as a head element or member of a substitution group.
- `extension`—Blocks the element from being used as the basis for an extension by another element.
- `restriction`—Blocks the element from being used as the basis for a restriction by another element.
- `list`—Blocks the element from being used as part of a list.
- `union`—Pblocks the element from being part of a union.

So, turning back to our `<item>` element, let's say we wanted it to be blocked from being part of a substitution group:

```
<element name="item" block="substitution"/>
```

Or if we wanted to provide a greater degree of protection, we could block everything related to the `<item>` element:

```
<element name="item" block="#all"/>
```

As we begin to build more complex content models in future chapters, the usefulness of the `block` attribute will become more apparent.

Tip

block="#all" is roughly equivalent to the final modifier in Java.

---

default

The default attribute allows you to specify a string as the default value for an element. So, if we wanted to declare a copyright element, we could use

```
<element name="copyright" default="Copyright 2001"/>
```

which would, if no other content were specified, cause the XML processor to treat the element as if it appeared in the XML document as

```
<copyright>Copyright 2001</copyright>
```

Default values are not *automatically* created in the XML document itself; however, the XML processor reading the document is responsible for filling in the content of default values when the document is parsed.

Specifying a default value can be quite useful for ensuring that vital elements in your document contain data, regardless of whether the document author neglects to include a value for a specific element. It can save the author some typing, but also serve to make sure that the element has a minimum default content (such as the minimum legally required copyright statement) should the author of the XML document neglect to customize the information.

final

The final attribute is another attribute which can be used to control how an element type is used by other element declarations, such as a restriction or an extension. Similar to block, the final attribute accepts a value of #all, extension, or restriction.

However, the final attribute does differ somewhat from block. The final attribute is typically used to prevent the further modification of an element by restriction or extension, whereas block is used to prevent the substitution of the element by a derived type (based on a restriction or extension). The difference is quite subtle.

Also, the <schema> element itself has an attribute called finalDefault which can be used to specify the default value for the final attribute within a Schema document. So, in the following example:

```
<schema finalDefault="extension">
<element name="item"/>
</schema>
```

Using the finalDefault attribute on the <schema> element has the same effect as using the final attribute:

```
<schema>
<element name="item" final="extension"/>
</schema>
```

We will discuss more about attributes like `block` and `final` when we start getting into more complex content models. Although we briefly covered the attributes here because they are valid attributes for the `<element>` declaration, the concepts involved in using these attributes inside a Schema are rather advanced and will be covered in greater detail in later chapters, such as Chapter 12, "Representing and Modeling Data."

fixed

The `fixed` attribute allows you to specify a string that will be the fixed value of an element. So, for example, if you declared

```
<element name="info" fixed="For information call 411"/>
```

then all of your `<info>` elements would be required to have a value of `For information call 411`:

```
<info>For information call 411<info/>
```

Fixed elements are one way to include information which you want to be a part of the instance document, but which you do not want the author to have the power to alter.

form

The `form` attribute accepts one of two values: `qualified` or `unqualified`. The attribute refers to whether the name of an element must appear in the instance document as a qualified or unqualified name. The qualified name, you might recall, takes the form `prefix:element` where the prefix and colon are used to denote the namespace of the element. Using the `form` attribute to force the use of the prefix and a qualified name is one way of ensuring that a namespace is used for your elements.

For example, if we had

```
<element name="myelement" type="xs:string" form="qualified"/>
```

when we used the element in an instance document, it would have to take the form

```
<prefix:myelement>
</prefix:myelement>
```

with the `prefix` being specified in the `xmlns` declaration in the instance document. Keep in mind that this mechanism only ensures that a namespace prefix be used with your element, not that the *correct* namespace is used.

id

The `id` attribute allows you to specify an ID for the element, which, like an ID in a DTD, serves as a unique identifier for the element. The `id` attribute actually accepts a value that is an `id` datatype, as specified in the XML Schema: Datatypes Recommendation. The `id` datatype can be represented in a number of different forms, which we will cover in later chapters when we discuss datatypes. For now, just remember that the `id` is a unique identifier for the element.

maxOccurs

If you remember from earlier chapters, when we were looking at a DTD, the syntax made use of +, *, and ? to denote how often an element could occur in a content model. Schema do away with this cryptic system, and instead make use of the maxOccurs and minOccurs attributes.

The maxOccurs attribute specifies the number of times an element may appear in the document (or in the content model). Its value may be a non-negative integer or unbounded, which means that the element may occur any number of times. The default value is 1. So, if we wanted to specify that a <part> element could occur up to 3 times, we would say

```
<element name="part" maxOccurs="3"/>
```

As you can see, this provides us with a great deal more flexibility than the +, ?, * of DTDs.

minOccurs

The minOccurs attribute goes hand-in-hand with maxOccurs. It is used to specify the minimum number of times an element may occur. The default value for minOccurs is also 1. So, let's say we were declaring an element called <features> for a clothing catalog, and we wanted to specify that each listing had to list at least two features of an item, but no more than six:

```
<element name="features" minOccurs="2" maxOccurs="6"/>
```

As you can see, using the minOccurs and maxOccurs attributes together provides a great deal of flexibility in the content model for your document.

Caution

Some combinations of minOccurs and maxOccurs are illegal. For example, you cannot have minOccurs="21" and maxOccurs="5" because this would cause an obvious conflict. The minOccurs can never be greater than the maxOccurs.

nillable

The nillable attribute is a Boolean which accepts the values of true or false. The default value is false. The nillable attribute is used to specify whether an element is nillable, that is, whether it can be set to the xsi:nil type, which is used to denote an EMPTY element which has a specific meaning, similar to a SQL NULL, rather than simply an empty string.

For example, if we created an element called <email> we might want to allow the element to be nillable:

```
<element name="email" type="string" nillable="true"/>
```

Which means that if the element has no data, it can be treated as nil, which means there is no value, not that the value is simply an empty string.

ref

The ref attribute is used to refer to a global element which has already been declared. In other words, if you want to reuse an element which has already been declared in the document, you can use a ref attribute to do so:

```
<schema>

  <element name="full_name" type="string"/>

  <element name="supervisor">
    <complexType>
      <element ref="full_name" />
    </complexType>
  </element>

  <element name="employee">
    <complexType>
      <element ref="full_name" />
    </complexType>
  </element>

</schema>
```

In this example, the <full_name> element is declared, and then it is referenced using the ref attribute inside the declarations for the <supervisor> and <employee> elements. It is very important to note here that the original element, <full_name>, is declared with a global scope. That is accomplished by declaring the element outside the content model of any other elements. In order to use ref to reference an element, the element being referenced either must be globally scoped or it must be in the same local scope as the ref attribute itself. It is also important to note that a ref attribute may not be used with a global element declaration itself, but only to reference that declaration.

So, in the previous example, you could not legally do

```
<schema>
  <element ref="full_name" type="string"/>
</schema>
```

because this would represent a ref used on a global element declaration.

substitutionGroup

The substitutionGroup element is used to create a grouping of elements that can be used *somewhat* interchangeably, provided that all of the elements in the substitution group are of the same datatype. The value of the substitutionGroup attribute takes the form of a qualified name.

Substitution groups themselves are composed of a head element which is a globally scoped (it must be globally scoped) element that serves as the element in the Schema that members of the substitution group may be substituted for, and the element members of the group, which may be substituted in the head element's place. Members of the substitution group do not have to be globally scoped, but they must be of the same type (or a derived type) as the head element.

We will talk more about substitution groups later in this chapter, in the section "Substitution Groups," including providing you with some examples of how they work.

type

The `type` attribute also accepts a qualified name as its value, and the value refers to the datatype of the element, which can be from the XML Schema: Datatypes specification or from another namespace.

There are many different datatypes which can be used in conjunction with your elements, but we will not go into detail on datatypes here. Datatypes are covered extensively in Part III, "XML Schema Datatypes," of this book.

That does it for the attributes that can be used with the `<element>` declaration. It's time now to move on to looking at the content models that you can use with element declarations and then move on to some examples of element declarations that you might find useful.

CONTENT MODELS

While there are some times when an empty element is useful in a document, most elements are not empty. Elements can have content that is of a simple, straightforward type, such as a string or a number, or they can have a mixture of text and other elements.

When an element contains only a text value and not other elements, we say that it has *simple content*. If an element is a parent element which contains only other elements as children, then the element has *element content*. And finally, when an element contains a mixture of character data and other elements, we say it has *mixed content*.

There is some confusing terminology used with XML Schema. For example, we have `simpleContent` and `simpleType`. We also have `complexContent` and `complexType`. While on the surface these components are similar, they do have different uses and applications. When it comes to defining straightforward content models, we should look to `simpleContent` and `complexContent`. Both `simpleType` and `complexType` are useful if we want to create specific element content types which can then be referenced or used again later.

The `<element>` declaration itself may contain any of the following:

- `<annotation>`
- `<simpleType>`
- `<complexType>`

An annotation is simply used to provide comments and other information to the document author or to an automated processing mechanism.

The `<simpleType>` element is used to specify content which is based on a built-in or derived simple type. Complex types are a little more flexible, and may be either restrictions or expansions of existing simple or complex types.

For example, let's say that you want to create an element which represents temperature. Since temperature can be expressed as a decimal representation, you could use a simple type to create a new `<temperature>` element. However, if you also wanted to include an attribute which specified whether the temperature was Centigrade or Fahrenheit, you would need to use a complex type, since simple types may not be extensions.

The most straightforward element content models, however, simply use the existing datatypes which are built in to the XML Schema Recommendation. These datatypes include (but are not limited to) `integer`, `decimal`, `date`, `boolean`, and `string`.

When using one of those built-in datatypes and content which is simply character data, that is, when the element does not contain any child elements, you can simply use a standalone element declaration. Let's look at some examples:

```
<xs:element name="quantity" type="xs:integer"/>
```

This declaration would create an element called `<quantity>` which would have an integer as its value. For example

```
<quantity>5</quantity>
```

We could also use a similar declaration with the decimal type, to declare an element called `temperature` which would be a decimal:

```
<xs:element name="temperature" type="xs:decimal"/>
```

Which would allow declaring

```
<temperature>98.6</temperature>
```

We can also make use of data structures which help standardize formats for commonly used data, such as the `date` datatype:

```
<xs:element name="holiday" type="xs:date"/>
```

The date datatype takes the form YYYY-MM-DD, so if we wanted to represent the U.S. holiday of the Fourth of July, it would look like this:

```
<holiday>2001-07-04</holiday>
```

A `boolean` type is useful for elements which will contain a value of either true or false. The value can be represented using `true` or `1` for a true value, or `false` or `0` for a false value:

```
<xs:element name="attendance" type="xs:boolean"/>
```

Which we could then use to indicate attendance, for example, an employee's presence at a meeting:

```
<attendance>true</attendance>
```

Finally, we could use a string datatype to declare an element which is character data:

```
<xs:element name="title" type="xs:string"/>
```

That would allow the following elements:

```
<title>SE Using XML Schema</title>
<title>Inside XML 3.5</title>
```

Now, these are by no means all of the datatypes which can be used. We will cover the datatypes that are built in to the XML Schema Recommendation, as well as the mechanisms for creating new datatypes, in greater detail in Part III.

However, with the knowledge that you can use these types, we can start creating element declarations, and the most basic declarations (as we have seen) take the form:

```
<element name="element name" type="some_datatype"/>
```

This works well for elements which have very simple content. However, in many cases, we need to represent elements which have more complex content, such as content which is another element, or content which is a mixture of data and other elements. So let's take a look at some other content models and the element declarations that accompany them.

<simpleType>

The <simpleType> element allows you to create an element with a content model that is still simple content, that is, content which contains only data and not child elements or mixed content. However, it provides a new level of flexibility: the ability to place restrictions on the existing datatype.

Why is this useful? One example might be declaring an element for inventory. Let's say that you have an inventory item, and you want to create an <inventory> element to represent that inventory. However, your storage space only allows you to store 100 of the item in your inventory, and you always reorder when there are only 12 in stock. We can use the <simpleType> to declare this kind of element:

```
<xs:element name="inventory">
  <xs:simpleType>
    <xs:restriction base="xs:integer">
      <xs:minInclusive value="12"/>
      <xs:maxInclusive value="100"/>
    </xs:restriction>
  </xs:simpleType>
</xs:element>
```

This will declare an element called <inventory>, which can legally have a value of any integer from 12 up to 100.

The <simpleType> element may only contain a restriction, a list, or a union. (We will talk more about lists and unions as we explore datatypes.) Therefore, if you need to extend an existing datatype, you cannot use a <simpleType>.

Additionally, the `<simpleType>` element does accept a number of attributes:

- `final`—This attribute accepts values of `#all`, `list`, `union`, or `restriction`, and indicates that the simple type declared is the final type, and may not be restricted further.
- `id`—This serves as an ID for the type.
- `name`—A name for the type, in the form of an NCName.

A nice side effect of the ability to create and name a simple type is that you can reuse the type in other declarations. For example, let's declare an element called `price` and define a simple type called `currency`:

```
<xs:simpleType name="currency">
  <xs:restriction base="xs:decimal">
    <xs:fractionDigits value="2"/>
  </xs:restriction>
</xs:simpleType>

<xs:element name="price" type="currency"/>
```

Now we have an element called `<price>`, which contains a decimal value with two decimal places. So any of the following values would be valid:

1.00

10.99

19.95

Now, since we have given our new `<simpleType>` a name, `currency`, you will notice that we did not nest the `<simpleType>` within the element declaration. That was deliberate, because if we nested the `<simpleType>` within the element declaration, it would be locally scoped. By declaring the `<simpleType>` first, and then using that type with our element declaration, we now have a globally scoped type called `currency` which we could use with another element:

```
<xs:element name="total" type="currency"/>
```

The power to reuse types that you define is one of the greatest flexibilities of Schema, and it's actually a datatype application. Although we are going to cover datatypes in detail in Part III, you can already see how pervasive they are, and you're already using them! So there is no need to be intimidated by datatypes; they can be a very useful tool for structuring your documents and data exactly as you want them to be.

`<complexType>`

Since XML Schema have a `<simpleType>` it follows that they also have a `<complexType>`. A *complex type* is used for developing content which is element content, mixed content, or both elements and data.

The representation of `<complexType>` is similar to the other components we have seen. It has a number of attributes that contribute to its customizability:

PART

II

CH

5

- abstract—A Boolean attribute which may be either `true` or `false`. An abstract complex type may not be referenced directly by an element, but may be used as a base for other derived types.
- block—Accepts values of `#all`, `extension`, or `restriction`, and denotes that the complex type may not be used in the specified manner.
- final—Also accepts values of `#all`, `extension`, or `restriction`, and indicates that the complex type is the final incarnation of the derivation.
- id—A unique ID for the complex type.
- mixed—A Boolean accepting `true` or `false` with a default value of `false`. A value of `true` is used to represent a `complexType` that has mixed content, that is both data and child elements.
- name—A name for the complex type, which can be referenced by element declarations, extensions, restrictions, and so on.

By using the `<complexType>` element with these attributes, you can create some very complicated content models for your elements, and in fact, you can go one step further and define the `complexType` globally, so that it can be used with more than one element.

The `<complexType>` element has a number of valid children, including

- `<simpleContent>`
- `<complexContent>`
- `<all>`
- `<group>`
- `<sequence>`

So now let's take a look at these subcomponents and see how they modify and define a `<complexType>`.

`<simpleContent>`

The `<simpleContent>` element is used to provide element content that is only character data, and does not contain any child elements. For example, if we wanted to declare an element called `<address>` which could only contain the address text, and no child elements, we could use `simpleContent` to do so.

The `<simpleContent>` element itself has only one attribute, `id`, which can be used to provide a unique identifier for the `<simpleContent>` element itself.

The content of the `<simpleContent>` element however, must be either an extension or a restriction. That is, the element being declared must be an extension or restriction of a built-in or derived datatype.

Let's take a look at an example. Say we are going to declare an element called `<title>` and we only want it to contain a text string. Well, since XML Schema: Datastructures provides a string type already, we can make our element a string type. So, our element declaration would look like this:

```
<element name="title" type="xs:string"/>
```

In this case, since we simply want an element which is a string, and contains only character data, we don't need to deal with anything but the type attribute.

What that leaves us with is a very simple element declaration for <title> which may contain a string as its value.

Similarly, we could also use a restriction to define our simple content. For example, if we wanted to create an element for quantity, which was limited to a dozen, we could use the following:

```
<element name="quantity">
  <simpleContent>
    <restriction base="positiveInteger">
      <maxInclusive value="12"/>
    </restriction>
  </simpleContent>
</element>
```

This creates a <quantity> element, which may have a positive integer up to and including 12 as its value.

That is all there is to creating simple content, and there are many instances when you will want to use simple content. But for many elements, you will want the content to be other elements, or a mixture of elements and element character data.

<complexContent>

Of course, if we have simpleType and complexType, it makes sense that since we have simpleContent, we also have complexContent. If the content is not simpleContent, then it's complexContent. But practically speaking, complex content is content which includes elements, either in an element content model or in a mixed content model.

So now let's take a look at the content models we can use complexContent to define.

ELEMENT CONTENT

When an element contains only other elements, that is called element content. An example of an element with element content might be an <address> element, which would contain <street>, <city>, <state>, and <zip> elements:

```
<xs:element name="address">
  <xs:complexType>
    <xs:element name="street" type="xs:string"/>
    <xs:element name="city" type="xs:string"/>
    <xs:element name="state" type="xs:string"/>
    <xs:element name="zip" type="xs:string"/>
  </xs:complexType>
</xs:element>
```

PART

II

CH

5

This would allow creating content of

```
<address>
<street> 1000 North Milwaukee</street>
<city>Chicago</city>
<state>IL</state>
<zip>60622</zip>
</address>
```

As you can see, all of the data in the value of the <address> element is actually data inside other elements.

When defining element content locally, as in the previous example, we can do so simply by using a complexType, without using complexContent at all. However, once again, if we want to provide flexibility, we can instead declare our complex type independently of the element declaration.

Let's take a look at another example. In this example, we want to end up with a customer element which contains the name of a contact and the contact's company. For the contact we want to have a first name and a last name. So we can start by declaring a complex type called full_name which will be composed of our <first_name> and <last_name> elements:

```
<xs:complexType name="full_name">
  <xs:element name="first_name" type="xs:string"/>
  <xs:element name="last_name" type="xs:string"/>
</xs:complexType>
```

Now we can declare our <contact> element:

```
<xs:element name="contact" type="full_name"/>
```

Next, we need to build our <customer> element, which will have element content, comprised of a <contact> element and a <company> element. If we want that company name to now become part of our <contact> element, we can do that with <complexContent>:

```
<xs:element name="customer">
  <xs:complexContent>
    <xs:extension base="full_name">
      <xs:sequence>
        <xs:element name="company" type="xs:string"/>
      </xs:sequence>
    </xs:extension>
  </xs:complexContent>
</xs:element>
```

Now we have a <customer> element which has complexContent. Since it is based on an extension of the <full_name> element, the <customer> content will include the <first_name> and <last_name> elements from the full_name type. Then the full_name type is extended with a sequence to add the <company> element to the complexContent for the <customer> element. The end result is an element called <customer> which takes the following form:

```
<customer>
  <contact>
    <first_name>David</first_name>
    <last_name>Gulbransen</last_name>
```

```
    </contact>
    <company>Vervet Logic</company>
  </customer>
```

As you can see, XML Schema provide a great deal of flexibility. In fact, there are often multiple ways to build any given component. How you construct your components will vary depending on how you need to reuse your data and make it available to other structures in the Schema. We will deal more with this in Chapter 8, "Example Schema: A Contact Schema," when we build an entire Schema from scratch, and later in Chapter 17, "Schema Best Practices," when we discuss best practices.

Mixed Content

A mixed content model is when an element has both data and child elements as its value. For example, let's say you have a notice you want to send customers:

```
<notice>
Dear <customer>John Doe</customer>,
We are happy you chose to purchase <product>Happy Fun Ball</product> however,
we are temporarily out of stock.

<company>Widgets Inc.</company>
</notice>
```

As you can see, we have an element `<notice>` that contains both text and elements. So how do we declare this? Let's take a look:

```
<xs:element name="notice">
  <xs:complexType mixed="true">
    <xs:sequence>
      <xs:element name="customer" type="xs:string"/>
      <xs:element name="product" type="xs:string"/>
      <xs:element name="company" type="xs:string"/>
    </xs:sequence>
  </xs:complexType>
</xs:element>
```

We start off by declaring the element `<notice>`, which contains a `complexType`. That type has a `mixed` attribute with a value of `true`, which is used to indicate that the following content model is mixed.

> **Caution**
>
> You might be familiar with mixed content models from XML and DTDs; however, in Schema there is one critical difference: The order of elements in a sequence is a validation constraint. That means if elements appear in the Schema in sequential order, then they must appear in the XML instance document in that order as well.

What follows next is a sequence of elements which are in the mixed content model. In this case, we have `<customer>`, `<product>`, and `<company>` elements within the content of the `<notice>` element.

Mixed content models can become very complex very quickly, so be careful when you are constructing elements with mixed content. The most common error made when working with mixed content in Schema is to forget that the ordering of elements in mixed content is important: Elements in the XML instance document must occur in the order and number in which they occur in the Schema document.

EMPTY ELEMENTS

There are instances when you might want to declare an empty element, for example, an element which only has attributes. This is possible to do by exploiting the `complexContent` element:

```
<xs:element name="emptyElement">
  <xs:complexType>
    <xs:complexContent>
      <xs:restriction base="xs:anyType"/>
    </xs:complexContent>
  </xs:complexType>
</xs:element>
```

We have declared an element called `emptyElement` and given it a complex type. Then we've specified that the `complexType` has `complexContent`, which is a restriction of the ur-type `anyType`. But because we do not give any restrictions, the element is treated as an empty element.

Of course, an empty element with no attributes is not really all that useful. However, as we explore attributes next in Chapter 6, we will revisit the empty element and see how we can add some attributes to the element to make better use of the empty element.

<all>, <choice>, AND <sequence>

The `<all>`, `<choice>`, and `<sequence>` elements are all related to particles and model groups, which we will be addressing in detail in Chapter 7, "Model Groups." For now, just keep in mind that a particle is a basic component which contributes to the building of a model group, and a model group in turn is a way to describe different kinds of element content.

SUBSTITUTION GROUPS

One new powerful feature of XML Schema is substitution groups. A substitution group is simply a grouping of elements which can be substituted for one another. The element which serves as the basis for the group is called the head element. Let's take a look at an example:

```
<xs:element name="customer" type="xs:string" />
<xs:element name="myspace:phone" type="xs:string" />

<xs:element name="USphone" type="xs:string"
       substitutionGroup="myspace:phone"/>

<xs:element name="INTphone" type="xs:string"
       substitutionGroup="myspace:phone"/>
```

```
<xs:element name="contact">
  <xs:complexType>
    <xs:sequence>
      <xs:element ref="contact"/>
      <xs:element ref="myspace:phone"/>
    </xs:sequence>
  <xs:complexType>
</xs:element>
```

In this example, we start by declaring a <customer> element for the name of our customer, and then declare a <phone> element for our customer phone number. Notice that we also declare the <phone> element with a namespace prefix. We do this because substitution groups must take the form of qualified names.

Next, we declare the <USphone> and <INTphone> elements, but you will notice that we added an attribute to these declarations called substitutionGroup. That attribute accepts a value in the form of a qualified name which represents the head element which the newly declared element may be substituted for.

Note

Elements in a substitution group must all be of the same type. For example, you could not have an element called <name> which was a string, and another called <quantity> which was an integer, and place them both in the same substitution group. In essence, substitution groups may not be used to create type unions.

Finally, we declare the <contact> element with an element content model that includes our <customer> and <phone> elements. The result is that all of the following XML instances are valid against our Schema declarations:

```
<contact>
<customer>John Doe</customer>
<myspace:phone>555-1212</myspace:phone>
</contact>

<contact>
<customer>John Doe</customer>
<myspace:USphone>312-555-1212</myspace:USphone>
</contact>

<contact>
<customer>John Doe</customer>
<myspace:INTphone>+1-312-555-1212</myspace:INTphone>
</contact>
```

In each case the only aspect that changes is the phone, Usphone, and INTphone elements, which may be substituted in the instance for one another, since they are all members of the same substitution group.

Substitution groups provide for a great deal of flexibility in the construction of XML instance documents. You can also use the block attribute with <element> declarations in order to prevent substitution of an element.

CONCLUSION

All of the terminology floating around with Schema can sometimes seem confusing, especially considering how similar some of the terms sound. However, when considering element declarations, try to keep it simple:

- An element declaration takes the form of the Schema `<element>` instance.
- Elements may have local or global scope. To reuse element declarations (in substitution groups or as base types, for example) an element must be declared globally.
- Element declarations may be altered through a number of attributes, such as `minOccurs` and `maxOccurs`.
- `minOccurs` and `maxOccurs` each have default values of `"1"`.
- Elements may have `simpleContent` as their content models only if they contain only data and not other elements.
- Elements which contain only other elements have an element only content model, which can be defined using `<complexType>` and `<complexContent>`.
- Elements which contain both data and elements have mixed content. Mixed content can be specified with `<complexContent>` and `<complexType>` elements and the `mixed` attribute.
- `<restriction>` and `<extension>` offer a way to reuse previous element types while altering their definitions slightly.
- Substitution groups provide a mechanism for interchanging elements that contain similar types of content.

Many of the concepts that we have examined in this chapter apply to more than element declarations. These Schema components can be used with element declarations, or they can stand on their own. So as we move forward with describing the syntax of Schema, don't be surprised if you see some of these concepts again. But don't worry; seeing them used in different contexts is a good thing: It will help you become more comfortable with the component and see how you might put it to creative uses when you are designing your own Schema.

Now that we have taken a look at elements, it's time to move on to another fundamental aspect of XML: attributes.

IN THE REAL WORLD

Element declarations are not that difficult to deal with. The vast majority of your element declarations will be one line long, simple declarations using one of the built-in datatypes from the Schema Recommendation. The most common element attributes you will use will be `type`, `minOccurs`, and `maxOccurs`.

Generally, even more complicated element types will probably not be represented in element declarations. Instead, you will more likely use the `complexType` element to declare your own type, which you can then apply to an element in a simple, one-line declaration.

Perhaps the best thing you can take away from this chapter is an appreciation for annotations. If you want to be able to exploit XML in some really innovative ways, keep annotations in mind. Many people will gloss over annotations, seeing them as some sort of enhanced comment, but in reality, the `appinfo` element gives you a lot of power to extend your Schema.

A perfect example of that can be found in the Schematron schema alternative/supplement. Schematron exploits the `appinfo` element, allowing you to nest entire Schematron schema *within* an XML Schema, eliminating the need for linking to an external file. You can use data nested in `appinfo` elements to customize your XML applications as well.

CHAPTER 6

ATTRIBUTES

In this chapter

ATTRIBUTES ARE FUNDAMENTAL

At the heart of the XML document is the element. Every XML document contains a root element, after all. But elements aren't the only fundamental component of XML documents; we also have attributes. Attributes are also a fundamental part of XML documents.

Elements and attributes go hand-in-hand, and often an attribute is a great way to augment an element. One way to think of it is to look at elements as the nouns and verbs of XML, and attributes as the adjectives and adverbs.

In this chapter, we're going to take a look at attribute declarations in XML Schema and how you can use them to declare attributes and manipulate the properties for your elements.

ATTRIBUTE PROPERTIES

You may recall from Chapter 4, "The Components of XML Schema," that the attribute declaration is a Schema component which has a number of properties that can be manipulated. Let's recap those properties:

- name—This property defines the name of the attribute. It must conform to the standard for NCNames in XML.

- target namespace—This property establishes the namespace for the declared attribute.

- type definition—The type definition property allows you to specify the datatype for the attribute. Attributes must be a simple type or a derivation of a simple type.

- scope—The scope property is defined by the placement of the attribute declaration within the Schema.

- value constraint—The value constraint property allows you to declare whether an attribute is optional or required, and allows you to set default or fixed values for the attribute.

- annotation—An annotation serves as a comment, documenting your attribute declaration.

Many of these properties are probably already familiar to you, as you have encountered them with element declarations. Some of them will be new, so let's go ahead and look at some actual attribute declarations.

Note

The properties of attributes aren't necessarily the same as the code used to declare attributes in XML Schema. Some properties, such as name, do have the same syntax, but that is not always the case.

DEFINING ATTRIBUTES WITH SCHEMA

Attributes are declared in an XML Schema using an `<attribute>` information element, which has a number of attributes itself. Those attributes are used to place constraints on the properties of the attribute declaration.

The scope of an attribute declaration is determined by its placement within the XML Schema. To declare a global attribute, you would declare the attribute as a child of the `<schema>` element:

```
<xs:schema>
  <xs:attribute name="myAttribute"/>
  <xs:element name="someElement" type="xs:string"/>
</xs:schema>
```

In this example, `myAttribute` would be declared globally, because it is the child of the `<schema>` element, and not the child of an element declaration. That means that the attribute could be referenced by any element or attribute group in the document.

If we wanted to locally declare an attribute so that it was only available to a specific element, we could do that by placing the attribute as a child of the element declaration itself:

```
<xs:schema>
  <xs:element name="someElement" type="xs:string">
  <xs:complexType>
    <xs:attribute name="myAttribute"/>
  </xs:complexType>
  </xs:element>
</xs:schema>
```

You'll notice that the element declaration has changed some: It now contains a `<complexType>` element, which in turn contains the attribute declaration. The attribute declaration itself hasn't changed at all; it is the same attribute declaration used before. However, since it is now a child of the `<complexType>` element *within* the `<element>` declaration, it is now scoped locally. We could not reference the attribute by another element.

This is how scope is defined for many components, including `<element>` declarations. So you should be careful when planning your Schema to determine whether you will need to reuse an element or attribute with other components. If you do, it would be best to declare the attribute globally, and then reference it in the element declaration.

`<attribute>`

Now that you have seen an attribute declaration, which takes the form of an `<attribute>` element that can have a number of attributes to define the declaration's properties, take a look at each of these attributes in detail.

name

The first attribute we use with the `<attribute>` declaration is the `name` attribute. This is used to specify the name of the attribute we are declaring. So, if you wanted to declare an attribute called `sku` for a sku number in a catalog, for example, you would use

```
<attribute name="sku"/>
```

The names of attributes must conform to the NCName rules, which basically means that they need to be valid XML names. Another aspect of naming to watch out for is naming conflicts. For example, you couldn't have two attributes declared using the same name:

```
<attribute name="sku" type="string"/>
<attribute name="sku" type="integer"/>
```

This would create a conflict because you would have two attributes with the same name, but different types. If they were declared globally, there would be no way to differentiate between the two attributes.

You can, however, have different components that have the same name. For example:

```
<element name="sku" type="xs:string" />
<attribute name="sku" type="xs:string" />
```

This is valid because one declaration is for an element, and the other is for an attribute.

default

The `default` attribute allows you to place a value constraint on the attribute being declared. By specifying a default value, you are defining what the value of the attribute will default to if the author of an XML instance document does not specify a value for the attribute. The `default` attribute takes a value in the form of a `string`.

For example, let's say that we have an attribute called `size` for items in a catalog. We want the author of an XML document to be able to specify a size, but we also don't ever want the `size` to be blank (or nil). We can use the `default` attribute to declare a default value for the attribute:

```
<attribute name="size" default="medium" type="xs:string" />
```

Now, with this declaration, if we had an item in an instance document

```
<shirt/>
```

even without having the `size` attribute listed, the value of `size` as determined by the XML processor would be `medium`.

fixed

There may be times when you want the value of an attribute to be fixed, for example, if there were an internal code that you wanted associated with an element, and didn't want the author of an XML document to be able to change the code. In that case, you could use the `fixed` attribute to declare a fixed value for the attribute declaration:

```
<attribute name="areacode" fixed="317" />
```

In this case, any time the areacode attribute is used in a document, the value will always be 317.

form

The form attribute allows you to specify the form that the attribute name will take when used in an instance document. The attribute accepts a value of qualified or unqualified, which is used to specify whether the name of the attribute, when used in an instance document, must be a QName or an NCName.

This can sometimes be a little confusing, so let's look at an example. Let's say we have a very simple Schema:

```
<schema xmlns="http://www.w3.org/2001/XMLSchema"
        targetNamespace="http://www.myserver.com/myschema">

<element name="contact">
  <complexType>
    <sequence>
      <element name="name" type="string">
        <complexType>
          <attribute name="title" form="qualified" type="string"/>
        </complexType>
      </element>
      <element name="phone" type="string"/>
    </sequence>
  </complexType>
</element>
</schema>
```

This Schema declares an element called contact, which has two child elements: <name> and <phone>. The <name> element has an attribute called title. You will note, however, that the attribute declaration for the title attribute has the form specified as qualified. That means that the name of the attribute, when used in an XML instance document, must take the form of a namespace qualified name.

There are two ways in which we can use this attribute in an instance document. The first is to declare the namespace in the instance document with a namespace prefix:

```
<?xml version="1.0" ?>
<my:contact
my:xmlns="http://www.myserver.com/myschema">
<my:name my:title="President">George Bush</my:name>
</my:contact>
```

In this example, in order to be a qualified name, we have to use the my prefix. Another way would be to simply declare a default namespace for the document, so that we do not need to use the prefix:

```
<?xml version="1.0" ?>
<contact
xmlns="http://www.myserver.com/myschema">
<name title="President">George Bush</name>
</contact>
```

In this example, the prefix isn't necessary because the namespace is declared as the default for the entire document. It's important to keep track of which namespaces apply where, because many XML components require qualified names, but being a qualified name doesn't *necessarily* mean that the prefix will be present, when the default namespace is declared globally as we have done here.

id

The `id` attribute is analogous to the ID in XML 1.0. This allows you to provide a unique identifier for the attribute, so that it can be referenced by other Schema components.

Tip

> In addition to reference by ID, you can also reference attributes by name, and in fact, that is the more common usage within an XML Schema. The `id` attribute in Schema is provided only as a mechanism for backward compatibility with DTDs.

ref

The `ref` attribute is used to provide a mechanism to reference another attribute declaration. There are some restrictions:

- A globally declared attribute may not contain a reference; it must contain a name.
- An attribute declaration which contains a `ref` may not also contain a name.

Here's an example. Let's say that we wanted to declare an attribute for a phone number, called `phone`, and that we wanted to be able to use it with multiple elements, such as `<business>` and `<personal>`:

```
<schema xmlns="http://www.w3.org/2001/XMLSchema"
        targetNamespace="http://www.myserver.com/myschema">

<element name="contact">
  <complexType>
    <element name="personal" type="string">
      <complexType>
        <attribute ref="phone"/>
      </complexType>
    </element>
    <element name="business" type="string">
      <complexType>
        <attribute ref="phone"/>
      </complexType>
    </element>
  </complexType>
</element>

<attribute name="phone" type="string"/>
</schema>
```

This example showcases a couple aspects of Schema. First, notice that each of the element declarations contains an attribute declaration that is actually a reference. Here, they are referencing the phone attribute declaration, which will enable both <personal> and <business> to have phone attributes. The actual <attribute> declaration is declared globally; otherwise it could not be referenced. You also will notice that the references occur in the Schema *before* the actual attribute declaration. That kind of forward reference is actually allowed in XML Schema.

Note

Forward references are not allowed in DTDs because DTDs are processed linearly, and therefore if the processor encounters something that has not been defined, it will cause an error. Schema (like most XML documents) are usually processed by building a tree representation, and therefore the restrictions imposed by linear processing are not a factor.

In an XML instance document, we could use the elements and attributes like this:

```
<?xml version="1.0" ?>
<contact>
<personal phone="317-555-1212">John Doe</personal>
<business phone="812-555-1212">My Company, Inc.</business>
</contact>
```

Using the ref attribute for references is a great way to make the structure of your Schema easier to read and more versatile. And references are not limited to attribute declarations; you may recall from Chapter 5, "Element Declarations," that you can use references with element declarations as well.

type

The type attribute is used to specify the datatype associated with the attribute value in the XML instance document. There are a number of built-in types which can be used for attribute values; some of these include

- boolean
- integer
- decimal
- float
- date
- time
- string

There are more types available as well, but all of the types have one thing in common: They are simple types. Unlike elements, attributes cannot be declared with complex types. Therefore, all attribute declarations have to be based either on the built-in simple types, or on a derived simple type, which itself would be based on a restriction of another simple type.

use

The use attribute is for limiting the usage of an attribute within an XML instance document. The attribute accepts one of three values:

- optional
- prohibited
- required

The default value (if none is specified in the attribute declaration) is optional. If an attribute use is defined as optional, then the attribute may or may not be used by the author of an instance document. If the use value is required then the attribute *must* be present in the XML instance document.

The final possible value for the use attribute is prohibited. If the attribute use is declared as prohibited then the attribute may not be used at all.

attributeGroup

We discussed earlier how you can make use of the ref tag to make a reference to an attribute which is declared globally within your Schema:

```
<schema xmlns="http://www.w3.org/2001/XMLSchema"
        targetNamespace="http://www.myserver.com/myschema">

<attribute name="sku" type="string"/>

<element name="catalog">
 <complexType>
  <element name="item" type="string">
   <complexType>
    <attribute ref="sku"/>
   </complexType>
  </element>
 </complexType>
</element>

</schema>
```

References are one way to organize and reuse your attributes; another way is the attribute group.

An <attributeGroup> allows you to declare attributes together within a common structure, and then reference that structure in place of individual attribute declarations.

For example, let's say you had a number of attributes:

```
<attribute name="sku" type="xs:string"/>
<attribute name="price" type="xs:string"/>
<attribute name="size" type="xs:string"/>
<attribute name="color" type="xs:string"/>
```

You could add all these to an element by using four different references. However, there is an easier way: Declare the attributes within an `<attributeGroup>`.

```
<attributeGroup name="itemInfoGroup">
  <attribute name="sku" type="xs:string"/>
  <attribute name="price" type="xs:string"/>
  <attribute name="size" type="xs:string"/>
  <attribute name="color" type="xs:string"/>
</attributeGroup>
```

Now, the entire set of attributes can be referred to in an element declaration using the name of the group:

```
<element name="catalog">
 <complexType>
  <element name="item" type="string">
   <complexType>
    <attribute ref="itemInfoGroup"/>
   </complexType>
  </element>
 </complexType>
</element>
```

There are several advantages to using an attribute group in this way. First, it enables you to declare a group of attributes with a global scope. This enables you to reuse the attributes as often as you need to, in more than just one element, simply with a reference to the attribute group.

Second, this can make your element declarations easier to read, by enabling you to use multiple attributes in the element declaration with a single reference.

The `<attributeGroup>` element itself accepts three attributes:

- id
- name
- ref

The `id` attribute allows you to specify an ID for the attribute group. The `name` attribute takes an NCName as its value, which is then used when referencing the attribute group. Finally, you can actually reference other attribute groups within an attribute group, which is why `<attributeGroup>` also accepts the `ref` attribute.

As for the content of the `<attributeGroup>` element itself, it may contain `<attribute>` declarations, as we saw in the previous example. It may also contain other attributeGroup elements as references to create a group of groups. Finally, it may contain `<anyAttribute>` as well, which is a special element discussed in the next section.

anyAttribute

The <anyAttribute> element is similar to the <any> element. If you recall from Chapter 5, the <any> element enables you to allow for the insertion of literally any element into your XML document, and to specify the namespace to which the new element can belong.

Similarly, <anyAttribute> allows that kind of flexibility with attributes. For example, let's say that you have an element called <comment> which is declared as a string:

```
<element name="comment" type="xs:string"/>
```

Now, let's say that you wanted the user to be able to use any attribute they wanted, no matter the namespace, in conjunction with the <comment> element:

```
<element name="comment" type="string">
  <complexType>
    <anyAttribute namespace="##any"
      processContents="skip"/>
  </complexType>
</element>
```

With this declaration, we have specified that the <comment> element may contain anyAttribute and that the attributes used with <comment> may be in ##any namespace.

The <anyAttribute> element has a number of attributes:

■ id

■ namespace

■ processContents

The id attribute is used to define a unique ID to identify the <anyAttribute> instance.

The namespace attribute is used to declare the namespace which the new attributes will be a part of. In this example, we specified ##any, which means that the new attributes may be a part of any namespace we want. The choices for the value of the namespace attribute include

■ ##any—This option denotes that the attributes may be a part of any namespace.

■ ##other—This option denotes that the attributes may be a part of any namespace other than the currently defined namespace.

■ ##local—This option denotes that the attributes do not need to be a part of any qualified namespace; they can simply be valid XML.

■ *URI*##targetNamespace—The URI of a specific namespace that the attributes must be a part of.

The final attribute which can be used with <anyAttribute> is the processContents attribute. This attribute specifies whether the contents of the attributes added should be processed or not. The values include

- **lax**—This indicates that the contents of the new attributes should be processed, but that the processing should be lax. What constitutes lax processing is really dependent on the parser processing the XML instance document.

- **skip**—This indicates that processing of the new attributes can be skipped altogether. This is a useful option if you want to skip over the new attributes an author might add to the instance document, because you anticipate that it might cause problems in the parsing of your document.

- **strict**—This indicates that the attributes should be processed strictly within the constraints of the XML and XML Schema Recommendations. This means not only that they must conform to the XML well-formedness and validity constraints, but that they must also conform to the appropriate namespace.

The default value for the processContents attribute is strict, which is the best choice for ensuring that your documents maintain their integrity. However, if you are allowing any attribute in any namespace, you might not care if the document strictly conforms, and therefore you could choose to skip processing of the new attributes entirely.

BUILT-IN ATTRIBUTES

There are a number of attributes which are built in to the XML Schema Recommendation. These are attributes which are defined for the XML Schema itself, and therefore do not require any additional declarations in order to be used.

These attributes include

- type

- nil

- schemaLocation

- noNamespaceSchemaLocation

Each one of these attributes is a part of the XML Instance namespace, and each has a global scope.

type

The type attribute is used to specify the type values for various Schema components. It has a QName type definition, which means that it accepts a qualified name (which is a simple type) as its value.

The type attribute is the same attribute used for both <element> and <attribute> declarations, and you will become very familiar with it as you begin to write your own Schema.

nil

The `nil` attribute is also built-in and a part of the XML Instance namespace. The `nil` attribute allows you to define an element within an instance document as being *nil*, which means it is essentially an empty element, even if the element is supposed to have content.

For example, let's say that you had an element called `stock` which is used to specify the quantity of an item in stock. Generally, the item would be expected to have a value greater than zero, provided the item was in stock, or a value of zero if the item were out of stock. But you might want to actually have a value of nil, for example if you were using the XML document in conjunction with a database, which would indicate that the item was not only out of stock, but that it would not be reordered.

In order to set the value to nil, the element must first be declared as being nillable:

```
<xs:element name="stock" type="xs:integer" nillable="true"/>
```

Once the element has been declared as nillable, you can then use the `nil` attribute to set the value of the element to nil:

```
<stock xsi:nil="true"></stock>
```

Although `nil` is a built-in attribute, it cannot actually be used for attributes. It can only be used to set the value for an element's content to nil; attribute content is not nillable.

schemaLocation

As we saw in Chapter 3, "Converting a DTD into a Schema," there needs to be a mechanism for instructing the XML parser to use an XML Schema. That mechanism is the `schemaLocation` attribute. The `schemaLocation` attribute, when used in an XML instance document, has two values: one is the namespace for the Schema, and the second is the location of the Schema file itself. So if we have an XML document in the `www.myserver.com/myNamespace` namespace, we could use the following:

```
<?xml version="1.0" ?>
<xmlns:xsi="http://www.w3.org/2001/XMLSchema-instance"
    xsi:schemaLocation="http://www.myserver.com/myNamespace
    http://www.myserver.com/mySchema.xsd">
<root>
</root>
```

This specifies that `mySchema.xsd` is to be used with the document. The `schemaLocation` attribute can also be used in some other cases. For example, if you are constructing a Schema from multiple files using the `<include>` element, you would also use `schemaLocation` to specify the location of the Schema that is to be included.

Similarly, the `schemaLocation` attribute is used with the `<import>` element, which can also be used to construct Schema from multiple files. The `<import>` element is used when you are constructing a Schema from multiple files in multiple namespaces.

Finally, the schemaLocation attribute can be used with the `<redefine>` element. The `<redefine>` element offers a mechanism for bringing in element declarations and complex type definitions from an outside Schema, and then redefining them for use in your own Schema.

We'll talk more about constructing Schema from multiple documents in Chapter 14, "Building Multipart Schema," but in order to do so, we will need to make use of the built-in schemaLocation attribute.

noNamespaceSchemaLocation

The schemaLocation attribute is used to indicate the location of Schema in relation to their namespace. However, Schema are not required to have a namespace. In those instances where you are using a Schema that does not have a namespace, you would need to make use of the noNamespaceSchemaLocation attribute in order to specify the Schema location.

However, noNamespaceSchemaLocation is only used with instance documents. Unlike the similar schemaLocation attribute, it is not used with include, import, or redefine.

IDs IN SCHEMA

The id attribute which we have seen with both elements and attributes is a holdover for compatibility from the XML 1.0 Recommendation. However, there are some key differences between how the ID functions in XML and how the id attribute is used in XML Schema.

The first and most important difference is that under XML 1.0, the ID is actually a type, which can be applied to an element or an attribute. For example, if we had the following XML:

```
<name phone="800-555-1212">Jane Doe</name>
```

under XML 1.0 with a DTD, it would be possible to declare that the phone attribute was actually an ID attribute, meaning that it always had to have a unique value (within the scope of the instance document) and that it could be referenced by the IDREF construct.

With XML Schema, however, we have the id attribute, and therefore we generally would not need to declare an attribute as an ID. However, to maintain compatibility with the ID from XML 1.0, XML Schema: Datatypes does include an id datatype which can be applied to attributes. Because it is a datatype, it could theoretically be applied to elements as well, although for compatibility's sake you should only use the id datatype with attributes.

ENUMERATIONS

Enumerations are simply lists. For example, if you had an address element, you might want it to include an attribute called state and you might want to force the user to choose from one of the fifty states in the U.S.

In XML 1.0, enumerations could only be used with attributes, which is why we are going to discuss them here. However, it is important for you to keep in mind that enumerations in XML Schema can actually be used with elements as well.

An enumeration is implemented by using a restriction of a `simpleType`. To define an enumeration, you would use the `<enumeration>` element as a child of the `<restriction>` element. Let's take a look at an example. Say you were defining an element called `<phone>` and you wanted the author to be able to specify an attribute called `location` from which they could choose one of `"work"`, `"home"`, `"fax"`, `"cell"`, or `"pager"` as the location of the phone number. That's a perfect use for an enumeration:

```
<xs:attribute name="location">
  <xs:simpleType>
    <xs:restriction base="xs:string">
      <xs:enumeration value="work">
      <xs:enumeration value="home">
      <xs:enumeration value="fax">
      <xs:enumeration value="cell">
      <xs:enumeration value="pager">
    </xs:restriction>
  </xs:simpleType>
</xs:attribute>

<xs:element name="phone">
  <xs:complexType>
  <xs:attribute ref="location"/>
  </xs:complexType>
</xs:element>
```

As you can see in the attribute declaration, the enumeration is formed by restricting a `simpleType`, in this case `string`.

Each choice for the enumeration is specified using an `<enumeration>` element which takes an attribute called `value`, which specifies the value for that enumeration choice.

Enumerations are found everywhere in computing applications, such as pull-down menus, so they are a very useful construct to be aware of when authoring your XML Schema.

CONCLUSION

Attributes are the complement to elements. Data in your XML documents which is used to expand on the content of an element, or describe element content in some way (like the way an adjective describes a noun), is often best used as an attribute. Here's a recap of some of the more important points about attributes:

- Attributes are declared using the `<attribute>` element within an XML Schema.
- Attribute scope is determined by the placement of the `<attribute>` element within the Schema. Attribute declarations which are children of the `<schema>` element are global. Attribute declarations which are children of `<element>` are local.
- Attributes can be declared with a `default` value or with a `fixed` value by using those attributes respectively.
- The use of an attribute in an XML instance document can be constrained with the `use` attribute. Attributes can be specified as `optional`, `required`, or `prohibited`.

- Attributes can be grouped together using the `<attributeGroup>` element, which allows a group of attributes to be referenced using one `ref` attribute.

- The XML Schema Recommendation contains a number of built-in attributes which are part of the XML Instance namespace: `type`, `nil`, `schemaLocation`, `noNamespaceSchemaLocation`.

- Attributes may appear in any order, so ordering is not important in attribute declarations.

- Attributes may be enumerations, which is a restriction of a `<simpleType>` that limits the value of an attribute to one from a list of choices.

Attributes and elements are the fundamental building blocks of XML, and because Schema are XML, they are the fundamental building blocks of Schema as well. Now that we have seen how you declare both elements and attributes in a Schema, we are going to talk about model groups and more advanced Schema structures. Then we'll round out this part with an example from start to finish of a Schema that makes use of the structures we've covered.

IN THE REAL WORLD

Attribute declarations will generally be one-line declarations, or enumerations. Most attributes will simply specify a `name` and a `type`, using one of the XML Schema built-in datatypes. The second most common form attributes take is an enumeration, as attributes are often used by developers as a way to communicate information to applications, such as pull-down menu choices in GUI apps.

If you are doing extensive work with databases, you should become very familiar with the built-in datatypes and `nil`, and should examine how they relate to the datatypes you are using in your database applications. You might find that the datatypes are a close match, but not perfect, and therefore need to tweak the built-in datatypes somewhat.

Finally, if you are authoring large Schema, you should make yourself very familiar with `attributeGroup`, because attribute groups function very similarly to parameter entities in DTDs. Groups enable you to define a set of attributes that you can then reference over and over again throughout your Schema, which can be a real time-saver with large sets of commonly used attributes.

PART
II

CH
6

MODEL GROUPS

In this chapter

MODEL GROUPS AND SCHEMA CONTENT

Elements and attributes make up the bulk of any XML instance document. The organization of those elements and attributes determines the structure of your document, and since XML is structured markup, that structure isn't just arbitrary; it is designed to reflect the intentions of the author for describing a set of information.

For example, you certainly want to be able to control which elements are nested within other elements. But you might also want to be able to control the order in which elements appear, or the number of times an element may occur. This type of control is why you are working with a schema. With only well-formed XML, there is no way to control the structure of the document; as long as a well-formed document is properly nested, with all tags closed, and so on, it is legitimate XML. Using a Schema, however, gives you more control. And one of the mechanisms that you can employ to give you that greater level of control is the model group.

WHAT IS A MODEL GROUP?

If an XML Schema component isn't defined as being empty, or as having a `simpleType` (such as a string or integer) as its content, then the content must consist of other components. It only stands to reason that there should be some mechanisms for defining content models.

In previous chapters, we saw how you can reference globally defined element or attribute declarations using the `ref` attribute. Once an element or attribute has been declared globally, you can then use that element or attribute again within the Schema by referencing it. This allows you to reuse components, which is one way in which you can begin building content models.

We have also already seen one way in which groups can be used to enhance content models: attribute groups. Attribute groups allow you to group attributes so that they may be used conveniently with element declarations.

While grouping attributes is a handy mechanism, most content models involve elements, so a mechanism that allows for the grouping of elements would be handy as well. Of course, element content models can be specified within the element declaration itself, within a `<complexContent>` or `<complexType>` element. Then, in conjunction with the `minOccurs` and `maxOccurs` attributes, it is possible to specify the number of times an element should occur within a content model.

Already, this provides more flexibility than was possible with DTDs; the `minOccurs` and `maxOccurs` attributes allow a much finer degree of control than the *, +, and ? of the DTD. But what if we wanted to specify that the element's content had to occur in a specific order? Or, that there could be a choice between different elements in the content? That's where model groups come into play. They allow you to create groupings of content with special meaning, to be used within your content models. Model groups are used in DTDs as well, but Schema provide some different mechanisms to create and reuse model groups.

MODEL GROUP PROPERTIES

A model group is a Schema component with a number of properties that can be constrained, similar to other Schema components. The properties which apply to the model group component are

- particles—A list of the individual particles in the model group, such as elements.
- compositor—May be all, choice, or sequence, which specify how that model group will be used.
- annotation—An annotation, or comment, for the model group.

The particle property allows you to define the list of particles which are a part of the model group. There are a number of particles which can be included in a model group.

The compositor property allows you to select what type of model group you are defining. We will look at the different types of model groups in more detail later in this chapter.

Finally, you can include an annotation in the model group as well, to document the structure and contents of the model group.

PARTICLES

If you think about physics, there are many examples of particles: electrons, neutrons, protons. These are the components of atoms, which in turn make up molecules, which comprise matter, and so on.

Similarly, in an XML Schema, a *particle* is a fundamental building block. Particles in XML Schema may consist of elements, wildcards, or other model groups. Now, that last part might sound confusing: How can a model group be a particle if it is constructed out of particles? Well, that is due to the recursive nature of XML Schema, and the value that can be found in grouping groups. Just like millions of kinds of molecules can be made from a limited number of atoms, which themselves are composed of only three kinds of subparticles, Schema become more versatile when we can build them piece by piece.

That is why you can actually have a model group made up of other model groups, and that is why a model group, *when* it is used within another model group, functions as a component.

PARTICLE SCHEMA COMPONENT

A particle is a Schema component as defined in the XML Schema Recommendation, and as such, it has the following properties:

- min occurs—A non-negative integer denoting the minimum number of occurrences for a particle.
- max occurs—A non-negative integer denoting the maximum number of occurrences for a particle.
- term—May be part of a model group, a wildcard, or an element declaration.

The min occurs property is expressed with the minOccurs attribute, which allows you to specify the minimum number of times the particle may appear. The max occurs property is expressed with the maxOccurs attribute, which allows you to specify the maximum number of times the particle may appear.

The term property refers to the particle definition itself, which is limited to being an element, a wildcard, or a group.

DEFINING MODEL GROUPS

Model groups are defined in XML Schema by using the <group> element, which accepts a number of children: <choice>, <sequence>, or <all>. These children dictate how the content of the model group is to be organized. The <group> element has the following attributes:

- id—Allows you to create a unique ID for the group.
- maxOccurs—Allows you to specify the maximum number of times the group may be used within a content model. maxOccurs has a default value of 1.
- minOccurs—Allows you to specify the minimum number of times the group may be used within a content model. maxOccurs has a default value of 1.
- name—Allows you to specify a name for the group so that the group can be referenced later, either by other groups or within a content model.
- ref—Allows you to reference another group, for example, declaring the model group globally, and then using it by reference in a local declaration.

These are the same attributes we've already seen for <element> declarations, and they function the same. Model groups can be named, and referred to by name, which makes them very powerful for building some very complex content models.

Now let's take a look at the possible child elements of group, and see how they can be used to make groups more flexible and powerful when designing a content model.

<choice>

The first option for a <group> is the <choice> element. The <choice> element enables you to define a list of elements from which an instance document's author may choose which one to use in the XML document itself.

For example, let's say that you had a catalog document, and you had several different types of items, from shirts to bulk candy. Shirts are sold by size, so it makes sense that you might want to have a <size> element. However, candy isn't usually sold by size; it's sold by weight, so you might want to have a <weight> element as well.

One way to do this might be as follows:

```
<element name="item">
 <complexType>
  <element name="size" type="string" minOccurs="0"/>
```

```
   <element name="weight" type="string" minOccurs="0"/>
  </complexType>
</element>
```

This would allow you to have an `<item>` that had either a `<size>` or a `<weight>` child, because with the `minOccurs` set to zero, you could always simply not include the element which was not appropriate. However, because both elements have a `minOccurs` of zero, an author could also choose to leave out *both* elements, or include both elements, which is not what you want the author to do. So a better solution would be to say that one of the elements was required, *either* a `<size>` element or a `<weight>` element. That is what `<choice>` is for:

```
<group>
 <choice>
  <element name="size" type="string"/>
  <element name="weight" type="string"/>
 </choice>
</group>
```

This defines a group, which then uses the `<choice>` element to specify that the group allows for a choice between the two elements, `<size>` and `<weight>`. The group could then be used in our `<item>` element's content model:

```
<element name="item">
 <complexType>
   <group>
    <choice>
     <element name="size" type="string"/>
     <element name="weight" type="string"/>
    </choice>
   </group>
 </complexType>
</element>
```

Now we have an element `<item>` which requires a choice between having either a `<size>` or a `<weight>` child. The `choice` element itself has a few options we can use with it as well. It can take the following attributes:

- `id`
- `minOccurs`
- `maxOccurs`

These attributes have the same meaning for the `<choice>` element just as they do for any other element, enabling you to dictate the number of occurrences of the choices described in the group.

Let's take a look at another `<choice>` example. Say we wanted to offer a choice between `<home>` and `<work>` children for both `<address>` and `<phone>` elements. We could declare a global model group, and then reference it from within the element declarations:

```
<group name="myChoice">
 <choice>
  <element name="home" type="string"/>
  <element name="work" type="string"/>
```

```
  </choice>
 </group>

 <element name="listing">
  <complexType>
   <element name="address">
    <complexType>
     <group ref="myChoice"/>
    </complexType>
   </element>
   <element name="phone">
    <complexType>
     <group ref="myChoice"/>
    </complexType>
   </element>
  </complexType>
 </element>
```

Here, we globally declare a model group which contains our <choice>, and then we reference the model group by name in the content model for our actual elements of <phone> and <address>.

<sequence>

Sometimes it is nice to have a <choice>, but other times, you may not want authors of your instance documents to have a choice over what is included in an element's content. In fact, you might want to be even more restrictive than you might normally be.

For example, if you are creating an <address> element based on the standard address format in the United States, the address takes the form

> Name
>
> Street Address
>
> City, State ZIP

If you were to write it

> City, Street Address
>
> ZIP, Name
>
> State

It *might* get to the proper place, but you would be making enemies at the post office, and relying on their good nature in order for your letter to be delivered. Since we can impose some rules in an XML document, why not state specifically that within an <address> element, there must be

```
<name>
<street>
<city>
<state>
<zip>
```

and that they must occur in that order? With the <sequence> element, you can do just that.
The <sequence> element lets you specify that the content must appear as it is outlined
within the <sequence> element itself, in order. Let's take a look:

```
<element name="address">
 <complexType>
  <group>
   <sequence>
    <element name="name" type="string"/>
    <element name="street" type="string"/>
    <element name="city" type="string"/>
    <element name="state" type="string"/>
    <element name="zip" type="string"/>
   </sequence>
  </group>
 </complexType>">
</element>
```

Now, the <sequence> element requires that all of the elements declared within it, <name>,
<street>, <city>, <state>, and <zip>, must appear in that same order when they are used in
an instance document. We could still provide some customization. For example, let's say we
wanted to make <name> optional, or offer a choice between <name> and <company>, and then
we also wanted to add an optional <street2> for a second street address line:

```
<element name="address">
 <complexType>
  <group>
   <sequence>
    <group>
     <choice>
      <element name="name" type="string"/>
      <element name="company" type="string"/>
     </choice>
    </group>
    <element name="street" type="string"/>
    <element name="street2" type="string" minOccurs="0"/>
    <element name="city" type="string"/>
    <element name="state" type="string"/>
    <element name="zip" type="string"/>
   </sequence>
  </group>
 </complexType>
</element>
```

Now, in this example, you'll notice that we have nested a <choice> within our <sequence>.
We can do that because model groups are treated as particles, and therefore, they can be
included in other model groups. The end result is that we now have a choice between a
<name> element or a <company> element for our address. Also, by adding the <street2>
declaration, we can have a second street address line; however, because it may occur zero
times, it is essentially optional. Therefore, in an instance document, we could have:

```
<address>
 <name>John Doe</name>
 <street>2135 North Damen</street>
```

PART

II

CH

7

```
<city>Chicago</city>
<state>IL</state>
<zip>60647</zip>
</address>
```

Or, we could have:

```
<address>
 <company>Widgets, Inc.</company>
 <street>1608 North Milwaukee</street>
 <street2>Suite 800</street2>
 <city>Chicago</city>
 <state>IL</state>
 <zip>60622</zip>
</address>
```

Both would fit the content model described by our use of the model groups as shown previously.

<all>

Finally, in addition to `<choice>` and `<sequence>`, there is another possible child element for the `<group>` element: `<all>`. Just as the `<sequence>` element is used to define a sequence of elements with a specific order of appearance in instance documents, and `<choice>` is used to define a choice between multiple elements, the `<all>` element is used to denote that *all* of the elements which are declared or referenced in the model group must appear in an instance document.

`<all>` is a little different than `<choice>` or `<sequence>`; however, there are some restrictions as to how `<all>` can be used:

- `<all>` must be the top level element in a content model. This means that an `<all>` element *cannot* be the child of a `<choice>` or `<sequence>`.

- `<all>` may contain only elements. This means that an `<all>` element may not contain a `<sequence>` or a `<choice>`; it can only contain an actual element declaration or the reference to an element declaration.

- You can use minOccurs and maxOccurs to specify occurrences within an `<all>` element; however, they can only have a value of 0 or 1 when used within an `<all>`.

Also, the `<all>` element does not place any restrictions on the order of the elements it contains; it merely means that they must be present. For example, let's say that we have a `<contact>` element, and we want to ensure that every contact has at least a name and a phone number:

```
<element name="contact">
 <complexType>
 <all>
  <element name="name" type="string"/>
  <element name="phone" type="string"/>
 </all>
 </complexType>
</element>
```

With this declaration, an instance document could be either

```
<contact>
<name>John Doe</name>
<phone>812-555-1212</phone>
</contact>
```

or

```
<contact>
<phone>812-555-1212</phone>
<name>John Doe</name>
</contact>
```

Since order is not important, the elements can appear in any order. However, you could *not* have

```
<contact>
<name>John Doe</name>
</contact>
```

This is not valid, because the `<all>` element specified that `<contact>` had to contain both a `<name>` *and* a `<phone>`, because the default value of the minOccurs and maxOccurs is 1.

As you can see, model groups give you a great deal of flexibility when it comes to defining content models for elements within your documents. When used correctly, they provide a much finer degree of control over the contents of an XML instance document than was ever possible with a DTD.

WILDCARDS

XML Schema can become complex very quickly. With the use of namespaces, Schema can contain elements from the Schema namespace, the XML Instance namespace, and even user-defined namespaces as well! And that is only the beginning. As namespaces become more commonplace in usage, you may find yourself with XML instance documents which take a number of elements or attributes from multiple namespaces.

So, how do you deal with allowing attributes and elements from other namespaces within your XML documents? Wildcards.

WILDCARD PROPERTIES

The wildcard component of XML Schema has a number of different properties which define how the wildcard functions:

- namespace constraint—Values of ##any, ##other, ##targetNamespace, or a URI. These keywords are used to specify how namespaces are to be used with the Schema document.
- process contents—May be skip, lax, or strict. Used to denote processing of the wildcard. There are no W3C definitions for what constitutes "lax" processing, so how these keywords are used will vary greatly, depending on the application processing the Schema.
- annotation—An annotation for the wildcard.

PART

II

CH

7

The namespace constraint properties enable you to specify how the wildcard relates to the namespaces you are using in your Schema and in instance documents. The process contents constraints enable you to instruct the XML parser on how it should treat the wildcard with respect to validation. And of course, you can add comments to a wildcard with an annotation.

USING WILDCARDS

Wildcards are expressed in an XML Schema using the `<any>` element, which accepts the following attributes:

- `id`
- `maxOccurs`
- `minOccurs`
- `namespace`
- `processContents`

By now, you are familiar with the `id`, `maxOccurs`, and `minOccurs` attributes. The `id` attribute enables you to set a unique ID for the `<any>` element, and the `maxOccurs` and `minOccurs` attributes enable you to specify the number of occurrences of a wildcard. The two attributes which are unique to the `<any>` element are the `namespace` attribute and the `processContents` attribute.

The `namespace` attribute enables you to specify the namespace which should be associated with the wildcard. It accepts the following keywords and values:

- `##any`—A keyword, specifying that any namespace may be used with the wildcard.
- `##other`—A keyword, specifying that any namespace, other than the current namespace, may be used with the wildcard.
- `##local`—A keyword, specifying that the wildcard is a member of the local namespace.
- `##targetNamespace`—A keyword, specifying that the wildcard should be a member of the specified target namespace.
- a URI—A value, which should specify the namespace for the wildcard with a URI.

The keyword `##any` denotes that the wildcard may be a part of *any* namespace, which pretty much leaves the gates wide open:

```
<xs:any namespace="##any"/>
```

You can specify that the wildcard may be a part of another namespace other than the document's declared target namespace using the `##other` keyword:

```
<xs:any namespace="##other"/>
```

That will allow the wildcard to be a part of any namespace which is not the target namespace as defined in the XML Schema. You can also specify the wildcard to be part of the local namespace by using the `##local` keyword:

```
<xs:any namespace="##local"/>
```

Similarly, you can declare the wildcard to be a member of the target namespace by using the ##targetNamespace keyword:

```
<xs:any namespace="##targetNamespace"/>
```

Finally, you can explicitly specify a namespace for the wildcard by providing a URI for the namespace as the value of the attribute:

```
<xs:any namespace="http://www.myServer.com/myNamespace"/>
```

In addition to specifying the namespace for the wildcard, you can also specify how the processor reading the Schema and instance document should treat wildcards by using one of the following values for the processContents attribute:

- lax
- skip
- strict

If lax is specified, then the parser should parse the wildcard, but how it validates it is really up to the parser. Each parser may give a different amount of leeway for validation. If skip is specified, then the parser should accept the wildcard without validation. If strict is specified, then the parser should treat the wildcard accordingly, and subject it to full validation in relation to the specified namespace for the wildcard.

So, what does this all mean, practically? Let's say that you have a document and you want to include a <comment> element. However, within the comment element, you want the author of the instance document to be able to include any other elements, from any other namespace that they want. You could do that with the following declarations:

```
<xs:element name="comment">
 <xs:complexType>
  <xs:complexContent>
   <xs:any namespace="##any" processContents="skip"/>
  </xs:complexContent>
 </xs:complexType>
</xs:element>
```

Here, we've declared the <comment> element using a standard element declaration. However, in the content model, instead of specifying another element, or attributes, we have used the <any> wildcard, and allowed it ##any namespace, with a skip processing instruction. Now, the author could use literally *any* element in the content of the <comment> element.

NOTATIONS

Notations are a means of including references to different types of (non-XML) data from within your XML document. Notations in Schema are included to allow backward compatibility with DTDs, as notations can be used with DTDs as well. For example, if you were developing an internal application for your company which helps people create company memos, and you wanted the memo.xml files to be able to include a .gif or a .jpeg of the

PART
II

CH
7

company logo, you could use a notation declaration. The notation declaration would allow you to pass information along to the XML parser about how to locate a helper application for dealing with the foreign data type.

NOTATION PROPERTIES

The notation declaration Schema component has the following properties:

- name
- target namespace
- system identifier
- public identifier
- annotation

The two properties which will stand out as different here are the system identifier and the public identifier. The system identifier is a URI which points to a defining resource for the notation type. The public identifier matches the PUBLIC identifier as specified in the XML 1.0 Recommendation; it is used to point to a public defining reference for the notation type. Only one of either the system or public identifiers is required to be present for a notation declaration.

Note

Practically speaking, the most common example I've seen of using a notation pertains to including binary data in an XML document. Frequently, notations are shown with .jpeg or .gif images, as a way of "including" those images in an XML instance document as a notation. However, there is no reasonable explanation, other than for the sake of backward compatibility, why a binary component would not be created as a special XML construct. XML Schema do offer some binary datatypes, hexBinary and base64Binary, which do allow you to specify a component with binary content. The result is that you rarely see notations in practical usage these days. It's good to know about them for compatibility, just in case the need should arise to use them in your documents, but don't be surprised if you don't use them very often, if at all.

USING NOTATIONS

Let's take a look at how you would declare a notation. Notations are declared using the <notation> element, which accepts the following attributes:

- id
- name
- public
- system

The id provides a unique ID for the notation. The name provides a name for the notation which can be used as a reference. The public and system attributes enable you to specify the public and system identifiers for the notation. So, let's look at an example. Let's say we wanted to create a memo and include a `.tiff` file of the company logo. First we would need to declare the notation:

```
<xs:notation name="tiff"
public="image/tiff" system="mspaint.exe "/>
```

Next, we would need to establish the element for the logo itself:

```
<xs:element name="logo">
 <xs:complexType>
  <xs:complexContent>
   <xs:extension base="xs:hexBinary">
    <xs:attribute name="format" type="xs:NOTATION"/>
   </xs:extension>
  </xs:complexContent>
 </xs:complexType>
</xs:element>
```

This would create a `<logo>` element with an attribute that would allow us to specify the logo format, in this case, `tiff`. So, our XML would may look something like this:

```
<logo format="tiff">the logo data</logo>
```

That's all there is to using notations with XML Schema. Chances are, though, that you will never use them.

ANNOTATIONS

Annotations are really just a more sophisticated method of commenting your XML Schema. They are structured to allow comments which are readable both by machines and by humans, so that you can pass along additional processing information to the applications which might be using your Schema, or so that you can provide documentation for another developer reading your Schema.

Let's take a look at the properties associated with annotations:

- application information—Annotation information designated for automatic processing.
- user information—Annotation information which is designed to be human readable.
- attributes—Allow for the inclusion of attributes from a user-defined namespace.

Annotations start with the `<annotation>` element, which has only one attribute, `id`, which can be used to specify a unique ID for the annotation.

The `<annotation>` element has two possible children, `<appinfo>` and `<documentation>`.

The `<appinfo>` element has one possible attribute, `source`, which accepts a URI as its value. The `<appinfo>` element is used to provide annotation information which is designed to be read by an automated processor reading the Schema. This could be used to pass along special processing instructions, for example. In this way, the `<appinfo>` element functions as a replacement for processing instructions (PIs) from DTDs.

The <documentation> element has two possible attributes: The first is a source attribute, which accepts a URI. The second is the xml:lang attribute, which can be used to specify the language in which the document is authored, for example, en for English.

Let's take a look at an annotation:

```
<xs:annotation>
<xs:documentation>User documentation about the contents of this schema.
➥</xs:documentation>
<xs:appinfo>Any Special Instructions for the application.</xs:appinfo>
</xs:annotation>
```

Annotations can be a great way to provide documentation for your Schema which in future applications could automatically be parsed out into manual pages, for example, so it is a good idea to use annotations when possible. But also keep in mind that annotations are not as easy to spot or read as comments, so judicious use is best.

Annotations should be used when you have detailed information to impart to the user, which would take longer to explain than a quick comment of a few words. For example, if you wanted to explain that something was an address, you might just use a comment to say "This is an address." But if you wanted to state that something was an address, and that it included state information and a postal code, and then to explain the format of the postal code, that would probably be better contained in an annotation. First, because it is long enough to format in an annotation and be easily read, but also because it is information that might be useful to pull out into a manual or help file for users. When information is contained in an annotation, XML applications can access that information, and make use of the information, unlike a comment, which parsers ignore.

COMMENTS

Annotations are fantastic and a great way to provide detailed information about your Schema to both an automated processor and other humans reading your Schema. However, because XML Schema are written in XML, you can always use the good old standard XML-style comment:

```
<!-- This is an XML Comment -->
```

There's nothing wrong with including a comment in this style in your schema, and in many cases, such as a quick, one-line comment, it is actually easier to read than an annotation. In general, when a brief, single line will do, comments are much better to use than annotations. For more detailed information, such as a few sentences or a paragraph of text, or to include application data in an <appinfo> element, you should use an annotation.

CONCLUSIONS

That does it for model groups, along with a few extras thrown in. You should now have a solid understanding of how model groups are defined, and how you can use them in building content models for your Schema. To recap:

- Model groups allow for the grouping of particles for easy use and reference.
- Particles are Schema components can be limited by `minOccurs` and `maxOccurs`, and can make up other content models.
- The `<all>` element enables you to create a model group which requires all of the child elements to be used in the XML instance document.
- The `<all>` element may not have any child elements or content models other than `<element>` declarations.
- The `<choice>` element enables you to declare a model group which specifies that an instance author may choose between one of several listed elements.
- The `<sequence>` element enables you to declare a model group in which all of the child elements declared must be present, and must be in the order they appear within the `<sequence>`.
- Both `<choice>` and `<sequence>` may contain other model group elements, such as `<all>`, `<choice>`, and `<sequence>`, as child elements, in addition to `<element>` declarations.
- Wildcards can be used to allow flexibility to the authors of instance documents.
- The `<any>` element is used to declare wildcards.
- Notations enable Schema authors to associate external resources with a notation, which can then be passed along to the XML processor as supplementary information for processing the external resource.
- Annotations provide a more detailed mechanism for commenting Schema, including enabling you to specify both human-readable and machine-readable comment information.
- Because XML Schema are XML, you can also still use XML-style comments.

That brings us to an end of the XML Schema: Structures portion of the Schema Recommendation. There are a few advanced topics which we did not address in this first section, as they relate more closely to datatyping and content building, which we will be covering in Part III, "XML Schema Datatypes." But you have learned a great deal about Schema so far, and are ready to begin applying that knowledge. So, in the final chapter of this part, we will be looking at the construction of a Schema from planning to execution.

IN THE REAL WORLD

Most, if not all, of the work you do with model groups will be in the form of element declarations and type definitions. Named groups are not common in everyday Schema, and you probably won't use them very often yourself.

That doesn't mean that model groups in themselves are not important, as the basic ideas are still applicable to creating element declarations and complex types, just that you probably won't use standalone model groups much.

Of the syntaxes used to create model groups, the ones you will find used most often are choice and sequence.

choice allows you to add flexibility in your Schema, so that users can customize their instance documents based on their needs, which is an important tool in making XML documents useful. Although choice is not quite as powerful as a conditional section, it still can provide a way for you to make your Schema more dynamic.

sequence is also a useful tool for enforcing order in your XML instance documents. Many people make the mistake of falsely assuming that because they wrote the elements in the Schema in a particular order, XML applications and authors will also use that order. This is not the case. Some applications may parse element declarations out of the Schema and choose to present them in some other order, such as alphabetical. Using sequence ensures that the order in which you want elements to appear is the order in which they will appear. Without it, order is not strictly enforced, and you could have any order in your documents. In many cases, that isn't a problem, because order is not always critical. But when order is important, consider using a sequence.

Wildcards are also important for keeping your Schema flexible. In the real world, if you are working solely within your own organization, you probably won't have a need for wildcards in your documents. Where wildcards really come in handy is for allowing interoperability with other organizations, who might be using a similar, but still slightly different XML syntax. Wildcards can also be used to provide some leeway for "forward compatibility," or the ability to add future elements to documents without necessarily revising the Schema. Of course, you should not really rely on wildcards to provide forward compatibility; your Schema should be kept as up to date as possible, but wildcards can be a way to give yourself a little breathing room.

Although notations are presented here in great detail, this is largely for the sake of backward compatibility. In the real world, you will likely never encounter a notation at all. While notations had some limited uses with XML 1.0 and DTDs, those functions (such as referencing binary data) are better served in XML Schema by mechanisms native to Schema, such as the binary datatypes.

In your everyday usage of Schema, you should really never use a notation unless it is necessary to ensure backward compatibility with an existing DTD. Otherwise, use the proper Schema mechanism.

Finally, the importance of annotations and comments in the real world cannot be stressed enough. Comments are useful as reminders to yourself and others about what you were intending for a specific small section, or line, of code. They can prove lifesavers when returning to an older piece of code which needs to be updated quickly and easily.

However, annotations are a very powerful tool for documentation and extensibility in XML Schema. Using the documentation element in an annotation, you can create an inline "user manual" of sorts, which can be parsed out by XML-aware applications to provide robust detail about the usage and implementation of your schema. This is a very important tool for documenting your Schema. Additionally, the appinfo element allows you to include virtually any kind of information with your Schema that can be passed along to the application parsing it. This provides functionality similar to Processing Instructions from XML 1.0, allowing information about the Schema to be passed directly to the application. In fact, this is such a useful tool that Schematron, a supplementary Schema validation tool, actually makes use of it to include Schematron instructions directly in XML Schema documents.

EXAMPLE SCHEMA:
A CONTACT SCHEMA

In this chapter

BUILDING AN XML SCHEMA

In the earlier chapters in this section we addressed the basics of components in XML Schema. We looked at properties, and how properties can be manipulated in element and attribute declarations to form the basic building blocks of your Schema. Then we looked at model groups, and how to build content models for your Schema elements.

Now it is time to pull all of that knowledge together into a practical sample Schema. In this chapter we are going to go step-by-step through the development of an XML Schema for a contact application. We'll look at the choices involved in planning the Schema and the structures used to author the Schema itself.

OUTLINING THE SCHEMA

One type of application that has become very common in usage on the Web is an Address Book. Many services offer online address books via the Web, some of which can even be synchronized with PDAs and wireless devices. The convenience of having your address book available to so many different resources should be obvious: Using any Web-enabled computer or wireless device, you can access your information.

So in this exercise, we are going to develop an XML Schema that can be used to describe an XML-based address book. The first step is to outline the elements and attributes that we will need to store the information. The second step will be to step through those outlines to produce the XML Schema syntax for the address book. And the final step will be to create an XML instance document that makes use of the Schema we have written.

OUTLINING THE ELEMENTS

The information that we will have in our address book will be text-based. In a more advanced version, we might allow for images (for company logos for example), but that really isn't necessary to the task at hand, which is storing contact information.

Because our data will be text data, there will be a number of elements that we can take advantage of. Let's look at some contact information which we might want to encode into XML:

> Bill Doe
>
> 25 Main Street
>
> New York, NY 20212
>
> 212-555-1212 home
>
> doe@billdoe.com

This represents some pretty common contact information that we might have for an individual. There's also some additional information that we might want to be able to keep track of. For example, is the address a home or work address? And we might want to add a pager number or a cell phone number. How about a Web site? It might also be nice to keep track of some other personal information as well, such as the contact's birthday, or if they are married with children, the name of their spouse and kids. For the names of children and spouses, we'll just use a single simple element. If the spouse is also in the contact book, they will have their own, more detailed record.

If we list all these various elements, we get the results shown in Table 8.1, which lists all of the elements we are going to use in the Address Book Schema.

TABLE 8.1   A SUMMARY OF THE ELEMENTS WHICH WILL BE DECLARED IN THE ADDRESS BOOK XML SCHEMA

Element	Description
address_book	Root element for the XML Instance document.
contact	Element for an individual contact record.
name	A parent element for the name of the contact record.
first	The first name of the contact.
middle	The middle name of the contact.
last	The last name of the contact.
company	The company of the contact.
address	A parent element for the address of the contact.
street	The street number and name of the contact's address.
city	The city of the contact's address.
state	The state of the contact's address.
zip	The ZIP code of the contact's address.
phone	A parent element for the phone numbers of the contact.
number	Each individual number, such as home, work, and so on.
internet	A parent element for Internet/electronic contact information.
email	The e-mail address of the contact.
web	The home page for the contact.
notes	A parent element for personal notes about the contact.
spouse	The name of the contact's spouse, if married.
child	The names of the contact's children, if any.
birthday	The birthday of the contact.
comments	Any additional comments for the contact record.

Now, although this list does contain all of the elements we are going to use in our document, it does not represent the relationships between those elements. For example, the table shows that we are going to have a <phone> element that will contain numbers. But the relationships are sometimes easier to see as a diagram, as shown in Figure 8.1.

Figure 8.1
The relationships
between the elements
of the Address Book
XML Schema.

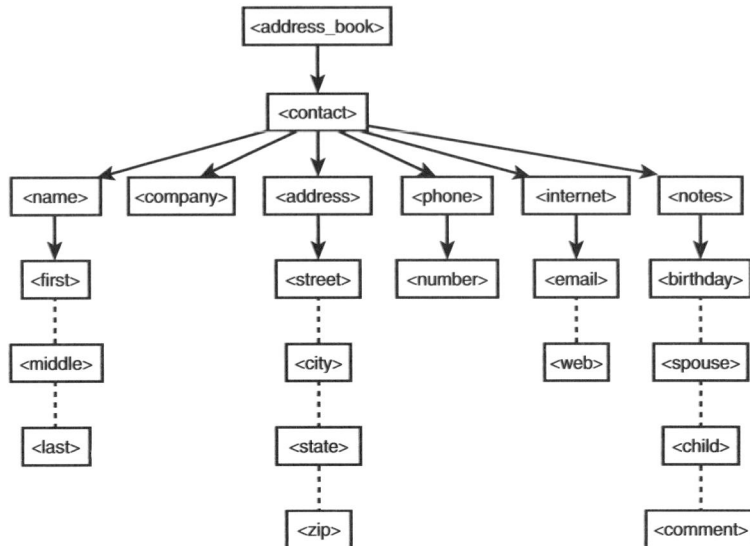

With the diagram it is a little easier to see how the elements relate to each other and which elements serve as parents to other elements. The elements joined by a line with an arrow have a parent-child relationship, while those joined by a dotted line have a sibling relationship.

The result is that we have 22 elements which will encapsulate the data in our address book. The document will start with an element called <address_book> which will serve as the root element for the document. Each record will then consist of a <contact> element, which contains the contact information for the entry.

The <name> element will have three children: <first>, <middle>, and <last>, which will be used to keep track of the contact's name. Breaking up the name entry in this manner will allow for sorting and searching of the records in an application based on the element content; for example, sorting by the <last> names for an alphabetical listing.

The <address> element in this case will have <street>, <city>, <state>, and <zip> children, because we are designing our address book for U.S. formatted addresses. However, as you will see when we begin writing the syntax later, abstracting a content model for the address will give us more flexibility, so that we could add other address types later.

The <phone> element will contain <number> elements for individual phone numbers. How will we deal with differentiating between home, work, cell, and so on? That is a perfect use for attributes.

Because electronic communication is so commonplace today, the <internet> element will have <email> and <web> children for electronic contact information.

And finally, the `<notes>` element will make use of child elements for us to keep track of our contact's `<spouse>`, `<child>`, and `<birthday>`, and will also contain a `<comment>` element for any additional comments we might want to keep track of.

That does it for the elements in our Schema. However, there are still a few things we need to address. For example, how might we express a category for the contact, such as a business contact as opposed to a personal contact? Or, how might we differentiate between a home address and a work address? We would do all this with attributes.

OUTLINING THE ATTRIBUTES

One question that always seems to come up when dealing with schema of any kind, DTDs or XML Schema, is "when should I use elements and when should I use attributes?"

To be honest, there is no easy answer to that question. For example, which one of these is correct:

```
<contact name="John Doe"/>
```

or

```
<contact>
<name>John Doe</name>
</contact>
```

Well, both are. They both are clearly contact information with a name, John Doe. Which is easier to work with? Well, that really depends on your application. There is no "right" way or "wrong" way to design your Schema. Why did we choose to encode most of the information in this Schema using elements? Simply to provide more flexibility and to concentrate on the fundamentals. But there are still some cases where attributes simply make sense, so let's take a look at those.

In our address book, we have three elements which can have multiple uses; that is, even though their values are clearly one type of data, that data might have multiple meanings.

For example, take the `<number>` element. It is clear that the value of the element (since it is a child of the `<phone>` element) is a phone number. However, is it a home phone? A work phone? We don't know. We could have just created an element called `<home_number>` and that would have been perfectly valid. However, the format of a phone number doesn't change between home, cell phones, or work. All share the same format, regardless of where the phone number rings. So, what we really care about is the number; that is the data we are after. Where that phone is located is descriptive information about the number itself. This number is a home phone number, but another one might be a cell phone number or a work phone number.

If we take a look at our elements, we have three elements which can really be used to hold information of multiple types. Those elements, and the attributes we have chosen to accompany them, are shown in Table 8.2.

TABLE 8.2   A SUMMARY OF THE ELEMENTS WITH ATTRIBUTES IN THE ADDRESS BOOK XML SCHEMA

Element	Attribute	Description
`<contact>`	`category`	An attribute that allows you to specify whether the contact is a business or personal contact.
`<address>`	`location`	An attribute which allows you to specify whether the address is a home or work address.
`<number>`	`type`	An attribute which allows you to differentiate between different phone numbers, such as home, work, fax, cell, and so on.

The first attribute we have is `category`, which we want to apply to the `<contact>` element so that we can tell whether the contact is a personal contact, a business contact, and so on.

Next, we need to be able to specify whether an address is a work address or a home address, so we will use the `location` attribute to keep track of the `<address>` element.

Finally, we have all those phone numbers to deal with, and we will use an attribute called `type` in conjunction with the `<number>` element to specify the type of phone number represented.

Now, you might notice a common trend among these attributes: They all basically offer a choice between one or more modifiers. That's one of the reasons we chose to represent this data with attributes, and why these attributes will be enumerations. Table 8.3 shows a summary of the attributes and the types we'll be using.

TABLE 8.3   A SUMMARY OF THE ATTRIBUTES WHICH WILL BE DECLARED IN THE ADDRESS BOOK XML SCHEMA AND THEIR TYPES

Attribute	Type	Notes
`category`	enumeration	Choice between `"business"` or `"personal"`
`location`	enumeration	Choice between `home` and `work`
`type`	enumeration	Choice between `home`, `work`, `fax`, `cell`, and `pager`

With our elements and attributes outlined, we're ready to get down to writing the XML Schema syntax itself. All of the work that we've done mapping out our elements and attributes will really pay off when it comes to writing the Schema. Now it will simply be a matter of translating the structure we already have into the syntax of XML Schema.

Another benefit of attributes over elements is the ability to designate units (such as weight, measurement, or currency) for the attribute value, which makes working with that type of data very easy.

BUILDING THE SCHEMA

The easiest way to go about building our Schema is to simply step through each of the components we outlined in the last section. In order to make things a little clearer, so that the overall structure of the Schema itself is more apparent, we will tackle the components starting with attributes, and then move on to standalone elements, and finish up with elements that contain other elements in their content models. Schema do actually allow forward references, so we don't have to do it that way; however, proceeding in this fashion will aid readability and give you a better understanding of how the components relate to each other.

So, let us begin with our attribute declarations. We will start with these so that you can see how they will be referenced when we build the elements that these attributes modify.

ATTRIBUTE DECLARATIONS

For each of our attribute declarations, we are going to have a very similar format. First, all of them will start with our generic attribute declaration:

```
<attribute name="">
</attribute>
```

Next, we know that our attributes have to be simple types. We also know, if you recall from Chapter 6, "Attributes," that an enumeration is a form of restriction of the string type. So now we have

```
<attribute name="">
 <simpleType>
  <restriction base="xs:string">
   <enumeration value=""/>
  </restriction>
 </simpleType>
</attribute>
```

That will form the basic shell for all of our individual attribute declarations.

category

For the category attribute, we are only going to have two enumeration values: personal and business. When we plug those values into our shell declaration, we get

```
<attribute name="category">
 <simpleType>
  <restriction base="xs:string">
   <enumeration value="personal"/>
   <enumeration value="business"/>
  </restriction>
 </simpleType>
</attribute>
```

If you wanted to expand the choices for the category, such as adding vendor or something similar, you could easily do that by simply adding another <enumeration> with the appropriate value.

That takes care of the first attribute declaration; now we can repeat the process for location.

location

The attribute declaration for our location attribute looks nearly identical to the category declaration. The only changes we've made are to the attribute name and the enumeration values:

```
<attribute name="location">
 <simpleType>
  <restriction base="xs:string">
   <enumeration value="home"/>
   <enumeration value="work"/>
  </restriction>
 </simpleType>
</attribute>
```

Those changes reflect the nature of what we are using the location attribute for. Of course, we could also easily add value choices here if we wanted to extend this attribute.

type

Our final attribute declaration is for our type attribute. This shouldn't be confused with the type attribute you might use with a Schema and datatypes. Our type attribute refers to the type of phone number which is represented in the <number> element. The attribute declaration itself should look familiar:

```
<attribute name="type">
 <simpleType>
  <restriction base="xs:string">
   <enumeration value="home"/>
   <enumeration value="work"/>
   <enumeration value="fax"/>
   <enumeration value="cell"/>
   <enumeration value="pager"/>
  </restriction>
 </simpleType>
</attribute>
```

As you can see, it is the same basic form as the other two attribute declarations. The difference is that we have simply added a few more values for the enumeration.

That's all there is to declaring our attributes. As you begin to author your own Schema, you will find that there may be common structures which you reuse often. That's because we tend to work with similar types of data repeatedly within a given field. In fact, you might be using and reusing components so frequently that it would make sense to build your Schema in a modular fashion, assembling them by including different Schema into one final Schema.

For this example, we're going to keep our Schema self-contained, but we will take a look at multiple-part Schema later, so that you can take advantage of segmenting your Schema as well.

ELEMENT DECLARATIONS

Now that we have our attribute declarations out of the way, we can move on to our element declarations. The easiest way to approach the element declarations is to start with the simple and move to the complex, so we will start off with the elements which have simple string content, and move forward to elements which have more complicated content models. At the end, we'll add some comments, and then pull together the final Schema!

CHILDLESS ELEMENTS

If you refer back to Table 8.1, you can see that there are a number of elements which do not have any children. These elements, such as `<company>`, `<spouse>`, or `<child>`, can also be scoped globally, so that we can reference them from within other element declarations.

Our simple element declarations will take the form

```
<element name="" type="xs:string"/>
```

So, we can step through a number of element declarations, simply by inserting the proper name for the name attribute:

```
<element name="company" type="xs:string" />
<element name="spouse" type="xs:string" />
<element name="child" type="xs:string" />
<element name="birthday" type="xs:date" />
<element name="comments" type="xs:string" />
<element name="email" type="xs:string" />
<element name="web" type="xs:string" />
<element name="first" type="xs:string" />
<element name="middle" type="xs:string" />
<element name="last" type="xs:string" />
```

See how easy it is to get started with element declarations? We now have 10 elements declared, and are ready to start moving on to more complicated element declarations.

```
<name>
```

The `<name>` element is going to be composed of three child elements, one each for the contact's first, middle, and last names. So, we start with the standard element declaration for the name element:

```
<element name="name"/>
```

We know that for the content model, we are going to have three elements, `<first>`, `<middle>`, and `<last>`. You may recall from Chapter 5, "Element Declarations," in the "Content Models" section, that when we have *complex content* in our content model, we need to add a `<complexType>` element, with the `<complexContent>` child element:

```
<element name="name">
 <complexType>
  <complexContent>
  </complexContent>
 </complexType>
</element>
```

Now, because our name will consist of a first, middle, and last name, in that order, we are going to use a sequence to limit the order in which the elements may appear. We want to make sure that we always have a first name and a last name, so we will leave the default values of 1 in place for min and max occurs. However, since we might not always know the middle name of our contact, we will make the <middle> element optional by setting minOccurs to 0:

```
<sequence>
 <element ref="first" />
 <element ref="middle" minOccurs="0"/>
 <element ref="last"/>
</sequence>
```

We don't declare the elements in the sequence by name; instead, we reference them using the ref attribute, because we have already defined those elements earlier. Since they were declared globally, we can reference them here without any difficulty. Now we can integrate the sequence into our <name> declaration, and get the final declaration for the <name> element in its entirety:

```
<element name="name">
 <complexType>
  <complexContent>
   <sequence>
    <element ref="first" />
    <element ref="middle" minOccurs="0"/>
    <element ref="last"/>
   </sequence>
  </complexContent>
 </complexType>
</element>
```

<internet>

The <internet> element can be defined quite simply. Since the element will only have two child elements, <email> and <web>, as the content, and we don't care about the order in which they appear, we can simply include them by reference in the <complexContent>:

```
<element name="internet">
 <complexType>
  <complexContent>
   <element ref="email" minOccurs="0" maxOccurs="unbounded"/>
   <element ref="web" minOccurs="0" maxOccurs="unbounded"/>
  </complexContent>
 </complexType>
</element>
```

The only tricky thing we've done here is change the number of minOccurs to zero, because not everyone will have an e-mail address or a Web page. Then we have set the maxOccurs to "unbounded" so that if someone has multiple e-mail addresses, as many people these days do, we can include them all, no matter how many.

`<notes>`

The notes element declaration will be very similar to that of the `<internet>` element. We are going to include a number of references in the content model, and also set the minOccurs so that the elements are not required to appear if they are not necessary.

```
<element name="notes">
 <complexType>
  <complexContent>
   <element ref="spouse" minOccurs="0"/>
   <element ref="child" minOccurs="0" maxOccurs="unbounded"/>
   <element ref="birthday" minOccurs="0"/>
   <element ref="comments" minOccurs="0"/>
  </complexContent>
 </complexType>
</element>
```

Here, we've included the `<spouse>`, `<child>`, `<birthday>`, and `<comments>` by reference, and we've set the minOccurs all to zero so that the elements don't have to be used if the author does not want to. For the maxOccurs, we've left most of the elements at the default value of 1, because no one can (legally) have more than one spouse. However, one could (theoretically) have any number of children, so for the `<child>` element, we set the value of maxOccurs to "unbounded". That will allow document authors to specify as many `<child>` elements as necessary.

`<phone>`

The `<phone>` element is another uncomplicated element declaration. It follows the same basic form as the other elements we have declared, using a reference to its only child element, the `<number>` element:

```
<element name="phone">
 <complexType>
  <complexContent>
   <element ref="number" maxOccurs="unbounded"/>
  </complexContent>
 </complexType>
</element>
```

Once again, we have specified the maxOccurs attribute to be "unbounded" so that instance authors will be able to include as many elements as is necessary. You might also note that we include the `<number>` element in the content model using a reference, but that we haven't actually declared the `<number>` element yet. That's okay; you can use forward references in XML Schema without any problem, as long as you do declare the referenced element at some point.

`<number>`

Since we have referenced the `<number>` element in the content model of our `<phone>` element declaration, now might be a good time to declare it.

This is the first element with which we will be using an attribute, so now it's time to pull out those attribute declarations we worked on earlier.

Overall, the structure of the <name> declaration takes on a familiar form:

```
<element name="number">
 <complexType>
 </complexType>
</element>
```

But since this is an element which will have character data as content, as well as an attribute, we need to add some more to the content model. We start by setting up the framework for our character data content:

```
<element name="number">
 <complexType>
  <simpleType>
   <extension base="xs:string">
   </extension>
  </simpleType>
 </complexType>
</element>
```

Now we have an element that is ready to go. In fact, all we need to do is add the attribute declaration, and the element is complete:

```
<element name="number">
 <complexType>
  <simpleType>
   <extension base="xs:string">
    <attribute name="type">
     <simpleType>
      <restriction base="string">
       <enumeration value="home"/>
       <enumeration value="work"/>
       <enumeration value="fax"/>
       <enumeration value="cell"/>
       <enumeration value="pager"/>
      </restriction>
     </simpleType>
    </attribute>
   </extension>
  </simpleType>
 </complexType>
</element>
```

We could have included the attribute declaration by reference, if we wanted to include the attribute declaration for the type attribute in the Schema as globally scoped. However, in this case, we thought it best to scope the attribute locally, since these attributes will not be reused with other elements. Therefore we just copied the attribute declaration from earlier into the <number> element declaration.

```
<address>
```

With the `<address>` element, we are going to use a mechanism to allow more flexibility in future versions of the Schema. Rather than declaring the `<complexType>` entirely locally, within the `<address>` element, we are actually going to create our own type called USaddress which will be a complex type content model for addresses in the format of the United States. This gives us a type for U.S. Addresses, which can be reused with other documents as well. Let's start with that declaration:

```
<complexType name="contact:USaddress">
 <sequence>
  <element name="street" type="xs:string" />
  <element name="city" type="xs:string" />
  <element name="state" type="xs:string" />
  <element name="zip" type="xs:string" />
 </sequence>
</complexType>
```

As you can see, this looks just like a `<complexType>` element that might occur in an element declaration, except that now it has been given a name. The name contact:USaddress is used to denote that the type is a part of the contact namespace (which we will need to define in our Schema element) and that it is called USaddress. If we declare this in the top level of our `<schema>`, it creates a global type which we can then reference in our element declarations. This is a preview of data structures and some of the methods we will be discussing in Chapter 11, "Derived Datatypes," and in Chapter 12, "Representing and Modeling Data."

The `<complexType>` definition then contains a `<sequence>` in which we declare the `<street>`, `<city>`, `<state>`, and `<zip>` elements, so they must occur in that order in an instance document. Now, we can use this type when we declare our `<address>` element:

```
<element name="address">
 <complexType>
  <extension type="contact:USaddress">
  </extension>
 </complexType>
</element>
```

The element declaration starts out the same as our previous declarations, with a name for the element, in this case address. What is different about this element declaration, however, is the content model itself. Here, we have used an extension, with the base type defined as the contact:USaddress type we defined earlier. We're extending it here so that we can include the attribute declaration for our location attribute. If we didn't want to extend the base type to add the attribute, we could use the type attribute in the element declaration.

With the attribute declaration in place, the declaration for the `<address>` element is complete:

```
<element name="address">
 <complexType>
  <extension type="contact:USaddress">
```

```
    <attribute name="location">
     <simpleType>
      <restriction base="string">
       <enumeration value="home"/>
       <enumeration value="work"/>
      </restriction>
     </simpleType>
    </attribute>
   </extension>
 </complexType>
</element>
```

`<contact>`

The `<contact>` element will serve as the parent element for each one of our contact records, which are constructed from all of the elements we have declared earlier. We know that each one of our contacts will possibly contain the following elements:

```
<name>
<company>
<address>
<phone>
<internet>
<notes>
```

Because we want to enforce some structure in our address book, to keep the organization of records consistent, we will use a `<sequence>` to declare the content model:

```
    <sequence>
     <element ref="name" />
     <element ref="company" minOccurs="0" />
     <element ref="address"  minOccurs="0" maxOccurs="2" />
     <element ref="phone" minOccurs="0" />
     <element ref="internet" minOccurs="0" />
     <element ref="notes" minOccurs="0"/>
    </sequence>
```

We've also used the `minOccurs` and `maxOccurs` attributes for declaring the number of occurrences allowed of the elements we have referenced. In most cases, we set the `minOccurs` to 0, which effectively makes those elements optional. The only exception is the `<name>` element, which uses the default value of 1, because there must be one and only one name associated with a contact record. Also, the `maxOccurs` value for the `<address>` element is set to 2 so that each record can contain up to two `<address>` elements, one for home and one for work.

Finally, we need to add the attribute declaration to the `<contact>` element, so that we can provide a "category" for each contact, to delineate whether the contact is a business or a personal contact.

When we bring it all together, we end up with

```
<element name="contact">
 <complexType>
  <complexContent>
   <sequence>
    <element ref="name" />
    <element ref="company" minOccurs="0" />
```

```
      <element ref="address"  minOccurs="0" maxOccurs="2" />
      <element ref="phone" minOccurs="0" />
      <element ref="internet" minOccurs="0" />
      <element ref="notes" minOccurs="0"/>
     </sequence>
     <attribute name="category">
      <simpleType>
       <restriction base="string">
        <enumeration value="personal"/>
        <enumeration value="business"/>
       </restriction>
      </simpleType>
     </attribute>
    </complexContent>
   </complexType>
  </element>
```

which completes the element declaration for the <contact> element.

THE ROOT ELEMENT: <address_book>

The only element we have left to declare is the root element for our document, the
<address_book> element. Even though the root element serves as the parent for our
entire document, the declaration for the element is actually quite simple:

```
<element name="address_book">
 <complexType>
  <complexContent>
   <element ref="contact" maxOccurs="unbounded"/>
  </complexContent>
 </complexType>
</element>
```

Since the root element in this case only has element content, we use <complexType> with a
<complexContent> child, and then simply include a reference to the <contact> element. The
only attribute we need to manipulate is maxOccurs, which we set to "unbounded" so that our
address book can contain an unlimited number of contacts.

ANNOTATING THE SCHEMA

Any time you are authoring a Schema, whether it is for public or internal use, it is a good
idea to provide some documentation. At the very least, you should identify what your Schema
is for. But it's also a good idea to provide some comments for your Schema to clarify what
purpose a component serves, or why you have declared something in a certain way. These
comments might not just help out someone else using your Schema, they might help you if
you have to go back and make revisions to your Schema at a later date.

With our Schema, we will include one annotation, which will let users know it is a Schema
for an address book:

```
<annotation>
 <documentation xml:lang="en">
 A sample XML Schema for an Address Book.
 </documentation>
</annotation>
```

> **Note**
>
> The `xml:lang` attribute is used to denote the language being used in the XML document, in this case, English. It is part of the "xml" namespace, which does not need to be explicitly declared.

For any additional commenting, we will insert XML-style comments:

```
<!-- Element declaration below -->
```

We chose to use these because they are simple, straightforward, and, for little notes throughout the Schema, are easier to read than full annotations.

Comments and annotations both are mechanisms to provide additional information to users of the Schema; however, they are used in different circumstances.

Comments should be used to provide quick notes, and are primarily used to document the Schema syntax itself, not the meaning of the structure. Annotations allow for much greater detail of information, and can be thought of as a way of providing documentation and supplemental information about the Schema. Annotations can also include `<appinfo>` elements, which function as a replacement for Processing Instructions.

BRINGING IT ALL TOGETHER

Now that we have all of our attribute and element declarations written, it's time to bring everything together into a Schema document. In order to do this, we must place all of our declarations inside a `<schema>` element.

You are not required to use namespaces by the XML Schema Recommendation; however, it is generally a good habit to develop. The Schema namespace should always be declared to ensure proper processing of the Schema. In this example, we are going to use three namespaces:

- A `contact` target namespace
- The XML instance namespace
- The XML Schema namespace

In order to declare the target namespace, we will use the `targetNamespace` attribute. Then we will also define a prefix for our target namespace, so that we can use that prefix when we declare our `USaddress` type. We define the `xsi` prefix for the XML instance namespace, and then finally we declare the XML Schema namespace as the default namespace. We could have also declared a prefix for the XML Schema namespace (by convention `xs`); however, for this simple example, we're not going to make extensive use of the `xs:` prefix, in order to help keep the Schema readable. Our declarations are still in the Schema namespace, because we declared it as the default.

Let's take a look at the `<schema>` element for our Address Book Schema:

```
<?xml version="1.0" encoding="UTF-8" ?>
<schema targetNamespace="http://www.myserver.com/contact"
```

```
    xmlns:contact="http://www.myserver.com/contact"
    xmlns:xsi="http://www.w3.org/2001/XMLSchema-Instance"
    xmlns="http://www.w3.org/2001/XMLSchema">

</schema>
```

Now we're ready to insert our element and attribute declarations. The code in Listing 8.1 shows the final Schema in its entirety—declarations, comments, and all.

LISTING 8.1 THE COMPLETE XML SCHEMA FOR AN ADDRESS BOOK APPLICATION

```xml
<?xml version="1.0" encoding="UTF-8" ?>
<schema targetNamespace="http://www.myserver.com/contact"
    xmlns:contact="http://www.myserver.com/contact"
    xmlns:xsi="http://www.w3.org/2001/XMLSchema-Instance"
    xmlns="http://www.w3.org/2001/XMLSchema">

<annotation>
 <documentation xml:lang="en">
  A sample XML Schema for an Address Book.
 </documentation>
</annotation>

<!-- Define the root element -->

<element name="address_book">
 <complexType>
  <complexContent>
   <element ref="contact" minOccurs="1" maxOccurs="unbounded"/>
  </complexContent>
 </complexType>
</element>

<!-- Define the contact element -->

<element name="contact">
 <complexType>
  <complexContent>
   <sequence>
    <element ref="name" />
    <element ref="company" minOccurs="0" />
    <element ref="address" minOccurs="0" maxOccurs="2" />
    <element ref="phone" minOccurs="0" />
    <element ref="internet" minOccurs="0" />
    <element ref="notes" minOccurs="0"/>
   </sequence>
   <attribute name="category">
    <simpleType>
     <restriction base="string">
      <enumeration value="personal"/>
      <enumeration value="business"/>
     </restriction>
    </simpleType>
   </attribute>
  </complexContent>
 </complexType>
</element>
```

LISTING 8.1   CONTINUED

```
<!-- Define the name element -->
<element name="name">
 <complexType>
  <complexContent>
   <sequence>
    <element ref="first"/>
    <element ref="middle" minOccurs="0"/>
    <element ref="last"/>
   </sequence>
  </complexContent>
 </complexType>
</element>

<element name="first" type="string"/>
<element name="middle" type="string"/>
<element name="last" type="string"/>

<!-- Define the company element -->

<element name="company" type="string" />

<!-- Define the address element, based on the USaddress type -->

<element name="address">
 <complexType>
  <extension type="contact:USaddress">
   <attribute name="location">
    <simpleType>
     <restriction base="string">
      <enumeration value="home"/>
      <enumeration value="work"/>
     </restriction>
    </simpleType>
   </attribute>
  </extension>
 </complexType>
</element>

<!-- Define the complex type for USaddress -->
<complexType name="contact:USaddress">
 <sequence>
  <element name="street" type="string" />
  <element name="city" type="string" />
  <element name="state" type="string" />
  <element name="zip" type="string" />
 </sequence>
</complexType>

<!-- Define the phone element -->
<element name="phone">
 <complexType>
  <complexContent>
   <element ref="number" maxOccurs="unbounded"/>
  </complexContent>
```

LISTING 8.1 CONTINUED

```
    </complexType>
  </element>

  <!-- Define the number element -->
  <element name="number">
   <complexType>
    <simpleType>
     <extension base="xs:string">
      <attribute name="type">
       <simpleType>
        <restriction base="string">
         <enumeration value="home"/>
         <enumeration value="work"/>
         <enumeration value="fax"/>
         <enumeration value="cell"/>
         <enumeration value="pager"/>
        </restriction>
       </simpleType>
      </attribute>
     </extension>
    </simpleType>
   </complexType>
  </element>

  <!-- Define the internet element -->
  <element name="internet">
   <complexType>
    <complexContent>
     <element ref="email" minOccurs="0" maxOccurs="unbounded"/>
     <element ref="web" minOccurs="0" maxOccurs="unbounded"/>
    </complexContent>
   </complexType>
  </element>

  <element name="email" type="string" />
  <element name="web" type="string" />

  <element name="notes">
   <complexType>
    <complexContent>
     <element ref="spouse" minOccurs="0"/>
     <element ref="child" minOccurs="0" maxOccurs="unbounded"/>
     <element ref="birthday" minOccurs="0"/>
     <element ref="comments" minOccurs="0"/>
    </complexContent>
   </complexType>
  </element>

  <element name="spouse" type="string"/>
  <element name="child" type="string"/>
  <element name="birthday" type="string"/>
  <element name="comments" type="string"/>

</schema>
```

With the Schema completed, anyone can now use it to author an XML instance document. An XML instance document based on the Schema would begin with the XML declaration, as should any XML instance document:

```
<?xml version="1.0" encoding="UTF-8" ?>
```

Next, we need to start off with the root element. The root element in this case will contain a number of namespace declarations. The namespace for the document itself is defined using a straightforward xmlns attribute:

```
xmlns="http://www.myserver.com/contact"
```

Next, we need to define the XML instance namespace, and define the xsi prefix to be used with it, so that we can use the schemaLocation attribute to specify the Schema we are going to use with our document:

```
xmlns:xsi="http://www.3.org/2001/XMLSchema-Instance"
```

Finally, we can link the Schema to our document using the schemaLocation attribute, along with the xsi prefix:

```
xsi:schemaLocation="http://www.myserver.com/contact
➥http://www.myserver.com/contact.xsd">
```

Bring that all together, and we have our root element:

```
<address_book
    xmlns="http://www.myserver.com/contact"
    xmlns:xsi="http://www.3.org/2001/XMLSchema-Instance"
    xsi:schemaLocation="http://www.myserver.com/contact
    http://www.myserver.com/contact.xsd">
</address>
```

Now all that is left to do is add some contacts! The code in Listing 8.2 shows an example of a complete XML instance document based on the Address Book Schema.

LISTING 8.2   A COMPLETE XML INSTANCE DOCUMENT BASED ON THE ADDRESS BOOK XML SCHEMA

```
<?xml version="1.0" encoding="UTF-8" ?>
<address_book
    xmlns="http://www.myserver.com/contact"
    xmlns:xsi="http://www.3.org/2001/XMLSchema-Instance"
    xsi:schemaLocation="http://www.myserver.com/contact
    http://www.myserver.com/contact.xsd">

  <contact category="personal">
   <name>
    <first>Bill</first>
    <last>Doe</last>
   </name>

   <address location="home">
    <street>25 Main Street</street>
    <city>New York</city>
    <state>NY</state>
```

LISTING 8.2   CONTINUED

```xml
  <zip>20212</zip>
 </address>

 <phone>
  <number type="home">212-555-1212</number>
  <number type="work">212-333-1212</number>
  <number type="cell">212-444-1212</number>
 </phone>

 <internet>
  <email>doe@billdoe.com</email>
  <web>www.billdoe.com</web>
 </internet>

 <notes>
  <spouse>Jane Doe</spouse>
  <child>Skip Doe</child>
  <child>Susie Doe</child>
  <comments>Just recently moved to NY</comments>
 </notes>

</contact>

<contact category="professional">
 <name>
  <first>Jane</first>
  <middle>K.</middle>
  <last>Doe</last>
 </name>

 <company>Global Corp</company>

 <address location="home">
  <street>25 Main Street</street>
  <city>New York</city>
  <state>NY</state>
  <zip>20212</zip>
 </address>

 <address location="work">
  <street>1 Wall Street</street>
  <city>New York</city>
  <state>NY</state>
  <zip>20201</zip>
 </address>

 <phone>
  <number type="home">212-555-1212</number>
  <number type="work">212-555-1000</number>
  <number type="fax">212-555-1001</number>
  <number type="cell">212-555-1002</number>
 </phone>

 <internet>
  <email>jane.doe@globalcorp.com</email>
```

LISTING 8.2   CONTINUED

```
  <web>www.globalcorp.com</web>
 </internet>

 <notes>
  <spouse>Bill Doe</spouse>
  <comments>See Bill Doe entry for family info.</comments>
 </notes>

 </contact>

</address_book>
```

CONCLUSION

Now you have worked through authoring a complete Schema, from the planning stage to writing the syntax for the element and attribute declarations. As you can see from the examples in this chapter, the actual writing of the Schema syntax can become just a mechanical exercise if you engage in proper planning for the elements and attributes in your Schema.

Planning and preparation will become more important as we begin to look at more complex Schema models. In the next part, we will begin to look at datatypes, which add a new dimension of power and complexity to your Schema. You've already had some exposure to datatypes, such as `simpleType` and `complexType`, but we haven't done anything very advanced with datatypes yet. We'll also look at building multiple-part Schema, and working with data, all of which will make your Schema much more complicated documents than the one we have just developed. However, if you take the time to carefully plan your datatypes, elements, and attributes before you begin authoring the Schema, even the most complex Schema can be an achievable goal.

IN THE REAL WORLD

You might not actually spend as much time rewriting components as we have here in this chapter. For example, rather than defining your own set of elements for names and phone numbers, it might be easier to simply import or include an existing Schema. Really, there are no right or wrong approaches to solving a problem such as this.

What is important is that you realize that when presented with a problem to solve, a dozen Schema authors will come up with a dozen different solutions to that problem. Because Schema are flexible and powerful, each author may tend to do some things slightly differently, and there really is no problem with that. That is why comments and annotations are important: for communicating your approach to the problem, and detailing your solution.

So, if you see a section in this chapter, or in any of the "Real World" example chapters, and you think to yourself "Hmmm, I would have done it this way instead," that simply means that you are doing well, getting the hang of Schema, and comfortable making the types of choices you will have to make when you are authoring your own Schema.

XML Schema Datatypes

CHAPTER

9

INTRODUCING DATATYPES

In this chapter

WHAT IS A DATATYPE?

There are really two broad divisions among the users of XML. First, there is the document camp. Those users are using XML to create structured documents in a format which we all think of as a "document"; that is, large blocks of text, such as a book or a letter. The document camp might have an XML document that looks like this:

```
<title>Introducing Datatypes</title>
<intro>This chapter introduces XML Schema Datatypes</intro>
<text> There are really two broad divisions among the users of XML. First,
there is the document camp... etc. </text>
```

This type of XML instance document reflects XML being used as a "document" format; that is, the XML describes a text-heavy set of information, similar to something you might want to edit in a word processor.

The second XML camp is the data camp. These might be replacements for traditional EDI applications, or other types of data interchange. The data users of XML are using XML for data applications which previously might or might not have had any standard; for example, a manufacturer keeping track of items in a database:

```
<item sku="3487112">
<manufacture_Date>2001-07-27</manufacture_Date>
<ship_Date>2001-07-27</ship_Date>
<warehouse>21200</warehouse>
<price>59.95<price>
</item>
```

These XML instance documents contain interrelated pieces of information, and the structure of the XML document is designed to reflect those relationships. This is also a perfectly legitimate use of XML.

XML documents provide a great way to exchange information which is primarily stored in data sets, such as application data, or data that would commonly be stored in a database. Because XML is a widely supported, W3C-based standard, any communication based on XML is also likely to be widely supported.

Another advantage of XML comes from making use of common base standards and a set of related standards (such as the standards in the XML family: XML, XML Schema, XSL, and so on) for accessing the information stored in XML documents. For example, previously, if two financial institutions used different formats for storing data about their transactions, they would need to build complicated customized translators in order to exchange data. XML provides a way for them to work together to build a common format, and even if translations are necessary, the translation is much easier because the documents in question are all based on the XML standards.

HOW DATATYPES ARE USEFUL

Interoperability is where datatypes really come in handy. A datatype is a way of defining a lexical meaning for the value of an element or an attribute.

For example, let's look at the following element:

```
<date>03-11-01</date>
```

What information is represented in this element? Well, as a human reader, we can surmise that it is a date from the element content, because we are used to seeing dates written in that format. But to an application processing it, the word `date` is just another string of letters; it doesn't necessarily have any meaning at all.

Then there is the matter of what this element's value means. Take a look at the date in the previous example. It could represent March 11, 2001; or it could represent November 3, 2001; or November 1, 2003; or January 11, 2003; or November 3, 1903. If we don't agree on what the number represents, in terms of YYYY-MM-DD or DD-MM-YYYY, there is no way for us to make real use of the data without the possibility of introducing errors into our data.

That is what datatypes really provide: a mechanism for us to agree on the representation of the data in our data set. The benefit is that when we all agree, for example, that a `date` should always be Year-Month-Day, then we all know that "2003-11-01" is November 1, 2003. That way our customer gets the item they ordered on time. Or, an item in stock that has an expiration date can be removed when it goes bad.

Datatypes are very useful in computing applications, and if you have done any programming with languages such as Java or C++, then you are probably already familiar with datatypes and their uses. Datatypes are also important for storing information in databases, for similar reasons to the ones we just outlined: They are a way to ensure the integrity of your data.

However, with the original XML specifications, datatypes were not included at all. Addressing that limitation was one of the major motivations for the XML Schema Recommendation.

Using XML and DTDs as specified in the XML 1.0 Recommendation, there was no way to define a datatype such as a date. Therefore, people who needed to use datatypes to restrict element and attribute values were limited to creating their own mechanisms to do so during XML parsing. But with no standard, people might implement datatypes differently, which takes data applications with XML back to square one.

Now, with the XML Schema: Datatypes Recommendation, there is not only a common set of datatypes that can be used by Schema and XML instance authors, but also a grammar for deriving new customized datatypes, so authors can create virtually any datatype they need for their documents, but in a specific way so that anyone using their Schema or documents can also use those same datatypes.

How Datatypes Function in Schema

The XML Schema: Datatypes Recommendation states how datatypes are defined and represented within an XML Schema. It also defines a number of commonly used "built-in" datatypes, defined in the Schema Recommendation so that you do not have to define them yourself, such as `date` and `string`.

The Schema Recommendation defines a datatype as a "3-tuple" consisting of

- a lexical space
- a value space
- facets

These three aspects come together to define datatypes in XML Schema, so let's take a look at each one and what they represent.

LEXICAL SPACE

Formally, the XML Schema Recommendation defines the *lexical space* as follows:

"A lexical space is the set of valid literals for a datatype."

What that means is that each datatype has a set of literals which can be used to represent values for the datatype. For example, if we had a datatype called `letter`, the lexical space (for an English alphabet) would consist of "a,b,c,d . . . w,x,y,z" or the 26 letters in the English alphabet (actually, because XML is case sensitive, it would consist of 52 characters, the 26 lowercase letters and 26 uppercase). Therefore, "4" would not be considered part of the lexical space for `letter` and would not be a valid value for the datatype.

INTEROPERABILITY

In order to encourage interoperability between XML Schema and other datatypes, the authors of the Schema Recommendation have made an effort to keep the lexical space for each datatype small. In fact, many times literals and values have a one-to-one mapping, as is the case with our "letter" example, where each literal (a–z) could also be a value. This helps keep the number of necessary translations to an absolute minimum when using schema and XML in conjunction with other applications.

BASIC READABILITY

As is the case with other aspects of XML, the literals for datatypes are text-based, not binary, so that reading an XML file which makes use of datatypes is still easy for both machines and humans.

EASE OF PARSING AND SERIALIZING

XML is not the first computing application to make use of datatypes. Many programming languages and applications such as databases already make use of datatypes, and have for a long time. Therefore, the XML Schema Recommendation makes use of the conventions already established for datatypes whenever possible. For example, when you use an `int` in XML to represent an integer, it has the same lexical literals (the values that can be stored in the datatype) as it would if you were using an `int` in Java, or C++, or with Oracle, and so on.

Caution

In theory, the lexical literals for datatypes in XML are similar to those in other programming languages. At least that is the goal. However, because programming languages vary, the maximum values for an `int` in C++ depend on the machine being used, while in Java it is set to 2^32. So, even though an `int` (and other datatypes) should be the same across many applications, be sure to check for compatibility.

CANONICAL LEXICAL REPRESENTATION

While most of the time there is a one-to-one mapping between literals and values for datatypes, occasionally, this is not the case. For example, what if we have a datatype called `time` and we want to say 9:00 a.m., in both New York and Los Angeles? We could express the time as

09:00:00-EST

09:00:00-PST

Both are valid representations of the same time, 0900 hours (in a 24-hour system) but one is in the Eastern Time Zone, as denoted by "EST", and the other is in the Pacific Time Zone, as denoted by "PST". Both, however, are valid parts of the lexical space for `time`. However, if you take a portion of the entire lexical space for `time` such as the Eastern Time Zone, then you have a canonical lexical representation, which does have that one-to-one mapping between the literals and the possible values.

VALUE SPACE

The *value space* for a datatype is the set of possible values for that datatype. For example, the datatype `integer` has a value space that consists of the numbers mathematically defined as being integers, that is { . . . –3, –2, –1, 0, 1, 2, 3 . . . }. The values are denoted by the use of a literal from the lexical space of the datatype.

Value spaces for datatypes can be defined

- axiomatically
- by enumeration
- by derivation
- by list or union

A value space defined axiomatically comes from a fundamental notation, and these are the built-in datatypes which are provided in the Recommendation for you. Defining the value space by enumeration involves providing a specific list of acceptable values, like you might do when creating an extension.

Defining the value space by derivation means that you would start with a built-in datatype and its value space, and then either by restricting or extending the possible values, create a new datatype which is *derived* from the base type. A derived datatype is based on one of the built-in datatypes, but altered in some way by a Schema author for a specific application.

Finally, lists and unions are mechanisms for combining value spaces from already defined datatypes when creating a new datatype. We will discuss lists and unions in more detail later on in this chapter.

FACETS

Facets provide a mechanism for manipulating the defining aspects of the value space for a datatype. The W3C Recommendation defines facets as

> "A facet is a single defining aspect of a value space. Generally speaking, each facet characterizes a value space along independent axes or dimensions."

For example, if we look at our sample datatype called `letter` which consisted of the letters in the English alphabet, a–z, we might have a facet called `case` which allowed us to specify whether the values for letters had to be lowercase letters or uppercase letters, or whether they could be mixed.

Facets provide a way for you to control the possible values of datatypes in your Schema/XML documents. There are both fundamental facets and constraining facets, which we will discuss later in this chapter.

NAMESPACES AND DATATYPES

As is the case with Schema in general, there are some namespace considerations when you are working with datatypes. There are two namespaces which are associated with XML Schema datatypes:

```
http://www.w3.org/2001/XMLSchema
http://www.w3.org/2001/XMLSchema-Datatypes
```

The first namespace can be used with datatypes in the Schema, and it is actually the namespace for the entire Schema Recommendation, both Part 1: Structures and Part 2: Datatypes. The second namespace is a namespace for just the datatypes, and it is provided to be used in applications where you need to reference the datatypes in the Schema Recommendation, but don't necessarily care about the other Schema components.

When you derive your own datatypes, they have their own namespace, which is the namespace of the Schema in which you are defining the new datatypes themselves.

PRIMITIVE AND DERIVED DATATYPES

Schema provide for two different types of datatypes, *primitive* and *derived*.

Primitive datatypes are defined within the Schema Part 2: Datatypes section of the Recommendation, and the only way that new primitive datatypes can be introduced is through the W3C adding them to the official recommendation.

The primitive datatypes included in the Recommendation are there for a number of reasons. First, these datatypes are datatypes which are already in common usage in other applications, such as databases and programming languages. Because of the likelihood that these common datatypes would be used in XML in addition to other computing applications, they were included in the Recommendation so that you don't have to expend energy defining them yourself.

Another reason for including the primitive datatypes is that they serve as the basis for building other kinds of datatypes. For example, you could build a house out of wood, brick, or stone. Those basic building materials would be the primitive datatypes which are used to construct additional, more complicated datatypes, which brings us to derived datatypes.

Derived datatypes are datatypes which are constructed from other datatypes, either through extension or restriction; that is, either extending the lexical and value spaces of a primitive datatype, or restricting the lexical and value spaces of a primitive datatype.

The Schema Recommendation also provides a number of derived datatypes, which are also commonly used datatypes provided for the convenience of XML Schema authors. However, Schema authors may also create their own derived datatypes, which we will discuss later in this and subsequent chapters.

BUILT-IN AND USER-DERIVED DATATYPES

As we mentioned before, the authors of the XML Schema Recommendation have included a number of datatypes which Schema authors have at their disposal. All of these datatypes are "built-in" datatypes, by definition. And those built-in datatypes break down into two categories, primitive datatypes and derived datatypes.

The various datatypes contained in the Schema Recommendation are shown in Table 9.1, broken down into primitive and derived types. The first column is simply a list of the primitive datatypes, and the second column is a list of derived types, but there is no relationship between the two columns.

TABLE 9.1   A SUMMARY OF THE BUILT-IN DATATYPES, BOTH PRIMITIVE AND DERIVED

Primitive Datatypes	Derived Datatypes
string	normalizedString
boolean	token
decimal	language
float	ID
double	IDREF
duration	IDREFS
dateTime	ENTITY

TABLE 9.1 CONTINUED

Primitive Datatypes	Derived Datatypes
time	ENTITIES
date	NMTOKEN
gYearMonth	NMTOKENS
gYear	Name
gMonthDay	NCName
gDay	integer
gMonth	nonPositiveInteger
hexBinary	negativeInteger
base64Binary	long
anyURI	int
QName	short
NOTATION	byte
	nonNegativeInteger
	unsignedLong
	unsignedInt
	unsignedShort
	unsignedByte
	positiveInteger

The primitive datatypes consist of types such as `string`, `boolean`, and `decimal`, which may serve as the basis for a number of other datatypes.

In fact, all of the built-in derived datatypes have one of the primitive datatypes as their base. These derived types can be used as-is by authors, or they can also be used as a base for deriving new datatypes.

In fact, Schema authors can create their own derived datatypes from any of the built-in datatypes, primitives or derived. We will examine all of these datatypes, starting with the primitive datatypes in Chapter 10, "Primitive Datatypes," and then derived datatypes in Chapter 11, "Derived Datatypes."

FACETS

We already introduced facets when we began this chapter, discussing the characteristics of datatypes. If you recall from the beginning of the chapter, all datatypes have three characteristics: lexical space, value space, and facets.

Facets are the individual characteristics which are used to define the properties of a datatype's value space. For example, a facet for a `string` might be `length`, which would enable you to define the length of a string when you are using it as a datatype.

Facets break down into two types: fundamental and constraining.

FUNDAMENTAL FACETS

The fundamental facets are actually facets that define the datatype, as opposed to placing limitations on the value space. The Schema Recommendation defines a *fundamental facet* as

> "A fundamental facet is an abstract property which serves to semantically characterize the values in a value space."

This means that fundamental facets are not properties that you can manipulate as a Schema author, but rather they are properties which are inherent in a given datatype, and define the characteristics that make it different from other datatypes.

There are five fundamental facets:

- equal
- order
- bounds
- cardinality
- numeric

Each of these facets applies to every datatype in the Schema Recommendation, and because even user-derived datatypes are based on the primitive datatypes, they will apply to your datatypes as well. So, now let's take a closer look at them.

EQUAL

The value space for every datatype supports the notion of "equality," and many of the mathematical properties which are associated with the idea of equality as well. Those include

- For a and b in a value space, either $a=b$ or $a!=b$. That is, if you have two values for a datatype, either they are equal to each other (a=b) or they are not (a!=b).
- You cannot have $a=b$ and $a!=b$ in the same value space. If a is equal to b in the value space, then it is not possible for a to also *not* be equal to b; that would be a logical contradiction.
- In the value space, $a=a$. The value of a datatype is always equal to itself.
- $a=b$ if and only if $b=a$. If two values are equal, then they are always equal, irrespective of order.
- If $a=b$ and $b=c$ then $a=c$. If two values are equal to each other, and a third value is equal to one of the first two values, then it is also equal to the other value as well.

■ If *a=b*, then *a* and *b* are indistinguishable. There is no mechanism for differentiating between two equal values within a datatype's value space. For example, "foo" and "foo" are both equal, and therefore, indistinguishable from one another.

ORDER

The concept of an order relation to value spaces is a mathematical concept, and there are two types of order relationships which can be imposed on a value space: a partial order or a total order.

A datatype is only "ordered" if there is an order relation established for the value space of the datatype.

A partial order is an order relation that is irreflexive, asymmetrical, and transitive, which means

■ For *a* in the value space, *a<a* is impossible. Because the equality facet dictates that *a* is equal to *a*, there is no way that *a* can be ordered in relation to itself. Unlike equality, order is not reflexive but irreflexive.

■ For *a* and *b* in the value space, if *a<b* then you cannot have a>b. Order is asymmetric.

■ For *a*, *b*, and *c*, *a<b* and *b<c* implies that *a<c*. Like equality, order is transitive, so that the relationship between *a* and *b* and the relationship between *b* and *c* implies a relationship between *a* and *c*.

A total order has all of the same properties as a partial order, but also adds that

$a<b$, or $b<a$, or a=b

which means that the order relationship is established and is rigidly enforced.

BOUNDS

The bounds fundamental facet involves establishing the boundaries for the value set of a datatype. There are two distinct types of bounds, inclusive and exclusive.

For an inclusive bound, the boundary includes the value set used to establish the boundary, and for exclusive, the value set does not. Each bounds facet consist of a pair of values, one serving as the lower bound, and one as the upper bound. Those combinations give us

■ inclusive lower bound
■ inclusive upper bound
■ exclusive lower bound
■ exclusive upper bound

Let's look at an example. Say we had a datatype called `digits` for which we wanted to have the value set of {0,1,2,3,4,5,6,7,8,9}. With this data set, we would say that the inclusive lower bound was "0" because that is the lower boundary, and it is included in the value set. The inclusive upper bound in this case is "9". If we wanted to use an exclusive upper bound, we would say "10" because it is the upper bound, but it is not included in the value set (because it is excluded, and 10 isn't a digit).

CARDINALITY

The cardinality of a value space has to do with the number of possible values in the value space. For example, in the `letters` example we used earlier in the "Lexical Space" section, the cardinality of the datatype is "52" because there are 26 letters in the English alphabet, but we treat lower- and uppercase as different values, bringing the total to 52.

There are two types of cardinality which generally apply to value spaces:

- Finite value space. This is a value space that has a limited number of values, which can be counted; for example, 1–10, or a–z, and so on.
- Countably infinite value space. This is a value space which can be counted (using the counting numbers) but could contain an infinite number of values. For example, "all positive integers" would be countable (in theory), starting with 1, 2, 3, 4, 5, 6, 7, ... However, since the positive integers continue indefinitely, the value is infinite.

There is also the possibility for an uncountable infinite value space, as would be the case with certain decimal values, but that case is less common.

NUMERIC

A *numeric* value set is a value set where the possible values are a part of any mathematical number set: integers, whole numbers, rational numbers, and so on.

If the values are not part of a number set, then the value set is non-numeric, which would be the case for strings, or for our previous sample datatype `letter`.

Now, all of the fundamental facets we have just discussed apply to all of the datatypes defined in the Schema Recommendation and to any datatypes which are derived from those datatypes. They are not facets which you will manipulate directly in most instances; rather, they are used for the fundamental definitions of the datatypes. Now we will take a look at the constraining facets, which are a set of optional facets for use with datatypes.

CONSTRAINING FACETS

Unlike the fundamental facets, the constraining facets are optionally applied to datatypes in order to constrain a datatype's value space.

When you constrain the value space of a datatype, you are also constraining the lexical space, and in fact, you are altering the datatype by restriction, which is one way of creating a new datatype.

We will talk more about creating your own datatypes by restriction in Chapter 12, "Representing and Modeling Data," in the "Derivation by Restriction" section. However, let's take a look now at the constraining facets and how they can be used to constrain value sets.

length

The length facet can be used to constrain the number of units of length for the value set of a datatype. The specific unit of length may vary from type to type.

For example, for strings, the length is determined by the number of characters, so for example, London has a length of "6" because the string contains six characters.

For the hexBinary and base64Binary datatypes, the length corresponds to octets, or 8-bit units of information.

Regardless of the datatype being restricted, the value of the length facet must always be a non-negative integer, such as 0, 1, 2, 3, 4, 5, ...

minLength

The minLength constraining facet corresponds to setting a minimum length for the value set of a datatype. For example, if we wanted to use the datatype string for a ZIP code, we might specify a minLength of "5" because that is the minimum length for a USPS ZIP Code:

```
<element name="zipCode">
 <simpleType>
  <restriction base="xs:string">
   <xs:minLength value="5"/>
  </restriction>
 </simpleType>
</element>
```

As with the length constraining facet, the minLength facet must be a non-negative integer.

maxLength

The maxLength constraining facet is analogous to the minLength facet. It can be used to specify the maximum length of the value set for a datatype. For example, if you were using a string type with a <name> element, you might want to limit the name to 25 characters, in which case you would set the maxLength facet equal to 25:

```
<element name="name">
 <simpleType>
  <restriction base="xs:string">
   <xs:maxLength value="25"/>
  </restriction>
 </simpleType>
</element>
```

And, just as with the length facet, the maxLength facet must be a non-negative integer as well.

pattern

The pattern constraining facet is actually a very powerful facet, because it enables you to restrict the value set of a datatype by using a regular expression. For example, let's say that you wanted to declare an element called <phone> for phone numbers, and you want them all to take the form of "(000) 000-0000". You could use the following:

```
<element name="phone">
 <simpleType>
  <restriction base="xs:string">
   <xs:pattern value="\([0-9]{3}*\)[0-9]{3}*-[0-9]{4}*"/>
  </restriction>
 </simpleType>
</element>
```

PART
III

CH
9

This element declaration uses <simpleType> and <restriction> to create a new type for the phone element, and also makes use of the pattern facet, to give a regular expression which will match phone numbers in that "(000) 000-0000" form.

We will talk more about regular expressions in Chapter 12, but they do provide a very powerful way to do complex matching for the value sets of datatypes.

enumeration

As we have seen when working with elements and attributes, an enumeration is a mechanism that allows you to specify a series of choices. For example, if your company offered three locations, and you wanted to have an element called <location> which required "United States", "England", or "France" as possible values, you would use an enumeration:

```
<element name="location">
 <simpleType>
  <restriction base="xs:string">
   <xs:enumeration value="United States"/>
   <xs:enumeration value="England"/>
   <xs:enumeration value="France"/>
  </restriction>
 </simpleType>
</element>
```

Each choice for the value is listed as an enumeration value, and when a type is restricted with this facet, the value specified for the element or attribute in an XML instance document must be one of the enumeration values.

whiteSpace

The whiteSpace facet controls how white space within a value set is treated. The facet accepts three possible values for how white space should be treated:

- preserve—This value specifies that the white space in the value is to be preserved. It is the same as "preserve" in the XML 1.0 Recommendation. For example, with preserve, "T h i s   S p a c e   " would remain exactly the same.

- replace—In this case, all instances of white space in the value set, such as tabs, carriage returns, and so forth, are all replaced with the #x20 white space character. That would change the value of the example to "T#x20h#x20i#x20s#x20#x20#x20#x20S#x20p#x20a# x20c#x20e#x20#x20#x20#x20".

- collapse—When collapse is specified, all leading and trailing white space characters are removed, and all white space which occurs in the value is collapsed as well, so that multiple spaces, for example, are reduced to a single #x20 character. With collapse the previous example would become "T#x20h#x20i#x20s#x20S#x20p#x20a#x20c#x20e".

The default value for whiteSpace is collapse for all datatypes except string, and this value cannot be altered by the author of a Schema. The only type which can make use of the whiteSpace facet is string, and therefore any datatype derived from string.

minInclusive

The minInclusive facet enables you to specify a minimum inclusive value for the value set for a datatype. The value of minInclusive has to be a valid possible member of the datatype; for example, if the datatype were integer, you could not specify a minInclusive facet of "Fred", because "Fred" is not an integer.

The minInclusive facet is inclusive, so if, for example, you set it to "25" for an integer type, the value could be "25" or anything greater than 25, but could not be less than 25.

maxInclusive

The maxInclusive facet is very similar to the minInclusive, but sets the maximum value for a value set, inclusive.

So, if we wanted to specify an element called <egg> which has a minimum value of a half-dozen, or six, and a maximum value of a dozen, we could use:

```
<element name="egg">
 <simpleType>
  <restriction base="xs:integer">
   <xs:minInclusive value="6"/>
   <xs:maxInclusive value="12"/>
  </restriction>
 </simpleType>
</element>
```

Because the facet is inclusive, both 6 and 12 could be used as values as well.

minExclusive

The minExclusive facet is analogous to minInclusive, with the one key difference being that the value stated in the facet may not be used in the value set.

maxExclusive

The `maxExclusive` facet is analogous to `maxInclusive`, with the one key difference being that the value stated in the facet may not be used in the value set. So, if we revisit the previous egg example, we cannot use the values of 6 and 12 for `minExclusive` or `maxExclusive` if we want to be able to use those in the value set. Therefore, the declaration would change to

```
<element name="egg">
 <simpleType>
  <restriction base="xs:integer">
   <xs:minExclusive value="5"/>
   <xs:maxExclusive value="13"/>
  </restriction>
 </simpleType>
</element>
```

That would have the same results as the previous declaration, but the values are changed to reflect that the facet is exclusive.

totalDigits

The `totalDigits` facet is only used with datatypes derived from `decimal` and is used to specify the total number of digits that are required for values. `totalDigits` is specified using a non-negative integer. So, let's say that we wanted to specify an element called `<CCnumber>` as an integer (which is derived from decimal), and we want to restrict it to a 16-digit number:

```
<element name="CCnumber">
 <simpleType>
  <restriction base="xs:integer">
   <xs:totalDigits value="16"/>
  </restriction>
 </simpleType>
</element>
```

This would create the element, and not allow any value for the element to be longer than 16 digits.

fractionDigits

The `fractionDigits` facet allows you to specify the number of digits used in the fractional portion of a datatype which has been derived from the `decimal` datatype.

This allows you to specify a degree of accuracy when dealing with the decimal places of a number. One useful application of this facet is to create an element for money, such as the U.S. dollar, which will have only 2 decimal places:

```
<element name="dollar">
 <simpleType>
  <restriction base="xs:decimal">
   <xs:fractionDigits value="2"/>
  </restriction>
 </simpleType>
</element>
```

Because `fractionDigits` has been limited to "2", you would need to specify all values of dollar with two decimal places, such as 1.99, 2.00, and so on, which is appropriate for dollar amounts.

Of course, each primitive and built-in datatype specified in the XML Schema: Datatypes Recommendation has a different set of constraining facets which can be applied to it. As we progress in Chapters 10 and 11 and take a look at those datatypes in more detail, we will also point out which facets can be applied to the datatype.

ATOMIC, LIST, AND UNION DATATYPES

The XML Schema Recommendation defines a datatype "dichotomy", which actually contains three different datatypes: atomic, list, and union.

> **Note**
>
> The W3C Recommendation actually defines the datatype "dichotomy" and calls it a dichotomy, even though it contains three types.

Atomic datatypes are datatypes which have value sets that are *indivisible*. For example, an `integer` is not an atomic datatype, because it is actually a very specific type of `decimal`: a decimal with no decimal digits.

In addition to the atomic type, there are also lists and unions. Let's take a closer look at lists and unions.

LIST

The list types are datatypes which have a value set that is a list, consisting of values which are an atomic datatype. The list is finite, so it has a limited number of values to choose from.

There are no primitive list datatypes; list datatypes are always derived. The values of the list are specified by listing them sequentially, separated by a white space character.

The definition of the list datatype is accomplished with the `itemType` atomic datatype. There are also a number of constraining facets that can be applied to constrain list values, including

- `length`
- `maxLength`
- `minLength`
- `enumeration`
- `pattern`
- `whiteSpace`

Let's look at an example. Say we wanted to create a type called `colors` which could be a list of colors for a clothing item. We could declare the list as follows:

```
<xs:simpleType name="colors">
 <xs:list itemType="xs:string"/>
</xs:simpleType>
```

This creates a simple list type called `colors` which can have strings as the value set. Then, in an instance document, we could make use of the list like this:

```
<shoes xsi:type="colors">black brown white</shoes>
```

That is a list of three values, because each value is separated by white space. If we had

```
<shoes xsi:type="colors">black brown white navy blue</shoes>
```

the list would actually have five values, because even though we might correctly read "navy blue" as one color, the white space separation reads each of those as separate list values.

Lists can be valuable in many applications; just keep in mind that they are derived from atomic types, and that list values are separated by white space.

UNION

The union type allows you to create a datatype that is the union of either two atomic datatypes or two lists. That means you can have multiple values of differing datatypes as the value set for an element or an attribute.

All unions are derived datatypes, and the union is specified by making use of the `memberTypes` attribute. Let's take a look at an example.

Let's say that you wanted to be able to keep track of the stock of an item, using an element called `<stock>`. But for the value of stock, you wanted to be able to use either an integer, representing the number of items in stock, or a string, specifying that the item is on back order or has been discontinued. A union provides a perfect mechanism for accomplishing this type of task.

First, you need to define the datatypes for your `quantity` integer, and the `status` string:

```
<simpleType name="quantity">
<restriction base="xs:integer">
<xs:minInclusive value="1"/>
</restriction>
</simpleType>

 <simpleType name="status">
  <restriction base="xs:string">
   <enumeration value="Back Ordered"/>
   <enumeration value="Discontinued"/>
  </restriction>
 </simpleType>
```

With these two datatypes defined, you can create the union type:

```
<simpleType name="inventory">
<union memberTypes="quantity status"/>
</simpleType>
```

Here the members of the union are specified as a list, in the value of memberTypes. Each type is a list item, separated by white space. Now we have a union type called inventory. We can now create a new element based on that union type:

```
<element name="item">
 <complexType>
  <element name="stock" type="inventory"/>
 </complexType>
</element>
```

Now we have an element called <stock> which can be used inside an <item>, and which is a union of the quantity and status datatypes. This means that in our XML instance document, any of the following would be considered valid values for the <stock> item:

```
<item>
 <stock>5</stock>
</item>

<item>
 <stock>Back Ordered</stock>
</item>

<item>
 <stock>Discontinued</stock>
</item>
```

As you can see, the union provides a powerful, yet easy way to make the value sets for your elements and attributes more flexible by providing a datatype which is a union of two other datatypes.

CONCLUSION

Datatypes are a very valuable new mechanism provided in the XML Schema Recommendation, which allows for a much greater degree of control over the content of XML instance documents than was previously possible under the XML 1.0 Recommendation.

To recap the basics of datatypes we covered in this chapter:

- Datatypes help ensure data integrity and interoperability with other applications, programming languages, and databases.

- Datatypes allow you to define a lexical space and value space for elements and attribute values.

- Primitive datatypes are datatypes defined in the Schema Recommendation which are not derived from other datatypes.

- Derived datatypes are datatypes which are based on another primitive datatype, and are either extensions or restrictions of a base type.

- The XML Schema Datatypes Recommendation contains a number of built-in datatypes, some of which are primitive types, and some of which are derived types.

- Facets are used to manipulate the properties of datatypes.

- Fundamental facets are facets which are inherent in the actual definition of the datatype itself, and cannot be manipulated by Schema authors.

- The fundamental facets are equal, order, bounds, cardinality, and numeric.

- Constraining facets are facets which authors can use to manipulate the value set of datatypes.

- The constraining facets are `length`, `minLength`, `maxLength`, `pattern`, `enumeration`, `whiteSpace`, `minInclusive`, `maxInclusive`, `minExclusive`, `maxExclusive`, `totalDigits`, and `fractionDigits`.

- Atomic datatypes are types which have values that are indivisible.

- List datatypes are types which consist of a list of values composed of a finite number of atomic datatypes.

- Union datatypes are types that consist of a union of multiple atomic or list types.

PART

III

CH

9

With those fundamentals of datatypes squared away, you are now ready to take an in-depth look at the built-in datatypes from the Schema Recommendation. In Chapter 10, we will examine the primitive built-in datatypes and their uses. Then, in Chapter 11 we will take a look at the derived datatypes and their uses, as well as take a closer look at defining your own derived datatypes.

IN THE REAL WORLD

The importance of datatypes cannot be overemphasized. Datatypes were one of the primary motivating factors for XML Schema, and you will encounter datatypes all the time in the real world.

It is also good practice to employ datatypes in your own Schema wherever appropriate, to ensure the integrity of your data, and to aid in compatibility with other computing applications.

The datatypes built in to the XML Schema Recommendation are designed to provide the base for creating your own datatypes, and to include a set of datatypes that mimics the functionality of datatypes in other computing applications. You should be sure to familiarize yourself with these built-in datatypes.

You should also be aware that sometimes even similar datatypes vary slightly from application to application, so when you are working with XML Schema and other applications (such as a programming language like Java, or a database) you should make sure to check and note any differences between datatypes the two applications might share.

The constraining facets provided with datatypes are all useful, but you are most likely to encounter the `enumeration` facet more than any other when working with Schema. You should be very familiar with its usage.

Also, the `pattern` facet provides a new kind of functionality in the ability to enforce pattern matching with regular expressions. You should be familiar with this facet as well, and know when it is appropriate to use it, as well as the syntax for using regular expressions in XML Schema (covered later in Chapter 12).

The other constraining facets are also useful, and it is likely you will encounter almost all of them at some point or another, so it is important that you are familiar with all of them. But more importantly, you should know how those facets might differ from type to type. For example the `length` facet applies to the number of characters in a `string` type, but to the number of items in a `list`. Failure to be aware of subtle differences such as this can introduce errors into your Schema at an alarming rate.

Lists and unions will also become more important as you work more closely with other applications, since these are advanced mechanisms for creating customized datatypes. You should keep these in the back of your mind as resources for customizing existing datatypes and creating new types to match the type from an application (such as a database) that you are working with.

CHAPTER 10

PRIMITIVE DATATYPES

In this chapter

INTRODUCING PRIMITIVE DATATYPES

There are a number of datatypes which are built in to XML Schema for the convenience of Schema authors, and to establish a set of primitives that can be used to derive more types. The first set of built-in datatypes is the primitive datatypes.

Primitive datatypes are types which serve as their own standalone definitions. That is, they are not built on top of another datatype (or derived), but often they serve as the base for building new datatypes. You cannot create a primitive datatype; the only way to add a new primitive datatype to XML Schema is for the W3C to add the primitive to the Recommendation.

The primitive datatypes are important for several reasons. First, there are many times when you will find that a primitive datatype does exactly what you need, and therefore you will not need to create your own datatype. Second, primitive datatypes can be used as the base for building new types. That is why it is important for you to have a good understanding of the primitive datatypes; in order to build your own datatypes using the primitives as your base, you will need to understand what each datatype represents and how its value set may be manipulated.

The primitive datatypes are all simple types. In fact, they are all descendents of the two *ur-types* which serve as the basis for all types. The hierarchy of the types is shown in Figure 10.1.

Figure 10.1
The hierarchy of the primitive datatypes, as descendents of the ur-types.

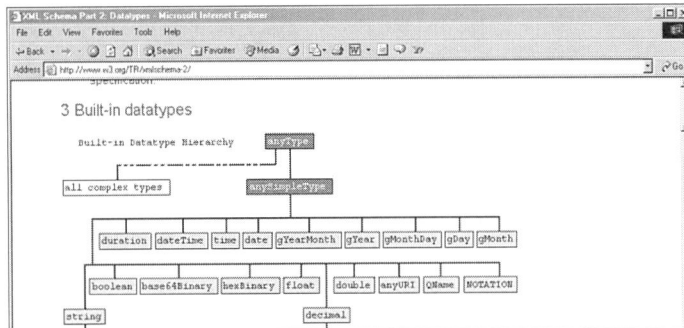

Copyright © 2001 W3C ® (MIT, INRIA, Keio), All Rights Reserved
W3C Recommendation, http://www.w3.org/TR/xmlschema-2/

The basis for all types in XML Schema, including complex types, is a type called anyType. All types are descendents of anyType. There is also a parent simple type called anySimpleType which is the ur-type for simple types. All simple types, including the primitives, are descendents of the anySimpleType and, in fact, are restrictions of that type.

So, now let's take a look at each one of the primitive datatypes and the types of data they can be used to represent.

string

The string datatype is a primitive datatype used to represent strings of characters. The character is considered the atomic unit of a string, and what constitutes a character is defined in the XML 1.0 Recommendation. The value set for a string will be dependent on the character set being used in the XML document, just as the characters in the English alphabet are different from the characters in the Cyrillic alphabet.

The constraining facets which can be used with the string datatype are

- length
- minLength
- maxLength
- pattern
- enumeration
- whiteSpace

The length, minLength, and maxLength facets accept values in the form of integers, which represent the number of characters in the string. The pattern facet accepts a value in the form of a regular expression that can be used for pattern matching against the value of the string.

The enumeration facet allows you to specify a list of choices for the value of a string, listing each choice for the value space as a separate enumeration facet. This is significant, because the enumeration values are provided individually, not as a simple list.

The whiteSpace facet, when applied to a string, enables you to specify how white space in the string is treated. The options for setting the value of this facet are preserve, replace, and collapse. Each of these values behaves here as described in Chapter 9, "Introducing Datatypes."

Let's take a look at a couple of examples using the string type. Let's say that you wanted to create an element called description which could contain a descriptive string:

```
<element name="description" type="string"/>
```

That's all there is to declaring an element using the string type. However, you can also create new datatypes using the string type by restricting those constraining facets. For example, we could create a new simple datatype called passwd based on the string type, and limit the number of characters in the password to fit into a range of 6–8 characters:

```
<simpleType name="passwd">
 <restriction base="string">
  <minLength value="6"/>
  <maxLength value="8"/>
 </restriction>
</simpleType>
```

By using the string type as a base, and then the minLength and maxLength constraining facets, we are left with a new datatype called passwd, which we could then use with an element declaration:

```
<element name="password" type="passwd"/>
```

If you were to use <password> in an instance document, the value of the element would have to be a string of characters at least 6 characters long, and a maximum of 8 characters long.

As you can see from these examples, each of the primitive types can be used directly in an element declaration, or they can be used in a type definition to create a new type.

boolean

A `boolean` is a datatype which is used to represent the mathematical concept of binary-valued logic. Practically speaking, that translates to true and false.

The `boolean` type has a predefined value set of {true, false, 0, 1}, where 1 is the same as true, and 0 is the same as false.

Because there are already a limited number of options in the value space, there are only two constraining facets:

- `pattern`
- `whiteSpace`

A `boolean` can be used when you need a datatype that represents a true or false condition. For example, if you wanted to create an element called `attendance` for keeping track of meeting attendees

```
<element name="attendance" type="xs:boolean"/>
```

In the instance document, the element could be either

```
<attendance>true</attendance>
```

or

```
<attendance>false</attendance>
```

depending on whether the person in question had attended or not. Booleans are a very useful datatype, so don't forget that they are available to you as a primitive.

NUMERIC DATATYPES

One of the most common uses of datatypes is to specify numeric data. These datatypes are commonly used in a number of computing applications, from programming languages and databases. The XML Schema Recommendation provides a number of these datatypes, which are designed to be compatible with other applications.

These datatypes are very important, as they form the basis of other numeric datatypes as well, such as derived datatypes, which we will discuss in Chapter 11, "Derived Datatypes."

decimal

There are not many data-centric XML documents where numbers won't play some role in the data, and that is where the `decimal` type comes in. The `decimal` type is used to represent decimal numbers with arbitrary precision.

The decimal type allows for a leading sign of "+" or "-" to specify a positive or negative number, although "+" is the default, so it is not necessary to use it. The type supports any theoretical number of digits to the right or left of the decimal point, although XML processors are required to support at least 18 total digits.

Some valid values for decimals include 4, 5.2, –6.3, or 3.14159.

There are a number of constraining facets which can be used with the decimal type. In fact, some of these are used to define other built-in types, such as Integer, that we will discuss in Chapter 11. The facets that apply to decimal include

- totalDigits
- fractionDigits
- pattern
- whiteSpace
- enumeration
- minInclusive
- maxInclusive
- minExclusive
- maxExclusive

The totalDigits facet can be used to constrain the total number of digits which are allowed in the decimal type. This applies to the digits on both the right and the left of the decimal point.

The fractionDigits facet enables you to limit the number of digits, or decimal places, to the right of the decimal point. This mechanism can effectively be used to determine precision.

The pattern, whiteSpace, and enumeration facets function as they do with other types; however, the decimal type also includes minInclusive, maxInclusive, minExclusive, and maxExclusive. These facets can be used to express a range for the value of the decimal, describing the bounds either inclusively or exclusively.

Let's take a look at some ways in which decimals can be used in XML Schema. One way is to create a datatype called dollar which could be used to keep track of monetary values. Because monetary values are expressed in the U.S. in decimal form, with two digits in the decimal place (such as $1.25), we can use a decimal type for dollar, if we limit the fractionDigits to 2:

```
<simpleType name="dollar">
 <restriction base="decimal">
  <fractionDigits value="2"/>
 </restriction>
</simpleType>
```

In addition to manipulating the fractionDigits, we can manipulate the totalDigits as well. For example, say we wanted to create a type for a PIN number. We could accomplish that by limiting the totalDigits to "4", and then limiting fractionDigits to "0", since PINs cannot have decimals:

```
<simpleType name="PIN">
 <restriction base="decimal">
  <totalDigits value="4"/>
  <fractionDigits value="0"/>
 </restriction>
</simpleType>
```

Of course, there are other types (such as integer) which might be easier to use; however, integer is based on decimal, with some of the limitations performed already. Another way to place limits is to make use of the min/max bounds. For example, if we wanted to set a price type which could not be more than $9.99, we could first use minInclusive set to "0" to ensure that we don't have a negative price. Then we could use maxExclusive with a value set to "10" to limit the value set to anything under 10, but since the bound is exclusive, the value could not be 10. Here's how we would define the type:

```
<simpleType name="price">
 <restriction base="decimal">
  <fractionDigits value="2"/>
  <minInclusive value="0"/>
  <maxExclusive value="10"/>
 </restriction>
</simpleType>
```

As you can see, decimal is a very flexible type, and although you might not make use of it directly in your Schema, many practical types can be derived from decimal.

float

The float datatype is used to represent a single-precision 32-bit floating point type, in accordance with the IEEE definition. The form of the float is a mantissa followed by an "E" or "e" and then an exponent (if either is used). The *mantissa* is the portion of a logarithm to the right of the decimal point.

> **Note**
>
> The float type is based on the standard definition published by the IEEE. If you'd like to read more about that definition, you can find it at:
>
> http://standards.ieee.org/reading/ieee/std_public/description/busarch/754-1985_desc.html

For example, –3E2, 3.1415E12, 84.23e–2, and 6.2 are all valid floats.

Leading and trailing zeros may not be used with a float, although there must be one digit to the right and left of the decimal point, so if that value is zero, it is not considered a leading zero: 0.3e2.

In addition, float has a number of special values. These values include

- Positive Zero: 0
- Negative Zero: –0
- Infinity: INF

- Negative Infinity: –INF
- Not a Number: NaN

Note

I have included these values in the interest of completeness because they are a part of Recommendation, not because I think you will find yourself working with these values often, if ever. However, if you are unclear about the mathematical differences between positive zero, negative zero, and so on, and you are curious, you can check out the following link:

`http://mathforum.com/dr.math/problems/king.10.5.99.html`

There are also a number of constraining facets that can be used with the `float` type.

- `pattern`
- `enumeration`
- `whiteSpace`
- `minInclusive`
- `maxInclusive`
- `minExclusive`
- `maxExclusive`

PART
III
CH
10

These constraining facets are all used with `float` similarly to how they would be used with a `decimal` type.

double

Like the `float` type, the `double` type is also based on the IEEE `double` datatype, which is similar to a `float`. The difference is that a `double` is a double-precision, 64-bit floating point type, rather than a 32-bit type.

The same special values apply to a `double` which apply to a `float`: 0, –0, INF, –INF, NaN.

As with the `float` type, the constraining facets for `double` are

- `pattern`
- `enumeration`
- `whiteSpace`
- `minInclusive`
- `maxInclusive`
- `minExclusive`
- `maxExclusive`

DATE AND TIME DATATYPES

There are a number of datatypes provided by the XML Schema Recommendation which can be used for specifying information about intervals of time, and date information. These types include

- duration
- dateTime
- time
- date
- gYearMonth
- gYear
- gMonthDay
- gDay
- gMonth

Now let's take a look at these datatypes in greater detail, including their usage and constraining facets.

duration

There are times when you might want to keep track of a length of time within an XML document, such as the end of contract, the expiration of perishable goods, or the end of a prison sentence.

For keeping track of a period of time, you can make use of the duration type, which allows you to keep track of a duration of time, using years, months, days, hours, minutes, and seconds.

Time periods specified in a duration take the following format:

PnYnMnDTnHnMnS

In this format, the "P" is a required symbol, and each n represents an integer specifying the length of time. The calendar portion (Year, month, day) is separated from the time portion by a "T" symbol, which can be omitted if there is no time specification. The time items also use integer values, with the exception of seconds, where n can be a decimal of arbitrary precision.

For example, let's say that we wanted to represent one year, six months, eight days, five hours, 15 minutes, and 30 seconds. We would use the duration

P1Y6M8DT5H15M30S

Or, if we wanted to represent 6 months, we could simply use

P6M

You can also use negative values of time, by preceding the "P" with a "-". So, negative one day, six hours, and 30 minutes would be

-P1DT6H30M

There are a number of constraining facets which can be used with the `duration` type:

- `pattern`
- `enumeration`
- `whiteSpace`
- `minInclusive`
- `maxInclusive`
- `minExclusive`
- `maxExclusive`

For example, we could create a datatype called `interval` which we could use to denote a time interval in hours, minutes, and seconds (with no decimals) by using the `pattern` facet and the `duration` type:

```
<simpleType name="interval">
<restriction base="duration">
<pattern value='PT[0-9]{2}H[0-9]{2}M[0-9]{2}S"/>
</restriction>
</simpleType>
```

This would require that the value of the type be represented in the form

PT09H30M15S

The `duration` type can be convenient when working with data from other applications, such as SQL databases.

dateTime

The `duration` type allows you to keep track of a period of time; however, it doesn't capture a moment in time, such as you might with a date/time stamp.

A date/time stamp can be recorded with the `dateTime` type, which defines a format for date and time in the following manner:

YYYY-MM-DDTHH:MM:SS

A four-digit representation of the year, followed by a two-digit representation of the month, and a two-digit representation of the day. A "T" then separates the time portion which is a two-digit hour, two-digit month, and two-digit seconds, separated by colons. The time is denoted in Coordinated Universal Time (UTC).

The term *Universal Time* is sometimes used in place of *Greenwich Mean Time,* which was formerly the standard for timekeeping. *Coordinated Universal Time (UTC)* is a standard based on a worldwide network of atomic clocks. Time in U.S. time zones can be expressed by subtracting the following values from UTC:

- Eastern Daylight Time –4:00
- Eastern Standard Time –5:00
- Central Daylight Time –5:00
- Central Standard Time –6:00
- Mountain Daylight Time –6:00
- Mountain Standard Time –7:00
- Pacific Daylight Time –7:00
- Pacific Standard Time –8:00

The time difference from UTC can be specified by using a + or - sign followed by hours and minutes (*HH:MM*) off UTC. So, for example, February 11, 2002, at 10:30 p.m. (PST) would be denoted as

2002-02-11T22:30:00-8:00

The constraining facets which can be used with `dateTime` include

- `pattern`
- `enumeration`
- `whiteSpace`
- `minInclusive`
- `maxInclusive`
- `minExclusive`
- `maxExclusive`

Each of the facets can be used to constrain the `dateTime` type, but if you are using it as a time stamp, it might not be necessary to constrain the type at all. In that case, we could use the type directly with an element declaration, such as

```
<element name="timeStamp" type="dateTime"/>
```

This would allow us to use the element as a time stamp as follows:

```
<timeStamp>2001-07-26T13:15:45-5:00</timeStamp>
```

which would represent July 26, 2001, 1:15:45 p.m. EST.

time

The `time` datatype exists for those instances where the date is not important but you want to record an instant of time.

The `time` type follows the same formatting as the time portion of the `dateTime` type

HH:MM:SS

and is also specified with the UTC time zone, or a "+" or "-" modifier with the offset to indicate other time zones. A "Z" can be used to denote UTC. For example,

13:30:00Z

represents 1:30 p.m. UTC, while to represent 1:30 p.m. EST you would use

13:30:00-5:00

The constraining facets you can use with `time` are the same as with `dateTime`:

- `pattern`
- `enumeration`
- `whiteSpace`
- `minInclusive`
- `maxInclusive`
- `minExclusive`
- `maxExclusive`

date

The `date` type represents a date, similar to the date portion of the `dateTime` type. The value refers to a date in the Gregorian calendar, and takes the YYYY-MM-DD format. So, May 16th, 2005 would be

2005-05-16

The constraining facets you can use with `date` also are the same as with `dateTime`:

- `pattern`
- `enumeration`
- `whiteSpace`
- `minInclusive`
- `maxInclusive`
- `minExclusive`
- `maxExclusive`

gYearMonth

The `gYearMonth` is a type which represents a year and month in the Gregorian calendar. The year/month pair is represented with a four-digit date and a two-digit month, in the format

YYYY-MM

So, the month of April, 2002, would be represented by

2002-04

The gYearMonth type has the following constraining facets:

- pattern
- enumeration
- whiteSpace
- minInclusive
- maxInclusive
- minExclusive
- maxExclusive

gYear

The gYear type represents a year in the Gregorian calendar. The year is represented by the four-digit year, with no other special characters. So the year 2003 is represented as

2003

There are no special provisions used to indicate a leap year, as all years are treated the same, regardless of the number of days.

The gYear type has the same constraining facets as the gYearMonth type:

- pattern
- enumeration
- whiteSpace
- minInclusive
- maxInclusive
- minExclusive
- maxExclusive

gMonthDay

The gMonthDay type represents a month/day pair in the Gregorian calendar. It takes a different form than the year/month pair, as it has a leading placeholder dash for the year. This helps parsers recognize it as a month/date pair, as opposed to some other pair, such as hour/min. The month is represented by a two-digit number, and the day is also represented by a two-digit number, each separated with a hyphen. The gMonthDay type takes the form

--MM-DD

So, the date of December 11th would be represented as

--12-11

The gMonthDay type has the same constraining facets as the gYearMonth type:

- pattern
- enumeration
- whiteSpace
- minInclusive
- maxInclusive
- minExclusive
- maxExclusive

gDay

The gDay type is used to represent a day in a Gregorian calendar month. The acceptable values for days range from 01 to 31, but no higher, as days in the Gregorian calendar don't have more than 31 days.

---DD

So, the day of March 15th would be represented as

---15

The gDay type has the same constraining facets as the gYearMonth type:

- pattern
- enumeration
- whiteSpace
- minInclusive
- maxInclusive
- minExclusive
- maxExclusive

gMonth

The gMonth type represents a month in the Gregorian calendar. It takes the format of a double-digit number representing the month, with leading and trailing dashes as placeholders:

--MM--

So, for example, the month of February would be represented as

--02--

As with gYear, this will represent the month of February regardless of the number of days in the month (as in a leap year).

The gMonth type has the same constraining facets as the gYearMonth type:

- pattern
- enumeration
- whiteSpace
- minInclusive
- maxInclusive
- minExclusive
- maxExclusive

There is one important consideration when working with dates and times, in addition to being mindful of time zones. That is that dates (years, months, and days) in the Gregorian calendar might not translate well to other calendars. Therefore, you should only make use of the "g" types if you know that you do not care about translation of the dates into another calendar system.

BINARY DATATYPES

In the XML 1.0 Recommendation, there are no datatype definitions at all, and the mechanisms provided for dealing with binary information are very rudimentary. The XML Schema Recommendation addresses the binary data issue directly with datatypes, providing two specific datatypes designed for binary information: hexBinary and base64Binary.

hexBinary

One of the limitations of the XML 1.0 Recommendation is the lack of real mechanisms for dealing with binary data. Binary data can be referenced in XML documents using notations; however, under the 1.0 Recommendation, there is no way to include binary data within an XML document.

> **Tip**
>
> There are some tricks that could be employed to use binary data in an XML document, such as using multiple CDATA sections (which, by the way, is a very bad idea), but these can introduce errors and is not a very good practice. If you need to use binary information in an XML document, datatypes and Schema are the way to go.

The ability to include binary data is one of the new features that comes with the XML Schema Recommendation. The first way to include binary data in an XML document is to use the hexBinary datatype.

The hexBinary type is used to represent hex-encoded binary data. That is binary data that has been converted from binary form (111110110111) into a binary octet hexadecimal form (0FB7).

Many applications are capable of converting between hexadecimal and binary formats, and it is a commonly used format for exchanging files. The advantage to using hexBinary types is that the information is encoded using ASCII text characters, so it will not cause conflicts with applications that can only handle text.

The constraining facets which can be used with the hexBinary type include

- length
- minLength
- maxLength
- pattern
- enumeration
- whiteSpace

There are some differences in how constraints apply to binary data versus text data.

First, length for binary data for (length, minLength, and maxLength) is specified in octets (8 bits). The length constraints, particularly the maxLength constraint, can be very useful for restricting the length of the binary information contained in the hexBinary type, to prevent documents from growing too large.

Second, the pattern, enumeration, and whiteSpace constraints, while technically applicable to the hexBinary type, are not really very practical. For example, pattern matching in a binary would be really difficult, and not very productive.

base64Binary

Another datatype which can be used to represent binary data in an XML document is the base64Binary type. This type is similar to the hexBinary type in that it allows you to include binary data in an XML document. Also, the base-64 encoded binary is *text-safe*, as the encoding method only uses ASCII and EBCDIC characters in the encoding, which limits the characters used to encode the binary information.

base64Binary is a good type to use for including binary information in your documents, because it is more compact, and it is also a very common format, used for exchanging MIME documents via applications.

The facets that can be used with the base64Binary type are the same as those used with the hexBinary type:

- length
- minLength
- maxLength

PART

III

CH

10

- pattern
- enumeration
- whiteSpace

As is the case with the hexBinary type, the length facets are far more practical than the other constraining facets that can be used with base64Binary.

For example, if you wanted to include a binary element in your XML document called <logo> which would allow you to include a base-64 encoded file with a logo, but you didn't want the file to be larger than 100KB, you could use the constraining facets.

The maxLength constraint can be used to specify the maximum length for the encoded file, in octets. An octet is equivalent to 8 bits, which is the same as one byte. We can convert that using the following:

1 Octet = 8 bits

8 bits = 1 Byte

1024 Bytes = 1KB

Therefore, 100 Kilobytes is equal to 102,400 bytes, and since a byte is the same as an octet, we now have our maximum length. So, our element declaration making use of the base64Binary type would look like this:

```
<element name="logo">
 <simpleType>
  <restriction base="base64Binary">
   <maxLength value="102400"/>
  </restriction>
 </simpleType>
</element>
```

This would allow you to include a logo, up to 100KB of information (this 100KB is *after* the file has been base-64 encoded, not before; the length constraint applies to the type in the XML document, which needs to have already been encoded) in an XML file using the <logo> element.

anyURI

The anyURI type represents a URI, or uniform resource identifier, as defined by the RFC 2396 and 2732 documents from the Internet Engineering Task Force (IETF). These define URIs as being references to resources, which can be absolute or relative identifiers.

Some examples of URIs include

```
http://www.w3.org
ftp://ftp.myserver.com
mailto:support@myorg.com
news:comp.text.xml
../images/mypic.gif
```

The constraining facets which can be used with `anyURI` include

- `length`
- `minLength`
- `maxLength`
- `pattern`
- `enumeration`
- `whiteSpace`

Let's take a look at an example. If we wanted to create an element called `<webpage>` which would have to have a value that was a valid URL (which is a type of URI), we could use the following declaration:

```
<element name="webpage">
 <simpleType>
  <restriction base="anyURI">
   <pattern value="http:\/\/[\.\~A-Za-z0-9]*"/>
  </restriction>
 </simpleType>
</element>
```

In this example, we make use of the `pattern` constraining facet to specify that the value for the `<webpage>` element has to begin with `http://` and that after that, it may contain any letter or number, a ~, or . characters. That might not guarantee that we get a valid URL for the value, but it certainly helps.

QName

The `QName` type is used to represent XML Qualified names; that is, names which belong to a specified namespace. Qualified names have two parts, the namespace name and the local part. The namespace name matches the `anyURI` type, and the local part has to be an NCName, or a valid XML name. The namespace part and the local part are also separated with the colon ':' character. Keep in mind though that a name can be a `QName` if the namespace is declared as a default, which would then not require the use of the prefix and colon.

The valid values for the `QName` type will be dependent on the namespaces declared with your Schema (such as `targetNamespace`), and they will be limited to those namespaces.

The constraining facets which can be used with the `QName` type are

- `length`
- `minLength`
- `maxLength`
- `pattern`
- `enumeration`
- `whiteSpace`

NOTATION

The NOTATION type is used to specify a NOTATION attribute type, which may be used in conjunction with any notations which have already been declared in the Schema document.

In this way, the NOTATION type functions slightly differently from the other types we have discussed. The NOTATION type specifically applies to attributes, so that you can make use of notations, similarly to notations in the XML 1.0 Recommendation. If there are no notations declared in your Schema then you cannot make use of the NOTATION type.

The constraining facets which can be used with the NOTATION type include

- length
- minLength
- maxLength
- pattern
- enumeration
- whiteSpace

Unlike most of the other types we've looked at so far, the NOTATION type actually *requires* that you use the enumeration constraining facet. The enumeration facet must be used to list the names of previously declared notations that can be used in conjunction with the NOTATION type.

Let's take a look at an example. Say you wanted to create an element called image, which could be a reference to either a JPEG or a GIF image. First, you would need to declare the notations themselves, using the <notation> declaration:

```
<notation name="gif" public="image/gif" system="mspaint.exe "/>
<notation name="jpg" public="image/jpeg" system="mspaint.exe "/>
```

This would create two notations, "gif" and "jpg", which are used to reference the declared notations. These are also the values which must be enumerated if you were to use the NOTATION datatype. So, let's take a look at what the element declaration looks like:

```
<element name="image">
 <complexType>
  <complexContent>
   <extension base="hexBinary">
    <attribute name="imageType">
     <simpleType>
      <restriction base="NOTATION">
       <enumeration value="gif"/>
       <enumeration value="jpg"/>
      </restriction>
     </simpleType>
    </attribute>
   </extension>
  </complexContent>
 </complexType>
</element>
```

We start by declaring the <image> element with a complex type and complex content. We then create an extension for the type, and define the extension as a hexBinary type, which will allow us to place the binary data for the image in our <image> tag.

Next, we define an attribute called imageType which we declare as being a NOTATION type. This is where we now have to make use of the enumeration facet, because the NOTATION type must have its value restricted to previously declared notations. In this case, we have to limit the choices to gif and jpg because those are the valid notation types.

With these declarations, we are free to use the <image> element to include a binary file for either a GIF or a JPEG in an XML instance document.

CONCLUSION

The datatypes we have just covered in this chapter are the only primitive datatypes in the XML Schema Recommendation. That doesn't mean that the W3C might not add new primitive types in future versions; however, only the W3C can add new primitive types. To summarize the properties of the primitive types:

- All primitive types are descended from the anyType and anySimpleType ur-types.

- All primitive types are simple types.

- Primitive datatypes can only be added by the W3C adding their definitions to the Schema Recommendation.

- Primitive datatypes can be used as the base for deriving new datatypes.

- The string type is used to represent strings of characters.

- The boolean type represents a mathematical binary logic, with values of "true", "false", "1", or "0".

- The decimal type represents a decimal number.

- The float and double types represent single precision 32-bit floating point and double precision 64-bit floating point numbers, respectively.

- The duration type represents a duration of time.

- The dateTime type represents a date and time stamp.

- The time and date types represent the time or the date portion of the date/time stamp separately.

- The gYearMonth, gYear, gMonthDay, gDay, and gMonth types represent their respective date and time information based on the Gregorian calendar.

- hexBinary and base64Binary are types which can be used to represent binary information in an XML document.

- The anyURI type represents any valid uniform resource identifier (URI), such as a URL.

- The QName type represents a valid Qualified name, which has a namespace component and a local component.

- The NOTATION type applies to attributes, and is used to specify the notation type, which must be a notation which has already been declared in the Schema.
- Constraining facets are length, minLength, maxLength, pattern, enumeration, whiteSpace, minInclusive, maxInclusive, minExclusive, maxExclusive, totalDigits, and fractionDigits.

The primitive simple types are very useful in representing data in your instance documents. Often, these types will suffice for your needs in their current forms. But one of the most powerful aspects of these types is that they can be used as the base for deriving new types. As we continue into Chapter 11, we will take a look at the built-in derived types, which are types based on the primitive types outlined here, but included in the XML Schema Recommendation for your convenience. Then as we move on, we will look at the mechanisms for deriving your own datatypes.

IN THE REAL WORLD

The primitive datatypes are very important in the real world. First, because they can often be used as-is in your documents. Datatypes such as string or boolean often do not need customization to be useful datatypes in your Schema documents.

Strings are a very common datatype, since nearly all of what we communicate using language can be stored as a string of characters. Booleans are also very common, useful for storing state information in documents, since they represent a binary condition: true/false, off/on, and so on.

In addition to these types, the numeric types are also very useful in computing applications. The float and double types will serve as the basis for a number of derived types, including integer. These datatypes allow you to work with numbers in applications with varying degrees of precision, and are very important types in the real world.

There is a caveat to working with numeric types in XML Schema, however. Although every effort has been made to include standard datatypes, such as float, the problem stems from the fact that not all float types are the same across all computing applications. The type of data is formatted the same; however, the bounds (the lower and upper limits of the value set) are often different. The bounds are set for XML in the XML Schema representation. However, using float as an example, the value set for a float in Java has different bounds than in Schema, and even different yet from C, where the bounds are determined by the machine being programmed on.

Because of subtle differences such as this, you should always be sure to double-check the bounds of the value set for your numeric datatypes, and make sure that they are similar across your applications. If they are not, you can use the primitive XML type to create your own compatible datatype to be used in your applications.

The various date types provided in the XML Schema are also important, as so much of what we do is linked to a date and/or time. However, you should keep in mind that not all of the world uses the same calendar system. Although Gregorian dates are undoubtedly the most common, other cultures might utilize other date formats. Just something to be aware of if you are working with global standards.

Finally, as we noted in previous chapters, the notation type is really only included for backward compatibility with DTDs. However, the hexBinary and base64Binary types are specifically designed to allow you to include binary information in Schema and XML documents. If you ever encounter a situation where a notation would be appropriate, make use of these types instead, unless you have a legacy DTD you need to work with.

PART

III

CH

10

CHAPTER 11

DERIVED DATATYPES

In this chapter

BUILT-IN DERIVED DATATYPES

In Chapter 10, "Primitive Datatypes," we took a look at a number of datatypes which were included in the XML Schema Recommendation as primitive types. In addition to the primitive datatypes, there are also a number of derived datatypes which are built in to the XML Schema Recommendation.

These datatypes are derived; that is, they are based on other datatypes, and are defined by limiting certain aspects of a datatype using the constraining facets in order to create a new datatype.

For example, say we wanted to create a datatype called range which expressed the depth of field of a camera, say 4ft–30ft. We could create a new datatype based on the integer type, and use the constraining facets to limit the value set so that only values between 4 and 30 would be valid. When we limit the possible values in a new datatype, what we are doing is deriving a new datatype from a base datatype.

This method of creating new types is one of the most powerful features of XML Schema, and allows you to create the exact custom datatypes that you need for your XML applications. However, there are a number of datatypes which come in handy in a variety of computing applications.

For example, computing programming languages and database applications have used datatypes for quite some time, and there are some datatypes, such as integer and byte, which have been in common usage for a long time. Additionally, there are some types which were specified in the XML 1.0 Recommendation that are necessary for compatibility, such as ID and ENTITY.

Because many of these datatypes are in common usage, and to ensure compatibility with the XML 1.0 Recommendation, the Schema authors have included a number of datatypes as "built-in" which are actually derived datatypes.

These datatypes include

- normalizedString
- token
- language
- Name
- NCName
- NMTOKEN and NMTOKENS
- ID, IDREF, and IDREFS
- ENTITY and ENTITIES
- integer

- nonPositiveInteger

- positiveInteger

- nonNegativeInteger

- negativeInteger

- int and unsignedInt

- long and unsignedLong

- short and unsignedShort

- byte and unsignedByte

These datatypes are derived from the built-in primitives, as shown in Figure 11.1.

Figure 11.1
The hierarchy of the built-in derived datatypes.

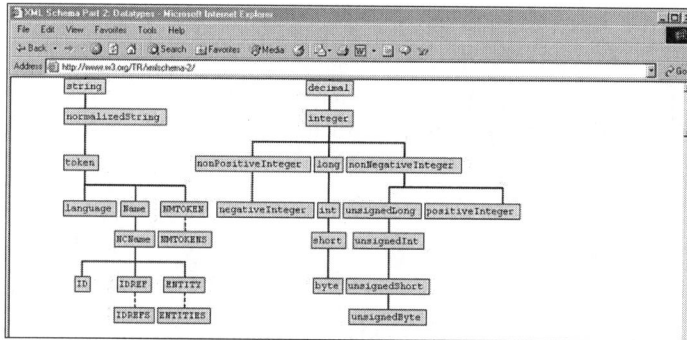

Copyright © 2001 W3C ® (MIT, INRIA, Keio), All Rights Reserved
W3C Recommendation, http://www.w3.org/TR/xmlschema-2/

PART
III

CH
11

These built-in derived datatypes are provided for the sake of convenience, and interoperability. This way, when you use an integer in your Schema, you can be sure other Schema authors are using the same definition of an integer. Unlike the primitive types, users can derive their own datatypes. We'll talk more about deriving your own datatypes later on in Chapter 12, "Representing and Modeling Data." But for now, let's take a look at the built-in derived datatypes in the Schema Recommendation.

normalizedString

A normalizedString type represents a string that has been white space-normalized. That means that the string has had the following characters removed:

- carriage return (#xD)

- line feed (#xA)

- tab (#x9)

The base type for `normalizedString` is `string`. However, even though `string`s may contain carriage returns and tabs, the `normalizedString` may not. Therefore, `normalizedString` is derived from `string` as a restriction.

The constraining facets which can be used with `normalizedString` include

- `length`
- `minLength`
- `maxLength`
- `pattern`
- `enumeration`
- `whiteSpace`

The `normalizedString` type isn't a type you are likely to use often in your own Schema, since one of the goals of XML is increasing human readability, and whitespace preservation helps accomplish that. However, it is an important type, as it serves as the base type for a number of other derived built-in types, such as `token`, which are very important to building your own types.

token

The `token` datatype is based on the `normalizedString` type, with some additional restrictions. Because it is derived from `normalizedString`, a `token` may not contain a carriage return, line feed, or tab character. But additionally, a `token` will have all leading and trailing white space trimmed. And a `token` may not have any internal sequences of more than one space (#x20) character in a row.

The constraining facets that apply to the `token` type include

- `length`
- `minLength`
- `maxLength`
- `pattern`
- `enumeration`
- `whiteSpace`

The `token` type is also not a type which you will use often, as it is mainly included for dealing with Names and other types. However, it is the base type for the `Name`, `language`, and `NMTOKEN` types, which are types that you might use.

language

The language type is derived from the token base type, and is used to represent a natural language identifier, as defined by the Internet Engineering Task Force (IETF) RFC-1766. It also includes the language identifiers specified in the XML 1.0 Recommendation. So, for example, the following are all valid language type values:

- "fr"—French
- "de"—German
- "en"—English
- "en-GB"—British English
- "en-US"—American English

The constraining facets which can be used with the language type:

- length
- minLength
- maxLength
- pattern
- enumeration
- whiteSpace

So, let's take a look at an example. If we wanted to create an attribute to specify the language of a speaker, we could base it on the language type:

```
<attribute name="speaker">
 <simpleType>
  <restriction base="language">
   <enumeration value="en"/>
   <enumeration value="fr"/>
   <enumeration value="de"/>
  </restriction>
 </simpleType>
</attribute>
```

This would create an attribute called speaker with acceptable values of "en", "fr", or "de" for English, French, and German.

PART

III

CH

11

The Compatibility Types

There are a number of datatypes defined in the XML Schema Recommendation which would not be included were it not for the fact that people relying on DTDs have made use of these types, which were available in the XML 1.0 Recommendation.

Therefore, for the sake of making XML Schema backward compatible with DTDs and the XML 1.0 Recommendation, these types are included in Schema as built-in datatypes as a matter of convenience. The types include ID, IDREF, IDREFS, ENTITY, ENTITIES, NMTOKEN, and NOTATION.

Most applications using these datatypes will need to also make use of a Document Type Definition as well, since many of them rely on declarations in the DTD for their value space. When authoring new Schema from scratch, it is unlikely that you will use many of these datatypes.

However, if you do run into a situation where you need to employ any of these types, keep in mind that they should (for the most part) be applied to attributes, as they are defined as attribute types in the XML 1.0 Recommendation. In each of the overviews for these datatypes, we have provided you with any compatibility information that might be relevant as well.

BACKWARD COMPATIBILITY

The following types, ID, IDREF, IDREFS, ENTITY, ENTITIES, NMTOKEN, and NMTOKENS are all provided in the XML Schema Recommendation for the sake of backward compatibility with DTDs and SGML.

These are types that you might not use when writing a Schema from scratch, as their functionality is better served with other types. However, if you are converting from DTDs, or working in an environment with both DTDs and Schema, you might encounter these types, or have a need for them.

ID

The ID type is provided for compatibility with the XML 1.0 Recommendation. An ID can serve as a means of uniquely identifying an element. However, because an ID in XML 1.0 is an attribute type, you should only use the ID type with attributes in order to maintain compatibility.

Note

There are other mechanisms in XML Schema for providing uniqueness, such as unique and key. The ID mechanism is provided mostly for backward compatibility. It should be used only when backward compatibility with DTDs is an issue.

The ID type is based on the NCName type, which means that its value must be an acceptable XML name.

The constraining facets for ID are

- length
- minLength
- maxLength
- pattern
- enumeration
- whiteSpace

For example, let's say that we wanted to create an attribute called code which would be a five-character client name, which would serve as an ID type:

```
<attribute name="sku">
 <simpleType>
  <restriction base="ID">
   <length value="5"/>
  </restriction>
 </simpleType>
</attribute>
```

Keep in mind that the value would need to conform to the naming conventions of XML, so the value could not begin with a digit, or with xml, and so forth.

IDREF

The IDREF type is used to represent a reference to an ID type, for the sake of compatibility with the XML 1.0 Recommendation. An IDREF is a reference to an ID value which has been previously assigned to an attribute.

The base type for an IDREF is NCName, and the value for an IDREF has to conform to the XML naming standards as well.

The constraining facets which can be used with the IDREF type are

- length
- minLength
- maxLength
- pattern
- enumeration
- whiteSpace

Because the IDREF type is used in the XML 1.0 Recommendation only with attributes, you should only use the IDREF type with attributes in your Schema as well.

IDREFS

The IDREFS type is based on the IDREF type, and allows for a list of IDREFs. The value space consists of only IDREFs which have been used in an XML instance document, and the list is limited to the number of valid IDREFs, each separated by a space.

The constraining facets for the IDREF type are

- length
- minLength
- maxLength
- enumeration
- whiteSpace

One thing to note with the constraining facets is that because the IDREFS type is derived from a list, the values for the length constraints are specified in the number of items in the list, not the number of characters.

As with the ID and IDREF types, the IDREFS type should only be used with attributes for the sake of compatibility with the XML 1.0 Recommendation.

ENTITY

The ENTITY type is based on the NCName type, and is a Schema representation of the ENTITY attribute type from the XML 1.0 Recommendation.

The value of an ENTITY type must conform to two rules:

- The ENTITY name must match the NCName restrictions.
- The ENTITY must have been declared in a DTD for the document.

The constraining facets which apply to the ENTITY type include

- length
- minLength
- maxLength
- pattern
- enumeration
- whiteSpace

As with many of the datatypes which have been defined for the purpose of backward compatibility, the ENTITY type should only be used with attribute declarations in an XML Schema.

ENTITIES

The ENTITIES type is based on the ENTITY type, and is simply a list of ENTITY types. The list must have at least one entity, and it must also have already been declared in the Document Type Definition.

The constraining facets for ENTITIES include

- length
- minLength
- maxLength
- enumeration
- whiteSpace

Because the ENTITIES type is derived from a list, the values for the length constraints are specified in the number of items in the list, not the number of characters.

NMTOKEN

The NMTOKEN type represents an NMTOKEN (a Name Token) as described in the XML 1.0 Recommendation. The NMTOKEN type is based on the token type.

The NMTOKEN type has the following constraining facets:

- length
- minLength
- maxLength
- pattern
- enumeration
- whiteSpace

And because the NMTOKEN is a type provided for compatibility, it should be used only with attributes.

NMTOKENS

The NMTOKENS type represents a list of valid NMTOKENs, each one separated by white space.

The constraining facets for the NMTOKENS type are

- length
- minLength
- maxLength
- enumeration
- whiteSpace

The values for the length constraints are specified in the number of items in the list, not the number of characters.

For the sake of compatibility with the XML 1.0 Recommendation, NMTOKENS should only be used with attributes.

Name

The Name type is the representation of a name which matches the Name production of the XML 1.0 Recommendation. If you recall from XML 1.0, that means that the name

- Must start with a letter
- May not start with "xml" or "XML"
- May include digits (although it may not start with a digit)

- May include the ".", "-", or "_" characters
- May include a colon ":", but this is bad form because the colon is reserved for name-space usage

The Name type is derived from the token type, and it has the following constraining facets:

- length
- minLength
- maxLength
- pattern
- enumeration
- whiteSpace

NCName

The NCName type represents a "non-colonized" name, as defined by the XML: Namespaces Recommendation. A non-colonized name is simply a name which does not contain a colon; in other words, one which is not in the prefix:name format. NCNames can be either qualified or unqualified, depending on how the namespace is declared in a document. However, when a name *must* be qualified, it is generally referred to as a QName.

The constraining facets which apply to the NCName type include

- length
- minLength
- maxLength
- pattern
- enumeration
- whiteSpace

integer

The integer type is used to represent an integer, as commonly defined mathematically. The integer type is derived from the decimal type, and the value set consists of any valid integer, in the set {. . ., -3, -2, -1, 0, 1, 2, 3, . . . }. Integers can be both positive and negative, with negative integers being marked with a "-" sign preceding the negative integer. Positive integers may have a preceding "+" sign, but if no sign is present, the integer is assumed to be positive.

Some valid examples of integers would include

–648, 0, 131, +156402, –3872, 9870123

The constraining facets that may be applied to an integer include

- totalDigits
- pattern
- whiteSpace
- enumeration
- minInclusive
- maxInclusive
- minExclusive
- maxExclusive

totalDigits constrains the total number of digits present in the integer, so limiting totalDigits to "4" would effectively limit the maximum value of the integer to "9999". To place bounding limits on an integer, you can also make use of the min/max Inclusive and Exclusive bounds.

For example, if we wanted to create an element called miles which would be an integer representing the total number of miles between destinations (rounded up to the nearest whole number of course) we could do so as follows:

```
<element name="miles" type="integer"/>
```

However, if we wanted to restrict it so that negative mileage couldn't be used, and the maximum distance was 25 miles, we would use

```
<element name="miles">
 <simpleType>
  <restriction base="integer">
   <minInclusive value="0"/>
   <maxInclusive value="25"/>
  </restriction>
 </simpleType>
</element>
```

That would restrict the values for the <miles> element to a range between 0–25 inclusive.

nonPositiveInteger

The nonPositiveInteger type is used to represent integers which do not fall into the "positive" range within the set of all available integers.

The nonPositiveInteger type is a restriction of the integer type, in which the maxInclusive value has been set to "0", which means that values for the type must fall into the range {. . . -3,-2,-1,0}. Leading zeros are prohibited with the nonPositiveInteger type, and the values must be preceded by a "-" minus sign, even for a "0" value. Some examples of valid nonPositiveInteger values include

−1, −5, −8931, −0, −78, −18238712

The constraining facets which may be applied to the `nonPositiveInteger` type include

- `totalDigits`
- `pattern`
- `whiteSpace`
- `enumeration`
- `minInclusive`
- `maxInclusive`
- `minExclusive`
- `maxExclusive`

negativeInteger

The `negativeInteger` type also represents a negative integer, similar to the `nonPositiveInteger` type. In fact, it is based on the `nonPositiveInteger` type, but with the `maxInclusive` value set to "-1", which results in a value set consisting only of the negative integers, but *not* zero.

So, some valid values for the `negativeInteger` type include

−8, −1, −12395137

The `negativeInteger` type has the same constraining facets as the `nonPositiveInteger` type:

- `totalDigits`
- `pattern`
- `whiteSpace`
- `enumeration`
- `minInclusive`
- `maxInclusive`
- `minExclusive`
- `maxExclusive`

nonNegativeInteger

The `nonNegativeInteger` type is used to represent integers which fall into the "positive" range within the set of all available integers.

The `nonPositiveInteger` type is a restriction of the `integer` type, in which the `minInclusive` value has been set to "0", which means that values for the type must fall into the range {0,1,2,3, . . . }. Leading zeros are prohibited with the `nonNegativeInteger` type, and the "+" plus sign is not necessary. Some valid `nonNegativeInteger` values include

79, 1, 9837921, 0, 53

The constraining facets which may be applied to the nonNegativeInteger type include

- totalDigits
- pattern
- whiteSpace
- enumeration
- minInclusive
- maxInclusive
- minExclusive
- maxExclusive

positiveInteger

The positiveInteger type also represents a positive integer, similar to the nonNegativeInteger type. In fact, it is derived from the nonNegativeInteger type, but with the minInclusive value set to "1", which results in a value set consisting only of the positive integers, but *not* zero.

So, some valid values for the positiveInteger type include

23, 1, 873, 380771

The positiveInteger type has the same constraining facets as the nonNegativeInteger type:

- totalDigits
- pattern
- whiteSpace
- enumeration
- minInclusive
- maxInclusive
- minExclusive
- maxExclusive

Note

A number of the remaining datatypes might seem as though they were added arbitrarily, since they will have value sets which on the surface don't seem to make much sense. However, most of these types are included because they are datatypes commonly used in other computing applications, specifically programming languages, and therefore, they are types which come in handy when writing Schema for XML-enabled applications. If you come across a type defined here, and you think "Now, I am never going to use that!" you might be right. However, should the situation arise where you need to take a datatype from C++ and somehow represent it in an XML document, you'll end up being glad these datatypes are included as built-in types.

long

The long type is derived from the integer type, and is a type which is commonly used in programming languages to represent large integer numbers.

The long type has a maximum value of 9223372036854775807 and a minimum value of −9223372036854775808. The long type exists because it is the range of integer numbers that can be stored in 8 bytes. Acceptable values for a long would be any integer falling into that range. A minus "-" sign must be used with longs to denote a negative number; however the "+" sign is optional. long values may not include leading zeros.

The constraining facets for the long type are similar to the integer type:

- totalDigits
- fractionDigits
- pattern
- whiteSpace
- enumeration
- minInclusive
- maxInclusive
- minExclusive
- maxExclusive

unsignedLong

An unsignedLong is the very similar to the long type; however, it does not make any distinctions between positive and negative numbers (no "+" or "-" signs are allowed at all). It is based on nonNegativeInteger, so the minimum value is "0", and the maximum value is set by defining the maxInclusive value as 18446744073709551615. Any integer within that range is a valid unsignedLong, and leading zeros are prohibited.

The constraining facets for the unsignedLong are

- totalDigits
- fractionDigits
- pattern
- whiteSpace
- enumeration
- minInclusive
- maxInclusive
- minExclusive
- maxExclusive

int

The int type is used to represent a range of integers, with the minInclusive value of —2147483648 and the maxInclusive value of 2147483647. Any integer within that range is considered a valid value for int, including "0". The int type is derived from the long type, so negative numbers must be prefixed with the "-" symbol, and positive numbers do not require a sign.

The constraining facets for the int type are

- totalDigits
- fractionDigits
- pattern
- whiteSpace
- enumeration
- minInclusive
- maxInclusive
- minExclusive
- maxExclusive

unsignedInt

The unsignedInt type is very similar to unsignedLong, and in fact it is derived from the unsignedLong type. unsignedInt consists only of integers in the positive set, including zero, and ranging up to an inclusive maximum value of 4294967295.

Because unsignedInt does not include negative numbers, no "+" sign is used with unsignedInt values.

The constraining facets for unsignedInt include

- totalDigits
- fractionDigits
- pattern
- whiteSpace
- enumeration
- minInclusive
- maxInclusive
- minExclusive
- maxExclusive

short

The short type is derived from the int type, and is used to represent "short" integers. The short type has a minimum inclusive value of −32768 and a maximum inclusive value of 32767. These values are the range of values of a 16-bit integer.

As with any signed type, negative numbers are denoted with the "-" sign. Zero is an accepted short value, and positive numbers do not require use of the "+" sign. Also, leading zeros are prohibited.

The constraining facets for the short type are

- totalDigits
- fractionDigits
- pattern
- whiteSpace
- enumeration
- minInclusive
- maxInclusive
- minExclusive
- maxExclusive

unsignedShort

An unsignedShort is a restriction of the unsignedInt type. The value set includes zero, and has a maximum inclusive limit of 65535. As with the other unsigned types, there is no use of the "+" or "-" sign with the type, and leading zeros are also prohibited.

The constraining facets for unsignedShort are

- totalDigits
- fractionDigits
- pattern
- whiteSpace
- enumeration
- minInclusive
- maxInclusive
- minExclusive
- maxExclusive

byte

The byte type is derived from the short type, and has a minInclusive value of −128, and maxInclusive value of 127. The "-" sign is used with byte to denote a negative number, while positive numbers do not use any sign. Leading zeros are prohibited as well.

The constraining facets which can be used with the byte type include

- totalDigits
- fractionDigits
- pattern
- whiteSpace
- enumeration
- minInclusive
- maxInclusive
- minExclusive
- maxExclusive

unsignedByte

The unsignedByte type is derived from the unsignedShort type. The maximum inclusive value for unsignedByte is 255. unsignedByte does not make use of either the "+" or "-" sign, and the value set does include "0".

The constraining facets for the unsignedByte include

- totalDigits
- fractionDigits
- pattern
- whiteSpace
- enumeration
- minInclusive
- maxInclusive
- minExclusive
- maxExclusive

CONCLUSION

That covers the built-in derived datatypes, and the facets which you can manipulate in order to customize the value sets of these datatypes. To recap the basics of the built-in derived types:

- The built-in datatypes include a number of derived datatypes in addition to the primitive types.
- The built-in derived datatypes are simple types, as they are derived by restriction from the primitive types, which themselves are derived from the anySimpleType ur-type.
- The string datatype serves as the basis for a number of built-in derived datatypes. They include normalizedString, token, language, Name, and NCName.

- There are a number of datatypes which are included for compatibility with the XML 1.0 Recommendation. Those types include NMTOKEN, NMTOKENS, ID, IDREF, IDREFS, ENTITY, and ENTITIES.

- Types which are included for compatibility should only be used with attributes to avoid errors.

- There are also a number of datatypes built-in for dealing with numbers. These include integer, nonPositiveInteger, nonNegativeInteger, negativeInteger, and positiveInteger.

- A number of datatypes for dealing with numbers are included for convenience when dealing with other computing applications. These include long, int, short, byte, unsignedLong, unsignedInt, unsignedShort, and unsignedByte.

That covers all of the datatypes which have been built in to the XML Schema Recommendation. They are a very robust set of datatypes, designed to allow you to build your own complex datatypes. In the following chapters, we will take a look at data modeling, and how you can use datatypes to your advantage. Then we'll look at an example of an XML Schema for a Purchase Order and Invoice which make extensive use of datatypes.

IN THE REAL WORLD

The strength of datatypes comes from the ability to derive new datatypes of your own, specific to the applications you need. The built-in, derived datatypes provided in the XML Schema Recommendation do serve as a great starting point, however, and a number of types have been included to make your life easier.

The most common types you will encounter are types such as integer, int, token, long, short, and byte. The other derived types, such as nonPositiveInteger, unsignedLong, and so on, are all types which you could derive yourself from the parent type. For example, if you wanted to have a type that could only be positive integers, you could use the constraining facets to create that type on your own easily enough. The positiveInteger type is included largely as a convenience. And while you might encounter some of these types, having all of them memorized isn't as important as understanding how they were derived from their parent types.

The types which we have called "Backward Compatibility" types in this chapter are types that should only rarely be used, and then only when compatibility with an existing DTD is essential. Unless you are working with legacy DTDs and Schema, it is unlikely that you will encounter these types at all. And unless your goal is compatibility with an existing DTD, these are types you probably should not use.

So, for real-world applications using the datatypes presented in this chapter, don't worry about memorizing them all. Be familiar with the parent types, and make sure you understand how their child types were derived, using the constraining facets. And be aware of the types provided for backward compatibility, but do not use them unless appropriate.

CHAPTER 12

REPRESENTING AND MODELING DATA

In this chapter

WORKING WITH DATA

For many people, working with Schema can seem very intimidating because of the complexity that comes along with the datatype portions of the Schema Recommendation. Now that you have seen the built-in datatypes, both the primitives and the derived, you can see that they are indeed powerful mechanisms.

We have also already seen some examples of defining your own datatypes, specifically in dealing with `<complexType>` and `<simpleType>` within element and attribute declarations. In this chapter we will revisit those methods for deriving datatypes, and look at some specific examples for how you can derive your own complex and simple types based on some of the types we have already seen.

We will also take a look at some of the tools useful for working with data modeling and XML Schema, such as the identity-constraint elements, like `<unique>` and `<key>`.

Finally, we will round out the chapter by taking a look at regular expressions, including how they function and how they are defined in XML Schema.

DERIVING SIMPLE TYPES

In Chapter 10, "Primitive Datatypes," we covered a number of simple types which were built in to the XML Schema Recommendation. Any of these types can be used as-is, without modifying their properties in the XML Schema. There are many times when you might want to do that, such as when you are just declaring a very straightforward element:

```
<element name="Brand" type="string"/>
```

In this example, we declare an element called `<Brand>` which has a type of `string`, and it is ready to go. Nothing else needs to be done.

However, if we wanted to limit the values of the `string` in any way, for example by limiting the length of the `string` to only 8 characters, we would need to derive our own type from the `string` type.

There are three primary ways to derive new simple types from an existing simple type: restriction, union, and list. You can't derive a new simple type by extending an existing simple type, because any simple type you extend becomes a complex type. So now, let's take a look at the ways we can derive new simple types.

DERIVATION BY RESTRICTION

The most common way of deriving a new simple type is through a restriction. If you recall from Chapter 10, each of the primitive types has a number of constraining facets which can be manipulated to influence the value set of a simple type. When deriving a new simple type by restriction, what you are doing is manipulating those constraining facets, by restricting the kinds of data that are acceptable values for the type.

Which constraining facets you have available to change will vary from type to type, so it's always a good idea to check and make sure that the facet you want applies, and to see what it expresses. But restrictions all take the same basic form.

For example, let's say we wanted to create a new type called Pen which we could then use with various elements in a stationary store catalog. We want the simple type to be a choice between Ball Point pens, Roller Ball pens, and Gel pens. Our type definition might look something like this:

```
<simpleType name="Pen">
 <restriction base="string">
  <enumeration value="BallPoint"/>
  <enumeration value="RollerBall"/>
  <enumeration value="Gel"/>
 </restriction>
</simpleType>
```

In this simple type definition, we name the new type Pen so that we can reference it in element or attribute declarations later in the Schema. Then we use the <restriction> element to denote that the type is a restriction, based on the string type. We then use the enumeration facet for string in order to specify that the value set of our new Pen type must consist of BallPoint, RollerBall, or Gel.

Restrictions can be used for any of the simple types. For example, if we wanted to use a restriction to define a new type called Quantity to limit the values between 1 and 144, we could do so:

```
<simpleType name="Quantity">
 <restriction base="integer">
  <minInclusive value="1"/>
  <maxInclusive value="144"/>
 </restriction>
</simpleType>
```

In this example, since the base type for the restriction was integer, we applied the minInclusive and maxInclusive constraining facets in order to limit the value set to the range we wanted.

All restrictions will follow this basic form, and by using the appropriate base class in conjunction with its constraining facets, you can create your own simple types which are more suited to your needs.

DERIVATION BY UNION

Another way in which you can derive new simple types is through a union. A *union* is simply a means for joining two simple types. The benefit of a union is that when you declare an element or an attribute as a union, the value of that element or attribute can be a part of the value set of either simple type used in the union.

For example, if we wanted to create an attribute for the size of the writing tip on a pen, we might want the size to be able to be expressed as a name, such as "Extra Fine", or as a decimal, such as ".05". So, we could start with defining a simple type for listing the size by using name tokens, or NMTOKEN:

```
<simpleType>
 <restriction base="NMTOKEN">
  <enumeration value="ExtraFine"/>
  <enumeration value="Fine"/>
  <enumeration value="Medium"/>
  <enumeration value="Large"/>
 </restriction>
</simpleType>
```

This would create a type with the value set {ExtraFine, Fine, Medium, Large}. Now, we could define another type, based on decimal, which had a value set between .01 and .99:

```
<simpleType>
 <restriction base="decimal">
   <minInclusive value=".01"/>
   <maxExclusive value="1.00"/>
  <fractionDigits value="2"/>
 </restriction>
</simpleType>
```

To combine these two value sets so that they could be used with an attribute called size, we would use a <union> to create a new simple type that was a union of our two types:

```
<attribute name="size">
 <simpleType>
  <union>
   <simpleType>
    <restriction base="NMTOKEN">
     <enumeration value="ExtraFine"/>
     <enumeration value="Fine"/>
     <enumeration value="Medium"/>
     <enumeration value="Large"/>
    </restriction>
   </simpleType>
   <simpleType>
    <restriction base="decimal">
      <minInclusive value=".01"/>
      <maxExclusive value="1.00"/>
     <fractionDigits value="2"/>
    </restriction>
   </simpleType>
  </union>
 </simpleType>
</attribute>
```

We could then declare an element which used our new attribute:

```
<element name="Pen">
 <complexType>
  <compexContent>
```

```
    <attribute ref="size"/>
   <complexContent>
  </complexType>
 </element>
```

And because the attribute consists of a union between our two simple types, either of the following would be legal values for the "size" attribute:

```
<Pen size=".05"/>
<Pen size="ExtraFine"/>
```

DERIVATION BY LIST

Finally, new simple types can be derived by *list*, which enables you to create a type that has a value set which consists of a list of acceptable values, rather than just one. Unlike and enumeration, which allows you to select one value from a predetermined set, lists allow you to combine more than one value.

For example, if you wanted to create an element called <color> that could have values of "Red", "Blue", "Green", "Black", and so on, you could use the following declaration:

```
<element name="color" type="string"></element>
```

But with that declaration, <color> could only have one value at a time. If an item were multicolored, we couldn't list all of the colors. Unless, we change the declaration to a new type, derived from list:

```
<element name="color">
 <simpleType>
  <list itemType="string">
   <restriction>
    <minLength value="1"/>
    <maxLength value="5"/>
   </restriction>
  </list>
 </simpleType>
</element>
```

Here, because the simple type includes a <list> with itemType defined as "string", the values for the <color> element could consist of a list of strings. The minLength and maxLength values do not refer to the lengths of the string, rather to the length of the list.

For example

```
<color>Red Green Blue</color>
```

would be an acceptable list. However, this would *not* be:

```
<color>Red Green Blue Black Orange Red Purple Brown</color>
```

This list is not valid, because it contains 8 list items, which is more than the maxLength of 5.

Lists can be useful for creating elements or attributes for which you want to be able to assign multiple values.

PART

III

CH

12

DERIVING COMPLEX TYPES

Simple datatypes offer a lot of power within an XML Schema, in terms of managing your data. However, they do lack the flexibility to define new complex representations of data within the content model of an element.

For defining complex types, XML Schema provide the `<complexType>` mechanism, which enables you to define your own complex types for element content models.

Complex types can also be defined independently of element declarations, so that they can be applied to multiple elements, or so that you may derive new complex types based on them. There are two mechanisms that you can use for deriving new complex types, restriction and extension.

COMPLEX TYPES BY RESTRICTION

Just as you can derive new simple types using a restriction, you can also use a restriction to define a new complex type. For example, let's start with the following complex type definition:

```
<complexType name="Beverages">
  <sequence>
   <element name="Name" type="string"/>
   <element name="Ingedients" type="string"/>
   <element name="Type" type="string"/>
  </sequence>
</complexType>
```

This creates a complex type called `Beverages` which has a number of child elements, such as `Name`, `Ingredients`, and `Type`. Now, in the complex type as we have defined it here, each one of these elements must occur once in this type.

Now, we could use this complex type as the base for a new type, called `Juice`, which would be used for specific kinds of `Beverages`. But suppose that with `Juice` we want the `Ingredients` type to be optional, and for the `Type` we want to have an enumeration of values, such as `Apple` and `Orange`.

We can do this with a restriction, because we aren't really adding any new elements or attributes to the type; instead, we are placing constraining facets on the existing elements in the type. So, our new type, which is a restriction of the `Beverages` type, would look like this:

```
<complexType name="Juice">
 <complexContent>
  <restriction base="Beverages">
   <sequence>
    <element name="Name" type="string"/>
    <element name="Ingedients" type="string" minOccurs="0"/>
    <element name="Type">
     <simpleType>
      <restriction>
       <enumeration value="Apple"/>
       <enumeration value="Orange"/>
      </restriction>
     </simpleType>
```

```
      </element>
     </sequence>
    </restriction>
   </complexContent>
 </complexType>
```

The first thing you will notice is that in the `<complexContent>` element within the type definition, we use the `<restriction>` element with a base of `Beverages`, which is the complex type we are restricting.

Next, we include the type definition for `<Name>`, just as it appears in the `Beverages` definition, because in a restriction, we have to include all of the definitions from the original complex type, even if we are not changing them. Next, however, we include the new declaration for the `<Ingredients>` element, with a new `minOccurs` attribute, set to `"0"` to denote that the element is optional.

Finally, we use a new declaration for the `<Type>` element, which uses another simple type definition, along with another restriction to specify the enumeration values for the new type:

```
<element name="Type">
 <simpleType>
  <restriction>
   <enumeration value="Apple"/>
   <enumeration value="Orange"/>
  </restriction>
 </simpleType>
</element>
```

The result is that we now have a type called `Juice` which is derived from the `Beverages` type. If we use this type with an element declaration, such as

```
<element name="Drink" type="Juice"/>
```

then the XML instance could look like this:

```
<Drink>
<Name>Natural Stuff</Name>
<Type>Apple</Type>
</Drink>
```

The advantage of deriving a complex type by restriction is that while you do have to duplicate a number of items between the two definitions, you establish a type hierarchy which defines a relationship between the different types.

COMPLEX TYPES BY EXTENSION

In addition to derivation by restriction, complex types can also be derived by extension. Deriving types by extension allows you to add new functionality to a complex type, to *extend* the base type with a new definition. For example, let's revisit the `Beverages` base class from before:

```
<complexType name="Beverages">
  <sequence>
   <element name="Name" type="string"/>
   <element name="Ingedients" type="string"/>
```

```
    <element name="Type" type="string"/>
  </sequence>
</complexType>
```

Now, let's say that we wanted to use all of the elements defined in the complex type definition for Beverages with a new Juice type, but rather than placing any restrictions on the new type, we want to extend the type by adding a new attribute called Temperature that we can use to indicate if Beverages is hot or cold.

The extension of our Beverages type would look like this:

```
<complexType name="Juice">
  <simpleContent>
   <extension base="bev:Beverages">
   <attribute name="Temperature">
    <simpleType base="string">
     <restriction>
      <enumeration value="Hot"/>
      <enumeration value="Cold"/>
     </restriction>
    </simpleType>
   </attribute>
   </extension>
  </simpleContent>
</complexType>
```

The first and most significant difference between the extension and restriction is that with an extension, it is not necessary to duplicate the elements defined in the original base type. These elements are assumed to be a part of the extension type, so all that we need to do is add the new element or attribute we are adding to the new, extended type. In this case, that is our new Temperature attribute declaration. With that added to the Juice type, our new complex type has all of the elements from our original Beverages type, but also includes our new attribute declaration.

So, if we declare a new element based on our new extended complex type

```
<element name="Drink" type="Juice"/>
```

The instance document might look like this:

```
<Drink Temperature="Cold">
<Name>Nature Made</Name>
<Ingredients>Apples, Water</Ingredients>
<Type>Apple</Type>
</Drink>
```

Creating a new extended type also helps establish a relationship between the new type and the base type, but unlike the restriction, it also provides a shorthand for including the declarations of the original base type, which saves you retyping the definitions.

ANONYMOUS VERSUS NAMED TYPES

In the last section, we actually employed two different kinds of type definitions: anonymous and named. A named type is a globally declared type definition, where the type is assigned a name:

```
<complexType name="Drink_Choices">
  <complexContent>
   <restriction base="string">
    <enumeration value="Coffee"/>
    <enumeration value="Tea"/>
    <enumeration value="Milk"/>
    <enumeration value="Water"/>
   </restriction>
  </complexContent>
 </complexType>
```

The name allows the type to be referenced elsewhere in the document, such as using the type as the base type for element declarations. Both simpleType and complexType can be named types. However, if you do not plan to reuse a type definition, or allow it to be used as a base type, you can reduce clutter in your documents by using anonymous types.

Just like named types, both simpleType and complexType can be used as anonymous types. An anonymous type is one that does not have a name attribute, and is local within an element declaration:

```
<element name="Drink">
  <complexContent>
   <restriction base="string">
    <enumeration value="Coffee"/>
    <enumeration value="Tea"/>
    <enumeration value="Milk"/>
    <enumeration value="Water"/>
   </restriction>
  </complexContent>
 </element>
```

The name attribute here applies to the element declaration, not the type, as in the previous example. Because the type is local to the element, it cannot be referenced by other elements. It also does not have a name which could be used to reference the type, making it anonymous.

SCOPE

We have discussed scope before in previous chapters, but it is worth taking a look at scoping one more time here, especially discussing how scope relates to type definitions.

If you recall from Chapter 5, "Element Declarations" in the section called "Scope," there are two ways in which both element declarations and type definitions can be scoped, globally and locally.

GLOBAL SCOPE

In order to declare a type or element globally, you would declare it as a child of the schema element, using the following structure:

```
<schema>
<type declaration/>
<element declaration1>

<element declaration2>
 <reference to element declaration1>
</element>

<element type="reference to type"/>
</schema>
```

In this structure, the type originally declared is global, because it is not nested in an element declaration. The first element declaration is also globally scoped, which makes it available to be used by reference in the content models of other elements.

Let's take a look at a sample Schema:

```
<schema>

<simpleType name="PaperType">
 <restriction base="string">
  <enumeration value="White"/>
  <enumeration value="Colored"/>
 </restriction>
</simpleType>

<simpleType name="PencilType">
 <restriction base="string">
  <enumeration value="Mechanical"/>
  <enumeration value="Wood"/>
 </restriction>
</simpleType>

<simpleType name="PenType">
 <restriction base="string">
  <enumeration value="BallPoint"/>
  <enumeration value="Gel"/>
 </restriction>
</simpleType>

<element name="Paper" type="PaperType"/>
<element name="Pencil" type="PencilType"/>
<element name="Pen" type="PenType"/>

<element name="Desk">
 <complexType>
  <sequence>
   <element ref="Paper"/>
   <element ref="Pencil"/>
   <element ref="Pen"/>
  </sequence>
 </complexType>
</element>
```

In this Schema, all of the simple types are declared globally, because they are children of the <schema> element. Then we also have three elements, <Paper>, <Pencil>, and <Pen>, which are also declared globally.

Because the simple types PaperType, PencilType, and PenType were all declared globally, we can use them with each of our element declarations. And because we declared the elements globally, we can construct the root element <Desk> by using references to the globally declared elements. An instance document based on this might look like:

```
<Desk>
<Paper>White</Paper>
<Pencil>Mechanical</Pencil>
<Pen>BallPoint</Pen>
</Desk>
```

Declaring your types and elements globally has several advantages. It helps keep the structure of your Schema simple, by avoiding complex nesting patterns which are hard to read. But the real advantage is reusability. Since the types and elements are declared globally, we could use them with as many new element declarations, and even attribute declarations, as we wanted.

For that reason, if you are defining a type which you think you might want to use with more than one element or attribute, it is best to declare it globally. Similarly, if you think that an element will be used in more than one content model, it's a good idea to declare it globally, so that it can then be used by reference throughout the Schema.

LOCAL SCOPE

The other way in which element declarations and type definitions may be scoped is locally. Local scoping is really new to XML Schema, because previously, using the <!ELEMENT declaration in a DTD was really a global declaration.

To scope a type or element declaration locally, the declaration or type definition must be a child of another element or type declaration. Here's the exact same Schema we used in the global scoping example, only modified so that everything is declared and defined locally:

```
<schema>

<element name="Desk">
 <complexType>
  <sequence>
   <element name="Paper">
    <simpleContent>
     <simpleType>
      <restriction base="string">
       <enumeration value="White"/>
       <enumeration value="Colored"/>
      </restriction>
     </simpleType>
    </simpleContent>
   </element>
   <element name="Pencil">
    <simpleContent>
```

```
    <simpleType>
     <restriction base="string">
      <enumeration value="Mechanical"/>
      <enumeration value="Wood"/>
     </restriction>
    </simpleType>
   </simpleContent>
  </element>
  <element name="Pen">
   <simpleContent>
    <simpleType>
     <restriction base="string">
      <enumeration value="BallPoint"/>
      <enumeration value="Gel"/>
     </restriction>
    </simpleContent>
   </simpleType>
  </element>
 </sequence>
</complexType>
</element>
```

The advantage to scoping everything locally is that the structure of the document is inherent in the Schema structure, since all the definitions follow their placement in the document structure. However, if we wanted to add a new element, and use one of our types in that element declaration, it would not be possible, since a locally scoped type cannot be referenced in another element declaration.

Scoping your elements and types locally can be useful to reveal structure through the Schema, or if you want to prevent the use of an element or type with a new declaration. However, it can lead to very complex models.

ABSTRACT TYPES

There may be times when you want to arrange your types in categories. This can be useful for organizational purposes, or for maintaining parity with other computing application design methodologies, such as object-oriented programming.

For example, if you were creating a Schema to describe food items in a restaurant supply catalog, you might want a type called Beverages which would be used to denote beverages that customers would be able to order. However, within the broad beverages category, you might also have two types, called Cola and Juice, to represent two different types of beverages.

Organizationally, this makes perfect sense, as both cola and juice are types of beverages. However, in an instance document, you might want to force the author to use the Cola and Juice types, rather than using the Beverages type.

You could do this by using an abstract type, which is a type that you define in the Schema, but because you would define it with the abstract value as "true", it would be prohibited from being used in an instance document.

The result is that you have a type which can be used to derive other types, but may not be applied to element or attribute declarations. Take a look at the following example:

```
<schema xmlns="http://www.w3.org/2001/XMLSchema"
        targetNamespace="http://www.myCompany.com/beverages"
        xmlns:bev="http://www.myCompany.com/beverages">

 <complexType name="Beverages" abstract="true"/>

 <complexType name="Cola">
  <complexContent>
   <extension base="bev:Beverages"/>
  </complexContent>
 </complexType>

 <complexType name="Juice">
  <complexContent>
   <extension base="bev:Beverages"/>
  </complexContent>
 </complexType>

 <element name="Drink" type="bev:Juice"/>

</schema>
```

In this example, we define a generic `complexType` called `Beverages` with the `abstract` attribute value of `"true"`. That means that the `Beverages` type cannot be used with any element or attribute declarations, but it can be used to derive new types. This is useful if you want to force the use of types which are related (in this case, all based on `Beverages`) but still have their own unique characteristics (specific kinds of beverages). The use of the abstract type establishes a relationship between the types, but still allows unique new types to be derived.

In the preceding example, the abstract `Beverages` type is used to derive two new types, `Cola` and `Juice`, which, because they are not abstract types, can be applied to element declarations in the Schema, as the `Juice` type is applied to the `<Drink>` element above.

While the example here is very simple, you could take the `Juice` type and extend its definition to make it as complicated as you needed, adding information about its freshness or expiration, for example. But because it was derived from the abstract type, you would always know that a `Juice` type was a type of `Beverages`.

CONTROLLING DERIVED TYPES

Taking advantage of scope and making use of abstract types are two ways to control the way your types are used and referenced. However, because Schema can be included or imported into other Schema, you might want a finer grain of control over your types.

Fortunately, the Schema Recommendation provides a few ways in which you can control types and how those types can be altered or manipulated down the road. These mechanisms include the `fixed`, `block`, and `final` attributes.

PART

III

CH

12

fixed

The first mechanism for controlling the use and content of Schema components is the `fixed` attribute. You may recall from dealing with elements and attributes that they may contain a `fixed` attribute in their declarations, which essentially assigns them a fixed value. For example,

```
<element name="SKU" fixed="310411"/>
```

will declare an element which has a fixed value of `"310411"`, so that any time the element appears in an instance document, it must appear in the form

```
<SKU>310411</SKU>
```

The same is true of an attribute which is declared with a fixed value. This is one method of controlling content.

However, the `fixed` attribute takes on a new meaning when it is used with a `<simpleType>` definition. In this case, the `fixed` attribute can be applied to a number of the constraining facets associated with the type definition (such as `Length`, `minInclusive`, `maxInclusive`, and so on). The `fixed` attribute is a `boolean` that has a value of `"true"` or `"false"`. The value is `false` by default.

The effect of using the `fixed` attribute with a constraining facet is that it denotes that the value of the facet is fixed, so that the facet value may not be altered in any future derivations. Let's look at an example.

Say we started with a type called `zip` for defining a U.S. ZIP code:

```
<simpleType name="zip">
 <restriction base="string">
  <length value="5" fixed="true"/>
  <pattern value="[0-9]{5}"/>
 </restriction>
</simpleType>
```

With this type definition, any five-digit string will match a ZIP code, but the length of the ZIP code is restricted to five digits, and because that facet has been set to `fixed="true"` we couldn't change it if we wanted to derive a new type. For example, if we wanted to create a new type for zip+4, and increase the length of the string to 10 characters, we couldn't do it. It would be illegal because the length of the string has been fixed in the base type.

block

Another mechanism you can use to control the derivation of new types is the `block` attribute. The `block` attribute can be used with elements as well, and you might recall from Chapter 5 that when used with an element, the `block` attribute can have the following values:

- `#all`—Blocks any derivation of any kind.
- `substitution`—Blocks the substitution of the element, if the element is a part of a substitution group.
- `extension`—Blocks the element from being extended.

- restriction—Blocks the element from being restricted.
- list—Blocks the element from being part of a list, or having a list as a value.
- union—Blocks the element from being part of a union, or having a union as a value.

The block attribute can be used with a <complexType> as well. However, when used with a complex type, the acceptable values for the block attribute are

- #all
- extension
- restriction

That is because a complex type cannot be a substitution, list, or union. But you can block the complex type from being used to create new types from an extension or restriction.

For example, let's say we start with a complex type for an address:

```
<complexType name="Address" block="extension">
 <sequence>
  <element name="street" type="string"/>
  <element name="city" type="string"/>
  <element name="state" type="string"/>
  <element name="zip" type="string"/>
 </sequence>
</complexType>
```

Because this type has been blocked from extension, if we wanted to create a new type called USaddress by extending the address type to add a <country> element with a value of "USA", we couldn't do it. Extensions have been blocked.

final

As is the case with both the fixed and block attributes, the final attribute can be used with an element, to denote that the element is the final version of the element. The final attribute can also be used with both <simpleType> and <complexType> definitions.

When the final attribute is used with a <simpleType> it can have the following values:

- #all
- list
- union
- restriction

This is because simple types can be declared as lists, unions, and restrictions, but not extensions. When the final attribute is used with <complexType>, it can have the following values:

- #all
- extension
- restriction

In either case, the result of using the `final` attribute is the same: It denotes that the type definition is the "final" derivation of that type that can occur. For example, let's look at a ZIP code example, in reverse. First, we start with a `zip4` type:

```
<simpleType name="zip4">
 <restriction base="string">
  <pattern value="[0-9]{5}\-[0-9]{4}"/>
 </restriction>
</simpleType>
```

Now, if we wanted to use this as a base to create a new type called `zip` for a five-digit ZIP code, we could use the following:

```
<simpleType name="zip" final="restriction">
 <restriction base="zip4">
  <length value="5" />
  <pattern value="[0-9]{5}"/>
 </restriction>
</simpleType>
```

Now, because we have declared this as the `final` restriction, the `zip` type could not be used as the basis for a new restriction. But this doesn't prevent the base `zip4` type from being used for other restrictions; it's more of a mechanism for ensuring that new derivations are made from the correct base type.

All of these mechanisms can be used to control how your types can be used as the basis for derivation. That might not be crucial when you are the sole author of a Schema; however, if you are working with multiple authors, that can help you control what other authors do with the types you define. And more importantly, these mechanisms can help ensure your types are used properly if you are building multiple-part Schema by including or importing one Schema into another. We will talk more about including and importing Schema later in Chapter 14, "Building Multipart Schema."

UNIQUENESS

With XML 1.0 and DTDs, it is possible to define an attribute as an ID, which means that it could serve as a unique ID. That ID could then be referenced using an IDREF.

While the ID attribute type does work, it also has some limitations. For example, only an attribute can serve as an ID type, so there is no way of specifying that an element content has to have a unique value.

With Schema, there is an improved mechanism for specifying that either an element or attribute has to have unique content. In fact, you can also define the scope in which the content has to be unique. Additionally, XML Schema provide a mechanism which enables you to specify an element or attribute as a Key, which serves as a unique identifier, and use Keyrefs to reference those keys. This provides a mechanism similar to those provided by some major databases for referencing content in your XML documents.

To see how uniqueness and keys work in Schema, we need to start with the basic building blocks, `<selector>` and `<field>`. Then we can use those to specify `<unique>`, `<key>`, and `<keyref>`.

selector

The `<selector>` element is used to select the scope of the element or attribute which is being identified as a key or for uniqueness. The `<selector>` element itself has no content, although it can have an annotation.

Instead, the `<selector>` element has two attributes, an `id` attribute, which can serve as a unique ID for the `<selector>`, and an `xpath` attribute, which is used to "select" the element or attribute using a subset of the XPath syntax.

So, a typical selector might look like this:

```
<selector xpath=".//state"/>
```

This would select a `<state>` element in the document. The `selector` works in conjunction with the `<field>` element, which also makes use of XPath.

> **Note**
>
> If you are unfamiliar with XPath and the XPath syntax, you can learn more at the W3C Web site's XPath section, located at `http://www.w3.org/TR/xpath`.

field

The `<field>` element also does not have any content, but can have an annotation. It also has an `id` attribute that can be used to give the `<field>` an ID, but its most important attribute is the `xpath` attribute which is used to specify the field being selected in a `<unique>` or `<key>` element. For example,

```
<field xpath="@zip"/>
```

This would select a `zip` attribute. If we combined it with the `<selector>` from earlier

```
<selector xpath=".//state"/>
<field xpath="@zip"/>
```

That would locate the `zip` attribute of the `<state>` element.

The `<selector>` and `<field>` elements work hand in hand. But you won't actually use them on their own; instead, you will use them as content for `<unique>` and `<key>` elements.

PART

III

CH

12

unique

The `<unique>` element can be used to specify an element or attribute that has to have a unique value within a certain scope. For example, let's look at a `contact` element:

```
<element name="contact">
 <complexType>
```

```
  <element name="name">
   <complexType>
    <complexContent>
     <attribute name="phone"/>
      <restriction base="string">
       <pattern value="[0-9]{3}\-[0-9]{4}"/>
      </restriction>
     </attribute>
    </complexContent>
   </complexType>
  </element>
 </complexType>
</element>
```

This would allow an instance document that looks like this:

```
<contact>
<name phone="555-1212">John Doe</name>
<name phone="345-1212">Jane Robinson</name>
<name phone="765-1212">Mark Smith</name>
</contact>
```

Now, let's say that we wanted the phone attribute to always be unique. We could specify that using a <unique> element.

The <unique> element has a name attribute that allows you to specify a name for <unique> element. The only content allowed in a <unique> tag are annotations and <selector> and <field> elements. In fact, you could use multiple <field> elements to denote combinations of elements or attributes which had to be unique. So, let's look at how we would specify a unique phone attribute:

```
<unique name="example">
<selector xpath=".//name"/>
<field xpath="@phone"/>
</unique>
```

Here, we use the <selector> and <field> elements to locate the phone attribute of the <name> element. And because it is specified in a <unique> element, the value of the phone attribute now must be unique.

key

Assigning keys works exactly the same as defining a <unique> element. The <key> element has two attributes, name and id. For its content, a <key> may have an annotation. But most importantly, the <key> can have a <selector> and multiple <field> elements for locating the key, using XPath expressions. So let's alter our Schema slightly:

```
<element name="contact">
 <complexType>
  <sequence>
   <element name="name" type="string"/>
   <element name="phone" type="string"/>
  </sequence>
 </complexType>
</element>
```

This will create a document such as

```
<contact>
<name>John Doe</name>
<phone>555-1212</phone>
</contact>
```

Now we have a `<name>` element and a `<phone>` element, and let's say we wanted to make the `<name>` element a `<key>`. We could do so like this:

```
<key name="nameKey">
<selector xpath=".//contact"/>
<field xpath="contact/name"/>
</key>
```

This would create a key based on the `<name>` child of the `<contact>` element. We could then use that key as an identifier, and use `<keyref>` to reference the key.

keyref

You can use the `<keyref>` element to create key references, which have a syntax almost identical to the `<unique>` element. The main difference is that the `<keyref>` also has a `refer` attribute, which is used to specify the `<key>` to which the reference is being created.

For example, if we wanted to make the previous example's `<phone>` element a key reference to `nameKey`, we would use

```
<keyref name="PhoneRef" refer="nameKey">
<selector xpath=".//contact"/>
<field xpath="contact/phone"/>
</keyref>
```

This would make the `<phone>` element a reference to the `<name>` element, establishing a key and a reference to the key.

Uniqueness and keys are very valuable mechanisms for working with your data, especially if you are working in a database context.

REGULAR EXPRESSIONS AND XML SCHEMA

If you have ever worked with Unix or PERL, then you have probably encountered regular expressions. If you haven't worked with regular expressions before, then get ready, as regular expressions can be used with XML Schema to provide pattern matching in a restriction for developing your own datatypes.

Caution

If you are familiar with regular expressions (such as PERL or AWK) you might still want to make sure to familiarize yourself with regexp for Schema and the differences to ensure they are used correctly.

A regular expression is simply a means of describing a pattern. For example,

`Match This`

is a regular expression. However, it's not a particularly useful one, because it only matches the string

Match This

exactly, and it does not match any other string. While there are times when you may want to match a string exactly, there are also many times when you will want to match any string that fits a certain pattern. For example, let's say that you wanted to match any three-letter word ending with "at", such as "cat" or "hat". You could use the regular expression

`.at`

This will match "hat", "cat", "fat", "bat", and so on, because the "." character means "Match any character here." In fact, it will also match "2at", "4at", and so on.

Regular expressions are a very flexible method for performing pattern matching, and because they are commonly used in many computing applications, chances are you've already used regular expressions, or will use them in the future.

SPECIAL CHARACTERS

There are a number of characters which have special meanings when used in regular expressions. We've already seen one, the period, which can be used as a wildcard for any character.

Each of the following characters has a special meaning or use in regular expressions:

- . Matches any valid XML character, with the exception of carriage returns and new lines.
- \ Is used to denote escape sequences, or to convert a special character, such as "*" or ".", into a literal.
- | Is used to group lists of regular expressions.
- * A special character denoting that the character (or parenthesized expression) that precedes it occurs zero or more times.
- + A special character denoting that the character (or parenthesized expression) that precedes it occurs one or more times.
- ? A special character denoting that the character (or parenthesized expression) that precedes it occurs zero or one times.
- {} Braces, used for defining category escapes and for iterations.
- () Parentheses, used to create a grouping of characters for repeat matching, or to create a subexpression.
- [] Brackets, used to denote a character set for expressions.

As we begin to get into constructing expressions, we will see how each of these characters functions in context.

SINGLE CHARACTER ESCAPES

The first character we'll put to use is the backslash "\", which is used to form sequences called "escapes". An *escape* is when we use a character (or characters) to represent a specific function or control character.

The backslash has two uses. The first is that when used with certain letters, it forms an escape for a character. For example,

- **\t** Tab
- **\n** New Line
- **\r** Carriage Return

So, if you wanted to match a tab, you couldn't just hit the tab key, as that would advance your cursor. So, you use "\t" to represent the tab in your pattern; that is a single character escape.

Caution

Matching whitespace in Schema can be a dangerous idea. Because whitespace in Schema can be collapsed or normalized, your regular expression searching for a tab, might only encounter spaces.

The second use for the backslash is when it is used with a special character. For example, what if we wanted to use the period in our pattern, such as ".com"? If you wrote

```
.com
```

that would match "acom" and "bcom" or "4com", and ".com". However, to match *only* ".com" you would use the backslash character to escape the period, turning it into the literal for the period rather than the wildcard special character:

```
\.com
```

That expression would match ".com" exactly and nothing more.

MULTIPLE CHARACTER ESCAPES

While single character escapes are used to represent a single character, such as a tab or newline, multiple character escapes are used to represent multiple characters.

Each multiple character escape is formed in the same manner as a single character escape: a backslash followed by the letter that represents the multiple characters the escape is representing. For example, to match digits, you would use a backslash followed by a lowercase "d":

```
\d
```

You can also use the same construction to mean "NOT" that character set, by using the uppercase "D" instead. So

```
\D
```

would match anything *not* a digit. Here's a list of multiple character escapes and their meanings:

- \s Spaces
- \S Non-spaces
- \i The first character in a name.
- \I Not the first character in a name.
- \c Any subsequent character of a name.
- \C Not the subsequent character of a name.
- \d Digits
- \D Non-digits
- \w Word characters
- \W Non word characters

So, for example, if you wanted to match two words, regardless of the spaces between them, you could use

```
word\sanother
```

Which would match "word another" or "word   another".

Multiple character escapes are useful, but another method for accomplishing similar matches is through the use of category escapes and character sets.

CATEGORY ESCAPES

Category escapes are another mechanism for matching a group of characters. The category escape is denoted by the "\p" sequence, followed by the category in a set of braces:

```
\p{category}
```

The categories are based on Unicode categories. For example, to represent the category of letters, you would use the "L" category in the braces:

```
\p{L}
```

and

```
\P{L}
```

Using the uppercase "P" denotes "NOT", so "\P{L}" means "not a letter". So, if we wanted to match the set of digits, we could use the "Nd" category:

```
\p{Nd}
```

and

```
\P{Nd}
```

Which would represent digits and not-digits, respectively.

We can also use Unicode block names, by using the `is` keyword inside the braces, followed by the Unicode block name. For example, to match characters in the Unicode "BasicLatin" block set you would use

```
\p{isBasicLatin}
```

To see an example of how you might use category escapes, let's say you wanted to match phone numbers, in the pattern xxx-xxx-xxxx:

```
\p{Nd}\-\p{Nd}\-\p{Nd}
```

That would match a set of digits, followed by a dash, another set of digits, a dash, and then a final set of digits. There is actually only one problem with this pattern. There is no mechanism for specifying the number of digits in the pattern. We'll see how to do that in just a little bit.

CHARACTER SETS

There is another syntax for specifying character sets within regular expressions, which involves specifying the character set as a range within a set of brackets.

For example, we can specify the character set of all the lowercase letters from a to z as follows:

```
[a-z]
```

Similarly, if we wanted to specify NOT the character set from a to z, we would use a caret "^" before the character set:

```
[^a-z]
```

Here's a rundown of some of the more common character sets used in regular expressions:

- **[a-z]** The character set of lowercase letters, a through z.
- **[^a-z]** NOT the character set of lowercase letters.
- **[A-Z]** The character set of uppercase letters, A through Z.
- **[^A-Z]** NOT the character set of uppercase letters.
- **[0-9]** The character set of digits, 1 through 9.
- **[^0-9]** NOT the character set of digits.

So, if we take a look at our previous phone example, we could also use

```
[0-9]*\-[0-9]*\-[0-9]*
```

to specify three ranges of digits, each separated by a dash. However, we still haven't specified the *number* of digits in each set, so we are not quite there.

COMBINING CHARACTER SETS

Character sets can also be combined in regular expressions, simply by combining the character set representations within the brackets. For example, if we wanted to define a character set consisting of all the uppercase and lowercase letters, we could combine the two sets into

```
[A-Za-z]
```

Or, we could combine a character set with a special character, or single character escape

```
[[A-Za-z^0-9]\.com]
```

which would match any letter, upper- or lowercase, followed by the string ".com", but *not* a digit in the 0–9 range.

CHARACTER SET SUBTRACTIONS

Character sets can also be subtracted from one another inside the brackets. For example, if you wanted to specify the characters in the Unicode "Basic Latin" block, excluding any characters which were also in the "General Punctuation" block, you could use the following:

```
[\p{isBasicLatin}-\p{isGeneralPunctuation}]
```

ADVANCED REGULAR EXPRESSIONS

Those are all the basics of regular expressions, which can be used to form a wide variety of patterns for use in your XML Schema. However, there are some additional features which will undoubtedly come in handy.

ITERATIONS

We've seen a number of examples using ranges of digits, which are very handy, given the use of numbers in our society. However, in the examples we've seen, such as a phone number, we haven't been able to specify the number of iterations of a pattern.

Regular expressions do have a number of mechanisms for specifying iterations. For example, the asterisk can be used to denote that a pattern may occur any number of times. For example, if we use it with a regular letter

```
Boo*
```

then we can have any number of "o" characters occurring after the initial "Bo". So, this expression would match:

> Bo
>
> Boo
>
> Booooo
>
> Boooooo

And so on. We can also use the "+" and the "?" symbols to express iteration. These might look familiar if you've worked with DTDs; they are also the symbols used for iteration in content models. The "+" indicates that an expression may occur one or many times, and the "?" indicates that the expression is optional, occurring zero or once.

Iterations can also be counted, which is very useful. Remember our phone number example? We wanted to create a pattern that matched a 10-digit phone number, in the XXX-XXX-XXXX form. Now we can use counted iterations to create that pattern:

```
[0-9]{3}\-[0-9]{3}\-[0-9]{4}
```

In this pattern, you will note that each of our ranges is followed by a pair of braces and an integer. That integer specifies the exact number of times the pattern must occur. We could also specify a range, in the form

```
[range]{min, max}
```

For example, to specify a number which must have at least one digit, but could have up to five, we would use

```
[0-9]{1,5}
```

which would match

```
0
412
15323
```

but not

```
3333214
```

because it has more than five digits.

Similarly, we could create a pattern to match Social Security numbers in the XXX-XX-XXXX form with the following expression:

```
[0-9]{3}\-[0-9]{2}\-[0-9]{4}
```

As you can see, counted iterations are very useful in regular expressions.

Parenthesized Expressions

Expressions can be placed into parentheses, forming subexpressions, which is especially useful with iterations. For example, we could use a pattern to match the word "The" with a space followed by a letter:

```
(The)\s[A-Za-z]
```

But if we wanted to specify that the word "The" was optional, we could use the "?" symbol:

```
(The)?\s[A-Za-z]
```

And finally, if we wanted to say that there could be an unlimited number of letters, we could use "*":

```
(The)?\s[A-Za-z]*
```

which would match any of the following:

The man

Man

The woman

The WoMaN

The   dog

ALTERNATIVE EXPRESSIONS

There is also a mechanism for allowing for a choice between two patterns or subexpressions in a regular expression, by making use of the "\" symbol. For example, if we wanted to match a specific string, such as a movie title, but we wanted to be able to match either the English title or the foreign language title, we could separate the strings with a "|":

```
Wings of Desire|Der Himmel Uber Berlin
```

This would match either the string "Wings of Desire" or the string "Der Himmel Uber Berlin". We can also build complex patterns using the alternate mechanism, such as matching a phone number, but limiting the number of area codes:

```
(773|312|847)\-[0-9]{3}\-[0-9]{4}
```

Which would match either of the following numbers:

773-555-1212

312-555-1212

But it would not match

317-555-1212

Regular expressions are very handy when building datatypes, as they can be used with the pattern constraining facet to provide a means for accomplishing specific formatting and pattern matching for datatype values.

These basics of regular expressions are very useful, not only in Schema, but in computing in general. So, if you have learned regular expressions before, you are now familiar with the syntax specifics when using them in XML Schema. And if you are new to regular expressions, you've just learned a skill which will serve you well in many different aspects of computing.

CONCLUSION

The Schema components we've discussed in this chapter are all mechanisms for controlling and manipulating your data models inside the Schema syntax. By using the techniques covered in this chapter, you can further customize your datatypes and content models to perform exactly as you want them to perform, and also place restrictions on what others can do with your datatypes.

How you end up using datatypes in your document will depend on your document needs, and the systems with which you are working, such as databases or document management systems. But with all the tools at your disposal now, you have the knowledge necessary to adapt XML Schema to your needs, with a little patience and practice. Let's refresh what we discussed in this chapter:

- New simple types can be derived from a base simple type by `restriction`, `list`, or `union`.

- A restriction involves placing new constraining facets on the value set of a previously defined type.

- A derivation by list involves creating a new value set that may consist of a list of potential values.

- A derivation by union involves creating a new value set which consists of the union of two value sets.

- New complex types can be derived from base complex types by extension or restriction.

- An extension involves adding new elements to the content model of the existing base type.

- Type definitions, element declarations, and attribute declarations may be scoped globally or locally.

- Globally scoped items are children of the `<schema>` element.

- Locally scoped items occur inside the content model of another definition or declaration.

- Abstract types allow you to create base types and declarations which are not allowed to not appear in XML instance documents.

- Derivation of types can be controlled by using the `fixed`, `final`, and `block` attributes.

- Uniqueness of element or attribute content can be achieved using the `<unique>` element.

- Unique content is selected and defined using `<select>` and `<field>`, and uses XPath expressions to locate values.

- Elements can be assigned keys, using `<key>`, so that the Schema component has a unique key for reference. This is handy for database compatibility.

- Keys can be referenced using `<keyref>`.

- Regular expressions enable you to create complex pattern matching constraints on type value sets.

PART

III

CH

12

Now you have all the tools necessary to work on full-featured, complex Schema. In the following chapters, we will be concentrating on writing some real-world Schema. We will be looking at the process of structuring a Schema and writing the Schema syntax. So, now let's move on to some practical Schema authoring to round out your Schema education.

IN THE REAL WORLD

In the real world, the majority of datatypes which you will use in your Schema will be types that you have derived yourself, either from `simpleTypes` or by creating your own `complexTypes`.

When working with simple types, the most common method of derivation will be `restriction`. Although both `list` and `union` are powerful methods of derivation, `restriction` is far more common, and you should be familiar with restrictions and how to use the constraining facets to create your own, new simple types. Complex types are commonly derived by `restriction` and `extension`, or by creating your own complex type with a model group.

When working with either simple types or complex types, you will need to determine if you want the type to be scoped locally or globally. The issue of named vs. anonymous types goes hand in hand with scope, as any type which is scoped globally must be a named type. Anonymous types, because they cannot be referenced by name, must be scoped locally.

When you are deriving your own types, you consider whether the type is likely to be reused, either within the Schema, or by other Schema. If the type is not likely to be reused (and many of your types will not), then it makes sense to scope the type locally as an anonymous type. This helps reduce clutter in the Schema, and helps avoid any potential conflicts. However, if you are going to reuse a type, then a globally declared named type is a good choice, as it allows you to reference the type by name, using it for multiple elements, or using it as a base type for further customization. A globally declared type can also be imported or included into other Schema.

Abstract types, `final` and `block`, are all useful tools when working with types, but if you are new to datatypes, don't worry about fully understanding the usefulness of these mechanisms. As you use datatypes more, and work with other applications, eventually you will encounter a situation where you want to create a type as a base, but not as a usable type, and that is when you will appreciate the value of `abstract`. However, until then, it is a pretty advanced feature of type derivation, and not one you are likely to encounter on a routine basis.

Finally, although `unique` and `key` provide valuable mechanisms for specifying uniqueness of elements and referencing elements by keys, you should use these features with caution. Although they are similar to mechanisms found in many major databases, the functionality may not always be identical, and the subtle differences can cause problems with your data. If you are working with XML and databases, you should spend some extra time comparing these features before assuming that a key in your database is compatible with a `key` in your Schema.

CHAPTER 13

EXAMPLE SCHEMA: CUSTOMER INVOICE

In this chapter

OUTLINING THE SCHEMA REQUIREMENTS

Now that you have a solid grasp of all the XML Schema structures and datatypes, you can bring them all together in a sample Schema that makes use of some of the datatypes covered in Chapters 10, "Primitive Datatypes," and 11, "Derived Datatypes." In this example for a customer invoice, we will be making use of the `string` datatype, the `date` type, and the `integer` type, as well as deriving our own types.

These datatypes are pretty common, and you will likely encounter them in your own Schema. They are also fairly typical, and the same techniques we use to manipulate these types and their constraining facets will be applicable to other datatypes you might use as well.

For this sample Schema, we are going to work with a customer invoice, which might look something like this:

```
- - - - - - - - - - - - - - - - - - - - - - - - - - - - - - - - - - - - - - - - - - - - - - -
Invoice    #00001
Job        #0021

Date: 04/11/02
Purchase Order: M34510-A
Reference: 982LG-233

Billing Address:       Mr. Widget Hydraulics
                       123 My Way
                       Grand Rapids, MI 60334

Shipping Address:    Use Billing Address


Item          Description   Quantity   Price/Rate      Amount
- - - -       - - - - - - - - - - -   - - - - - - - -   - - - - - - - - - -   - - - - - -
089SD2        Torque Hub    1            234.00         234.00
3432D2        Flange Valve  4             25.00         100.00

                                       Subtotal        334.00
                                       Taxes            16.70
                                       Shipping         35.00

                           Total/Balance Due           385.70

Terms: Due Net 30
Sales Representative: DLG
Memo: Thank you for choosing Large Company, Ltd!
- - - - - - - - - - - - - - - - - - - - - - - - - - - - - - - - - - - - - - - - - - - - - - -
```

This is a pretty generic format for a customer invoice, created to show you the basic structure of a possible application. In reality, your specific data might look slightly different, but that is the nature of proprietary data. There is no way for us to address every possible structure for common documents, so we've chosen a deliberately generic example to showcase the techniques of using Schema and datatypes, rather than provide a specific detailed example that would not fit anyone's needs. As presented, the example is serviceable. But most importantly, with the techniques you learn in this and the following chapters, you will be able to easily extend and customize the Schema to your specific needs.

So for this application, we're going to create a generic customer invoice Schema, which could be used for storing customer invoice data, exchanging invoices with suppliers, or formatting via a mechanism such as XSLT.

An application such as this is a good candidate for a Schema using datatypes due to the nature of the information which we are describing. In this case, we will be working with part numbers, quantities, and dollar amounts, all of which lend themselves very nicely to certain datatypes.

So, let's take a look at the specific information that we want to include in our Schema. The basic information breaks down into data about the customer, and data about the items being invoiced.

For the customer related data, we are going to need to keep track of

- The invoice number
- Any job number associated with the invoice
- The invoice date
- The customer's billing address
- The customer's shipping address
- A Purchase Order from the customer
- Any customer-supplied reference number (such as an internal PO from a reseller)
- The customer's sales representative (our employee)
- The customer's payment terms

For the invoice related data, we will need to keep track of

- The Item or Service number
- A description of the item or service
- The quantity of items ordered, or duration of service
- The per-item or per-unit price
- The line item total cost
- The subtotal of the invoice
- Any applicable shipping charges
- Any applicable taxes
- The total amount due

The items we want to use on our invoice, along with a description of the item and its role, are shown in Table 13.1.

TABLE 13.1   AN OVERVIEW OF THE TYPES OF INFORMATION TO BE USED IN THE INVOICE

Invoice Items	Description
Invoice Number	A reference number for the invoice.
Job Number	A reference number for a specific customer job.
Purchase Order Number	A customer purchase order number.
Reference Number	A reference number for the customer's internal use, if supplied.
Date	The date of the invoice.
Representative	Our company's sales representative.
Billing Address	The billing address for the invoice.
Shipping Address	The shipping address for the invoice.
Items/Services	The items or services being invoiced.
Description	A description of the items or services.
Quantity	The quantity of items, or the duration unit of the service.
Price/Rate	The price per item or rate per service unit.
Amount	The amount of the invoice line item.
Subtotal	The subtotal for the invoice.
Shipping/Handling	Any additional shipping or handling charges.
Tax	Any applicable taxes, such as sales tax or V.A.T.
Total	The total amount for the invoice.
Payment Terms	The payment terms of the invoice.
Message	A message for the invoice, such as "Thanks for doing business with us".
Notes	Any internal notes we might have about the invoice.

By stepping through the list of items we find on our invoice, we can come up with the elements and attributes we will want in our final XML instance document, which is the same list of elements and attributes that we need to declare in our Schema.

First, we need a root element for the invoice, which will contain all of the child elements which describe the content of a particular invoice. We also need some way of keeping track of a particular invoice (the invoice number) and how the invoice relates to a customer (the job number). Because the invoice number and the job number relate to the invoice itself, we can make them attributes:

```
<invoice number="00001" job="0021">
```

Next, we need to keep track of the date on which the invoice is issued. So, we create a date element to specify the invoice date:

```
<date>04/11/02</date>
```

Now that we have an invoice and a date, we also need to keep track of the information that relates to the customer purchase or purchase order that started the whole order process. In this case, we'll use an element called PO and some attributes to keep track of the PO:

```
<PO PONumber="M34510-A" ref="982LG-233"/>
```

The PONumber attribute references the customer's purchase order number. The ref attribute is optional, and we can use it to specify an internal reference number for the customer, such as whether the customer was a reseller and needed to reference one of *their* customer's purchase orders.

With all the tracking information out of the way, we need to specify some information about the company we are billing, and where the merchandise (or services) are to be delivered.

For this, we can make use of two elements, billingAddress and shippingAddress. Both will be able to contain a number of child elements which relate to the address information:

- company
- contact
- department
- address1
- address2
- city
- state
- zip
- phone
- fax
- email
- altPhone
- altContact

This gives us a great deal of flexibility in keeping track of billing and shipping information, including some alternate contact info, just in case personnel changes at our customer's organization. The result is a billingAddress element which looks like this:

```
<billingAddress>
  <company>Mr. Widget Hydraulics</company>
  <contact>Bill Widget</contact>
  <address1>123 My Way</address1>
  <city>Grand Rapids</city>
  <state>MI</state>
  <zip>60334</zip>
  <phone>703-333-1231</phone>
  <fax>703-333-0001</fax>
  <email>mr.widget@widget.com</email>
</billingAddress>
```

Of course, all this information could be easily duplicated for the shipping address, or different information could be specified as well. But in that case where all the shipping and billing information is the same, we'll create a special attribute that can be used called useBilling:

```
<shippingAddress useBilling="yes"/>
```

This will save us the trouble of duplicating all that address and contact information, and let anyone using the invoice XML document know that they should simply use the billing address information if this attribute's value is "yes".

Now that we have the contact information out of the way, we're ready to move on to the section of the invoice that describes the items being invoiced. For this, we need to keep track of the code (such as the part number) for an item, as well as the item's description, the quantity of the item ordered, the per-unit price or rate of the item, and then also the total price for all of that particular item (or service) ordered. For example

```
<item code="089SD2">
 <description>Torque Hub</description>
 <quantity>1</quantity>
 <price_rate>234.00</price_rate>
 <amount>234.00</amount>
</item>
```

Here we have an item, identified by the item code, which is described as a "Torque Hub". The quantity is also specified, along with a price/rate. The final amount is derived by multiplying the rate and the quantity, giving us an amount total for that line item.

We can have multiple items in our invoice, but when the prices of all the items are added together, we get a subtotal for the invoice:

```
<subtotal>334.00</subtotal>
```

Of course, with some items, there may be taxes associated, so we will need to add any applicable taxes. We also can make use of a rate attribute to keep track of the tax rate being assessed for that invoice:

```
<tax taxRate=".05">16.70</tax>
```

There may be additional charges associated with the invoice as well. For example, if the invoice is paid on credit, there may be a finance charge. Or if the items are to be shipped, there may be a shipping charge. To keep track of these additional charges, we will use a charges element, with a type attribute that allows the specification of the type of charges being applied:

```
<charges type="shipping">35.00</charges>
```

Finally, when all of the costs are added, we are left with a total for the invoice:

```
<total>385.70</total>
```

We also might provide a balanceDue element, in case there is a difference in the total and the amount due, as a result of financing or partial payments:

```
<balanceDue>385.70</balanceDue>
```

And with respect to payments, some customers might have extended credit terms, such as having the net balance due in 30 days, while others might have to pay upon receipt of the invoice. To specify the terms, we'll use a `term` element:

```
<term>Due Net 30</term>
```

To help us deal with the customer account internally, we'll want to keep track of the representative who generated the invoice, as well as their department. We can do this with a `rep` element which makes use of `name` and `dept` attributes:

```
<rep name="DLG" dept="sales"/>
```

Finally, at the end of the invoice, we might want to print a custom message, such as a thank you. We can specify that message with a message element:

```
<message>Thank you for choosing Large Company, Ltd!</message>
```

And we can make use of a `notes` element to keep track of internal notes which are not printed on the final invoice, but kept in our records for future interaction with the customer:

```
<notes>A good, loyal customer. Always prompt payment.</notes>
```

There are a number of elements and attributes put to use in the invoice example, and they are summarized in Table 13.2.

TABLE 13.2   THE ELEMENTS AND ATTRIBUTES TO BE DEFINED IN THE INVOICE SCHEMA

Element	Child Elements	Attributes
invoice	(root element)	number, job
date	N/A	
billingAddress	company	
	department	
	contact	
	address1	
	address2	
	city	
	state	
	zip	
	phone	
	fax	
	email	
	altPhone	
	altContact	
shippingAddress	company	useBilling

TABLE 13.2 THE ELEMENTS AND ATTRIBUTES TO BE DEFINED IN THE INVOICE SCHEMA

Element	Child Elements	Attributes
	department	
	contact	
	address1	
	address2	
	city	
	state	
	zip	
	phone	
	fax	
	email	
	altPhone	
	altContact	
PO		PONumber, reference
rep		name, dept
term		
item		code
service		
description		
quantity		
price_rate		
amount		
subtotal		
tax		taxRate
charges		type
total		
balanceDue		
message		
notes		

When all of these elements and attributes are pulled together into an XML instance document, the result is something like the code shown in Listing 13.1.

LISTING 13.1 A SAMPLE INVOICE XML INSTANCE DOCUMENT

```xml
<?xml version="1.0" encoding="UTF-8" ?>

<invoice number="00001" job="0021">

 <date>04/11/02</date>

 <billingAddress>
  <company>Mr. Widget Hydraulics</company>
  <contact>Bill Widget</contact>
  <address1>123 My Way</address1>
  <city>Grand Rapids</city>
  <state>MI</state>
  <zip>60334</zip>
  <phone>703-333-1231</phone>
  <fax>703-333-0001</fax>
  <email>mr.widget@widget.com</email>
 </billingAddress>

 <shippingAddress useBilling="yes"/>

<PO PONumber="M34510-A" reference="982LG-233"/>

 <item code="089SD2">
  <description> Torque Hub</description>
  <quantity>1</quantity>
  <price_rate>234.00</price_rate>
  <amount>234.00</amount>
 </item>

 <item code="3432D2">
  <description>Flange Valve</description>
  <quantity>4</quantity>
  <price_rate>25.00</price_rate>
  <amount>100.00</amount>
 </item>

 <subtotal>334.00</subtotal>
 <tax taxRate=".05">16.70</tax>
 <charges type="shipping">35.00</charges>
 <total>385.70</total>

 <balanceDue>385.70</balanceDue>

 <term>Due Net 30</term>

 <rep name="DLG" dept="sales"/>

 <message>Thank you for choosing Large Company, Ltd!</message>
 <notes>A good, loyal customer. Always prompt payment.</notes>

</invoice>
```

By outlining all of the elements and attributes we're going to use in our invoice documents, we now have a clear road map for developing the Schema itself. Now we can start with the

Schema by looking at how we will use datatypes with these elements and attributes, and then we'll be ready to step through the declarations for each element and attribute.

DEFINING THE DATATYPES

The next step to constructing our Schema will be to go through our elements and attributes to see if there are datatypes from the Schema which might be applicable to our information. We also need to keep in mind that we can derive new datatypes as well, and in some cases, that might be a valid approach for the invoice Schema. So, let's take a look.

The invoice element itself is the root element, so we don't need a datatype there. We can also identify a number of elements which will be strings, such as <company> or <department>. There are also some elements where it might seem like we would want to use a datatype, such as <PONumber>, but where doing so can cause a problem.

For example, if we were to limit the Purchase Order Number to being an integer, what would happen if a company submitted a PO to us with the PO number 34GDF-2? This isn't an integer, so it would violate our type. With an element or attribute such as the invoice number, we control the number, since we are assigning it. That means we can easily specify that it needs to be an integer. But with information being supplied by an outside source, such as customers or suppliers, it's safe to go with string unless we have an agreement whereby we can enforce that the data they are providing will meet our requirements.

That said, there are a few numbers we do control, such as the number and job attributes for the invoice. Since those are numbers we are generating, we can easily make them integer types, so that the formatting of invoice numbers and job numbers is similar.

Similarly, the <quantity> element we use to specify the quantity of a line item can be an integer, unless we have a reason to do fractional quantities. In this case, we're going to assume that our items are all sold as whole pieces, or that services are billed in one-hour minimum blocks, so <quantity> can be typed as an integer as well. If we wanted to specify quantities of fractional values, we could use a decimal type here as well.

Now we can turn to the other elements and types. One perfect example of employing a type is our <date> element, used for the invoice date. Since the date type is built in to the XML Schema Recommendation, this is a perfect place to make use of the datatype in the exact fashion it was intended.

Finally, the last built-in datatype we're going to make use of is the boolean type, which if you recall allows the value to be "true" or "false" (yes, or no). The attribute we're going to make a boolean is the useBilling attribute for the <shippingAddress> element. That's because we want this attribute to only accept two possible values: "yes" if the billing and shipping addresses are the same, or "no" if the addresses are different.

That wraps up the built-in datatypes which our Schema will take advantage of. There are a few more types we can make use of in the Invoice Schema, but they are types we are going to need to derive for ourselves.

THE DERIVED DATATYPES

In our Schema there are an additional six datatypes we are going to use as examples for derived datatypes. These datatypes are for data that has specific structural requirements, such as the formatting of a ZIP code. They are also types which may be reused in other Schema, and therefore might benefit from being abstracted into their own types. They are

- `address`
- `state`
- `zip`
- `phone`
- `currency`
- `percentage`

The `address` type will be a complex type, used to describe an address (and the child elements in an address) based on the U.S. address format. We're only assuming this is a U.S. domestic invoice for this exercise. One of the reasons is so that in Chapter 14, "Building Multipart Schema," we can show you how to abstract this type and build modular Schema in order to make your Schema more flexible.

Because we are using a U.S. address format, we can also develop a `state` type, which will be used to express an address's state using the standard two-letter abbreviation. Similarly, we can develop a `zip` type which will restrict our usage of postal codes to the U.S. ZIP Code and ZIP+4 formats.

There are also places where we employ phone numbers on the invoice, for the customer phone, fax, and alternate phone. We want to restrict our phone numbers to the U.S. standard 10-digit area code and number format.

Finally, we are dealing with a number of elements which specify a currency amount as their value, so it makes sense that we create a `UScurrency` type to express dollar amounts. Along these same lines, when we express the `taxRate` attribute for assessing tax charges, that rate can be specified as a percentage, which can also be defined as a type.

That takes care of all the datatypes we are going to be using in this Schema. The elements and attributes which we are going to use in this Schema, along with their datatypes, are summarized in Table 13.3.

PART

III

CH

13

TABLE 13.3   THE ELEMENTS AND ATTRIBUTES FOR THE INVOICE SCHEMA AND THEIR DATATYPES

Element/Attribute	Datatype	Type
invoice	(root element)	N/A
number	string	Built-in
job	integer	Built-in
date	date	Built-in

TABLE 13.3 CONTINUED

Element/Attribute	Datatype	Type
billingAddress	address	Derived (Complex)
shippingAddress	address	Derived (Complex)
useBilling	boolean	Built-in
company	string	Built-in
department	string	Built-in
contact	string	Built-in
address1	string	Built-in
address2	string	Built-in
city	string	Built-in
state	state	Derived (Simple)
zip	zip	Derived (Simple)
phone	phone	Derived (Simple)
fax	phone	Derived (Simple)
email	string	Built-in
altPhone	phone	Derived (Simple)
altContact	string	Built-in
PO	(element)	
PONumber	string	Built-in
reference	string	Built-in
rep	(element)	
name	string	Built-in
dept	string	Built-in
term	string	Derived (enumeration)
item	string	Built-in
service	string	Built-in
description	string	Built-in
quantity	integer	Built-in
price_rate	UScurrency	Derived (Simple)
amount	UScurrency	Derived (Simple)
subtotal	UScurrency	Derived (Simple)
tax	UScurrency	Derived (Simple)
taxRate	percentage	Derived (Simple)

TABLE 13.3   CONTINUED

Element/Attribute	Datatype	Type
charges	UScurrency	Derived (Simple)
type	string	Derived (enumeration)
total	UScurrency	Derived (Simple)
balanceDue	UScurrency	Derived (Simple)
message	string	Built-in
notes	string	Built-in

Figure 13.1 demonstrates the elements and their hierarchies.

Figure 13.1
The elements of the
Invoice Schema.

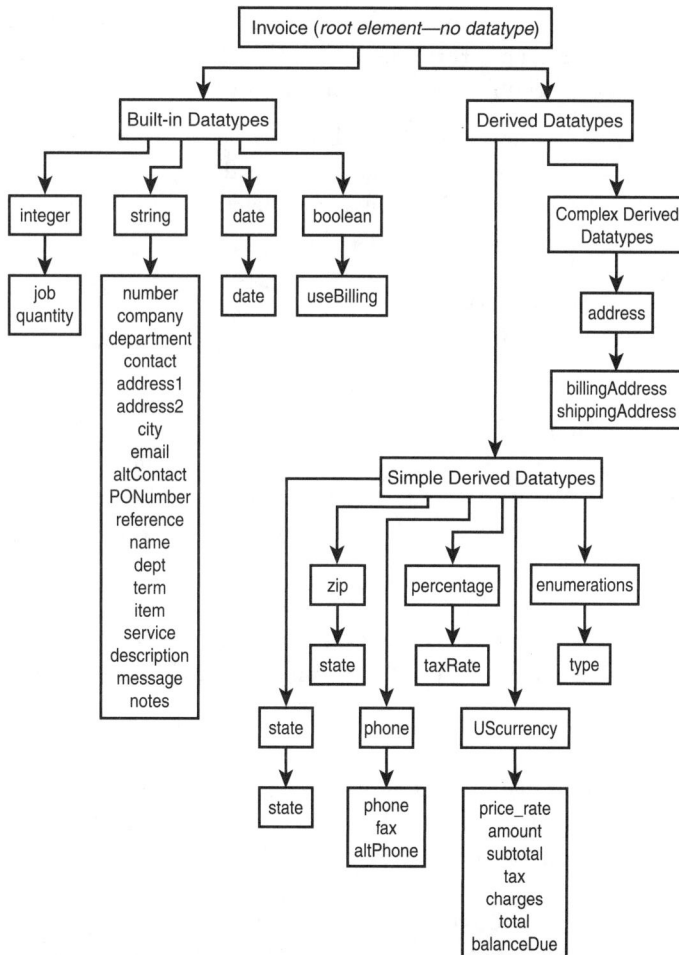

Now, with a clear road map for our datatypes, we're ready to start work on the Schema itself. For the elements using built-in types, we will specify the type in the element and attribute declarations themselves. But for our derived types, we need to define the datatypes by hand.

> **Note**
>
> You will notice that in all of the next sections, we make extensive use of the xs namespace prefix in our declarations. That is because when we integrate each of these segments into the final Schema, we will be making use of the XML Schema namespace, with the xs prefix. So we make use of the prefix in the code snippets so you get used to seeing it in your Schema documents.

state

Let's start with the state type. We need this type to build our ADDRESS type, so it's good to get it out of the way. The state type is essentially a string; however, it is a string that is limited to a two-letter abbreviation, in capital letters.

The best way to develop a state type, therefore, is to use a restriction based on the string type, and use a regular expression and pattern matching to restrict the state values to two uppercase letters. If you recall from previous chapters, a restriction is a form of a simpleType, so our definition looks like this:

```
<xs:simpleType name="state">
 <xs:restriction base="xs:string">
  <xs:pattern value="[A-Z]{2}"/>
 </xs:restriction>
</xs:simpleType>
```

If you recall from the regular expression tutorial in Chapter 12, "Representing and Modeling Data," what we are doing with the [A-Z]{2} pattern is specifying a range of values, from the character set of the uppercase letters of the English alphabet. The braces and the 2 indicate the number of letters that must be in the pattern to match.

ZIP

Another part of our address that we want to restrict is the ZIP Code, which can take one of two formats: either a five-digit code, or a nine-digit code in the form 00000-0000.

Because what we are doing here is once again pattern matching, we are going to employ a restriction based on the string type. If we weren't allowing for the ZIP+4 option, we could have also used an integer type. Our ZIP type looks like this:

```
<xs:simpleType name="ZIP">
 <xs:restriction base="xs:string">
  <xs:pattern value="[0-9]{5}(\-[0-9]{4})?"/>
 </xs:restriction>
</xs:simpleType>
```

Once again, we've employed ranges in our pattern, this time limiting the range to digits. And we've also made use of some optional sections of the expression, such as (\-[0-9]{4})? which makes the dash optional and the "+4" section of the ZIP Code optional.

phone

The final type we're going to define that will make use of a string and pattern matching is phone, which will specify a format for phone numbers which we can then use with either our <phone> or <fax> elements:

```
<xs:simpleType name="phone">
 <xs:restriction base="xs:string">
  <xs:pattern value="[0-9]{3}\-[0-9]{3}\-[0-9]{4}"/>
 </xs:restriction>
</xs:simpleType>
```

Once again, we use a restriction, and we make use of ranges of digits to specify a 10-digit phone number, which takes the form of 000-000-0000.

UScurrency

There are a number of elements in our invoice which deal with currency amounts:

- amount
- subtotal
- charges
- tax
- total
- balanceDue

Each of these elements should contain a value in the form of a decimal, limited to two decimal places, which is how currency is described for the U.S. dollar. To define a UScurrency type, we are going to use a restriction of the decimal type which will look like this:

```
<xs:simpleType name="UScurrency">
 <xs:restriction base="xs:decimal">
  <xs:fractionDigits value="2"/>
 </xs:restriction>
</xs:simpleType>
```

Here, we've defined the UScurrency type, which is simply a decimal that uses the fractionDigits constraining facet to limit the decimal places to "2".

percentage

We also want to be able to make use of a percentage for the taxRate attribute so that we can express the sales tax rate being assessed as a percent: for example, .0875 or .05. To do this, we are again going to make use of a restriction of the decimal type, only this time we are going to limit both the fractionDigits and the totalDigits to "4", so that the percentage may not contain more than four decimal places:

PART
III

CH
13

```
<xs:simpleType name="percentage">
 <xs:restriction base="xs:decimal">
  <xs:fractionDigits value="4"/>
  <xs:totalDigits value="4"/>
 </xs:restriction>
</xs:simpleType>
```

Now, with all of our simple derived types defined, we are ready to move on to build the last of our derived types, a complex type for the addresses in our invoice.

ADDRESS

Because we are going to be reusing addresses in our invoice, it makes sense to abstract the address structure into a complexType which can be reused. This type of abstraction is also good preparation for Chapter 14, when we will be abstracting addresses into their very own Schema as well.

If you recall from Chapter 11, "Derived Datatypes," derived complex types have a form very similar to an element declaration, only it makes use of the <complexType> element.

In this case, we are going to make use of a <sequence> which will then contain the actual element declarations used for the elements in our ADDRESS type. That way, if we declare any elements later in our Schema as being of type ADDRESS, they too will contain the ADDRESS child elements in their content models. Let's take a look:

```
<xs:complexType name="ADDRESS">
 <xs:sequence>
  <xs:element name="company" type="xs:string" minOccurs="0"/>
  <xs:element name="department" type="xs:string" minOccurs="0"/>
  <xs:element name="contact" type="xs:string"/>
  <xs:element name="address1" type="xs:string"/>
  <xs:element name="address2" type="xs:string" minOccurs="0"/>
  <xs:element name="city" type="xs:string"/>
  <xs:element name="state" type="state"/>
  <xs:element name="zip" type="ZIP"/>
  <xs:element name="phone" type="phone"/>
  <xs:element name="fax" type="phone" minOccurs="0"/>
  <xs:element name="email" type="xs:string" minOccurs="0"/>
  <xs:element name="altPhone" type="phone" minOccurs="0"/>
  <xs:element name="altContact" type="xs:string" minOccurs="0"/>
 </xs:sequence>
</xs:complexType>
```

First, we declare the type, followed by the sequence. Next, we declare our <company> and <department> elements, which are both strings, and which both are optional, so we set their minOccurs to zero.

Next, we have <contact> and <address1> elements, also strings but required this time, followed by another optional <address2> element. A required <city> element follows, and then we have a chance to make use of our previously defined datatypes of state and ZIP. When we declare the <state> element, we define the type to be state and the <zip> element to be of type ZIP so that now, the restrictions of those type definitions apply to those elements.

In the remaining declarations, we also make use of previously defined types with the `<phone>`, `<altPhone>`, and `<fax>` elements, which are `phone` types, and which are also optional. The `<email>` element is a simple `string` as is the `<altContact>` element, bringing our ADDRESS type to a close.

Now, with all of our types defined, we are ready to move on to the element and attribute declarations of the Schema.

WRITING THE SCHEMA

Now we are ready to begin writing the Schema, but here's a little surprise: You already have been writing the Schema! The type definitions that we worked on in the last section are a part of the final Schema, just the same as the element and attribute declarations we're about to continue with. So now, let's finish up the Invoice Schema with the elements and attributes which constitute the bulk of information.

DECLARING THE ELEMENTS

Our Invoice instance document is pretty element-heavy. That is by design, as elements lend themselves to much of the information contained in our invoice, and using elements (as opposed to attributes) does increase the human readability of the document some. This might not be as important if you are working with a strictly data application, but since human readability is a concern to us here, elements are very appropriate. So, let's start our declarations.

The first element we declare will be our `<date>` element, which, if you recall from the last section, is going to make use of the Schema built-in `date` type:

```
<xs:element name="date" type="xs:date"/>
```

The declaration is very straightforward, as is our next declaration, for the `<billingAddress>` element:

```
<xs:element name="billingAddress" type="ADDRESS"/>
```

With this declaration, you will note that the type is ADDRESS, which is a complex type that we defined earlier. Because the `<billingAddress>` element is an ADDRESS it will automatically contain all of the elements we declared for the `address` type, so even though this declaration is straightforward, the content for the `<billingAddress>` element is not necessarily.

Next, we want to declare the `<shippingAddress>` element. We could use a simple declaration similar to the one we just used for billing; however, we also want to add an attribute `useBilling` to the `<shippingAddress>` element, so that if the shipping address is the same as the billing address, we can indicate that. Therefore, we actually have to use an extension in this case:

```
<xs:element name="shippingAddress">
 <xs:complexType>
  <xs:complexContent>
   <xs:extension base="ADDRESS">
```

```
       <xs:attribute ref="useBilling"/
    </xs:extension>
   </xs:complexContent>
  </xs:complexType>
</xs:element>
```

This extension allows us to add an attribute reference. We use a reference here because we will be defining the attribute later in the Schema, and as you might recall, Schema allow forward references.

The <PO> element and the <rep> element both have very similar element declarations. Both are straightforward declarations with complex content, with each declaration containing two attribute references; in the case of the <PO> element, the attributes are PONumber and reference. In the case of the <rep> element, the attributes are name and dept. Here's what the declarations look like:

```
<xs:element name="PO">
 <xs:complexType>
  <xs:complexContent>
   <xs:attribute ref="PONumber"/>
   <xs:attribute ref="reference"/>
  </xs:complexContent>
 </xs:complexType>
<xs:element>

<xs:element name="rep">
 <xs:complexType>
  <xs:complexContent>
   <xs:attribute ref="name"/>
   <xs:attribute ref="dept"/>
  </xs:complexContent>
 </xs:complexType>
<xs:element>
```

The next element we're going to declare is the <term> element, used to specify the payment terms for our invoice. This is a special element, because we want the choices of the value to be limited to a fixed number of terms. To do this, we're going to make use of an enumeration, which is a form of restriction, and in this case, our base type is going to be string.

So our element declaration will look like this:

```
<xs:element name="term">
 <xs:simpleType>
  <xs:restriction base="xs:string">
   <xs:enumeration value="Net15"/>
   <xs:enumeration value="Net30"/>
   <xs:enumeration value="Net60"/>
   <xs:enumeration value="Due on Receipt"/>
   <xs:enumeration value="PAID"/>
   <xs:enumeration value="PAST DUE"/>
  </xs:restriction>
 </xs:simpleType>
</xs:element>
```

This is an element declaration containing a locally scoped simple type, which is a restriction and enumeration limited to the value set specified. We could have also created our own type for these terms, and we will abstract this further in Chapter 14. However, for this example, we wanted to show you how you could still create your own type definitions within an element declaration, resulting in a local scope.

Next, we need to define our `<item>` and `<service>` elements, which will also have similar content: Both will have a `code` attribute, and child elements of `<description>`, `<quantity>`, `<price_rate>`, and `<amount>`. Because each of these elements is used twice, once in the `<item>` element and once in the `<service>` element, we will define them globally, and in these declarations will only include the child elements by reference:

```
<xs:element name="item">
 <xs:complexType>
  <xs:complexContent>
   <xs:attribute ref="code"/>
   <xs:sequence>
    <xs:element ref="description"/>
    <xs:element ref="quantity"/>
    <xs:element ref="price_rate"/>
    <xs:element ref="amount"/>
   </xs:sequence>
  </xs:complexContent>
 </xs:complexType>
</xs:element>

<xs:element name="service">
 <xs:complexType>
  <xs:complexContent>
   <xs:attribute ref="code"/>
   <xs:sequence>
    <xs:element ref="description"/>
    <xs:element ref="quantity"/>
    <xs:element ref="price_rate"/>
    <xs:element ref="amount"/>
   </xs:sequence>
  </xs:complexContent>
 </xs:complexType>
</xs:element>
```

To define the `<quantity>` element, we will make use of another restriction. Since we determined that for our invoice, quantities had to be whole integers (no fractional quantities) and that even services would be measured in whole units, we can make our `<quantity>` element a restriction of `integer`, and set it so that the `<quantity>` has a minimum value of "1":

```
<xs:element name="quantity">
 <xs:simpleType>
  <xs:restriction base="xs:integer">
   <xs:minInclusive value="1"/>
  </xs:restriction>
 </xs:simpleType>
</xs:element>
```

The next two elements from our <item> and <service> declarations are <price_rate> and <amount>. These are going to express values as currency, so we can make use of the UScurrency type we defined earlier. In fact, we might as well declare all of the elements which are going to express currency now, since they will have nearly identical declarations:

```
<xs:element name="price_rate" type="UScurrency"/>
<xs:element name="amount" type="UScurrency"/>
<xs:element name="subtotal" type="UScurrency"/>
<xs:element name="total" type="UScurrency"/>
<xs:element name="balanceDue" type="UScurrency"/>
```

In fact, we have two more elements which are also UScurrency: <tax> and <charges>. However, these elements also have attributes. The <tax> element has the taxRate attribute to express the rate of tax, and the <charges> element has the type attribute to specify the type of charges being applied.

So, for these declarations, we will use the UScurrency type as a base, but we will also extend the type to provide the necessary attribute references:

```
<xs:element name="tax">
 <xs:complexType>
  <xs:complexContent>
   <xs:extension base="UScurrency"/>
    <xs:attribute ref="taxRate"/>
   </xs:extention>
  </xs:complexContent>
 </xs:complexType>
</xs:element>

<xs:element name="charges"/>
 <xs:complexType>
  <xs:complexContent>
   <xs:extension base="UScurrency"/>
   <xs:attribute ref="type"/>
   </xs:extention>
  </xs:complexContent>
 </xs:complexType>
</xs:element>
```

Finally, there are only three elements left to declare: <description>, <message>, and <notes>, all of which are simple declarations, based on the string type:

```
<xs:element name="description" type="xs:string"/>
<xs:element name="message" type="xs:string"/>
<xs:element name="notes" type="xs:string"/>
```

With those declarations out of the way, all of the elements for our Invoice Schema have now been declared. We're ready to finish out the attribute declarations, and then we will be ready to pull everything together into the final Invoice Schema.

DECLARING THE ATTRIBUTES

The attribute declarations for this Schema are also pretty straightforward. We'll start by declaring the number attribute, used to keep track of the Invoice Number. Since our organization will be generating the invoices, we can control the form that this number will take. We could make the invoice number a series of digits, a combination of digits and letters, or really, anything we want. However, in order to keep things simple, we'll make the invoice number an `integer`, with no less than four digits, and no more than six. This is a luxury we have in this situation, because we are defining the invoice number. In practice, however, you might have to use a regular expression, or some other mechanism to match invoice numbers, if your company already has established a system of invoicing. We can do that using a simple type and a restriction of the `integer` type:

```
<xs:attribute name="number">
 <xs:simpleType>
  <xs:restriction base="xs:integer">
   <xs:minLength value="4"/>
   <xs:maxLength value="6"/>
  </xs:restriction>
 </xs:simpleType>
</xs:attribute>
```

We have the same degree of freedom over the job number, since we control its generation. In this case, we'll use a similar restriction for the job number as well:

```
<xs:attribute name="job">
 <xs:simpleType>
  <xs:restriction base="xs:integer">
   <xs:minLength value="4"/>
   <xs:maxLength value="6"/>
  </xs:restriction>
 </xs:simpleType>
</xs:attribute>
```

Next, we have the `useBilling` attribute, which we want to only have a value of `"yes"` or `"no"` (true or false), which makes it perfect for the `boolean` type:

```
<xs:attribute name="useBilling" type="xs:boolean"/>
```

The `type` attribute, which we will use with the `<charges>` element to specify a type of charges, will be based on `string`, but restricted to an enumeration, so we can restrict the type of charges being applied:

```
<xs:attribute name="type">
 <xs:simpleType>
  <xs:restriction base="xs:string">
   <xs:enumeration value="Shipping"/>
   <xs:enumeration value="Late Fee"/>
   <xs:enumeration value="Finance"/>
  </xs:restriction>
 </xs:simpleType>
</xs:attribute>
```

This will limit the `type` values to only `"Shipping"`, `"Late Fee"`, or `"Finance"`.

Next, we need to declare the `taxRate` attribute for our `<tax>` element:

```
<xs:attribute name="taxRate" type="percentage"/>
```

Because we wanted the tax rate to be specified as a percentage, we used the `percentage` type we defined earlier.

Finally, we have a number of attributes which are simply strings. These include the PONumber, reference, name, department, and code attributes:

```
<xs:attribute name="PONumber" type="xs:string"/>
<xs:attribute name="reference" type="xs:string"/>
<xs:attribute name="name" type="xs:string"/>
<xs:attribute name="department" type="xs:string"/>
<xs:attribute name="code" type="xs:string"/>
```

With all of the attributes declared, it's now time to pull everything together into a declaration for the root <invoice> element, and put everything in our <schema> container.

PULLING IT ALL TOGETHER

Now that we have all of our elements and attributes declared, and our datatypes defined, it's time to pull everything together into our root element, the <invoice>.

Because we have declared our elements and attributes globally, the content model for our root <invoice> element will be specified using references to the appropriate elements and attributes. We start off building a complexType, with complexContent, and first add our attribute references for the <invoice> element itself, our number and job attributes. Next, we add the content for the <invoice> inside a <sequence> element, starting with the <date> and working our way down through to the <notes>. The result looks like this:

```
<xs:element name="invoice">
 <xs:complexType>
  <xs:complexContent>
   <xs:attribute ref="number"/>
   <xs:attribute ref="job"/>
   <xs:sequence>
    <xs:element ref="date"/>
    <xs:element ref="billingAddress"/>
    <xs:element ref="shippingAddress"/>
    <xs:element ref="PO"/>
    <xs:element ref="item" minOccurs="0" maxOccurs="unbounded"/>
    <xs:element ref="service" minOccurs="0" maxOccurs="unbounded"/>
    <xs:element ref="subtotal"/>
    <xs:element ref="tax" minOccurs="0"/>
    <xs:element ref="charges" minOccurs="0"/>
    <xs:element ref="total"/>
    <xs:element ref="balanceDue" minOccurs="0"/>
    <xs:element ref="term"/>
    <xs:element ref="rep"/>
    <xs:element ref="message" minOccurs="0"/>
    <xs:element ref="notes" minOccurs="0" maxOccurs="unbounded"/>
   </xs:sequence>
  </xs:complexContent>
 </xs:complexType>
</xs:element>
```

Each element is included as a reference and we have added minOccurs and maxOccurs where necessary to specify reoccurring elements. Of note are the <item> and <services> element references, which have maxOccurs of "unbounded", so that they can appear in our invoice an unlimited number of times.

Now, with all elements, including our root element, declared, we are ready to place everything into a <schema> element. With this Schema, we are going to make use of namespaces, and we will start by establishing the xs prefix for the XML Schema namespace:

```
xmlns:xs="http://www.w3.org/2001/XMLSchema"
```

We'll also include the XML Instance namespace:

```
xmlns:xsi="http://www.w3.org/2001/XMLSchema-Instance"
```

And finally, we will specify the target namespace for our Invoice Schema, and make that the default namespace for the document. We do this because declaring the target namespace as the default namespace is considered a "best-practice" for reasons we will go into in detail in Chapter 17, "XML Schema Best Practices." But basically, it ensures that if we make this Schema modular, or import/export it into other Schema, we won't have problems resulting from namespace conflicts.

```
targetNamespace="http://www.myserver.com/invoice"
xmlns="http://www.myserver.com/invoice"
```

So our final <schema> element looks like this:

```
<?xml version="1.0" encoding="UTF-8" ?>
<xs:schema xmlns:xs="http://www.w3.org/2001/XMLSchema"
    xmlns:xsi="http://www.w3.org/2001/XMLSchema-Instance"
    targetNamespace="http://www.myserver.com/invoice"
    xmlns="http://www.myserver.com/invoice">

</xs:schema>
```

When we bring all of our datatype definitions, element declarations, and attribute declarations together into the final Schema form, and add some comments for readability, the result is a full Invoice XML Schema, as shown in Listing 13.2.

LISTING 13.2   THE COMPLETE INVOICE XML SCHEMA

```
<?xml version="1.0" encoding="UTF-8" ?>
<xs:schema xmlns:xs="http://www.w3.org/2001/XMLSchema"
    xmlns:xsi="http://www.w3.org/2001/XMLSchema-Instance"
    targetNamespace="http://www.myserver.com/invoice"
    xmlns="http://www.myserver.com/invoice">

<xs:annotation>
 <xs:documentation xml:lang="en">
  A sample XML Schema for a Customer Invoice.
 </xs:documentation>
</xs:annotation>

<!-- Define the root invoice element -->

<xs:element name="invoice">
 <xs:complexType>
  <xs:complexContent>
   <xs:attribute ref="number"/>
   <xs:attribute ref="job"/>
```

LISTING 13.2 CONTINUED

```
  <xs:sequence>
   <xs:element ref="date"/>
   <xs:element ref="billingAddress"/>
   <xs:element ref="shippingAddress"/>
   <xs:element ref="PO"/>
   <xs:element ref="item" minOccurs="0" maxOccurs="unbounded"/>
   <xs:element ref="service" minOccurs="0" maxOccurs="unbounded"/>
   <xs:element ref="subtotal"/>
   <xs:element ref="tax" minOccurs="0"/>
   <xs:element ref="charges" minOccurs="0"/>
   <xs:element ref="total"/>
   <xs:element ref="balanceDue" minOccurs="0"/>
   <xs:element ref="term"/>
   <xs:element ref="rep"/>
   <xs:element ref="message" minOccurs="0"/>
   <xs:element ref="notes" minOccurs="0" maxOccurs="unbounded"/>
  </xs:sequence>
 </xs:complexContent>
</xs:complexType>
</xs:element>

<!-- Define the Number attribute -->
<xs:attribute name="number">
 <xs:simpleType>
  <xs:restriction base="xs:integer">
   <xs:minLength value="4"/>
   <xs:maxLength value="6"/>
  </xs:restriction>
 </xs:simpleType>
</xs:attribute>

<!-- Define the Job attribute -->
<xs:attribute name="job">
 <xs:simpleType>
  <xs:restriction base="xs:integer">
   <xs:minLength value="4"/>
   <xs:maxLength value="6"/>
  </xs:restriction>
 </xs:simpleType>
</xs:attribute>

<!-- This section will define our elements and attributes-->

<!-- Define the Date element -->
<xs:element name="date" type="xs:date"/>

<!-- Define the BillingAddress element -->
<xs:element name="billingAddress" type="ADDRESS"/>

<!-- Define the ShippingAddress element -->
<xs:element name="shippingAddress">
 <xs:complexType>
  <xs:complexContent>
   <xs:extension base="ADDRESS">
    <xs:attribute ref="useBilling"/>
```

LISTING 13.2   CONTINUED

```
    </xs:extension>
   </xs:complexContent>
  </xs:complexType>
</xs:element>

<!-- Define the UseBilling attribute -->
<xs:attribute name="useBilling" type="xs:boolean"/>

<!-- Define the PurchaseOrder element -->
<xs:element name="PO">
 <xs:complexType>
  <xs:complexContent>
   <xs:attribute ref="PONumber"/>
   <xs:attribute ref="reference"/>
  </xs:complexContent>
 </xs:complexType>
<xs:element>

<!-- Define the PONumber attribute -->
<xs:attribute name="PONumber" type="xs:string"/>

<!-- Define the Reference attribute -->
<xs:attribute name="reference" type="xs:string"/>

<!-- Define the Representative element -->
<xs:element name="rep">
 <xs:complexType>
  <xs:complexContent>
   <xs:attribute ref="name"/>
   <xs:attribute ref="dept"/>
  </xs:complexContent>
 </xs:complexType>
</xs:element>

<!-- Define the Name attribute -->
<xs:attribute name="name" type="xs:string"/>

<!-- Define the Department attribute -->
<xs:attribute name="department" type="xs:string"/>

<!-- Define the Term element -->
<xs:element name="term">
 <xs:simpleType>
  <xs:restriction base="xs:string">
   <xs:enumeration value="Net15"/>
   <xs:enumeration value="Net30"/>
   <xs:enumeration value="Net60"/>
   <xs:enumeration value="Due on Receipt"/>
   <xs:enumeration value="PAID"/>
   <xs:enumeration value="PAST DUE"/>
  </xs:restriction>
 </xs:simpleType>
</xs:element>

<!-- Define the Item element -->
```

PART

III

CH

13

LISTING 13.2 CONTINUED

```
<xs:element name="item">
 <xs:complexType>
  <xs:complexContent>
   <xs:attribute ref="code"/>
   <xs:sequence>
    <xs:element ref="description"/>
    <xs:element ref="quantity"/>
    <xs:element ref="price_rate"/>
    <xs:element ref="amount"/>
   </xs:sequence>
  </xs:complexContent>
 </xs:complexType>
</xs:element>

<!-- Define the Service element -->
<xs:element name="service">
 <xs:complexType>
  <xs:complexContent>
   <xs:attribute ref="code"/>
   <xs:sequence>
    <xs:element ref="description"/>
    <xs:element ref="quantity"/>
    <xs:element ref="price_rate"/>
    <xs:element ref="amount"/>
   </xs:sequence>
  </xs:complexContent>
 </xs:complexType>
</xs:element>

<xs:attribute name="code" type="xs:string"/>

<!-- Define the Description element -->
<xs:element name="description" type="xs:string"/>

<!-- Define the Quantity element -->
<xs:element name="quantity">
 <xs:simpleType>
  <xs:restriction base="xs:integer">
   <xs:minInclusive value="1"/>
  </xs:restriction>
 </xs:simpleType>
</xs:element>

<!-- Define the price_rate element -->
<xs:element name="price_rate" type="UScurrency"/>

<!-- Define the Amount element -->
<xs:element name="amount" type="UScurrency"/>

<!-- Define the Subtotal element -->
<xs:element name="subtotal" type="UScurrency"/>

<!-- Define the Tax element -->
<xs:element name="tax">
 <xs:complexType>
```

LISTING 13.2   CONTINUED

```xml
  <xs:complexContent>
   <xs:extension base="UScurrency"/>
    <xs:attribute ref="taxRate"/>
   </xs:extension>
  </xs:complexContent>
 </xs:complexType>
</xs:element>

<!-- Define the TaxRate attribute -->
<xs:attribute name="taxRate" type="percentage"/>

<!-- Define the Charges element -->
<xs:element name="charges"/>
 <xs:complexType>
  <xs:complexContent>
   <xs:extension base="UScurrency"/>
   <xs:attribute ref="type"/>
   </xs:extension>
  </xs:complexContent>
 </xs:complexType>
</xs:element>

<!-- Define the Type attribute -->
<xs:attribute name="type">
 <xs:simpleType>
  <xs:restriction base="xs:string">
   <xs:enumeration value="Shipping"/>
   <xs:enumeration value="Late Fee"/>
   <xs:enumeration value="Finance"/>
  </xs:restriction>
 </xs:simpleType>
</xs:attribute>

<!-- Define the Total element -->
<xs:element name="total" type="UScurrency"/>

<!-- Define the BalanceDue element -->
<xs:element name="balanceDue" type="UScurrency"/>

<!-- Define the Message element -->
<xs:element name="message" type="xs:string"/>

<!-- Define the Notes element -->
<xs:element name="notes" type="xs:string"/>

<!-- This section will define our datatypes -->
<!-- Define the state type -->
<xs:simpleType name="state">
 <xs:restriction base="xs:string">
  <xs:pattern value="[A-Z]{2}"/>
 </xs:restriction>
</xs:simpleType>

<!-- Define the ZIP type -->
<xs:simpleType name="ZIP">
```

LISTING 13.2   CONTINUED

```
 <xs:restriction base="xs:string">
  <xs:pattern value="[0-9]{5}(\- [0-9]{4})?"/>
 </xs:restriction>
</xs:simpleType>

<!-- Define the phone type -->
<xs:simpleType name="phone">
 <xs:restriction base="xs:string">
  <xs:pattern value="[0-9]{3}\-[0-9]{3}\-[0-9]{4}"/>
 </xs:restriction>
</xs:simpleType>

<!-- Define the ADDRESS type -->
<xs:complexType name="ADDRESS">
 <xs:sequence>
  <xs:element name="company" type="xs:string" minOccurs="0"/>
  <xs:element name="department" type="xs:string" minOccurs="0"/>
  <xs:element name="contact" type="xs:string"/>
  <xs:element name="address1" type="xs:string"/>
  <xs:element name="address2" type="xs:string" minOccurs="0"/>
  <xs:element name="city" type="xs:string"/>
  <xs:element name="state" type="state"/>
  <xs:element name="zip" type="ZIP"/>
  <xs:element name="phone" type="phone"/>
  <xs:element name="fax" type="phone" minOccurs="0"/>
  <xs:element name="email" type="xs:string" minOccurs="0"/>
  <xs:element name="altPhone" type="phone" minOccurs="0"/>
  <xs:element name="altContact" type="xs:string" minOccurs="0"/>
 </xs:sequence>
</xs:complexType>

<!-- Define the UScurrency type -->
<xs:simpleType name="UScurrency">
 <xs:restriction base="xs:decimal">
  <xs:fractionDigits value="2"/>
 </xs:restriction>
</xs:simpleType>

<!-- Define the percentage type -->
<xs:simpleType name="percentage">
 <xs:restriction base="xs:decimal">
  <xs:fractionDigits value="4"/>
  <xs:totalDigits value="4"/>
 </xs:restriction>
</xs:simpleType>

</xs:schema>
```

This Schema is ready to be used in conjunction with an XML instance document, such as the one shown here in Listing 13.3. This isn't the last we'll see of this Schema though. As we continue into the next section, we'll be taking a closer look at this Schema in Chapter 14 Schema.

LISTING 13.3 A COMPLETE XML INSTANCE DOCUMENT BASED ON THE INVOICE XML SCHEMA

```xml
<?xml version="1.0" encoding="UTF-8" ?>

<invoice xmlns="http://www.myserver.com/invoice"
      xmlns:xsi="http://www.3.org/2001/XMLSchema-Instance"
      xsi:schemaLocation="http://www.myserver.com/invoice
      http://www.myserver.com/invoice.xsd"
         number="33421" job="0023">

<date>04-11-02</date>

<billingAddress>
 <company>Defunkt Dot Com</company>
 <contact>Ms. Moneypenny</contact>
 <department>Accounts Payable</department>
 <address1>123 Easy Street</address1>
 <address2>Room 304</address2>
 <city>San Francisco</city>
 <state>CA</state>
 <zip>94503</zip>
 <phone>415-324-0210</phone>
 <fax>415-324-0215</fax>
 <email>money@defunkt.com</email>
</billingAddress>

<shippingAddress useBilling="no">
 <company>Defunkt Dot Com</company>
 <contact>Mr. Big</contact>
 <address1>45 Trendy Lane</address1>
 <city>San Francisco</city>
 <state>CA</state>
 <zip>94503</zip>
 <phone>415-324-0210</phone>
</shippingAddress>

<PO PONumber="33134D"/>

<item code="442A">
 <description>Deluxe Executive Board Leather Chair</description>
 <quantity>10</quantity>
 <price_rate>875.00</price_rate>
 <amount>8750.00</amount>
</item>

<item code="503D">
 <description>Solid Teakwood Executive Table</description>
 <quantity>1</quantity>
 <price_rate>15000.00</price_rate>
 <amount>15000.00</amount>
</item>

<subtotal>23750.00</subtotal>
<tax taxRate=".0875">2078.13</tax>
<charges type="finance">499.95</charges>
<total>26328.08</total>
<balanceDue>26328.08</balanceDue>
```

LISTING 13.3   CONTINUED

```
<term>PAST DUE</term>

<rep name="DLG" dept="Sales"/>

<message>Payment is Past Due. Please contact us immediately.</message>
<notes>First invoiced on 1/1/98.</notes>
<notes>Currently working to repossess.</notes>

</invoice>
```

CONCLUSION

Designing and implementing a Schema can seem a daunting task, and it certainly is not without its challenges. However, the best way to approach it is by following some simple guidelines:

- Clearly identify the goals and requirements of both the XML instance documents and the Schema that will describe them.
- Create a sample XML instance document to serve as a reference.
- Make a complete table of all elements and attributes for the Schema.
- Make a table outlining the datatypes necessary for the Schema.

Once you've done this, you are ready to start stepping through the outlined elements, attributes, and type definitions to build the Schema itself.

We mentioned several times in this chapter that there are multiple ways to approach any given element or attribute. There is no one solution to a Schema any more than there is one solution to solving a complex math problem, or writing a song. What works here is one solution, but certainly it is not the only solution. You might want to tweak the Schema design, or change some elements and attributes to make them more appropriate to your application. Or you might find that a Schema heavy in attributes better describes an invoice. That is one of the beauties of XML and the fact that Schema are XML documents: They are flexible.

As we move on to Part IV, "Developing a Purchase Order Schema," we will be taking another look at this invoice Schema, and how we can further adapt it to make it even more powerful and flexible than it already is.

IN THE REAL WORLD

The development of a Schema for your organization will never be as simple as it is outlined in a chapter in a computer book. The reality of authoring Schema is that they involve a lot of input from a lot of different departments and personnel, and that kind of input is virtually impossible to duplicate in a textbook setting. How you author your Schema, the approach you take, and the compromises that you make will depend on a number of variables. The important thing for you to keep in mind during the process is this: If the Schema does not meet the needs of your customers (in the case of IT, the users are your customers) then you need to re-evaluate your progress.

How you approach meeting those needs will depend upon your organization, and unfortunately, a great deal of office politics. You might have to make a number of design compromises in order to appease various entities within your particular situation.

For example, in the example we used in this chapter, we have two types of numbers that could be used to identify invoices: our invoice number and the PONumber. If you recall, we made our invoice number an integer, because we had that luxury. Chances are, when working with a very large organization, you will not. A more likely case would be similar to the PONumber, where we chose to make the number a string; that way it could be represented however we needed it to be, and if we wanted to enforce a specific kind of string, we could always add a regular expression pattern later.

So why did we not do the same with the invoice in this example? To provide you with some contrast about how these types of numbers might be handled. Because the example is customized to teach, we had that luxury. But it is very rare that decisions such as this will come down to the developer. They are usually made by constraints placed on your design by working with legacy data, or by mandate from another department within your company.

That is why we tried to stress adequate planning before jumping into the Schema authoring. So many decisions will be hashed out and rehashed that it is a good idea to have a clear map of where you are headed, and to make sure everyone involved is on-board before you set out to write the final Schema.

PART

III

CH

13

Developing a Purchase Order Schema

CHAPTER 14

BUILDING MULTIPART SCHEMA

In this chapter

ADVANTAGES OF MULTIPART SCHEMA

If you were writing a dictionary, you would probably not keep all of the dictionary entries in one single word processing file. If you did, accessing the file could be painfully slow, and if the file became corrupt, you would lose all of your data. Instead, you might divide the dictionary up into smaller files, for example, one for each letter of the alphabet.

XML Schema are simply documents that are used to define other documents. And as the documents they describe become more complex, the Schema themselves can quickly become large and unwieldy. In order to help keep complex Schema under control, and to provide some mechanisms for making Schema easier to use, the Schema Recommendation contains some provisions for carving your Schema up into multiple documents, so that a Schema can be built from a series of smaller Schema. This type of multipart Schema is really just a single Schema which is created by importing or including a series of smaller individual Schema documents or fragments. Each one of these smaller Schema might function on its own as a Schema, or might not. However, when linked together, they can be used as a large-scale, fully functional Schema. This allows for easier management and reuse of your Schema files.

There are several advantages to working with a Schema as multiple documents, as long as you are careful when designing the Schema originally.

First, using multiple documents improves readability. By segmenting the Schema in a way that makes sense, such as grouping all of a certain type of definition together in one file, you can make it easier to follow the structures being defined. As you start building complicated Schema which rely on many datatypes, this can be especially important.

Second, a multiple-document Schema can be easier to maintain. By localizing certain types of definitions and declarations into a single file, it can be quicker and easier to locate declarations for updates, or review for the most current definitions. For example, if in the future your company changes the format of its Purchase Order Numbers, it might be easier to locate and edit a small PO.xsd file than one massive file containing all purchasing documents, including invoices, checks, and so on.

Third, security and ownership are easier to control with multiple documents. For example, you might want the accounting department of your organization to maintain their own Schema, while sales maintains theirs. However, these Schema will undoubtedly share some information, which is where generating a single, multipart Schema comes in handy. Multipart Schema can be authored and maintained by the most appropriate party, but still be accessible to all. You might also want to share your schema with your suppliers and customers in order to improve your organization's efficiency and lower costs.

Finally, reuse is another key advantage to using multiple-document Schema. For example, many XML documents, and therefore many XML Schema, will make use of address information. One way to handle this is to author a new set of standards for address elements and attributes each time your Schema needs to use an address. But another way is to reuse the address components you have already defined by including a previously authored Schema. A good modular design when working with your Schema will help you create "libraries" of Schema that you can reuse in order to streamline your authoring process and help keep your data in adherence to standards.

COMBINING MULTIPLE SCHEMA INTO A SINGLE SCHEMA

There really is not any special syntax that you need to be aware of when you are authoring the Schema documents that make up a multipart (or multiple-document) Schema. Each Schema that you are working with should follow the same general structure that you would normally follow when authoring a Schema.

However, there are some special syntaxes that you need to be aware of when you want to combine your multiple Schema into a single document. For that you will need to make use of one of three different mechanisms:

- `include`
- `import`
- `redefine`

Each mechanism has its own set of advantages, disadvantages, and caveats. So now, let's take a closer look at each one and see how they function in relation to a multipart Schema.

include

The first, and also the easiest, method for joining together definitions and declarations from multiple Schema is the `include` statement.

Unlike other Schema components, the `include` statement isn't really a component at all. It can only be used to include the contents of one Schema inside another, and it must be used as a child of the `<schema>` component.

Additionally, the `<include>` statement must appear as the first child (or children, as multiple `includes` are allowed) of the `<schema>` component.

The structure the `<include>` statement takes is

```
<include id="ID" schemaLocation="URI"/>
```

The `id` is optional; however, the `schemaLocation` must have a valid URI which points to the Schema which is to be included.

The effect of including a Schema is that the contents of the other Schema are all included in the same namespace as the original Schema. The effect is to create one large Schema. For example, if we have

```
<schema targetNamespace="http://www.myserver.com/dummySchema"
        xmlns="http://www.w3.org/2001/XMLSchema">

 <element name="something" type="string"/>

</schema>
```

PART
IV

CH

14

as our first Schema, and we then include this Schema into a second schema. This `import` statement assumes that the `dummy.xsd` Schema is located at the stated address on the Web site:

```
<schema targetNamespace="http://www.myserver.com/dummySchema"
        xmlns="http://www.w3.org/2001/XMLSchema">

<include schemaLocation="http://www.myserver.com/dummy.xsd"/>

 <element name="something_else" type="string"/>

</schema>
```

The effect is the same as if we had both element declarations in the same document:

```
<schema targetNamespace="http://www.myserver.com/dummy.xsd"
   xmlns="http://www.w3.org/2001/XMLSchema">

 <element name="something" type="string"/>
 <element name="something_else" type="string"/>
</schema>
```

You can also use multiple `<include>` statements to bring together multiple files, but keep in mind that when you include an existing Schema into your Schema, you are also including any other Schema *that* Schema may have included.

One consideration when including Schema is that only globally declared definitions and declarations are included. For example, let's take a look at the following schema:

```
<schema targetNamespace="http://www.myserver.com/Contact"
        xmlns="http://www.w3.org/2001/XMLSchema">

 <element name="phone">
  <complexType>
   <attribute name="location">
    <restriction base="xs:string">
     <enumeration value="home"/>
     <enumeration value="work"/>
    </restriction>
   </attribute>
  </complexType>
 </element>

</schema>
```

Here we have a Schema which contains an element declaration, for `<phone>`, and an attribute for the `phone` element, called `location`, which we could use to specify a `"work"` phone number or a `"home"` phone number. Now, let's say we included this in a bigger contact Schema:

```
<schema targetNamespace="http://www.myserver.com/Contact"
        xmlns="http://www.w3.org/2001/XMLSchema">

<include schemaLocation="http://www.myserver.com/dummy.xsd"/>

</schema>
```

We could now make use of the <phone> element by reference:

```
<element name="contact">
 <complexType>
  <complexContent>
   <element ref="phone"/>
  </complexContent>
 </complexType>
</element>
```

This is valid, because the previous Schema included the <phone> element declaration. However, if we wanted to use the location attribute (outside of the phone element it is already a part of) we could not, because it was not declared globally. So we *could not* use

```
<element name="address">
 <complexType>
  <attribute ref="location"/>
 </complexType>
</element>
```

because this example references an attribute that has never been declared. The locally declared attribute from our previous Schema is *not* included in the new Schema, because there is no difference between components declared in included Schema and the including schema.

There is, however, another major consideration when including Schema: *All included schema must have the same targetNamespace.* That's because when the Schema are parsed, what is really happening is that included Schema are being parsed, and the elements, attributes, and types of the included Schema are being added to the existing targetNamespace. You can include two Schema which do not have any targetNamespace, but not two Schema that have two different targetNamespaces. For example, you could not use <include> with the following two schema:

```
<schema targetNamespace="http://www.myserver.com/dummySchema"
        xmlns="http://www.w3.org/2001/XMLSchema">
 <element name="something" type="string"/>
</schema>
```

and

```
<schema targetNamespace="http://www.myserver.com/TotallyNewNamespace"
        xmlns="http://www.w3.org/2001/XMLSchema">
 <element name="something_different" type="string"/>
</schema>
```

because these two Schema do not share a common namespace. However, if the first Schema looked like this:

```
<schema xmlns="http://www.w3.org/2001/XMLSchema">
 <element name="something" type="string"/>
</schema>
```

with no targetNamespace defined, it could be included.

There is a mechanism for bringing together Schema that do not share a common namespace. To do that, you will need to use the import statement rather than include.

PART

IV

CH

14

import

The <import> mechanism works similarly to the <include> mechanism, but with one major difference: It allows you to import Schema from other namespaces into your current Schema.

The <import> statement takes the form of

```
<import id="id" namespace="URI" schemaLocation="URI"/>
```

This statement allows you to specify the namespace for the Schema you are importing, as well as the schemaLocation. One thing to remember is that you should also declare the imported namespace in your <schema> element, as well as specify a prefix in order to best make use of the imported namespace components.

Let's look at an example. We'll start with a simple contact Schema:

```
<xs:schema xmlns:xs="http://www.w3.org/2001/XMLSchema"
    targetNamespace="http://www.myserver.com/Contact"
    xmlns="http://www.myserver.com/Contact">

<xs:elment name="name" type="xs:string"/>
<xs:elment name="phone" type="xs:string"/>

<xs:complexType name="address">
 <xs:elment name="street" type="xs:string"/>
 <xs:elment name="city" type="xs:string"/>
 <xs:elment name="state" type="xs:string"/>
 <xs:elment name="zip" type="xs:string"/>
</xs:complexType>

<xs:element name="contact">
 <xs:complexType>
  <xs:complexContent>
   <xs:extension base="address">
    <xs:element ref="name"/>
    <xs:element ref="phone"/>
   </xs:extension>
  </xs:complexContent>
 </xs:complexType>
</xs:element>

</schema>
```

This Schema defines an instance valid with respect to this Schema:

```
<contact>
<name>John Doe</name>
<phone>800-555-1212</phone>
<street>23 Parkway</street>
<city>Bloomington</city>
<state>IN</state>
<zip>47408</zip>
</contact>
```

Because the `<name>` and `<phone>` elements are globally declared, we can access them in an imported Schema. The same is true of the address complex type, which we can also access. But the individual elements within the address complex type cannot be accessed because they are only declared locally, not globally.

Now we can create a new Schema for Customer Records, and import the contact Schema in order to make use of those definitions and declarations. We start by declaring the schema element, and within the schema element, we create a namespace for the contact Schema:

```
<xs:schema xmlns:xs="http://www.w3.org/2001/XMLSchema"
    xmlns:contact="http://www.myserver.com/Contact"
    targetNamespace="http://www.myserver.com/CustomerRecords"
    xmlns="http://www.myserver.com/CustomerRecords">
```

Next, we can import the `contact.xsd` Schema:

```
<import namespace="http://www.myserver.com/Contact"
    schemaLocation="http://www.myserver.com/contact.xsd"/>
```

And now we are ready to go. We can now include any globally declared components in our new Schema that we want. For example, if we wanted to make use of the name element from the contact Schema, we could use

```
<xs:element ref="contact:name"/>
```

Note that when referencing the imported element, we make use of the namespace prefix we declared in the `<schema>` element. A complete Schema that uses the name and phone elements from the contact Schema might look like this:

```
<xs:schema xmlns:xs="http://www.w3.org/2001/XMLSchema"
    xmlns:contact="http://www.myserver.com/Contact"
    targetNamespace="http://www.myserver.com/CustomerRecords"
    xmlns="http://www.myserver.com/CustomerRecords">

<import namespace="http://www.myserver.com/Contact"
    schemaLocation="http://www.myserver.com/contact.xsd"/>

<xs:element name="customer">
 <xs:complexType>
  <xs:complexContent>
   <xs:element ref="contact:name"/>
   <xs:element name="account" type="xs:string"/>
   <xs:element ref="contact:phone"/>
   <xs:element name="sales_rep" type="xs:string"/>
  </xs:complexContent>
 </xs:complexType>
</xs:element>

</xs:schema>
```

This Schema would import the `contact.xsd` Schema, and allow us to create instance documents that looked like this:

```
<customer>
 <name>Marc Doe</name>
 <account>38873</account>
```

```
<phone>708-555-1212</phone>
 <sales_rep>John Smith</sales_rep>
</customer>
```

As you can see, importing Schema allows you a little more flexibility than including them. However, it also means that you need to keep close track of the namespace issues surrounding imported components and how those are used.

redefine

One problem with both `include` and `import` is that both of these mechanisms require that you work with the components from the imported Schema in exactly the form in which they were imported. For example, if you imported a phone element which was defined as

```
<element name="phone" type="string"/>
```

You would be stuck using the `phone` element as-is. You couldn't restrict it to massage the phone number into the format you wanted, such as by enforcing pattern matching.

Fortunately, XML Schema allow the possibility of including an external Schema *and* redefining the components with the use of the `<redefine>` element.

The `<redefine>` element takes the following form:

```
<redefine id="ID" schemaLocation="URI"> </redefine>
```

One thing you will notice is that unlike the previous `<include>` and `<import>` examples, we've shown a closing tag for `<redefine>`. That's because the `<redefine>` element will actually contain the definitions and declarations you are using to redefine components from the Schema you are importing.

The `<redefine>` element functions very similarly to the `<include>` element. It has many of the same restrictions:

- `<redefine>` must be the first child of the `<schema>` element, before any type definitions or declarations.
- Only Schema belonging to the same `targetNamespace`, or not having any namespace at all, can be redefined.
- Only components which have been declared globally can be redefined.

In addition to these restrictions, all of the redefinitions themselves must be contained in the `<redefine>` element, so you have to group any redefinitions together. You cannot redefine any components outside of the `<redefine>` tag.

Let's take a look at an example. Suppose we start with another contact Schema, which looks like this:

```
<xs:schema xmlns:xs="http://www.w3.org/2001/XMLSchema"
        xmlns="http://www.myserver.com/Contact">

<xs:elment name="name" type="xs:string"/>
<xs:elment name="ID" type="xs:string"/>
```

```
<xs:element name="phone" type="xs:string"/>
<xs:element name="address">
 <xs:complexType>
  <xs:complexContent>
   <xs:elment name="street" type="xs:string"/>
   <xs:elment name="city" type="xs:string"/>
   <xs:elment name="state" type="xs:string"/>
   <xs:elment name="zip" type="xs:string"/>
  </xs:complexContent>
 </xs:complexType>
</xs:element>

</schema>
```

Here we have a simple Schema which has defined <name>, <ID>, <phone>, and <address> elements. These are the only elements we can access to redefine, because they are the only components which have been declared globally. We cannot alter the <street>, <city>, <state>, or <zip> elements, because they are only declared locally to the <address> element. Note also that the Schema we are going to be redefining does not contain a targetNamespace.

Now, let's say that we wanted to create a Schema for retirement benefit recipients. We want to be able to use the same contact information, but we want to make the <ID> element take the form of a Social Security number (000-00-0000). We can do this with redefine:

```
<redefine schemaLocation="http://www.myserver.com/contact.xsd">

<xs:elment name="ID">
 <xs:simpleType>
  <xs:restriction base="xs:string">
   <xs:pattern value="[0-9]{3}\-[0-9]{2}\-[0-9]{4}"/>
  </xs:restriction>
 </xs:simpleType>
</xs:element>

</redefine>
```

Here the redefine element specifies the location of the Schema we are including and redefining. Next, we insert the new definition for our <ID> element. This redefinition will take the place of the declaration in the imported Schema; however, all of the other Schema components will be included unaltered, so we can make use of those as well. If we wanted to redefine any other components, we'd have to do it here as well.

Namespaces are also a consideration when using redefine. In order to use redefine, the external components from the Schema that we are redefining either have to be in the same targetNamespace as the new Schema, or they have to have no namespace at all. When you use redefine with components that have no namespace, they become members of the targetNamespace of your new Schema when they are redefined.

When we integrate the redefinition into our new Schema, it looks like this:

```
<xs:schema xmlns:xs="http://www.w3.org/2001/XMLSchema"
    targetNamespace="http://www.myserver.com/Benefits"
    xmlns="http://www.myserver.com/Benefits">
```

PART

IV

CH

14

```
<redefine schemaLocation="http://www.myserver.com/contact.xsd">

<xs:elment name="ID">
 <xs:simpleType>
  <xs:restriction base="xs:string">
   <xs:pattern value="[0-9]{3}\-[0-9]{2}\-[0-9]{4}"/>
  </xs:restriction>
 </xs:simpleType>
</xs:element>

</redefine>

<xs:element name="recipient">
 <xs:complexType>
  <xs:complexContent>
   <xs:element ref="name"/>
   <xs:element ref="ID" />
   <xs:element ref="phone"/>
   <xs:element ref="address"/>
  </xs:complexContent>
 </xs:complexType>
</xs:element>

</xs:schema>
```

With this Schema, we can make use of contact elements from the first Schema, and make use of our new redefined <ID> element as well. An XML instance document could look like this:

```
<recipient>
 <name>Jane Doe</name>
 <ID>312-00-2311</ID>
 <phone>703-555-1212</phone>
 <address>
  <street>410 Evergreen Rd.</street>
  <city>Milpitas</city>
  <state>CA</state>
  <zip>97013</zip>
 </address>
</recipient>
```

TYPE LIBRARIES

One of the best applications for using multiple Schema documents is creating your own Schema type libraries. For example, contact information is something that is frequently used and reused throughout an organization. People maintain business contacts and personal contacts, and those contacts get used on billing information, payment information, contracts, delivery schedules, and so forth.

So it makes a whole lot of sense that if you need to develop Schema for all of these applications, rather than rewriting all of the contact component definitions and declarations each time, you should write them once and then reuse them! You could do this by cutting and pasting, but then if you updated the contact elements to include a new service (for example, we didn't always have cell phones; what new technology will be used next?), you would need to edit all of your documents manually.

Conversely, if you have defined a contact Schema, and then reference that Schema in your other Schema by importing or including, then when you make changes to the original Schema, those changes will be automatically reflected throughout your Schema set. The result is a very flexible system, easy to manage.

So as you approach your own Schema projects, you should look at the type of data and documents you are defining, and when you see areas in which that data might be reused, think about abstracting that section of your Schema out into a separate Schema to create a "type library." A little forethought during the design process can save you a great deal of work down the road.

WORKING WITH NAMESPACES

When you are working with multiple-document Schema, the biggest challenge you will face will be to keep track of namespaces and to avoid namespace collisions (when you have two components with the same declaration in the same namespace).

The trick to avoiding problems with namespace and multiple Schema documents is to follow a few simple guidelines.

When you are working with a Schema that you did not develop, such as one being published by another organization or developer, it is best to import the Schema, and to use prefixes with qualified names when using imported Schema components. That helps keep your documents up to date with respect to the imported Schema, so that validators (those that check, that is) are properly aware of the namespace components you are importing. It also has the added benefit of eliminating the bloat in your own Schema that would result from constantly cutting and pasting new components in. Similarly, if you are authoring Schema that are designed to be shared outside of your organizations, it is a good idea to use a `targetNamespace` to help prevent namespace collisions.

When you are working with your own multiple-document Schema, which will not be used outside your organization, and over which you have more control, the easiest approach is to actually use target namespaces as little as possible. By creating small Schema with no target namespaces, you can easily include them in your documents wherever necessary.

We'll discuss more of the issues surrounding namespaces and Schema, as well as the best approaches to use, in Chapter 17, "XML Schema Best Practices."

AN EXAMPLE: THE INVOICE SCHEMA REVISITED

Now that we have seen three ways of working with multiple-document Schema, let's take a look at the customer invoice Schema that we designed in Chapter 13, "Example Schema: Customer Invoice," and see how it might benefit from being split up into multiple documents.

First, the data that we are working with in the Invoice example falls into three basic categories:

- **Contact Information.** This is the information regarding the customer contacts, billing information, shipping information, and so on.
- **Accounting Information.** Information such as the Purchase Order number, Subtotals, Tax information, payment terms, and so forth.
- **Invoice Specifics.** Information such as the line-items and services, which are specific to the invoice itself.

Using these categories as a guideline, you can divide the `invoice.xsd` Schema from Chapter 13 into four parts:

- `contact.xsd`
- `accounting.xsd`
- `line-item.xsd`
- `invoice-modular.xsd`

Let's take a look at these parts, what kinds of information each individual Schema contains, and then how to bring all of the individual Schema together again to describe our invoice.

contact.xsd

Contact information is one of the most frequently used types of information among our data set, so abstracting the contact components into their own Schema makes a great deal of sense. Also, in order to maintain more flexibility with the contact information (such as publishing the Schema to our customers and suppliers) we have given it its own namespace. That doesn't really have a significant impact on the authoring of the `contact.xsd` schema itself, but it does mean that we will need to use the `<import>` mechanism to import the `contact.xsd` Schema into our modular invoice Schema.

Most of the definitions in our new `contact.xsd` Schema will look familiar to you from Chapter 13. However, we have made some improvements. The following two sections describe the most notable of these.

THE us_address TYPE

Because not all of our customers will be based in the United States, we've created a new type called us_address which allows us to keep track of addresses in the U.S. format. By abstracting this type, we could now easily add other types of addresses, such as uk_address, and then apply those types to our `<billing_address>` or `<shipping_address>` elements to accommodate non-U.S. addresses:

```
<xs:complexType name="us_address">
 <xs:sequence>
  <xs:element name="address" type="xs:string"/>
  <xs:element name="address2" type="xs:string" minOccurs="0"/>
  <xs:element name="city" type="xs:string"/>
  <xs:element name="state" type="state"/>
```

```
    <xs:element name="zip" type="zip"/>
  </xs:sequence>
</xs:complexType>
```

THE state TYPE

We've also made some changes to the state type from the previous chapter. If you recall, we had restricted the state type to being two uppercase letters. While that is the format for state abbreviations in U.S. addresses, it also allows entries such as "CX", which isn't a state.

In the new type definition, we have restricted the value space using enumerations, and listed one for each of the valid state abbreviations:

```
<xs:simpleType name="state">
 <xs:restriction base="xs:string">
  <xs:enumeration value="AK"/>     <!--Alaska -->
  <xs:enumeration value="AL"/>     <!--Alabama -->
<!-- The Full Definitions for all states are provided in the accompanying
➥example file -->
  <xs:enumeration value="WI"/>     <!--Wisconsin -->
  <xs:enumeration value="WY"/>     <!--Wyoming -->
 </xs:restriction>
</xs:simpleType>
```

BRINGING IT ALL TOGETHER

We've also reorganized the way all of the contact pieces fit together, declaring new <billing> and <shipping> elements to contain the relevant contact information for each section.

The remaining declarations and definitions are pretty much the same as in Chapter 13. The major difference is that they are now in their own Schema file. The complete code for our new contact.xsd Schema is shown in Listing 14.1.

LISTING 14.1   THE CONTACT SCHEMA WITH CONTACT INFORMATION FOR THE INVOICE SCHEMA

```
<?xml version="1.0" encoding="UTF-8" ?>
<xs:schema xmlns:xs="http://www.w3.org/2001/XMLSchema"
    xmlns:xsi="http://www.w3.org/2001/XMLSchema-Instance"
    targetNamespace="http://www.myserver.com/Contact"
    xmlns="http://www.myserver.com/Contact">

<xs:complexType name="contact">
 <xs:element name="company" type="xs:string" minOccurs="0"/>
 <xs:element name="department" type="xs:string" minOccurs="0"/>
 <xs:element name="contact_name" type="xs:string"/>
 <xs:element name="phone" type="us_phone_number"/>
 <xs:element name="fax" type="us_phone_number" minOccurs="0"/>
 <xs:element name="email" type="xs:string" minOccurs="0"/>
 <xs:element name="alt_phone" type="us_phone_number" minOccurs="0"/>
 <xs:element name="alt_contact" type="xs:string" minOccurs="0"/>
</xs:complexType>
```

Listing 14.1   Continued

```
<xs:complexType name="us_address">
 <xs:sequence>
  <xs:element name="address" type="xs:string"/>
  <xs:element name="address2" type="xs:string" minOccurs="0"/>
  <xs:element name="city" type="xs:string"/>
  <xs:element name="state" type="state"/>
  <xs:element name="zip" type="zip"/>
 </xs:sequence>
</xs:complexType>

<xs:simpleType name="state">
 <xs:restriction base="xs:string">
  <xs:enumeration value="AK"/>       <!--Alaska -->
  <xs:enumeration value="AL"/>       <!--Alabama -->
<!-- The Full Definitions for all states are provided in the accompanying
➥example file -->
  <xs:enumeration value="WI"/>       <!--Wisconsin -->
  <xs:enumeration value="WY"/>       <!--Wyoming -->
 </xs:restriction>
</xs:simpleType>

<xs:simpleType name="zip">
 <xs:restriction base="xs:string">
  <xs:pattern value="[0-9]{5}(\-)?([0-9]{4})?"/>
 </xs:restriction>
</xs:simpleType>

<xs:simpleType name="us_phone_number">
 <xs:restriction base="xs:string">
  <xs:pattern value="[0-9]{3}\-[0-9]{3}\-[0-9]{4}"/>
 </xs:restriction>
</xs:simpleType>

<xs:element name="billing">
 <xs:complexType>
  <xs:element name="billing_contact" type="contact"/>
  <xs:element name="billing_address" type="us_address"/>
 </xs:complexType>
</xs:element>

<xs:element name="shipping">
 <xs:complexType>
  <xs:complexContent>
  <xs:element name="shipping_contact" type="contact"/>
  <xs:element name="shipping_address" type="us_address" minOccurs="0"/>
  <xs:attribute name="useBilling" type="xs:boolean" use="required"/>
  </xs:complexContent>
 </xs:complexType>
</xs:element>

</xs:schema>
```

accounting.xsd

Any invoice deals with a number of components which involve accounting data. Information such as totals, subtotals, and so on need to be kept as monetary values, in a currency format.

In order to make better use of these components, we've assembled them into a new Schema called `accounting.xsd`. For this example, we have not given this Schema its own namespace, because we don't intend to distribute the Schema to our clients in any way. By keeping it free of a `targetNamespace`, we can easily use either `<include>` or `<redefine>` when we are working with the Schema as well.

We've cleaned up some of the declarations in the Schema, and reorganized some of the declarations to be local, so that only the main types and elements are declared globally, and therefore accessible when included.

However, the most major change we've made to this Schema is that we have changed the `us_currency` type, which was used in Chapter 13 to specify a `decimal` value for currency, and replaced it with `monetary_value`, which has the same declaration. We did this so we could create a new attribute called `currency`:

```
<xs:attribute name="currency">
<xs:simpleType>
 <xs:restriction base="xs:string">
  <xs:enumeration value="USD"/>
  <xs:enumeration value="EUR"/>
  <xs:enumeration value="UK"/>
 </xs:restriction>
</xs:simpleType>
</xs:attribute>
```

This attribute allows us to specify the type of currency values being used, such as U.S. dollars, British pounds, the Euro, and so on. Since we're updating our address information to allow for the inclusion of international addresses, it makes sense to deal with international currency.

The complete listing for our new `accounting.xsd` Schema is shown in Listing 14.2.

LISTING 14.2 THE ACCOUNTING SCHEMA WHICH DEFINES THE TYPES AND ELEMENTS USED IN CONJUNCTION WITH ACCOUNTING FOR THE INVOICE SCHEMA

```
<?xml version="1.0" encoding="UTF-8" ?>
<xs:schema xmlns:xs="http://www.w3.org/2001/XMLSchema"
    xmlns:xsi="http://www.w3.org/2001/XMLSchema-Instance"
    xmlns="http://www.w3.org/2001/XMLSchema">

<xs:simpleType name="monetary_value">
 <xs:restriction base="xs:decimal">
  <xs:fractionDigits value="2" fixed="true"/>
 </xs:restriction>
</xs:simpleType>

<xs:simpleType name="percentage">
 <xs:restriction base="xs:decimal">
  <xs:fractionDigits value="4"/>
```

PART

IV

CH

14

LISTING 14.2   CONTINUED

```
  <xs:totalDigits value="4" fixed="true"/>
  <xs:minInclusive value="0" fixed="true"/>
  <xs:maxInclusive value="1" fixed="true"/>
 </xs:restriction>
</xs:simpleType>

<xs:attribute name="currency">
 <xs:simpleType>
  <xs:restriction base="xs:string">
   <xs:enumeration value="USD"/>
   <xs:enumeration value="EUR"/>
   <xs:enumeration value="UK"/>
  </xs:restriction>
 </xs:simpleType>
</xs:attribute>

<xs:attribute name="job_number">
 <xs:simpleType>
  <xs:restriction base="xs:integer">
   <xs:Length value="5"/>
  </xs:restriction>
 </xs:simpleType>
</xs:attribute>

<xs:attribute name="charge_type">
 <xs:simpleType>
  <xs:restriction base="xs:string">
   <xs:enumeration value="Shipping"/>
   <xs:enumeration value="Late Fee"/>
   <xs:enumeration value="Finance Charge"/>
  </xs:restriction>
 </xs:simpleType>
</xs:attribute>

<xs:element name="purchase_order">
 <xs:complexType>
  <xs:complexContent>
   <xs:attribute name="PO_number" type="xs:string"/>
   <xs:attribute name="customer_reference" type="xs:string"/>
  </xs:complexContent>
 </xs:complexType>
</xs:element>

<xs:element name="term">
 <xs:simpleType>
  <xs:restriction base="xs:string">
   <xs:enumeration value="Net15"/>
   <xs:enumeration value="Net30"/>
   <xs:enumeration value="Net60"/>
   <xs:enumeration value="Due on Receipt"/>
   <xs:enumeration value="PAID"/>
   <xs:enumeration value="PAST DUE"/>
  </xs:restriction>
 </xs:simpleType>
</xs:element>
```

LISTING 14.2   CONTINUED

```xml
<xs:element name="tax">
 <xs:complexType>
  <xs:complexContent>
   <xs:extension base="monetary_value">
    <xs:attribute name="taxRate" type="percentage" use="required"/>
   </xs:extension>
  </xs:complexContent>
 </xs:complexType>
</xs:element>

<xs:element name="charges">
 <xs:complexType>
  <xs:complexContent>
   <xs:extension base="monetary_value">
   <xs:attribute ref="charge_type" use="required"/>
   </xs:extension>
  </xs:complexContent>
 </xs:complexType>
</xs:element>

<xs:element name="sub_total">
 <xs:complexType>
  <xs:complexContent>
   <xs:extension base="monetary_value">
   <xs:attribute ref="currency"/>
   </xs:extension>
  </xs:complexContent>
 </xs:complexType>
</xs:element>

<xs:element name="total">
 <xs:complexType>
  <xs:complexContent>
   <xs:extension base="monetary_value">
   <xs:attribute ref="currency"/>
   </xs:extension>
  </xs:complexContent>
 </xs:complexType>
</xs:element>

<xs:element name="balance_due">
 <xs:complexType>
  <xs:complexContent>
   <xs:extension base="monetary_value">
   <xs:attribute ref="currency"/>
   </xs:extension>
  </xs:complexContent>
 </xs:complexType>
</xs:element>

</xs:schema>
```

PART

IV

CH

14

line-item.xsd

The last of our multiple Schema documents is `line-item.xsd`. This Schema is going to deal with very specific information which is going to be used on the invoice for line items, such as part numbers being invoiced, or services being billed.

It would be possible to just include the components in this Schema in our `invoice-modular.xsd` file, so why did we create this new Schema? For two reasons:

- First, by placing this information in a separate document, we open the possibility that someday we could use this Schema and its components in another application, such as a catalog, for example. Just because we don't have a use for the components other than our invoice right now does not mean that will always be the case.

- Second, although we do not do so here, you could easily restrict `<item>` and/or `<service>` values by enumerations; that would be useful if you only sold five items, or offered a few services. We've left it more open and generic here, but if you wanted to strictly limit the line-item choices, it would be much easier to access and edit them in this separate file.

The component declarations in this chapter are pretty much the same as they are in Chapter 13. However, there are two features of this Schema we should point out.

First, we have once again not specified a `targetNamespace` for this Schema, which means we can freely and easily include it inside our `invoice-modular.xsd` Schema.

Second, we have included the `accounting.xsd` Schema in this Schema:

```
<include schemaLocation="http://www.myserver.com/accounting.xsd"/>
```

We've done this so that we can access the `monetary_value` type, for elements such as `<amount>`. Because neither Schema has a `targetNamespace`, we can easily include the `accounting.xsd` Schema in the `line-item.xsd` Schema.

The complete code for the line-item Schema is shown below in Listing 14.3.

LISTING 14.3   THE LINE-ITEM SCHEMA WHICH DEFINES THE TYPES AND ELEMENTS USED IN CONJUNCTION WITH LINE ITEMS FOR THE INVOICE SCHEMA

```
<?xml version="1.0" encoding="UTF-8" ?>
<xs:schema xmlns:xs="http://www.w3.org/2001/XMLSchema"
    xmlns:xsi="http://www.w3.org/2001/XMLSchema-Instance"
    xmlns=" http://www.w3.org/2001/XMLSchema ">

<include schemaLocation="http://www.myserver.com/accounting.xsd"/>

<xs:element name="item">
 <xs:complexType>
  <xs:complexContent>
   <xs:attribute name="item_code" type="xs:string"/>
   <xs:sequence>
    <xs:element ref="description"/>
```

LISTING 14.3   CONTINUED

```
    <xs:element ref="quantity"/>
    <xs:element ref="price_rate"/>
    <xs:element ref="amount"/>
   </xs:sequence>
  </xs:complexContent>
 </xs:complexType>
</xs:element>

<xs:element name="service">
 <xs:complexType>
  <xs:complexContent>
   <xs:attribute name="service_code" type="xs:string"/>
   <xs:sequence>
    <xs:element ref="description"/>
    <xs:element ref="duration"/>
    <xs:element ref="price_rate"/>
    <xs:element ref="amount"/>
   </xs:sequence>
  </xs:complexContent>
 </xs:complexType>
</xs:element>

<xs:element name="description" type="xs:string"/>

<xs:element name="quantity">
 <xs:simpleType>
  <xs:restriction base="xs:integer">
   <xs:minInclusive value="1"/>
  </xs:restriction>
 </xs:simpleType>
</xs:element>

<xs:element name="duration">
 <xs:simpleType>
  <xs:restriction base="xs:decimal">
   <xs:minInclusive value="1"/>
   <xs:fractionDigits value="1"/>
  </xs:restriction>
 </xs:simpleType>
</xs:element>

<xs:element name="price_rate" type="monetary_value"/>

<xs:element name="amount" type="monetary_value"/>

</xs:schema>
```

invoice-modular.xsd

With our three modular Schema defined, we are now ready to bring them all together into the invoice-modular.xsd Schema, which will serve as the basis for our XML instance documents.

The first step to constructing our modular Schema is to define the `<schema>` element:

```
<xs:schema xmlns:xs="http://www.w3.org/2001/XMLSchema"
    xmlns:xsi="http://www.w3.org/2001/XMLSchema-Instance"
    targetNamespace="http://www.myserver.com/Invoice"
    xmlns:contact="http://www.myserver.com/Contact"
    xmlns="http://www.myserver.com/Invoice">
```

You should note the namespace declarations here. We have specified a `targetNamespace` for the invoice, so that we can publish the Schema more easily. However, the important detail here is that we have also specified the `contact` namespace and prefix, because as you might recall, we had given `contact.xsd` its own `targetNamespace`.

That means when we reference components from the `contact.xsd` Schema, we will need to make use of the `contact` prefix:

```
<xs:element ref="contact:billing"/>
<xs:element ref="contact:shipping"/>
```

Next, we need to bring together our other Schema components. First, we can include the `line-item.xsd` Schema, which does not have a `targetNamespace` defined, so we can use `<include>`:

```
<include schemaLocation="http://www.myserver.com/line-item.xsd"/>
```

Including this Schema has an additional benefit. Remember that we used `<include>` within the `line-item.xsd` Schema to include the `accounting.xsd` schema. That means we do not have to include the accounting Schema here, because the nested `<include>` makes that Schema accessible to the `invoice-modular.xsd` Schema as well. If we were to go ahead and include the Schema here again, the components which were included in the `line-time.xsd` from our accounting Schema would once again be included, and the processor would need to resolve the resulting conflicts. Since the declarations are the same in this case, it should still function correctly. This is not illegal in XML Schema, according to the Recommendation, but as it taxes the Schema processor, it is strongly discouraged.

Next, we can `<import>` the `contact.xsd` Schema:

```
<import namespace="http://www.myserver.com/Contact"
    schemaLocation="http://www.myserver.com/contact.xsd"/>
```

which gives us access to our contact components. Now we're ready to go with the definitions for our invoice document. The complete listing for the final, modular version of the invoice Schema is shown in Listing 14.4.

LISTING 14.4   THE FINAL, MODULAR INVOICE SCHEMA

```
<?xml version="1.0" encoding="UTF-8" ?>
<xs:schema xmlns:xs="http://www.w3.org/2001/XMLSchema"
    xmlns:xsi="http://www.w3.org/2001/XMLSchema-Instance"
    targetNamespace="http://www.myserver.com/Invoice"
    xmlns:contact="http://www.myserver.com/Contact"
    xmlns="http://www.myserver.com/Invoice">
```

LISTING 14.4 CONTINUED

```
<xs:annotation>
 <xs:documentation xml:lang="en">
  A sample XML Schema for a Customer Invoice.
  Modular Version, based on importing the Accounting, Contact,
➥and LineItem Schema.
 </xs:documentation>
</xs:annotation>

<!-- Import the other Schema Modules -->
<include schemaLocation="http://www.myserver.com/line-item.xsd"/>
<import namespace="http://www.myserver.com/Contact"
    schemaLocation="http://www.myserver.com/contact.xsd"/>

<xs:element name="invoice">
 <xs:complexType>
  <xs:complexContent>
   <xs:attribute name="invoice_number">
    <xs:simpleType>
     <xs:restriction base="xs:integer">
      <xs:minLength value="6"/>
     </xs:restriction>
    </xs:simpleType>
   </xs:attribute>
   <xs:attribute ref="job_number"/>
   <xs:sequence>
    <xs:element name="date" type="xs:date"/>
    <xs:element ref="purchase_order"/>
    <xs:element ref="contact:billing"/>
    <xs:element ref="contact:shipping"/>
    <xs:element ref="item" minOccurs="0" maxOccurs="unbounded"/>
    <xs:element ref="service" minOccurs="0" maxOccurs="unbounded"/>
    <xs:element ref="sub_total"/>
    <xs:element ref="tax" minOccurs="0"/>
    <xs:element ref="charges" minOccurs="0"/>
    <xs:element ref="total"/>
    <xs:element ref="balance_due" minOccurs="0"/>
    <xs:element ref="term"/>
    <xs:element name="representative">
     <xs:complexType>
      <xs:complexContent>
       <xs:attribute name="name" type="xs:string"/>
       <xs:attribute name="department" type="xs:string"/>
      </xs:complexContent>
     </xs:complexType>
    </xs:element>
    <xs:element name="message" type="xs:string" minOccurs="0"/>
    <xs:element name="notes" type="xs:string" minOccurs="0"
➥maxOccurs="unbounded"/>
   </xs:sequence>
  </xs:complexContent>
 </xs:complexType>
</xs:element>

</xs:schema>
```

With this Schema complete, we can now create instance documents for our invoices, such as the one shown in Listing 14.5.

LISTING 14.5 AN XML INSTANCE DOCUMENT BASED ON THE NEW MODULAR INVOICE SCHEMA

```
<?xml version="1.0" encoding="UTF-8" ?>

<invoice xmlns="http://www.myserver.com/invoice"
      xmlns:xsi="http://www.3.org/2001/XMLSchema-Instance"
      xsi:schemaLocation="http://www.myserver.com/invoice"
      http://www.myserver.com/invoice-modular.xsd"
         invoice_number="283412" job_number="00032">

<date>2002-11-04</date>

<purchase_order PO_Number="34123GA" customer_reference="231-22D"/>

<billing>
 <billing_contact>
  <company>Corner Stores, Inc.</company>
  <department>Accounts Payable</department>
  <contact_name>Jim Doe</contact_name>
  <phone>312-333-0001</phone>
  <fax>312-333-0050</fax>
  <email>j.doe@csi.com</email>
 </billing_contact>
 <billing_address>
  <address>PO Box 78993</address>
  <city>Chicago</city>
  <state>IL</state>
  <zip>90210</zip>
 </billing_address>
</billing>

<shipping useBilling="no">
 <shipping_contact>
  <company>Corner Stores, Inc.</company>
  <department>Store #58</department>
  <contact_name>Bill Ruthford</contact_name>
  <phone>312-333-0231</phone>
 </shipping_contact>
 <shipping_address>
  <address>2534 West West Parkway</address>
  <city>Mumford</city>
  <state>IL</state>
  <zip>34231</zip>
 </shipping_address>
</shipping>

<item item_code="LP-1000">
 <description>New Lock Cylinder</description>
 <quantity>1</quantity>
 <price_rate>37.50</price_rate>
 <amount>37.50</amount>
</item>
```

LISTING 14.5 CONTINUED

```
<service service_code="INST">
 <description>Tumbling and Installation</description>
 <duration>1.5</duration>
 <price_rate>60.00</price_rate>
 <amount>90.00</amount>
</service>

<sub_total>127.50</sub_total>
<tax taxRate".0875">3.28</tax>
<total>130.78</total>
<term>Net30</term>

<representative>
 <name>Dale Evans</name>
 <department>Insallation</department>
</representative>

<messages>Thanks for Choosing Lock Pro!</messages>
</invoice>
```

As you can see from this example and the others in this chapter, using multiple documents to construct your Schema can provide you with a great deal of flexibility. There is no one right or wrong way to organize your multipart Schema. But you should consider the full impact of future uses and possibilities when designing your Schema, to make the most of what the XML Schema Recommendation allows.

CONCLUSIONS

Multiple-document Schema enable you to create sets of Schema and type libraries for reusing components. This allows you to write things once and then reuse them when necessary to save valuable development time. The key points to building multiple-part Schema are

- <include> enables you to include one Schema inside another, provided both are part of the same namespace, or no targetNamespace has been declared.

- <import> enables you to import a Schema into another with a different targetNamespace.

- When using <import> statements, be sure to keep careful track of namespace declarations and prefixes to avoid namespace collisions.

- <redefine> functions similarly to <import>, but allows you to redefine the components from the Schema being imported.

- <import>, <include>, and <redefine> must all appear as the first child elements of a <schema> element, before any other declarations or definitions.

- All redefined components must be contained within the <redefine> element.

Next, in Chapter 15, "An Example Schema: Human Resources," we will follow another Schema example from start to finish, dedicating Chapter 15 to the planning and development of the Schema, and Chapter 16, "Building and Using the Schema," to the detailed, step-by-step writing of the Schema itself.

IN THE REAL WORLD

You are more likely to find Schema all lumped into one very large file. There are various reasons for this, the biggest being that it is easier for people to simply cut and paste other code into their own Schema than to import and include and worry about namespace issues, or keep track of someone else's Schema. It is unfortunate, because it does make for longer, more burdensome Schema, and it also leads to sloppy work.

So, if you are unlikely to encounter lots of multipart Schema in the real world, why did we spend a whole chapter covering them? Because they are a good idea, and you *should* be using them yourself. Especially with large-scale internal projects, where you aren't relying on outside Schema, using multiple Schema really will help you retain your sanity.

The biggest real-world issue that you will encounter with regard to multipart Schema will revolve around namespaces. When you are working with Schema from other sources, you will need to be mindful of namespaces and the potential for namespace collisions. The best approach for this is that when working with Schema from outside sources, they should always have a declared targetNamespace, and you can then use the import mechanism to bring those Schema into your own. If you are working with multiple-part Schema which are controlled entirely by your organization, then they should all be a part of the same targetNamespace, and you can use the include mechanism.

CHAPTER 15

AN EXAMPLE SCHEMA: HUMAN RESOURCES

In this chapter

OUTLINING THE PROJECT

In Chapters 15 and 16 we're going to walk through the process of solving a problem using XML Schema, from start to finish. Chapter 15, "An Example Schema: Human Resources," will primarily be a chapter of lists and descriptions, while Chapter 16, "Building and Using the Schema," will be a chapter very heavy in code.

The reason we've set it up into two chapters is to help you learn about how to organize your Schema writing process. Just sitting down and starting to write the Schema immediately will likely lead you down a few blind alleys, and introduce potential problems and conflicts into your Schema. Remember, the Schema you write is going to serve as the foundation for all of your XML instance documents, so careful planning is very important.

Now let's start the exercise.

THE SCENARIO

The human resources department at a small company has recently decided to engage in a project to make all of its employee records (as much as possible, anyway) electronic. We've been asked to write a Schema which will allow XML instance documents to meet the following goals:

- Store an employee profile
- Store employee contact information
- Store employee benefits information
- Store employee reviews

Right now, the company is small. There are only 23 employees, but it is anticipating rapid growth over the next year to two. Therefore, it wants a set of simple Schema which will address its current needs, but also which are able to grow with the organization. These Schema will be used for a variety of applications. The first stage of implementing the new human resources system will be entering the data for employees in instance documents by hand; however, the eventual goal is to create a Web-based system, using XSLT to allow employees to access their data via an internal Web site, and also to allow the HR department to edit the data via a GUI over the Web as well. Although we won't be discussing the mechanisms for building a GUI here (that is a topic worthy of its own book), this is one of the considerations when approaching this project.

This type of Schema is a pretty typical example of how early adopter organizations are using XML Schema currently. More commonly, XML Schema are being used with very specific data applications, but following the authoring of such a schema involves an intimate knowledge of the company's documents and procedures. With the example, we've tried to create a practical, real-world situation, but still remain abstract enough so that you can follow the design process and see how the project is structured. The end goal is to produce a Schema which you could actually put into use at an organization; but hopefully, the real goal is to show you the framework for building the Schema, so you can take this structure, and then customize and alter it for your organization's specific needs.

A SAMPLE INSTANCE DOCUMENT

The first thing we'll do is sit down and draft an XML instance document which contains all the types of information that are required. We do this in conjunction with the human resources manager, in order to make sure this is the information set that's needed.

It's very important that you listen carefully to the information needs of the community you are authoring a Schema for. In applications where you are writing a Schema for your own instance documents, that's pretty easy. However, when you are working with others, a good approach is to start with the instance document. Work with a complete instance document, containing all the data, even optional elements or attributes, which will find their way into your final Schema. This gives you a broad picture of the structure of your documents, and gives you a handy reference guide to use as you begin writing the Schema.

The complete instance document we developed to use as our guideline is shown in Listing 15.1.

LISTING 15.1   THE BASE XML INSTANCE DOCUMENT FOR CREATING A HUMAN RESOURCES SCHEMA

```
<employee>

 <profile>
  <name>Joe Doe</name>
  <SOC>231-98-9912</SOC>
  <DOB>1968-03-15</DOB>
  <spouse>Kathy Doe</spouse>
  <child>Billy Doe</child>
  <department>Sales</department>
  <title>Manger</title>
  <supervisor>Bill Krafty</supervisor>
  <salary type="hourly">13.00</salary>
  <bonus reason="performance">500.00</bonus>
  <hire date="2001-02-02">Hotjobs</hire>
  <termination></termination>
 </profile>

 <contact>
  <home>
   <address>1792 North Elm</address>
   <address>Apt. 3</address>
   <city>Chicago</city>
   <state>IL</state>
   <zip>60633</zip>
   <phone type="primary">312-773-1456</phone>
   <phone type="pager">312-313-3321</phone>
  </home>

  <work>
   <address>1121 North Ave</address>
```

LISTING 15.1   CONTINUED

```
   <city>Elgin</city>
   <state>IL</state>
   <zip>60647</zip>
   <phone type="office">312-829-0121</phone>
  </work>
 </contact>

 <benefits>
  <healthcare>
   <plan>HMO</plan>
   <provider>Providian</provider>
   <start_date>2001-03-01</start_date>
   <termination_date></termination_date>
   <options>Dental</options>
   <options>Eye</options>
  </healthcare>

  <retirement>
   <plan>401k</plan>
   <start_date>2001-05-01</start_date>
   <maturity>2038-01-01</maturity>
   <payroll_deduction>127.00</payroll_deduction>
  </retirement>

  <personal_days allocation="3" used="1" remaining="2">
   <used date="2001-07-05"/>
  </personal_days>

  <vacation allocation="7" used="1" remaining="6">
   <used date="2001-06-21"/>
  </vacation>
 </benefits>

 <review status="">
  <date>2001-6-01</date>
  <period>6 month</period>
  <supervisor>Bill Krafty</supervisor>
  <reviewer>Mark Johnson</reviewer>
  <goal status="met">Meet company sales quota</goal>
  <goal status="future">Increase sales 5%</goal>
  <responsibility status="current">Manage local sales team</responsibility>
  <responsibility status="desired">Manage regional sales team</responsibility>
  <strength>Excellent with clients</strength>
  <weakness>Needs to improve vendor relationships</weakness>
  <training>2001 Sales Training</training>
  <performance>Above Average</performance>
  <employee_comments>Great working environment, would like to move up in
➥organization.</employee_comments>
  <supervisor_comments>Strong employee skills, very promotable
➥</supervisor_comments>
  <reviewer_comments>Good departmental relationship</reviewer_comments>
  <next>2001-12-15</next>
  <raise rate="hourly">2.00</raise>
 </review>

</employee>
```

The first section of our instance document is used to describe information about the employees themselves:

```
<profile>
 <name>Joe Doe</name>
 <SOC>231-98-9912</SOC>
 <DOB>1968-03-15</DOB>
 <spouse>Kathy Doe</spouse>
 <child>Billy Doe</child>
 <department>Sales</department>
 <title>Manger</title>
 <supervisor>Bill Krafty</supervisor>
 <salary type="hourly">13.00</salary>
 <bonus reason="performance">500.00</bonus>
 <hire date="2001-02-02">Hotjobs</hire>
 <termination date=""></termination>
</profile>
```

Within this structure, we have elements describing

- The employee's name
- The employee's Social Security number
- The employee's date of birth
- The name of the employee's spouse (if married)
- The names of the employee's children (if they have children)
- The department the employee works for within the company
- The employee's job title
- The employee's immediate supervisor
- The employee's salary, including how it's calculated
- Any bonuses the employee has received, including the reason for the bonus
- The date on which the employee was hired and the method by which he or she was hired
- The date on which the employee was terminated (if they have left the company) including the reason for termination

In the next section, we have the contact information for the employee outlined in the profile:

```
<contact>
 <home>
  <address>1792 North Elm</address>
  <address>Apt. 3</address>
  <city>Chicago</city>
  <state>IL</state>
  <zip>60633</zip>
  <phone type="primary">312-773-1456</phone>
  <phone type="pager">312-313-3321</phone>
 </home>

 <work>
  <address>1121 North Ave</address>
```

```
    <city>Elgin</city>
    <state>IL</state>
    <zip>60647</zip>
    <phone type="office">312-829-0121</phone>
  </work>
 </contact>
```

Here we store the address and telephone information of the employee, both for their home contact information and their work contact information (for multiple company locations).

Next, we keep track of the benefit programs the employee is eligible for, or has elected to participate in. This company is small, and only offers limited benefits. There is a healthcare plan, a retirement plan, personal days, and vacation time.

In the section that describes the healthcare benefits

```
  <healthcare>
   <plan>HMO</plan>
   <provider>Providian</provider>
   <start_date>2001-03-01</start_date>
   <termination_date></termination_date>
   <options>Dental</options>
   <options>Eye</options>
  </healthcare>
```

We are keeping track of information related to the employee's medical insurance. This includes

- The name of the plan they are enrolled in
- The plan provider
- The start date for their healthcare benefits
- The termination date for their healthcare benefits (when they leave the company)
- Any optional benefits, such as maternity coverage for a spouse

The next section describes any retirement benefits the employee is eligible for:

```
  <retirement>
   <plan>401k</plan>
   <start_date>2001-05-01</start_date>
   <maturity>2038-01-01</maturity>
   <payroll_deduction>127.00</payroll_deduction>
  </retirement>
```

This includes

- The name of the retirement plan
- The start date of enrollment
- The date the plan reaches maturity
- The amount of payroll deduction the employee has elected to use

Of course, these sections could contain a lot more data, but with a company this small, they are just basic sections. However, as the company grows, these are two sections we'll want to keep a close eye on and be able to update easily. This makes them an idea candidate for abstraction into their own Schema.

Next, we have two sections to keep track of how the employee is using their time off:

```
<personal_days allocation="3" used="1" remaining="2">
 <used date="2001-07-05"/>
</personal_days>

<vacation allocation="7" used="1" remaining="6">
 <used date="2001-06-21"/>
</vacation>
```

Each of these elements allows us to keep track of information regarding the employee's personal days, and their vacation time, including

- The number of days allocated annually
- The number of days currently used
- The number of days remaining
- The date a personal day or vacation day was taken

That wraps up the benefits information we'll be tracking. The last section of information we need to keep track of for our employees involves performance reviews. This company has just started a process of an employment review every six months, with the review being conducted between the supervisor and the employee and overseen by an independent third-party reviewer.

The section of our instance document describing the reviews looks like this:

```
<review status="">
 <date>2001-6-01</date>
 <period>6 month</period>
 <supervisor>Bill Krafty</supervisor>
 <reviewer>Mark Johnson</reviewer>
 <goal status="met">Meet company sales quota</goal>
 <goal status="future">Increase sales 5%</goal>
 <responsibility status="current">Manage local sales team</responsibility>
 <responsibility status="desired">Manage regional sales team</responsibility>
 <strength>Excellent with clients</strength>
 <weakness>Needs to improve vendor relationships</weakness>
 <training>2001 Sales Training</training>
 <performance>Above Average</performance>
 <employee_comments>Great working environment, would like to move up in
➡organization.</employee_comments>
 <supervisor_comments>Strong employee skills, very promotable
➡</supervisor_comments>
 <reviewer_comments>Good departmental relationship</reviewer_comments>
 <next>2001-12-15</next>
 <raise rate="hourly">2.00</raise>
</review>
```

This information allows us to contain a complete review inside an instance document, so that the employee's performance history is maintained in their file. The information we're storing includes

- The review status (pending, approved, etc.)
- The date of the review

- The period of the review
- The employee's supervisor for the review
- The independent reviewer
- Goals and their status. This includes goals set during previous reviews, and goals set to work on for the next review
- Responsibilities, including current employee responsibilities, and responsibilities they'd like in the future
- Employee strengths
- Employee weaknesses
- Comments from the employee about their performance and review
- Comments from the supervisor about the employee's performance
- Comments from the reviewer about the relationship and review
- The date of the next review
- Any raise being assigned, and the method of calculation

That completes all of the information that is contained in our XML instance document. It also gives us a good overview of the type of information we'll be dealing with for our Schema. Now we have a reference document to use in writing the Schema which we can turn to if we need to answer a question during the Schema authoring process.

ESTABLISHING RELATIONSHIPS

The next step we'll take in designing our Schema is to make a list of all the elements and attributes in our document, along with their children.

This helps us establish the relationships between the various elements and attributes. The results are shown in Table 15.1.

TABLE 15.1   A LISTING OF ALL THE ELEMENTS AND ATTRIBUTES IN THE HUMAN RESOURCES DOCUMENT, DETAILING THEIR RELATIONSHIPS

Element	Attribute	Children
employee		all (root element)
profile		name, SOC, DOB, spouse, child, department, title, supervisor, salary, bonus, hire, termination
name		
SOC		
DOB		
spouse		

TABLE 15.1 CONTINUED

Element	Attribute	Children
child		
department		
title		
supervisor		
salary	type	
bonus	reason	
hire	date	
termination	date	
contact		home, work
home		address, city, state, zip, phone
work		address, city, state, zip, phone
address		
city		
state		
zip		
phone	type	
benefits		healthcare, retirement, personal_days, vacation
healthcare		plan, provider, start_date, termination_date, options
plan		
provider		
start_date		
termination_date		
options		
retirement		plan, start_date, maturity, payroll_deduction
maturity		
payroll_deduction		
personal_days	allocation, used, remaining	used
used	date	
vacation	allocation, used, remaining	used

Table 15.1   Continued

Element	Attribute	Children
review	status	name, date, period, supervisor, reviewer, goal, responsibility, strength, weakness, performance, employee_comments, supervisor_comments, reviewer_comments, next, raise
name		
date		
period		
reviewer		
goal	status	
responsibility	status	
strength		
weakness		
performance		
employee_comments		
supervisor_comments		
reviewer_comments		
next		
raise	rate	

Now we have a convenient place where we can easily reference the structure of the document, without looking at the data in the instance document. Another approach to this might have been to work through the instance document, removing any data from the document, and retaining only the structure of elements, attributes, and so on. That would provide you with a tree overview of the document's structure. Either way accomplishes the same goal, and is mostly a matter of personal preference.

Summarizing Components

To do lists can often be handy pieces of information. They allow you to keep track of what's been done and what remains. Similarly, it is a good idea to have lists of all the elements and all the attributes in our completed instance document.

This will allow us to double-check our schema, since we already know we will be working with a multipart Schema, to make sure that we have not left any elements or attributes undeclared.

So each of the following tables will serve as a visual list that you can use to cross off components as they are declared in the Schema, giving you a visual way of making sure that everything is properly defined. The order of the elements and attributes in these tables is roughly similar to that of the instance document, and the order that we will follow when we write the Schema.

The results of our summary are shown in Table 15.2 and Table 15.3.

TABLE 15.2   A SIMPLE SUMMARY OF ALL THE ELEMENTS TO BE DECLARED FOR OUR HR SCHEMA

Elements

employee	profile	name
DOB	spouse	child
SOC	title	supervisor
department	bonus	hire
salary	contact	home
termination	address	city
work	zip	phone
state	healthcare	plan
benefits	start_date	termination_date
provider	retirement	plan
maturity	options	personal_days
used	payroll_deduction	review
date	vacation	reviewer
goal	period	strength
weakness	responsibility	employee_comments
supervisor_comments	performance	next
raise	reviewer_comments	

TABLE 15.3   A SUMMARY OF ALL THE ATTRIBUTES TO BE DECLARED FOR OUR HR SCHEMA

Attributes

type (salary)	reason	date
type (phone)	allocation	used
remaining	status (review)	rate
status (goal)	status (responsibility)	

These tables will essentially function as "to-do" lists for us in Chapter 16, allowing us to cross each element and attribute off after we have declared it.

ESTABLISHING THE DATATYPES

Next, we need to take a look at how we will make use of datatypes in our Schema.

There are many types of data which we can utilize as datatypes, as we've seen in previous examples:

- dates
- phone numbers
- ZIP codes
- Social Security numbers
- currency

And, because we are dealing with names and text, we will likely have a lot of `strings` as well. So, the next step we take is to return to our template instance document, and walk through the document, listing each component and the datatype we'll use in conjunction with it.

At the same time, since we're walking through the instance document anyway, we're also going to make a note of what we think will be the best number of `minOccurs` and `maxOccurs` for each component. In doing so, we have to consider the needs of the particular organization. For example, in this organization, employees can only participate in up to three different areas, so we are limiting the number of `department`, `supervisor`, and `title` to a maximum of three. Similarly, this organization's review guidelines specify a minimum of three goals/responsibilities and a maximum of five. This is the way its performance reviews have been established in the past, and so we are retaining those conventions here. Of course, none of this is set in stone; however, chances are it will make the authoring process fly by if we already know this information.

The results of summarizing all of our datatypes are shown in Table 15.4.

TABLE 15.4   A LISTING OF ALL THE COMPONENTS FOR THE HR SCHEMA, ALONG WITH THEIR DATATYPES AND THEIR `minOccurs` AND `maxOccurs` USAGE

Name	Component	Datatype	minOccurs	maxOccurs
employee	root element	complex	n/a	n/a
profile	element	complex	1	1
name	element	string	1	1
DOB	element	date	1	1
SOC	element	social_security (derived)	1	1
spouse	element	string	0	1

TABLE 15.4   CONTINUED

Name	Component	Datatype	minOccurs	maxOccurs
child	element	string	0	unbounded
department	element	string	1	3
title	element	string	1	3
supervisor	element	string	1	3
salary	element	currency (derived)	1	1
bonus	element	currency (derived)	0	unbounded
hire	element	string (enumeration)	1	1
termination	element	string	0	1
contact	element	complex	1	1
home	element	complex	1	1
work	element	complex	1	1
address	element	string	1	3
city	element	string	1	1
state	element	state (enumeration)	1	1
zip	element	zip (derived)	1	1
phone	element	phone (derived)	1	4
benefits	element	complex	1	1
healthcare	element	complex	0	1
plan	element	string (enumeration)	1	1
provider	element	string (enumeration)	1	2
start_date	element	date	1	1
termination_date	element	date	0	1
options	element	string (enumeration)	0	6
retirement	element	complex	0	1
maturity	element	date	0	1
payroll_deduction	element	currency (derived)	0	1
personal_days	element	complex	1	1
used	element	integer	0	unbounded
vacation	element	complex	1	1

TABLE 15.4   CONTINUED

Name	Component	Datatype	minOccurs	maxOccurs
review	element	complex	0	unbounded
date	element	date	1	1
period	element	string	1	1
reviewer	element	string	1	1
goal	element	string	3	5
responsibility	element	string	3	5
strength	element	string	3	5
weakness	element	string	3	5
performance	element	string	1	1
employee_comments	element	string	1	1
supervisor_comments	element	string	1	1
reviewer_comments	element	string	1	1
next	element	date	1	1
raise	element	currency	0	1
type (salary)	attribute	enumeration	n/a	n/a (use=required)
reason (bonus)	attribute	string	n/a	n/a (use=required)
date	attribute	date	n/a	n/a (use=required)
type (phone)	attribute	enumeration	n/a	n/a (use=required)
allocation	attribute	integer	n/a	n/a (use=required)
used	attribute	integer	n/a	n/a (use=required)
remaining	attribute	integer	n/a	n/a (use=optional)
status (review)	attribute	enumeration	n/a	n/a (use=required)
status (goal)	attribute	enumeration	n/a	n/a (use=required)
status (responsibility)	attribute	enumeration	n/a	n/a (use=required)
rate	attribute	enumeration	n/a	n/a (use=required)

The majority of our types are strings, as predicted. However, aside from the complex element types we'll build from other elements, there are a few derived types we'll want to define on our own.

First, in the contact section, we will want to define datatypes for state abbreviations, ZIP Codes, and phone numbers. The state abbreviations we will define as an enumeration, as we did in Chapter 14, "Building Multipart Schema," (in fact, we could include those type definitions). The ZIP Codes, phone numbers, and Social Security numbers we will define as restrictions of strings, making use of pattern matching and regular expressions.

We also need to address several elements which will contain currency values, such as salary, raise, and so on. So we will need to define our own currency type, as a restriction of the decimal type.

Finally, there are a number of elements and attributes which we have defined as enumerations. These are components where the HR department has a limited number of choices for the values, and has asked us to restrict the possible values to those choices.

Just as with the state abbreviations, this is a good application for enumerations, so we'll make another list. This time, we list all of the components which are enumerations, as well as the acceptable values for those enumerations. This way, we can easily refer back to the data shown in Table 15.5 when we need to know what the possible values for a component are.

TABLE 15.5   A LISTING OF ALL THE COMPONENTS USING ENUMERATIONS, AND THE VALUE SET FOR THEIR ENUMERATIONS

Enumerated Component	Value Set
hire	probationary
	full-time
	part-time
	contract
state	All two-letter state abbreviations
plan (healthcare)	HMO
	PPO
	Managed
	Personal
provider	Blue Shield
	Ecma
	COBRA
	Providian
options	Dental, Optical, Maternity, Life, Disability, Orthodontic
plan (retirement)	401K, IRA, Stock Program

Table 15.5 Continued

Enumerated Component	Value Set
type *(salary)*	hourly
	monthly
	annually
type *(phone)*	primary
	cellular
	pager
	fax
status *(review)*	pending
	approved
status *(goal)*	met
	not-met
	future
status *(responsibility)*	current
	desired
rate *(raise)*	hourly
	monthly
	annually

Planning the Multiple Schema

All this information serves a useful purpose for planning our Schema. However, we still have to plan for the Schema themselves.

As we mentioned earlier in the chapter, the HR department wants a Schema design which can grow with it as its needs grow. This is a perfect application for modular Schema, especially since we might want to be able to create separate, standalone instance documents based on some of the information, such as benefits or reviews.

When we look at the instance document, we see a natural breakdown among the information, so we'll use that as the basis for our Schema documents. The main, master Schema will be employee.xsd, which will comprise four distinct Schema:

- profile.xsd—This Schema will define the profile information about the employee, but keep contact information separate, so that the profile can be viewed without releasing private information such as a home address.

- contact.xsd—This Schema will define the contact information for the employee, but should remain generic enough that it could be used in other Schema for vendors, and so forth. This is one reason the currency type will be defined here: because the contact Schema is the most portable.

- benefits.xsd—This Schema will be used to define the information about employee benefit programs. Currently, because the programs are small, it can all be contained in one Schema. However, in the future, this could be further modularized into healthcare.xsd and retirement.xsd Schema, and so on.

- review.xsd—This Schema will define the employee review information. It will also be structured so that the review can be used as a standalone XML instance document, to provide the capability for employees and supervisors to access reviews later as document fragments without accessing other confidential information.

This breakdown will allow maintenance work on one Schema, without impacting the others (with the exception of the employee.xsd Schema, which will always be affected). The results of the multiple document breakdown are shown in Table 15.6.

TABLE 15.6   A BREAKDOWN OF THE SCHEMA DOCUMENTS WHICH WILL BE USED TOGETHER TO DESCRIBE AN EMPLOYEE'S PERSONNEL FILE

Schema	Type Definitions	Elements	Attributes
profile.xsd	social_security	name	
		SOC	
		DOB	
		spouse	
		child	
		department	
		title	
		supervisor	
		salary	type
		bonus	reason
		hire	date
		termination	date
contact.xsd	phone_number	home	
	state	work	
	zip	address	
	currency	city	
		state	

TABLE 15.6   CONTINUED

Schema	Type Definitions	Elements	Attributes
		zip	
		phone	type
benefits.xsd	currency (include from contact.xsd)	benefits	
		healthcare	
		plan	
		provider	
		start_date	
		termination_date	
		options	
		retirement	
		plan	
		start_date	
		maturity	
		payroll_deduction	
	personal_days	allocation, used, remaining	
		used	date
	vacation	allocation, used, remaining	
review.xsd		review	status
		name (included from contact.xsd)	
		date	
		period	
		supervisor	
		reviewer	
		goal	status
		responsibility	status
		strength	
		weakness	
		training	
		performance	
		employee_comments	

TABLE 15.6   CONTINUED

Schema	Type Definitions	Elements	Attributes
		supervisor_comments	
		reviewer_comments	
		next	
		raise	rate
employee.xsd		profile	
		contact	
		benefits	
		review	

Now we have a complete set of templates which we can use to begin writing our Schema. We can reference each one of the tables we've created to give us detailed information about the component we're declaring. Table 15.6 will serve as our starting point, allowing us to map out our multiple Schema and be sure we include the correct declarations in each one.

CONCLUSIONS

As you can see, the planning stage for writing our Schema has consisted of making a lot of lists. However, now we have a complete understanding of the requirements for our Schema document and all of the definitions and declarations we will need to use in order to get there. This gives us a solid foundation for the next step: authoring. And hopefully, because of the groundwork we've laid out here, the authoring process will be simple and easy, just stepping through our lists.

To recap the process we've followed for planning our Schema in this chapter:

- Work closely with the people who will be your Schema's end-users, to ensure it meets their needs
- Create a reference XML instance document for building the Schema
- Create a structural view of the data, either as a table or tree
- Create a list of all the elements which need to be declared
- Create a list of all the attributes which need to be declared
- Chart the datatypes which will be used in your Schema, including datatypes you will need to derive
- Make a list of any enumerations or special value sets you will need to define
- Create a breakdown of your multiple Schema documents, including which definitions and declarations will be contained in each Schema document

Now, armed with all this planning, we're ready to write the schema. Chapter 16 details the Schema authoring process step by step.

IN THE REAL WORLD

A project such as this is likely to go through several incarnations before you finally arrive at a solution. In fact, this is a real-world example, actually still in the process of being developed for a small company which is just beginning to grow its human resources department. Many of the details have been changed slightly, however, to protect the internal data of the company.

One of the problems you will face in the real world, when trying to learn Schema by example, is that many internal Schema are just that: internal. They represent proprietary data that a company uses internally, and therefore, is not anxious to share with the outside world. This flies in the face of the goal of the Web and XML, which is to facilitate the sharing of structured data, but that is the reality of the world of corporate information technology. Knowledge management tools represent a competitive edge, and therefore, are usually held pretty close to the chest. Even though most of the actual data is stored in XML instance documents, many companies are hesitant to share any kind of internal documentation, and therefore, it can be hard to sometimes find real-world examples of Schema, other than open source or community standards projects, even though both can be excellent sources for learning about Schema.

The other hurdle you will face in the real world of Schema development is that the planning stage will never, under any circumstances, go as smoothly as is outlined in this chapter. Typically, the requirements of your Schema will change several times before you even start writing it, and then change several more times once you have begun. Unfortunately, to illustrate this effect, we'd have to walk you through the development of a schema, and then, 25 pages into the chapter, say "Oh, hold on a second. We actually don't want to do this at all, we really want to do that."

You will find that in planning most Schema the end-users of the Schema will provide valuable planning resources, but will then almost certainly ask for changes in your completed work. That is the real world, and no matter how satisfied you are with your Schema, or how proud you are of its elegance, you have to be ready to roll with the changes, since a Schema developed completely without user input is likely to be a Schema completely without users.

CHAPTER 16

BUILDING AND USING THE SCHEMA

In this chapter

GETTING STARTED

Armed with our careful planning from Chapter 15, "An Example Schema: Human Resources," we're ready to start assembling the definitions and declarations which will comprise our final `employee.xsd` Schema for the human resources department.

From time to time throughout this chapter we will be making references back to the tables contained in Chapter 15. Here's a summary of the information in those tables to refresh your memory:

- Table 15.1: A listing of the relationships between components for the XML instance document.
- Table 15.2: A summary of all the element components.
- Table 15.3: A summary of all the attribute components.
- Table 15.4: A complete listing of the components and their datatypes, as well as the `minOccurs` and `maxOccurs` for each element.
- Table 15.5: Enumerated components and their value sets.
- Table 15.6: Modular Schema breakdown by file.

Since this information will be our guide through the writing process, occasionally referencing these tables will be necessary. Now, on to the Schema.

THE MODULAR APPROACH

Taking a look at Table 15.6, we see how the individual files which are each going to serve as a module for our complete Schema are constructed. We have five schema in total:

- `profile.xsd`—The Schema defining the profile information about the employee, such as name, date of birth, and so forth.
- `contact.xsd`—The Schema defining contact information, such as address and phone number.
- `benefits.xsd`—The Schema defining the benefit programs offered by this particular company.
- `review.xsd`—The Schema outlining the employee review document.
- `employee.xsd`—The "glue" Schema which brings the four previous Schema into a complete, comprehensive employee human resources record.

So, let's start with the first Schema on our list: the `profile.xsd` Schema.

THE `profile.xsd` SCHEMA

By taking a look at the information in Table 15.6, we know the component definitions which we will need to include in the `profile.xsd` Schema. We need to declare one type, for Social Security numbers, and the remaining components are elements and attributes.

Table 15.4 outlines each component's datatype, minOccurs, and maxOccurs. Using that as our guideline, we can start right in with our components. First, we need to define our social_security type, which is simply a string. Because Social Security numbers are nine-digit numbers which all share the same "000-00-0000" format, we can use a regular expression to define a pattern for the SS number. If you recall from our earlier chapters on datatypes, using a regular expression as a pattern is part of a restriction, which means that our social_security type can be a restriction of a simpleType, the string datatype. That yields the following type definition:

```
<xs:simpleType name="social_security">
 <xs:restriction base="xs:string">
  <xs:pattern value="[0-9]{3}\-[0-9]{2}\-[0-9]{4}"/>
 </xs:restriction>
</xs:simpleType>
```

This type can now be applied to an element declaration in order to define the element's content as being of the social_security type. We see from the table that the SOC element will play that role, so it can be declared with a straightforward element declaration:

```
<xs:element name="SOC" type="social_security"/>
```

Looking through the listing of the components we're using, we find that the DOB element also has a straightforward declaration, based on the built-in primitive type date, so we can easily get that declaration out of the way as well:

```
<xs:element name="DOB" type="xs:date"/>
```

In this first section of the profile.xsd Schema, there are also a number of elements which are simple declarations based on the built-in string primitive type. Keep in mind that we are going to be building a parent element for these elements called profile later, which is why we are not defining the minOccurs and maxOccurs for these elements now. When we reference these element declarations later, we will specify the minOccurs and maxOccurs values. In the meantime, the declarations for the individual elements are

```
<xs:element name="name" type="xs:string"/>
<xs:element name="spouse" type="xs:string"/>
<xs:element name="child" type="xs:string"/>
<xs:element name="department" type="xs:string"/>
<xs:element name="title" type="xs:string"/>
<xs:element name="supervisor" type="xs:string"/>
```

Next, we have a series of element declarations which are a bit more involved. The first among these elements is the <salary> element, which we see from the table needs to be a currency type. But it also contains an attribute which specifies the salary type, and that attribute is an enumeration.

Because we want the attribute to be only used with the <salary> element, we'll declare the attribute locally within the element declaration. That way, it will be scoped locally and not accessible to other declarations or documents. The declaration looks like this:

```
<xs:element name="salary">
 <xs:complexType>
  <xs:simpleContent>
```

```
    <xs:extension base="contact:currency">
     <xs:attribute name="type">
      <xs:simpleType>
       <xs:restriction base="xs:string">
        <xs:enumeration value="hourly"/>
        <xs:enumeration value="monthly"/>
        <xs:enumeration value="annually"/>
       </xs:restriction>
      </xs:simpleType>
     </xs:attribute>
    </xs:extension>
   </xs:simpleContent>
  </xs:complexType>
</xs:element>
```

We start with the element declaration, naming our `salary` element, and defining that it will be a `complexType` containing `simpleContent`, and that it will be an extension (because we're adding the attribute) of the `currency` type. Now, you might have noticed that we have not defined a currency type yet. That's okay. The `currency` type is actually going to be defined in the `contact.xsd` file, which we will then `import` in this Schema later, giving us access to that type. Because the `contact.xsd` Schema will have its own namespace, though, we need to use the namespace prefix here, in order to correctly identify the `currency` type as belonging to the `http://www.myserver.com/Contact` namespace.

Finally, we declare the attribute. Because it is an enumeration, it is a restriction of the `string` type, and we then make use of the `<enumeration>` information item to define each of the possible enumeration values (looked up from Table 15.5).

Next, we have a similar declaration for the `<bonus>` element, with the primary difference being that the `reason` attribute for the element is not an enumeration. So we start the declaration in the same manner, but when we get to the attribute declaration, we can use a simple declaration, declaring the `reason` attribute to be a `string` type:

```
<xs:element name="bonus">
 <xs:complexType>
  <xs:simpleContent>
   <xs:extension base="contact:currency">
    <xs:attribute name="reason" type="xs:string"/>
   </xs:extension>
  </xs:simpleContent>
 </xs:complexType>
</xs:element>
```

Next, we have the `<hire>` element, which is a little different because this element itself is an enumeration. That means we start off with a typical element declaration, with a `complexType` and `complexContent`. However, we have to define that the element is a restriction of the `string` type, and then specify those possible enumeration values as we did for the attribute earlier.

Once we close the restriction, we can move on to the attribute declaration for the `<hire>` element, which is a straightforward attribute declaration based on the `date` type:

```
<xs:element name="hire">
 <xs:complexType>
```

```
 <xs:complexContent>
  <xs:restriction base="xs:string">
  <enumeration value="probationary"/>
  <enumeration value="fill-time"/>
  <enumeration value="part-time"/>
  <enumeration value="contract"/>
  </xs:restriction>
   <xs:attribute name="date" type="xs:date"/>
 </xs:complexContent>
 </xs:complexType>
</xs:element>
```

For the <termination> element, we don't need to worry about an enumeration, and we only have one attribute, which is a date:

```
<xs:element name="termination">
 <xs:complexType>
  <xs:simpleContent>
   <xs:extension base="xs:string">
    <xs:attribute name="date" type="xs:date"/>
   </xs:extension>
  </xs:simpleContent>
 </xs:complexType>
</xs:element>
```

Now, with all of our elements and attributes declared, we're ready to bring together everything into our <profile> element, which will serve as the parent element for the employee profile information. Because we've already declared all of the child elements, when we add them to the profile declaration, we will do so by reference. This is also where we will make use of Table 15.4 again, to specify the minOccurs and maxOccurs for each element, should they deviate from the default values of "1".

Here's what the <profile> element declaration looks like:

```
<xs:element name="profile">
 <xs:complexType>
  <xs:complexContent>
   <xs:sequence>
    <xs:element ref="name"/>
    <xs:element ref="SOC"/>
    <xs:element ref="DOB"/>
    <xs:element ref="spouse" minOccurs="0"/>
    <xs:element ref="child" minOccurs="0" maxOccurs="unbounded"/>
    <xs:element ref="department" maxOccurs="3"/>
    <xs:element ref="title" maxOccurs="3"/>
    <xs:element ref="supervisor" maxOccurs="3"/>
    <xs:element ref="salary"/>
    <xs:element ref="bonus"/>
    <xs:element ref="hire"/>
    <xs:element ref="termination" minOccurs="0"/>
   </xs:sequence>
  </xs:complexContent>
 </xs:complexType>
</xs:element>
```

Finally, to bring the entire Schema together, we need to wrap it all in a `<schema>` element. Because we are going to `include` this Schema into the `employee.xsd` schema later, we know that we don't want to complicate the `include` process by defining a target namespace. So we can declare the XML Schema and XML Instance namespaces, but leave out a default namespace for the document.

Caution

> Although we are choosing not to define a `targetNamespace` for our Schema in this example, we are only doing so because these Schema are being designed to be used in an internal environment only, where we can keep a better eye on possible namespace clashes. If we were intending these Schema for use by any other organization, or other application, a `targetNamespace` should be declared.

Also, if you recall from earlier in this section, we are making use of the `currency` type which will be defined in the `contact.xsd` Schema, so we need to `import` the `contact.xsd` Schema within this Schema. We have to use the import mechanism here, because the `contact.xsd` Schema makes use of a different namespace than our `profile.xsd` Schema:

When we combine all of our declarations together into the final `profile.xsd` Schema, together with an annotation which lets readers know the purpose of this Schema, the results are as shown in Listing 16.1.

LISTING 16.1   THE COMPLETE CODE LISTING FOR THE `profile.xsd` XML SCHEMA

```
<?xml version="1.0" encoding="UTF-8" ?>
<xs:schema xmlns:xs="http://www.w3.org/2001/XMLSchema"
    xmlns:xsi="http://www.w3.org/2001/XMLSchema-Instance"
    xmlns:contact="http://www.myserver.com/Contact"
    xmlns="http://www.w3.org/2001/XMLSchema">
<xs:annotation>
 <xs:documentation xml:lang="en">
  A sample XML Schema for a Human Resources modular schema.
  This is the "profile.xsd" schema for employee profile information.
 </xs:documentation>
</xs:annotation>

<import namespace="http://www.myserver.com/Contact"
    schemaLocation="http://www.myserver.com/contact.xsd"/>


<xs:element name="profile">
 <xs:complexType>
  <xs:complexContent>
   <xs:sequence>
    <xs:element ref="name"/>
    <xs:element ref="SOC"/>
    <xs:element ref="DOB"/>
    <xs:element ref="spouse" minOccurs="0"/>
    <xs:element ref="child" minOccurs="0" maxOccurs="unbounded"/>
    <xs:element ref="department" maxOccurs="3"/>
    <xs:element ref="title" maxOccurs="3"/>
```

LISTING 16.1 CONTINUED

```
      <xs:element ref="supervisor" maxOccurs="3"/>
      <xs:element ref="salary"/>
      <xs:element ref="bonus"/>
      <xs:element ref="hire"/>
      <xs:element ref="termination" minOccurs="0"/>
    </xs:sequence>
  </xs:complexContent>
 </xs:complexType>
</xs:element>

<xs:simpleType name="social_security">
 <xs:restriction base="xs:string">
  <xs:pattern value="[0-9]{3}\-[0-9]{2}\-[0-9]{4}"/>
 </xs:restriction>
</xs:simpleType>

<xs:element name="name" type="xs:string"/>
<xs:element name="SOC" type="social_security"/>
<xs:element name="DOB" type="xs:date"/>
<xs:element name="spouse" type="xs:string"/>
<xs:element name="child" type="xs:string"/>
<xs:element name="department" type="xs:string"/>
<xs:element name="title" type="xs:string"/>
<xs:element name="supervisor" type="xs:string"/>

<xs:element name="salary">
 <xs:complexType>
  <xs:simpleContent>
   <xs:extension base="contact:currency">
    <xs:attribute name="type">
     <xs:simpleType>
      <xs:restriction base="xs:string">
       <xs:enumeration value="hourly"/>
       <xs:enumeration value="monthly"/>
       <xs:enumeration value="annually"/>
      </xs:restriction>
     </xs:simpleType>
    </xs:attribute>
   </xs:extension>
  </xs:simpleContent>
 </xs:complexType>
</xs:element>

<xs:element name="bonus">
 <xs:complexType>
  <xs:simpleContent>
   <xs:extension base="contact:currency">
    <xs:attribute name="reason" type="xs:string"/>
   </xs:extension>
  </xs:simpleContent>
 </xs:complexType>
</xs:element>

<xs:element name="hire">
 <xs:complexType>
```

PART
IV

CH
16

LISTING 16.1 CONTINUED

```
  <xs:complexContent>
   <xs:restriction base="xs:string">
   <enumeration value="probationary"/>
   <enumeration value="fill-time"/>
   <enumeration value="part-time"/>
   <enumeration value="contract"/>
   </xs:restriction>
    <xs:attribute name="date" type="xs:date"/>
  </xs:complexContent>
 </xs:complexType>
</xs:element>

<xs:element name="termination">
 <xs:complexType>
  <xs:simpleContent>
   <xs:extension base="xs:string">
    <xs:attribute name="date" type="xs:date"/>
   </xs:extension>
  </xs:simpleContent>
 </xs:complexType>
</xs:element>

</xs:schema>
```

THE `contact.xsd` SCHEMA

The next Schema we need to write is the `contact.xsd` Schema. The `contact.xsd` Schema is a perfect example of how in Schema authoring you will often find it easier to reuse components than to write them from scratch.

We've worked with contact information many times throughout this book, and in fact, many of the declarations we are going to use here we already defined in other chapters.

In this case, because we are working with an example of limited scope, we are going to "cut and paste" some of these declarations from other chapters. However, if we were working on an organizational level, what we would really need to do would be to coordinate the Schema between all of the departments making use of them.

However, for now we won't reinvent the wheel. So, if you recall from Chapter 14, "Building Multipart Schema," we had developed a type for U.S. State abbreviations, which was an enumeration that contained all of the possible abbreviations:

```
<xs:simpleType name="state">
 <xs:restriction base="xs:string">
  <xs:enumeration value="AL"/>        <!-- Alabama -->
  <!-- Etc... etc... -->
  <xs:enumeration value="WY"/>        <!-- Wyoming -->
 </xs:restriction>
</xs:simpleType>
```

That works perfectly for our needs here as well. So does the `zip` type we defined, which uses regular expressions to format ZIP Codes as either their five-digit form, or the ZIP+4 form:

```xml
<xs:simpleType name="zip">
 <xs:restriction base="xs:string">
  <xs:pattern value="[0-9]{5}(\-)?([0-9]{4})?"/>
 </xs:restriction>
</xs:simpleType>
```

And of course, we can bring these elements together to form the basis of a USaddress type, which will create a type for address information relative to the U.S.:

```xml
<xs:complexType name="USaddress">
 <xs:sequence>
  <xs:element name="address" type="xs:string" minOccurs="1" maxOccurs="3"/>
  <xs:element name="city" type="xs:string"/>
  <xs:element name="state" type="state"/>
  <xs:element name="zip" type="zip"/>
 </xs:sequence>
</xs:complexType>
```

But our reuse of types doesn't stop there. Remember when we defined a type for phone numbers, to match the 10-digit U.S. phone number? Here it is again:

```xml
<xs:simpleType name="phone_number">
 <xs:restriction base="xs:string">
  <xs:pattern value="[0-9]{3}\-[0-9]{3}\-[0-9]{4}"/>
 </xs:restriction>
</xs:simpleType>
```

And finally, we need to define that currency type we used in our profile.xsd file. That too has appeared as an example earlier in this title:

```xml
<xs:simpleType name="currency">
 <xs:restriction base="xs:decimal">
  <xs:fractionDigits value="2"/>
 </xs:restriction>
</xs:simpleType>
```

As you can see, reusing previously defined types has allowed us to rocket through this Schema. However, even though we're cutting and pasting from other chapters, if we were working in an organization which had already developed a contact Schema, we would be smarter just to include that Schema here. Cutting and pasting, though, means that we now have to maintain these elements. For example, if our organization already had a Schema with all of these components declared, and we just cut and pasted them into our Schema, we wouldn't know it if the original document were updated. That's why in general it's much better to include and import previously defined components.

Now, we do have one specialized component which we are altering significantly from our previous definitions. That is the <phone> element. In this contact Schema, the phone element will have its base type as the phone_number type declared earlier, but we are also giving it a required attribute called type, which will be used to denote what type of phone number is listed, such as a pager number, cell, and so on.

So, we start with the element declaration, and then extend the base phone_number type with an attribute declaration for type. You might be wondering how we can use the name "type" here for this attribute, since there is already an attribute called type. Well, remember that we do not have a targetNamespace, and also that the Schema syntax has its own namespace. So actually, the type attribute we use to declare a datatype exists in a separate namespace (xs:type) than the phone number type we are currently defining. The phone number type is also an enumeration, so we grab the values from Table 15.5, and the final declaration looks like this:

```
<xs:element name="phone">
 <xs:complexType>
  <xs:complexContent>
   <xs:extension base="phone_number">
    <xs:attribute name="type" use="required">
     <xs:simpleType>
      <xs:restriction base="xs:string">
       <xs:enumeration value="primary"/>
       <xs:enumeration value="cellular"/>
       <xs:enumeration value="fax"/>
       <xs:enumeration value="pager"/>
      </xs:restriction>
     </xs:simpleType>
    </xs:attribute>
   </xs:extension>
  </xs:complexContent>
 </xs:complexType>
</xs:element>
```

We have two types of contact information for our human resources needs: home contact information and work contact information. So we bring together our address redefinitions and phone definitions with two new elements, <home> and <work>:

```
<xs:element name="home">
 <xs:complexType>
  <xs:complexContent>
   <xs:extension base="USaddress">
    <xs:element ref="phone" maxOccurs="4"/>
   </xs:extension>
  </xs:complexContent>
 </xs:complexType>
</xs:element>

<xs:element name="work">
 <xs:complexType>
  <xs:complexContent>
   <xs:extension base="USaddress">
    <xs:element ref="phone" maxOccurs="4"/>
   </xs:extension>
  </xs:complexContent>
 </xs:complexType>
</xs:element>
```

Here we've also specified our minOccurs and maxOccurs for the elements, to give us complete elements we can use for home contact information and work contact information. Now, unlike with the <profile> element, we are *not* going to create a wrapper contact element for this Schema. The reason is that we want this Schema to be portable within our organization, so that all of these elements can be reused (without cutting and pasting!) by other departments. So we will take care of the <contact> element in the employee.xsd file, so that the contact section we define will only be local to human resources.

Now we're ready for the <schema> element. With the contact.xsd Schema, we are creating a Schema which we know will be reused, and which is a good candidate for sharing with outside entities, such as healthcare providers, payroll companies, and so on. Because we might want to distribute this Schema, it makes sense to place it in its own namespace, so in the <schema> element, we declare a targetNamespace and a default namespace for the contact.xsd Schema:

```
<?xml version="1.0" encoding="UTF-8" ?>
<xs:schema xmlns:xs="http://www.w3.org/2001/XMLSchema"
    xmlns:xsi="http://www.w3.org/2001/XMLSchema-Instance"
    targetNamespace="http://www.myserver.com/Contact"
    xmlns="http://www.myserver.com/Contact">

</xs:schema>
```

We bring this all together into the resulting contact.xsd Schema, as shown in Listing 16.2.

LISTING 16.2   THE COMPLETE CODE LISTING FOR THE contact.xsd XML SCHEMA

```
<?xml version="1.0" encoding="UTF-8" ?>
<xs:schema xmlns:xs="http://www.w3.org/2001/XMLSchema"
    xmlns:xsi="http://www.w3.org/2001/XMLSchema-Instance"
    targetNamespace="http://www.myserver.com/Contact"
    xmlns="http://www.myserver.com/Contact">

<xs:annotation>
 <xs:documentation xml:lang="en">
  A sample XML Schema for a Human Resources modular schema.
  This is the "contacts.xsd" schema for employee contact information.
 </xs:documentation>
</xs:annotation>

<xs:element name="home">
 <xs:complexType>
  <xs:complexContent>
   <xs:extension base="USaddress">
    <xs:element ref="phone" maxOccurs="4"/>
   </xs:extension>
  </xs:complexContent>
 </xs:complexType>
</xs:element>

<xs:element name="work">
 <xs:complexType>
  <xs:complexContent>
   <xs:extension base="USaddress">
    <xs:element ref="phone" maxOccurs="4"/>
   </xs:extension>
  </xs:complexContent>
 </xs:complexType>
</xs:element>

<xs:element name="phone">
 <xs:complexType>
  <xs:complexContent>
```

LISTING 16.2 CONTINUED

```
  <xs:extension base="phone_number">
   <xs:attribute name="type" use="required">
    <xs:simpleType>
     <xs:restriction base="xs:string">
      <xs:enumeration value="primary"/>
      <xs:enumeration value="cellular"/>
      <xs:enumeration value="fax"/>
      <xs:enumeration value="pager"/>
     </xs:restriction>
    </xs:simpleType>
   </xs:attribute>
  </xs:extension>
 </xs:complexContent>
</xs:complexType>
</xs:element>

<xs:complexType name="USaddress">
 <xs:sequence>
  <xs:element name="address" type="xs:string" minOccurs="1" maxOccurs="3"/>
  <xs:element name="city" type="xs:string"/>
  <xs:element name="state" type="state"/>
  <xs:element name="zip" type="zip"/>
 </xs:sequence>
</xs:complexType>

<xs:simpleType name="state">
 <xs:restriction base="xs:string">
  <xs:enumeration value="AL"/>       <!-- Alabama -->
  <xs:enumeration value="AK"/>       <!-- Alaska -->
  <xs:enumeration value="AZ"/>       <!-- Arizona -->
  <xs:enumeration value="AR"/>       <!-- Arkansas -->
  <xs:enumeration value="CA"/>       <!-- California -->
  <xs:enumeration value="CO"/>       <!-- Colorado -->
  <xs:enumeration value="CT"/>       <!-- Connecticut -->
  <xs:enumeration value="DE"/>       <!-- Delaware -->
  <xs:enumeration value="FL"/>       <!-- Florida -->
  <xs:enumeration value="GA"/>       <!-- Georgia -->
  <xs:enumeration value="HI"/>       <!-- Hawaii -->
  <xs:enumeration value="ID"/>       <!-- Idaho -->
  <xs:enumeration value="IL"/>       <!-- Illinois -->
  <xs:enumeration value="IN"/>       <!-- Indiana -->
  <xs:enumeration value="IA"/>       <!-- Iowa -->
  <xs:enumeration value="KS"/>       <!-- Kansas -->
  <xs:enumeration value="KY"/>       <!-- Kentucky -->
  <xs:enumeration value="LA"/>       <!-- Louisiana -->
  <xs:enumeration value="ME"/>       <!-- Maine -->
  <xs:enumeration value="MD"/>       <!-- Maryland -->
  <xs:enumeration value="MA"/>       <!-- Massachusetts -->
  <xs:enumeration value="MI"/>       <!-- Michigan -->
  <xs:enumeration value="MN"/>       <!-- Minnesota -->
  <xs:enumeration value="MS"/>       <!-- Mississippi -->
  <xs:enumeration value="MO"/>       <!-- Missouri -->
  <xs:enumeration value="MT"/>       <!-- Montana -->
  <xs:enumeration value="NE"/>       <!-- Nebraska -->
  <xs:enumeration value="NV"/>       <!-- Nevada -->
```

LISTING 16.2   CONTINUED

```
   <xs:enumeration value="NH"/>    <!-- New Hampshire -->
   <xs:enumeration value="NJ"/>    <!-- New Jersey -->
   <xs:enumeration value="NM"/>    <!-- New Mexico -->
   <xs:enumeration value="NY"/>    <!-- New York -->
   <xs:enumeration value="NC"/>    <!-- North Carolina -->
   <xs:enumeration value="ND"/>    <!-- North Dakota -->
   <xs:enumeration value="OH"/>    <!-- Ohio -->
   <xs:enumeration value="OK"/>    <!-- Oklahoma -->
   <xs:enumeration value="OR"/>    <!-- Oregon -->
   <xs:enumeration value="PA"/>    <!-- Pennsylvania -->
   <xs:enumeration value="RI"/>    <!-- Rhode Island -->
   <xs:enumeration value="SC"/>    <!-- South Carolina -->
   <xs:enumeration value="SD"/>    <!-- South Dakota -->
   <xs:enumeration value="TN"/>    <!-- Tennessee -->
   <xs:enumeration value="TX"/>    <!-- Texas -->
   <xs:enumeration value="UT"/>    <!-- Utah -->
   <xs:enumeration value="VT"/>    <!-- Vermont -->
   <xs:enumeration value="VA"/>    <!-- Virginia -->
   <xs:enumeration value="WA"/>    <!-- Washington -->
   <xs:enumeration value="DC"/>    <!-- Washington,D.C. -->
   <xs:enumeration value="WV"/>    <!-- West Virginia -->
   <xs:enumeration value="WI"/>    <!-- Wisconsin -->
   <xs:enumeration value="WY"/>    <!-- Wyoming -->
  </xs:restriction>
 </xs:simpleType>

<xs:simpleType name="zip">
 <xs:restriction base="xs:string">
  <xs:pattern value="[0-9]{5}(\-)?([0-9]{4})?"/>
 </xs:restriction>
</xs:simpleType>

<xs:simpleType name="phone_number">
 <xs:restriction base="xs:string">
  <xs:pattern value="[0-9]{3}\-[0-9]{3}\-[0-9]{4}"/>
 </xs:restriction>
</xs:simpleType>

<xs:simpleType name="currency">
 <xs:restriction base="xs:decimal">
  <xs:fractionDigits value="2"/>
 </xs:restriction>
</xs:simpleType>

</xs:schema>
```

THE benefits.xsd SCHEMA

The most restrictive Schema we're going to develop in this exercise is the benefits.xsd
Schema. You'll notice that in this Schema, we're going to declare a number of components
locally, with no exposure for including or importing. That's because, as we mentioned in the
outline for the project in Chapter 15, this is the least-well-defined area for human resources.

As a small company, the HR benefits to this point have been minimal, and as the company grows things are changing rapidly. So as things change, this Schema will likely undergo many changes. Therefore, not exposing many of the elements will prevent other users from using components outside of the benefits context which are likely to be changed. This provides some protection from building new Schema based on the benefits.xsd Schema, but users can still use the elements from this schema in their instance documents. Of course, as this Schema evolves, those instance documents will need to be revised along with it, which is an issue to consider when working with legacy data.

So, we start this Schema with a complicated declaration for the <healthcare> element:

```
<xs:element name="healthcare">
 <xs:complexType>
  <xs:complexContent>
   <xs:element name="plan">
    <xs:simpleType>
     <xs:restriction base="xs:string">
      <xs:enumeration value="HMO"/>
      <xs:enumeration value="PPO"/>
      <xs:enumeration value="Managed"/>
      <xs:enumeration value="Personal"/>
     </xs:restriction>
    </xs:simpleType>
   </xs:element>
   <xs:element name="provider">
    <xs:simpleType>
     <xs:restriction base="xs:string">
      <xs:enumeration value="Blue Shield"/>
      <xs:enumeration value="Ecma"/>
      <xs:enumeration value="COBRA"/>
      <xs:enumeration value="Providian"/>
     </xs:restriction>
    </xs:simpleType>
   </xs:element>
   <xs:element name="start_date" type="xs:date"/>
   <xs:element name="termination_date" type="xs:date"/>
   <xs:element name="options">
    <xs:simpleType>
     <xs:restriction base="xs:string">
      <xs:enumeration value="Dental"/>
      <xs:enumeration value="Optical"/>
      <xs:enumeration value="Maternity"/>
      <xs:enumeration value="Life"/>
      <xs:enumeration value="Disability"/>
      <xs:enumeration value="Orthodontic"/>
     </xs:restriction>
    </xs:simpleType>
   </xs:element>
  </xs:complexContent>
 </xs:complexType>
</xs:element>
```

While on the surface, this declaration looks complicated due to the amount of information, examine it a little more closely. You will notice that it is actually composed of a number of smaller, more manageable declarations, which have been nested here so that they are scoped locally.

We start out by declaring that the `<healthcare>` element will be a `complexType`, with `complexContent`. But then we simply are inserting another declaration for the `<plan>` element, which is just an enumeration with the values outlined in Table 15.5:

```
<xs:element name="plan">
 <xs:simpleType>
  <xs:restriction base="xs:string">
   <xs:enumeration value="HMO"/>
   <xs:enumeration value="PPO"/>
   <xs:enumeration value="Managed"/>
   <xs:enumeration value="Personal"/>
  </xs:restriction>
 </xs:simpleType>
</xs:element>
```

Next, we have another simple enumeration, this time for the `<provider>` element, also just based on a restriction of the `string` type, with enumeration values specified limiting the value set for the element:

```
<xs:element name="provider">
 <xs:simpleType>
  <xs:restriction base="xs:string">
   <xs:enumeration value="Blue Shield"/>
   <xs:enumeration value="Ecma"/>
   <xs:enumeration value="COBRA"/>
   <xs:enumeration value="Providian"/>
  </xs:restriction>
 </xs:simpleType>
</xs:element>
```

Next, we have two very straightforward element declarations, both for date information, the `<start_date>` and the `<termination_date>` elements:

```
<xs:element name="start_date" type="xs:date"/>
<xs:element name="termination_date" type="xs:date"/>
```

Then, to round out the seemingly complicated `<healthcare>` declaration, we finish with another element that is an enumeration, and a restriction of the `string` type:

```
<xs:element name="options">
 <xs:simpleType>
  <xs:restriction base="xs:string">
   <xs:enumeration value="Dental"/>
   <xs:enumeration value="Optical"/>
   <xs:enumeration value="Maternity"/>
   <xs:enumeration value="Life"/>
   <xs:enumeration value="Disability"/>
   <xs:enumeration value="Orthodontic"/>
  </xs:restriction>
 </xs:simpleType>
</xs:element>
```

Next, we have a similar situation with the `<retirement>` element declaration:

```
<xs:element name="retirement">
 <xs:complexType>
  <xs:complexContent>
   <xs:element name="plan">
```

```
  <xs:simpleType>
   <xs:restriction base="xs:string">
    <xs:enumeration value="401K"/>
    <xs:enumeration value="IRA"/>
    <xs:enumeration value="Stock Program"/>
   </xs:restriction>
  </xs:simpleType>
 </xs:element>
 <xs:element name="start_date" type="xs:date"/>
 <xs:element name="maturity" type="xs:date"/>
 <xs:element name="payroll_deduction" type="contact:currency"/>
  </xs:complexContent>
 </xs:complexType>
</xs:element>
```

A close examination of the declaration will reveal that it is simply a nesting of simpler declarations, beginning with an enumeration for the <plan> element, and then followed by three very straightforward element declarations for <start_date>, <maturity>, and <payroll_deduction>. You'll also notice that we make use of the currency type here as well, which means we will need to be importing the contact.xsd Schema in order to access that datatype.

After those lengthy declarations, we can declare the <used> element, which will be a date, and the allocation, used, and remaining attributes, all of which will be used for personal days and vacation time:

```
<xs:element name="used" type="xs:date"/>
<xs:attribute name="allocation" type="xs:integer"/>
<xs:attribute name="used" type="xs:integer"/>
<xs:attribute name="remaining" type="xs:integer"/>
```

We can now use the <used> element declaration and the attributes in the declarations for <personal_days> and <vacation>, both of which take on a virtually identical structure, with the key difference being in the maxOccurs for the <used> element in each, since employees are allotted 5 personal days, and a maximum of 21 vacation days:

```
<xs:element name="personal_days">
 <xs:complexType>
  <xs:complexContent>
  <xs:element ref="used" minOccurs="0" maxOccurs="5"/>
  <xs:attribute ref="allocation"/>
  <xs:attribute ref="used"/>
  <xs:attribute ref="remaining"/>
  </xs:complexContent>
 </xs:complexType>
</xs:element>

<xs:element name="vacation">
 <xs:complexType>
  <xs:complexContent>
  <xs:element ref="used" minOccurs="0" maxOccurs="21"/>
  <xs:attribute ref="allocation"/>
  <xs:attribute ref="used"/>
  <xs:attribute ref="remaining"/>
```

```
    </xs:complexContent>
  </xs:complexType>
</xs:element>
```

The <schema> element for this one will look familiar as well. There will be no
targetNamespace declared, so reuse will be simplified, and we also need to import the
contact.xsd Schema in order to access the currency type:

```
<?xml version="1.0" encoding="UTF-8" ?>
<xs:schema xmlns:xs="http://www.w3.org/2001/XMLSchema"
    xmlns:xsi="http://www.w3.org/2001/XMLSchema-Instance"
    xmlns:contact="http://www.myserver.com/Contact">

<import namespace="http://www.myserver.com/Contact"
    schemaLocation="http://www.myserver.com/contact.xsd"/>

</xs:schema>
```

We now bring it all together into the complete code for the benefits.xsd Schema, as shown
in Listing 16.3.

LISTING 16.3 THE COMPLETE CODE LISTING FOR THE benefits.xsd XML SCHEMA

```
<?xml version="1.0" encoding="UTF-8" ?>
<xs:schema xmlns:xs="http://www.w3.org/2001/XMLSchema"
    xmlns:xsi="http://www.w3.org/2001/XMLSchema-Instance"
    xmlns:contact="http://www.myserver.com/Contact">


<xs:annotation>
 <xs:documentation xml:lang="en">
  A sample XML Schema for a Human Resources modular schema.
  This is the "benefits.xsd" schema for employee benefit information.
 </xs:documentation>
</xs:annotation>

<import namespace="http://www.myserver.com/Contact"
    schemaLocation="http://www.myserver.com/contact.xsd"/>


<xs:element name="benefits">
 <xs:complexType>
  <xs:complexContent>
   <xs:element ref="healthcare"/>
   <xs:element ref="retirement"/>
   <xs:element ref="personal_days"/>
   <xs:element ref="vacation"/>
  </xs:complexContent>
 </xs:complexType>
</xs:element>

<xs:element name="healthcare">
 <xs:complexType>
  <xs:complexContent>
   <xs:element name="plan">
    <xs:simpleType>
```

LISTING 16.3 CONTINUED

```
     <xs:restriction base="xs:string">
      <xs:enumeration value="HMO"/>
      <xs:enumeration value="PPO"/>
      <xs:enumeration value="Managed"/>
      <xs:enumeration value="Personal"/>
     </xs:restriction>
    </xs:simpleType>
   </xs:element>
   <xs:element name="provider">
    <xs:simpleType>
     <xs:restriction base="xs:string">
      <xs:enumeration value="Blue Shield"/>
      <xs:enumeration value="Ecma"/>
      <xs:enumeration value="COBRA"/>
      <xs:enumeration value="Providian"/>
     </xs:restriction>
    </xs:simpleType>
   </xs:element>
   <xs:element name="start_date" type="xs:date"/>
   <xs:element name="termination_date" type="xs:date"/>
   <xs:element name="options">
    <xs:simpleType>
     <xs:restriction base="xs:string">
      <xs:enumeration value="Dental"/>
      <xs:enumeration value="Optical"/>
      <xs:enumeration value="Maternity"/>
      <xs:enumeration value="Life"/>
      <xs:enumeration value="Disability"/>
      <xs:enumeration value="Orthodontic"/>
     </xs:restriction>
    </xs:simpleType>
   </xs:element>
  </xs:complexContent>
 </xs:complexType>
</xs:element>

<xs:element name="retirement">
 <xs:complexType>
  <xs:complexContent>
   <xs:element name="plan">
    <xs:simpleType>
     <xs:restriction base="xs:string">
      <xs:enumeration value="401K"/>
      <xs:enumeration value="IRA"/>
      <xs:enumeration value="Stock Program"/>
     </xs:restriction>
    </xs:simpleType>
   </xs:element>
   <xs:element name="start_date" type="xs:date"/>
   <xs:element name="maturity" type="xs:date"/>
   <xs:element name="payroll_deduction" type="contact:currency"/>
  </xs:complexContent>
 </xs:complexType>
</xs:element>
```

LISTING 16.3 CONTINUED

```
<xs:element name="personal_days">
 <xs:complexType>
  <xs:complexContent>
  <xs:element ref="used" minOccurs="0" maxOccurs="5"/>
  <xs:attribute ref="allocation"/>
  <xs:attribute ref="used"/>
  <xs:attribute ref="remaining"/>
  </xs:complexContent>
 </xs:complexType>
</xs:element>

<xs:element name="vacation">
 <xs:complexType>
  <xs:complexContent>
  <xs:element ref="used" minOccurs="0" maxOccurs="21"/>
  <xs:attribute ref="allocation"/>
  <xs:attribute ref="used"/>
  <xs:attribute ref="remaining"/>
  </xs:complexContent>
 </xs:complexType>
</xs:element>

<xs:element name="used" type="xs:date"/>
<xs:attribute name="allocation" type="xs:integer"/>
<xs:attribute name="used" type="xs:integer"/>
<xs:attribute name="remaining" type="xs:integer"/>

</xs:schema>
```

THE review.xsd SCHEMA

The review.xsd Schema will be designed to define information relating to an employee review document which was developed by HR. Turning back to Tables 15.4 and 15.6, we can start in on the element declarations for the Schema. We know that we will link the review document to the employee and supervisor by name, so we know that we will need to include the profile.xsd Schema. But there are also a number of very straightforward element declarations.

We start with the declarations for <date> and <next>, both of which are date types:

```
<xs:element name="date" type="xs:date"/>
<xs:element name="next" type="xs:date"/>
```

Next, there are a number of elements which are based on the string type:

```
<xs:element name="period" type="xs:string"/>
<xs:element name="reviewer" type="xs:string"/>
<xs:element name="strength" type="xs:string"/>
<xs:element name="weakness" type="xs:string"/>
<xs:element name="training" type="xs:string"/>
<xs:element name="performance" type="xs:string"/>
<xs:element name="employee_comments" type="xs:string"/>
<xs:element name="supervisor_comments" type="xs:string"/>
<xs:element name="reviewer_comments" type="xs:string"/>
```

With that series of "one-liner" element declarations, the bulk of our element declarations are done. The next two declarations will take a very similar form:

```
<xs:element name="goal">
 <xs:complexType>
  <xs:complexContent>
   <xs:extension base="xs:string">
    <xs:attribute name="status" use="required">
     <xs:simpleType>
      <xs:restriction base="xs:string">
       <xs:enumeration value="met"/>
       <xs:enumeration value="not-met"/>
       <xs:enumeration value="future"/>
      </xs:restriction>
     </xs:simpleType>
    </xs:attribute>
   </xs:extension>
  </xs:complexContent>
 </xs:complexType>
</xs:element>
```

The declaration starts by naming the element, and specifying `complexType` and `complexContent`. The element itself will contain a `string`, but is an extension of the `string` type, since it will contain an attribute. The attribute declaration is an enumeration which is a restriction of the `string` type, and the enumeration values are looked up in Table 15.5. The result is our declaration for the `<goal>` element, with a `status` attribute which can have a value of `"met"`, `"not-met"`, or `"future"`.

The `<responsibility>` element takes on nearly the exact same form, with only the element name and the enumeration values changed:

```
<xs:element name="responsibility">
 <xs:complexType>
  <xs:complexContent>
   <xs:extension base="xs:string">
    <xs:attribute name="status" use="required">
     <xs:simpleType>
      <xs:restriction base="xs:string">
       <xs:enumeration value="current"/>
       <xs:enumeration value="desired"/>
      </xs:restriction>
     </xs:simpleType>
    </xs:attribute>
   </xs:extension>
  </xs:complexContent>
 </xs:complexType>
</xs:element>
```

The `<raise>` element also follows this same pattern, adding an attribute with an enumeration as part of the declaration. However, the base for the extension in this declaration is `currency`, which you might recall was defined in the `contact.xsd` Schema. This isn't a problem, as long as we are sure to `<include>` the contact Schema into the review Schema when we write the Schema headers:

```
<xs:element name="raise">
 <xs:complexType>
  <xs:complexContent>
   <xs:extension base="currency">
    <xs:attribute name="rate" use="required">
     <xs:simpleType>
      <xs:restriction base="xs:string">
       <xs:enumeration value="hourly"/>
       <xs:enumeration value="monthly"/>
       <xs:enumeration value="annually"/>
      </xs:restriction>
     </xs:simpleType>
    </xs:attribute>
   </xs:extension>
  </xs:complexContent>
 </xs:complexType>
</xs:element>
```

To create the parent `<review>` element that will contain the contents of the review, we will reference the previously declared elements. Here, we can also reference Table 15.4 for information about the `minOccurs` and `maxOccurs` for each element as well.

The only additional declaration we have nested within the `<review>` declaration is for the status attribute of the `<review>` element, which is an enumeration with a choice of values between pending and approved:

```
<xs:element name="review">
 <xs:complexType>
  <xs:complexContent>
   <xs:sequence>
    <xs:element ref="name"/>
    <xs:element ref="date"/>
    <xs:element ref="period"/>
    <xs:element ref="supervisor"/>
    <xs:element ref="reviewer"/>
    <xs:element ref="goal" minOccurs="3" maxOccurs="5"/>
    <xs:element ref="responsibility" minOccurs="3" maxOccurs="5"/>
    <xs:element ref="strength" minOccurs="3" maxOccurs="5"/>
    <xs:element ref="weakness" minOccurs="3" maxOccurs="5"/>
    <xs:element ref="training" minOccurs="0" maxOccurs="unbounded"/>
    <xs:element ref="performance"/>
    <xs:element ref="employee_comments"/>
    <xs:element ref="supervisor_comments"/>
    <xs:element ref="reviewer_comments"/>
    <xs:element ref="next"/>
    <xs:element ref="raise" minOccurs="0"/>
   </xs:sequence>
   <xs:attribute name="status" use="required">
    <xs:simpleType>
     <xs:restriction base="xs:string">
      <xs:enumeration value="pending"/>
      <xs:enumeration value="approved"/>
     </xs:restriction>
    </xs:simpleType>
   </xs:attribute>
  </xs:complexContent>
 </xs:complexType>
</xs:element>
```

Finally, when we bring this all together under the <schema> element, things are a little different from our previous examples. For the review.xsd Schema, we *are* going to specify a targetNamespace, to aid in the creation of robust XML instance documents. This means that when we incorporate the review.xsd Schema into the employee.xsd Schema, we will need to make use of the <import> element, rather than <include>.

We also need to include the profile.xsd Schema here, so that we can access the <name> and <supervisor> element declarations. We also get the added bonus of access to the currency type, which although defined in the contact.xsd Schema, is here by virtue of it being imported in the profile.xsd Schema.

```
<?xml version="1.0" encoding="UTF-8" ?>
<xs:schema xmlns:xs="http://www.w3.org/2001/XMLSchema"
    xmlns:xsi="http://www.w3.org/2001/XMLSchema-Instance"
    targetNamespace="http://www.myserver.com/Review"
    xmlns="http://www.myserver.com/Review">


<include schemaLocation="http://www.myserver.com/profile.xsd"/>

</xs:schema>
```

We now bring all of these declarations together into their final form; the resulting review.xsd Schema is shown in Listing 16.4.

LISTING 16.4 THE COMPLETE CODE LISTING FOR THE review.xsd XML SCHEMA

```
<?xml version="1.0" encoding="UTF-8" ?>
<xs:schema xmlns:xs="http://www.w3.org/2001/XMLSchema"
    xmlns:xsi="http://www.w3.org/2001/XMLSchema-Instance"
    targetNamespace="http://www.myserver.com/Review"
    xmlns="http://www.myserver.com/Review">


<xs:annotation>
 <xs:documentation xml:lang="en">
  A sample XML Schema for a Human Resources modular schema.
  This is the "review.xsd" schema for employee review information.
 </xs:documentation>
</xs:annotation>

<include schemaLocation="http://www.myserver.com/profile.xsd"/>

<xs:element name="review">
 <xs:complexType>
  <xs:complexContent>
   <xs:sequence>
    <xs:element ref="name"/>
    <xs:element ref="date"/>
    <xs:element ref="period"/>
    <xs:element ref="supervisor"/>
    <xs:element ref="reviewer"/>
    <xs:element ref="goal" minOccurs="3" maxOccurs="5"/>
    <xs:element ref="responsibility" minOccurs="3" maxOccurs="5"/>
    <xs:element ref="strength" minOccurs="3" maxOccurs="5"/>
    <xs:element ref="weakness" minOccurs="3" maxOccurs="5"/>
    <xs:element ref="training" minOccurs="0" maxOccurs="unbounded"/>
```

LISTING 16.4 CONTINUED

```
  <xs:element ref="performance"/>
  <xs:element ref="employee_comments"/>
  <xs:element ref="supervisor_comments"/>
  <xs:element ref="reviewer_comments"/>
  <xs:element ref="next"/>
  <xs:element ref="raise" minOccurs="0"/>
  </xs:sequence>
  <xs:attribute name="status" use="required">
   <xs:simpleType>
    <xs:restriction base="xs:string">
     <xs:enumeration value="pending"/>
     <xs:enumeration value="approved"/>
    </xs:restriction>
   </xs:simpleType>
  </xs:attribute>
  </xs:complexContent>
 </xs:complexType>
</xs:element>

<xs:element name="date" type="xs:date"/>
<xs:element name="period" type="xs:string"/>
<xs:element name="reviewer" type="xs:string"/>

<xs:element name="strength" type="xs:string"/>
<xs:element name="weakness" type="xs:string"/>
<xs:element name="training" type="xs:string"/>
<xs:element name="performance" type="xs:string"/>
<xs:element name="employee_comments" type="xs:string"/>
<xs:element name="supervisor_comments" type="xs:string"/>
<xs:element name="reviewer_comments" type="xs:string"/>
<xs:element name="next" type="xs:date"/>

<xs:element name="goal">
 <xs:complexType>
  <xs:complexContent>
   <xs:extension base="xs:string">
    <xs:attribute name="status" use="required">
     <xs:simpleType>
      <xs:restriction base="xs:string">
       <xs:enumeration value="met"/>
       <xs:enumeration value="not-met"/>
       <xs:enumeration value="future"/>
      </xs:restriction>
     </xs:simpleType>
    </xs:attribute>
   </xs:extension>
  </xs:complexContent>
 </xs:complexType>
</xs:element>

<xs:element name="responsibility">
 <xs:complexType>
  <xs:complexContent>
   <xs:extension base="xs:string">
    <xs:attribute name="status" use="required">
```

LISTING 16.4 CONTINUED

```
    <xs:simpleType>
     <xs:restriction base="xs:string">
      <xs:enumeration value="current"/>
      <xs:enumeration value="desired"/>
     </xs:restriction>
    </xs:simpleType>
   </xs:attribute>
  </xs:extension>
 </xs:complexContent>
 </xs:complexType>
</xs:element>

<xs:element name="raise">
 <xs:complexType>
  <xs:complexContent>
   <xs:extension base="currency">
    <xs:attribute name="rate" use="required">
     <xs:simpleType>
      <xs:restriction base="xs:string">
       <xs:enumeration value="hourly"/>
       <xs:enumeration value="monthly"/>
       <xs:enumeration value="annually"/>
      </xs:restriction>
     </xs:simpleType>
    </xs:attribute>
   </xs:extension>
  </xs:complexContent>
 </xs:complexType>
</xs:element>

</xs:schema>
```

The review.xsd Schema is designed to be used with its own standalone XML instance documents. That's one of the reasons we gave it its own namespace, as it is a prime candidate for distribution as well. Listing 16.5 shows an example of an XML instance document based on the review.xsd Schema.

LISTING 16.5 AN EXAMPLE OF A STANDALONE XML INSTANCE DOCUMENT USING THE review.xsd XML SCHEMA

```
<?xml version="1.0" encoding="UTF-8" ?>

<review xmlns="http://www.myserver.com/Review"
      xmlns:xsi="http://www.3.org/2001/XMLSchema-Instance"
      xsi:schemaLocation="http://www.myserver.com/Review
      http://www.myserver.com/review.xsd"
      status="approved">

<name>Brian Baker</name>
<date>2001-07-15</date>
<period>6 month</period>
<supervisor>Darby Collins</supervisor>
<reviewer>Michael Clark</reviewer>
```

Listing 16.5   Continued

```xml
<goal status="met">Identify XML technologies to pursue organizationally.</goal>
<goal status="met">Develop internal documentation standards.</goal>
<goal status="future">Implement company documentation policy.</goal>
<goal status="future">Identify XML compatible database solutions.</goal>
<goal status="future">Develop XML roadmap for organizational IT needs.</goal>

<responsibility status="current">Design and implementation of XML
➥documents.</responsibility>
<responsibility status="current">Design and implementation of
➥databases.</responsibility>
<responsibility status="desired">Managing Development Team.</responsibility>

<strength>Strong grasp of existing technologies.</strength>
<strength>Ability to rapidly acquire new skills.</strength>
<strength>Strong interpersonal skills.</strength>

<weakness>Reports are occasionally too technical in nature.</weakness>
<weakness>Technology evaluation process often moves beyond established
➥deadlines.</weakness>
<weakness>Has been late to work on numerous occasions.</weakness>

<training>XML 2000 Conference</training>
<performance>Excellent.</performance>

<employee_comments>
I recognize that occasionally my desire to completely investigate a technology
has on occasion delayed projects. In the future I will try to make more
efficient assessments without sacrificing the quality of my reports.
</employee_comments>

<supervisor_comments>
Brian exhibits superior technical skills and is great working with the
technology. My only criticism of his performance would be that occasionally
he is overly thorough in his evaluations, pushing back project deadlines.
</supervisor_comments>

<reviewer_comments>
Employee and Supervisor are in agreement on the employee assessment contained
in this performance review. Both exhibit professional and healthy relationships
within the department.
</reviewer_comments>

<next>2001-12-15</next>
<raise rate="annually">2500.00</raise>

</review>
```

Bringing It All Together

With the four modules written, we're now ready to bring them all together into the final `employee.xsd` Schema. Of course, each of these Schema can be used on their own, but they were all designed with the idea of joining them together, so now let's do that.

THE employee.xsd SCHEMA

We start off the employee.xsd Schema with the XML declaration, and the `<schema>` element:

```
<?xml version="1.0" encoding="UTF-8" ?>
<xs:schema xmlns:xs="http://www.w3.org/2001/XMLSchema"
    xmlns:xsi="http://www.w3.org/2001/XMLSchema-Instance"
    targetNamespace="http://www.myserver.com/Employee"
    xmlns:review="http://www.myserver.com/Review"
    xmlns="http://www.myserver.com/Employee">
```

The important aspect of the schema element to note here is that we have declared a targetNamespace for the Employee namespace associated with the employee.xsd document. But we have also declared a namespace and prefix for the Review namespace associated with the review.xsd document. That's because, if you recall, we defined a Review namespace and targetNamespace with the review.xsd document. That means that in this Schema, we will need to `<import>` the review Schema, which means we have to use the namespace prefix and qualify references to the components defined in the review.xsd Schema.

Next, we can `<include>` the profile.xsd and benefits.xsd Schema. We get the contact.xsd Schema as a bonus, because it was included in the profile.xsd Schema:

```
<include schemaLocation="http://www.myserver.com/profile.xsd"/>
<include schemaLocation="http://www.myserver.com/benefits.xsd"/>
```

Then we need to `<import>` the review.xsd schema:

```
<import namespace="http://www.myserver.com/Review"
    schemaLocation="http://www.myserver.com/review.xsd"/>
```

Finally, we are ready to build the `<employee>` root element which will contain all of our employee information. We start with a basic element declaration, a complexType with complexContent, which will be a sequence of child elements:

```
<xs:element name="employee">
 <xs:complexType>
  <xs:complexContent>
   <xs:sequence>
```

Next, we include a reference to the `<profile>` element, as defined in the profile.xsd Schema:

```
    <xs:element ref="profile"/>
```

Then, we can define a `<contact>` element to keep track of content information. You'll recall that in the contact.xsd Schema, we didn't establish a `<contact>` element to keep the Schema more flexible, so we do that here, and then add references to the `<home>` and `<work>` elements from the contact.xsd Schema:

```
    <xs:element name="contact">
     <xs:complexType>
      <xs:complexContent>
       <xs:element ref="home"/>
       <xs:element ref="work"/>
```

```
    </xs:complexContent>
   </xs:complexType>
  </xs:element>
```

Next, a simple reference to the `<benefits>` element:

```
<xs:element ref="benefits"/>
```

And then a reference to the `<review>` element. Remember, the `review` element is in the `http://www.myserver/Review` namespace, so we need to use the prefix when referencing the element:

```
<xs:element ref="review:review" minOccurs="0" maxOccurs="unbounded"/>
```

PART

IV

CH

16

And with that we are done! The `employee.xsd` Schema is now complete, and ready to be used in XML instance documents. The final version of the completed `employee.xsd` Schema is shown in Listing 16.6.

LISTING 16.6   THE COMPLETE CODE LISTING FOR THE `employee.xsd` XML SCHEMA

```xml
<?xml version="1.0" encoding="UTF-8" ?>
<xs:schema xmlns:xs="http://www.w3.org/2001/XMLSchema"
    xmlns:xsi="http://www.w3.org/2001/XMLSchema-Instance"
    targetNamespace="http://www.myserver.com/Employee"
    xmlns:review="http://www.myserver.com/Review"
    xmlns="http://www.myserver.com/Employee">

<xs:annotation>
 <xs:documentation xml:lang="en">
  A sample XML Schema for Human Resources.
  Modular Version, based on the profile.xsd, contact.xsd, benefits.xsd and
➥review.xsd XML Schema.
 </xs:documentation>
</xs:annotation>

<!-- Import the other Schema Modules -->

<include schemaLocation="http://www.myserver.com/profile.xsd"/>
<include schemaLocation="http://www.myserver.com/benefits.xsd"/>

<import namespace="http://www.myserver.com/Review"
    schemaLocation="http://www.myserver.com/review.xsd"/>

<xs:element name="employee">
 <xs:complexType>
  <xs:complexContent>
   <xs:sequence>
    <xs:element ref="profile"/>
    <xs:element name="contact">
     <xs:complexType>
      <xs:complexContent>
       <xs:element ref="home"/>
       <xs:element ref="work"/>
      </xs:complexContent>
     </xs:complexType>
    </xs:element>
```

LISTING 16.6   CONTINUED

```
   <xs:element ref="benefits"/>
   <xs:element ref="review:review" minOccurs="0" maxOccurs="unbounded"/>
  </xs:sequence>
 </xs:complexContent>
 </xs:complexType>
</xs:element>

</xs:schema>
```

Using the `employee.xsd` Schema as the basis, it is now possible to write a complete XML instance document based on all of our Schema modules, functioning together as one Schema.

Incorporating employee profile information, contact information, benefit information, and a review, our complete `employee.xml` instance document is shown in Listing 16.7.

LISTING 16.7   AN `employee.xml` XML INSTANCE DOCUMENT WHICH IS BASED ON THE FINAL `employee.xsd` XML SCHEMA

```
<?xml version="1.0" encoding="UTF-8" ?>

<employee xmlns="http://www.myserver.com/Employee"
      xmlns:xsi="http://www.3.org/2001/XMLSchema-Instance"
      xsi:schemaLocation="http://www.myserver.com/Employee
      http://www.myserver.com/employee.xsd">

 <profile>
  <name>Brian Baker</name>
  <SOC>485-90-3528</SOC>
  <DOB>1967-03-15</DOB>
  <spouse>Susan Baker</spouse>
  <department>Corporate IT</department>
  <title>Technologist</title>
  <supervisor>Darby Collins</supervisor>
  <salary type="annually">47500.00</salary>
  <hire date="2001-2-11"></hire>
 </profile>

 <contact>
  <home>
   <address>1613 Cottonwood Circle</address>
   <address>Apt 3C</address>
   <city>Redwood City</city>
   <state>CA</state>
   <zip>94708</zip>
   <phone type="primary">415-336-0823</phone>
  </home>

  <work>
   <address>1 Hi-Tek Center</address>
   <city>Sunnyvale</city>
   <state>CA</state>
   <zip>94981</zip>
```

LISTING 16.7 CONTINUED

```
  <phone type="primary">408-352-1221</phone>
  <phone type="fax">408-352-1400</phone>
  <phone type="pager">408-879-4922</phone>
  <phone type="cellular">408-321-4981</phone>
 </work>
</contact>

<benefits>
 <healthcare>
  <plan>HMO</plan>
  <provider>Ecma</provider>
  <start_date>2001-4-01</start_date>
  <termination_date>2001-10-01</termination_date>
  <options>Dental</options>
  <options>Optical</options>
  <options>Maternity</options>
 </healthcare>

 <retirement>
  <plan>401K</plan>
  <start_date>2001-4-01</start_date>
  <maturity>2042-01-01</maturity>
  <payroll_deduction>238.57</payroll_deduction>
 </retirement>

 <personal_days allocation="5" used="1" remaining="4">
  <used date="2001-5-05"/>
 </personal_days>

 <vacation allocation="14" used="0" remaining="14"/>
</benefits>

<review status="approved">
 <name>Brian Baker</name>
 <date>2001-07-15</date>
 <period>6 month</period>
 <supervisor>Darby Collins</supervisor>
 <reviewer>Michael Clark</reviewer>

 <goal status="met">Identify XML technologies to pursue
➥organizationally.</goal>
 <goal status="met">Develop internal documentation standards.</goal>
 <goal status="future">Implement company documentation policy.</goal>
 <goal status="future">Identify XML compatible database solutions.</goal>
 <goal status="future">Develop XML roadmap for organizational IT needs.</goal>

 <responsibility status="current">Design and implementation of XML
➥documents.</responsibility>
 <responsibility status="current">Design and implementation of
➥databases.</responsibility>
 <responsibility status="desired">Managing Development Team.</responsibility>

 <strength>Strong grasp of existing technologies.</strength>
 <strength>Ability to rapidly acquire new skills.</strength>
 <strength>Strong interpersonal skills.</strength>
```

LISTING 16.7 CONTINUED

```
    <weakness>Reports are occasionally too technical in nature.</weakness>
    <weakness>Technology evaluation process often moves beyond established
➥deadlines.</weakness>
    <weakness>Has been late to work on numerous occasions.</weakness>

    <training>XML 2000 Conference</training>
    <performance>Excellent.</performance>

    <employee_comments>
     I recognize that occasionally my desire to completely investigate a
     technology has on occasion delayed projects. In the future I will try to make
     more efficient assessments without sacrificing the quality of my reports.
    </employee_comments>

    <supervisor_comments>
     Brian exhibits superior technical skills and is great working with the
     technology. My only criticism of his performance would be that occasionally
     he is overly thorough in his evaluations, pushing back project deadlines.
    </supervisor_comments>

    <reviewer_comments>
     Employee and Supervisor are in agreement on the employee assessment contained
     in this performance review. Both exhibit professional and healthy
     relationships within the department.
    </reviewer_comments>

    <next>2001-12-15</next>
    <raise rate="annually">2500.00</raise>
   </review>
</employee>
```

USING THE SCHEMA

This set of Schema was designed to work together in the final `employee.xml` document which would provide a comprehensive file for each employee of this particular company. However, there is no reason that each Schema can't be used on its own for specific applications as well.

We've already seen how the `review.xsd` Schema can be used to create standalone XML review documents. Similarly, we could use the `profile.xsd` Schema as a reference for validation of standalone profile documents.

But one of the more significant uses for these Schema lies in the `contact.xsd` schema, which can and should be used throughout this organization in order to provide a standard basis for defining contacts. By making use of one central Schema for this task, anyone in the entire organization, not just human resources, can be sure that their contact information conforms to the organizational standard.

CONCLUSIONS

In Part I, "XML Schema Basics," you learned about the legacy, history, and basics of XML Schema. In Part II, "XML Schema Structures," you learned about Schema structures, including how to write your own simple Schema. In Part III, "XML Schema Datatypes," you learned all about datatypes, and how they can be used to enhance the functionality of your Schema.

Now, you've followed the development of a complex set of Schema from start to finish, and are probably ready to start tackling your own Schema projects. But before you do, we're going to present you with a few more important pieces of information. In Chapter 17, "XML Schema Best Practices," we will take a look at some of the "best practices" standards being developed in relation to XML Schema, so that you will have a good idea of the best methods for addressing complicated issues that might arise with your own Schema. And then, finally, in Chapter 18, "Schema Alternatives and Future Directions," we will take a look at some of the alternatives which are being promoted to address the shortcomings of the XML Schema Recommendation, as well as the future of the XML Schema Recommendation itself.

IN THE REAL WORLD

One of the biggest issues you will face regarding this type of Schema development relates to using namespaces. Schema which are going to be made public, or published for your partners, should have their own `targetNamespace`. Providing namespaces is an important step toward preventing namespace clashes in the future. For smaller Schema, or internal-only Schema, you can sometimes side-step the issue of a namespace; however, in the real world, this can really cause problems down the road. In practice, writing Schema means dealing with and mastering namespaces.

Another controversial issue we have touched on here in this chapter is that of code reuse. Not controversial because anyone would argue that reusing code is inherently bad; in fact, the vast majority of all coders reuse a significant percentage of their code.

However, many developers "reuse" code by simply cutting and pasting it from one piece of source to the other. In spite of years of preaching about code reuse, and object-oriented programming, surprisingly few developers actually practice what they preach.

Some would argue, in the case of Schema, that including or importing other Schema could cause your applications to break, should the imported Schema be updated or changed at a later date. While this is true, it is still a very weak argument against code reuse. In fact, if anything it highlights a shortcoming of the development community in not adequately planning and anticipating code reuse. For example, any Schema which is designed to be published and shared publicly could easily be versioned. Just as standards evolve, Schema do too, and keeping track of versions will always be necessary. This could be done through annotations, or even through naming conventions for namespaces. The point being that in reality, this is a weak argument against sharing and reusing code.

The real reasons are complicated. Most stem from the fact that developers are often under a lot of stress to provide solutions quickly, not eloquently, and therefore the added work of keeping track of revisions, publishing revision histories, and so on is work that often isn't mission critical, and therefore never gets done. It's not really the fault of developers, just a consequence of the pace of technology development, and the growing demands placed on information management everyday.

So, in practice, you are probably not likely to encounter a lot of code reuse, or modularity in design. That should not stop us from encouraging you to do so as you begin to develop Schema, however, as it is a good way to build better Schema for you and your organization in the long run.

CHAPTER 17

XML SCHEMA BEST PRACTICES

In this chapter

SCHEMA BEST PRACTICES

The purpose of the XML Schema Recommendation is to bring everyone into a consensus regarding the methodologies for writing a grammar for XML instance documents. Everyone writes an element declaration the same way, which is one of the reasons software developers can write applications which know how to interpret those declarations and use them as the basis for validating an XML document.

At the most basic level, it is the Recommendation itself that establishes the way to accomplish a task. For example, to declare an element, we know we have to use

```
<element name="something"/>
```

No matter how much we might like to shortcut, and say

```
<element="something"/>
```

we cannot do that, because it is not how the Recommendation says we declare an element, and therefore, no applications are likely to understand that as an element declaration.

But what about Schema issues which are not clearly established in the Recommendation? For example, when should we use an element declaration vs. a type definition? When should you use an attribute vs. an element? When and how should you make use of namespaces? There are many valid questions to approaching Schema authoring which do not have clear-cut answers.

However, in most cases, thinking hard about how your Schema will be used will help dictate the choices you make. For example, when should you split a Schema into multiple documents? Obviously, the choice to split or not to split will depend on your applications. What is the best choice for a particular application? That is what "best practices" attempt to address. Best practices are not formally defined by any sanctioning body, but rather by building a consensus among XML developers.

This chapter tries to address some of the issues which you might be confronted with and explains the various options provided by XML Schema, including which option might be best in a particular situation. And as much as the author would like to take credit for resolving all these issues, best practices are rarely developed by a single person; instead they evolve from a considerable mass of knowledge, and such is true with the best practices we will present here. This chapter relies heavily on the work of the developers on the xml-dev list, and owes a special acknowledgment to Roger Costello and his work in archiving and documenting the discussions from that list.

MULTIPART SCHEMA

One issue you might face which we discussed in Chapter 14, "Building Multipart Schema," is the issue of whether to split a Schema into multiple documents, or to write the Schema as one large document.

As we have seen already, sometimes the document you are working to describe will have a natural structure which will lend itself to being divided into multiple parts; for example, a book is naturally broken down into chapters, paragraphs, sentences, and so on. Other types of data, such as parts in a catalog, might have common groupings, but the order might not be as important as the order of a story in a book. Of course, just as often a document won't have a clear-cut delineation; scientific data might simply need to be recorded from an instrument as it is read, but might not have a specific grouping that becomes apparent until later analysis. In those circumstances, the best approach is to examine what components from the Schema might be useful in other applications. If there is a large amount of reusable information, you might consider creating a multipart schema in order to conveniently group those elements which are reusable.

The major issues to consider when you are breaking a Schema into multiple parts are

- Namespaces—Be sure to keep careful track of namespaces so that you can avoid possible namespace collisions when you combine Schema.

- Declarations and Definitions—Be sure that you have only declared a component or defined a datatype in one location.

- Watch `includes` and `imports`—If you are including and importing multiple Schema, you should check to see how the Schema might be nested.

Another caveat applies to when you are importing or including a Schema from another source. If you did not author the Schema you are importing, it's important that you read the Schema and understand all of the declarations and definitions, as well as check to make sure importing/including it will not create a conflict with any of your components. This is another important role for namespaces.

As with many of the issues surrounding best practices, there is no clear-cut answer here. But if you follow your instincts, in conjunction with the caveats above, you should come to an appropriate solution.

ELEMENTS AND DATATYPES

One question that is as fundamental as "element or attribute?" is "element or datatype?" While there is really no easy answer to either question, there are some guidelines we can apply to the element vs. datatype question in order to help guide your decision.

The debate stems from the fact that you can declare an element directly, or use a type definition, and then declare the element from there. For instance, take an address example. We could declare an `address` element, containing `street`, `city`, `state`, and `zip` elements:

```
<xs:element name="xs:address">
 <xs:complexType>
  <xs:complexContent>
   <xs:element name="street" type="xs:string"/>
   <xs:element name="city" type="xs:string"/>
   <xs:element name="state" type="xs:string"/>
```

```
    <xs:element name="zip" type="xs:string"/>
   </xs:complexContent>
  </xs:complexType>
</xs:element>
```

That would be defining address as an element. Defining address as a type would be

```
<xs:complexType name="address">
 <xs:complexContent>
   <xs:element name="street" type="xs:string"/>
   <xs:element name="city" type="xs:string"/>
   <xs:element name="state" type="xs:string"/>
   <xs:element name="zip" type="xs:string"/>
 </xs:complexContent>
</xs:complexType>
```

Keep in mind that we can always easily turn the type into an element with a simple declaration:

```
<xs:element name="address" type="address"/>
```

There isn't a problem using the same name for the element and the type, because they inhabit different symbol spaces (one for elements and the other for types), so there is no conflict.

In fact, it's so easy to make a type into an element that in general you will actually want to use a type rather than an element, except in one specific case: when you need to make the element part of a substitution group. In that case, you have to use an element declaration because types cannot be a part of a substitution group. For example, if we wanted to have a generic element for address, but be able to substitute a <USaddress>, <UKaddress>, or <CNaddress>, we'd need to use an element declaration.

Of course for straightforward applications or declarations, such as

```
  <xs:element name="city" type="xs:string"/>
```

an element declaration is the best choice, because we are using the built-in string type. There is no point in complicating your Schema needlessly.

However, there are several instances when it is best to use a type definition, and then declare an element of that type.

For example, if you are likely to reuse the type repeatedly as the base for other elements, a type definition is appropriate. We would want to define our address as a type if we wanted to be able to create elements such as <home_address> or <work_address> which would both be a form of our address type:

```
<xs:element name="home_address" type="address"/>
<xs:element name="work_address" type="address"/>
```

In this case a type definition is more appropriate.

Another reason to use types is that they are easily extensible. You can use the type as the basis for a restriction or an extension. For example, if we wanted to declare a new address form and add a <country> element, we could do that with a type:

```
<xs:element name="xs:address">
 <xs:complexType>
  <xs:complexContent>
   <xs:extension base="address">
    <xs:element name="country" type="xs:string"/>
   </xs:extension>
  </xs:complexContent>
 </xs:complexType>
</xs:element>
```

Because address was originally defined as a type, we can use it as the base type for our <address> element, but still extend it with our own declarations.

As you can see, there is no pat answer, but as is the case with most best practices if you look closely at the intended use of your information, the choice for your authoring approach will generally become apparent.

SCOPE ISSUES

As we discussed in earlier chapters, Schema components can either be declared locally, nested within content models, or they can be declared globally as children of the <schema> element, and then referenced in the content model. For example

```
<xs:element name="global_element">
 <xs:complexType>
  <xs:complexContent>
   <xs:element name="local_element" type="xs:string"/>
   <xs:element ref="second_global_element"/>
  </xs:complexContent>
 </xs:complexType>
</xs:element>

<xs:element name="second_global_element" type="xs:string"/>
```

In this example, we have three elements: The first is <global_element>, which is indeed a global element. It contains a declaration for a <local_element>, and a reference to another globally declared element, <second_global_element>.

The issue of whether to declare an element as a local element or a global element is really an issue related to the overall structure of your Schema. It brings to the front such issues as

- Should the components be accessible to other Schema authors, via include/import?
- Are the components being designed to be reusable, either in multiple places within the same document, or within other Schema documents?
- What is the intended impact on other documents, should the element declaration change in the original document?

To examine these issues, let's take a look at three methodologies for designing the structure of XML Schema.

RUSSIAN DOLL DESIGN

The Russian Doll design for Schema involves nesting all of the component definitions and declarations within the Schema structure itself. Everything is declared locally with the exception of the parent element of the document.

The result is a Schema that can be hard to read, but directly reflects the design of the XML instance document it describes. For example, let's look at a Schema for a newspaper article:

```
<?xml version="1.0" encoding="UTF-8" ?>
<xs:schema xmlns:xs="http://www.w3.org/2001/XMLSchema"
    xmlns="http://www.w3.org/2001/XMLSchema">

<xs:element name="article">
 <xs:complexType>
  <xs:complexContent>
   <xs:element name="headline">
    <xs:simpleType>
     <xs:restriction base="xs:string">
      <maxLength value="50"/>
     </xs:restriction>
    </xs:simpleType>
   </xs:element>
   <xs:element name="dateline">
    <xs:complexType>
     <xs:complexContent>
      <xs:element name="submission" type="xs:date"/>
      <xs:element name="publication" type="xs:date"/>
     </xs:complexContent>
    </xs:complexType>
   </xs:element>
   <xs:element name="byline" minOccurs="0">
    <xs:simpleType>
     <xs:restriction base="string">
      <maxLength value="25"/>
     </xs:restriction>
    </xs:simpleType>
   </xs:element>
   <xs:element name="text" type="xs:string"/>
  </xs:complexContent>
 </xs:complexType>
</xs:element>
</xs:schema>
```

With a Schema written using the Russian Doll design, we have a Schema that reflects the structure of an instance document:

```
<article>
 <headline>Mars Invades Earth</headline>
 <dateline>
  <submission>2001-04-01</submission>
  <publication>2001-04-01</publication>
 </dateline>
 <byline>Alan Smithee</byline>
 <text>Today the planet of Mars launched an invasion...</text>
</article>
```

In a Russian Doll design, all of the components, save the parent element, are declared locally. The Russian Doll Design does have some advantages.

First, we already mentioned that it follows the structure of the instance document. Therefore, following a Russian Doll Schema to build an instance document is often quite easy.

Because all of the declarations are local in scope, and self contained, there can't be references to a declared component in another section of the Schema. As a result, what you see is what you get.

Another advantage is that the namespaces are localized. If we declared a targetNamespace for our Schema, and our Schema were then imported into another Schema, we would only need to worry about namespace qualification with the <article> element, as the other elements would be local to <article>. For example, had we declared a namespace for the previous example, say "xmlns:article" in an instance document, our code would look like this:

```
<article xmlns="http://www.myserver.com/article">
 <headline>Mars Invades Earth</headline>
 <dateline>
  <submission>2001-04-01</submission>
  <publication>2001-04-01</publication>
 </dateline>
 <byline>Alan Smithee</byline>
 <text>Today the planet of Mars launched an invasion...</text>
</article>
```

Part
IV

Ch

17

Note that only the parent <article> document has the namespace declaration, because the other elements are local to the <article> element by definition. This can help avoid namespace confusion and clutter in instance documents.

This does also have the advantage of shielding instance documents somewhat, because if your Schema is included in another Schema, only the parent element is exposed. That means that the integrity of the element is harder to compromise. (Not impossible; it could still be redefined, for example. However, the child elements cannot be accessed out of the context of the parent element.)

For example, our <article> might be included into a Schema describing a <magazine>. That magazine might include other types of content, such as a <review> or <editorial>. Now, because all of our elements are locally scoped, if we change the declaration for anything within an <article>, it only affects the article, not any of the other elements. But had we, say, declared <byline> globally, and then our <byline> element were included as the byline for <review> or <editorial>, if we now make a change to our article Schema, the impact is broader than just the <article> element. This can be seen as an advantage, or a disadvantage, almost entirely dependent on how much control you want to exert over the original Schema, and how you want to allow others to reuse your design.

However, reuse of components is one of the great features of Schema, and the Russian Doll design lacks the flexibility to reuse components. The Russian Doll design is not solely without merit, however. Because of its simplicity, the development time for a Russian Doll Schema can be relatively short, and therefore, it can serve as a good starting point for modification into other paradigms later.

SALAMI SLICE DESIGN

The "Salami Slice" design approach to structuring your Schema involves splitting the component declarations into smaller segments, and then building the complete parent element by reference to the previous declarations.

The Salami Slice design still relies heavily on element declarations as opposed to type definitions, but most of the element declarations are declared globally, so they are potentially exposed to other Schema, and are free to be referenced in other locations within your own Schema document.

Let's take a look at the same example we used for the Russian Doll Design, only now the Schema has been modified to reflect the Salami Slice design:

```
<?xml version="1.0" encoding="UTF-8" ?>
<xs:schema xmlns:xs="http://www.w3.org/2001/XMLSchema"
xmlns="http://www.w3.org/2001/XMLSchema">

<xs:element name="headline">
 <xs:simpleType>
  <xs:restriction base="xs:string">
   <maxLength value="50"/>
  </xs:restriction>
 </xs:simpleType>
</xs:element>

<xs:element name="dateline">
 <xs:complexType>
  <xs:complexContent>
   <xs:element name="submission" type="xs:date"/>
   <xs:element name="publication" type="xs:date"/>
  </xs:complexContent>
 </xs:complexType>
</xs:element>

<xs:element name="byline">
 <xs:simpleType>
  <xs:restriction base="string">
   <maxLength value="25"/>
  </xs:restriction>
 </xs:simpleType>
</xs:element>

<xs:element name="text" type="xs:string"/>

<xs:element name="article">
 <xs:complexType>
  <xs:complexContent>
   <xs:element ref="headline"/>
   <xs:element ref="dateline"/>
   <xs:element ref="byline" minOccurs="0"/>
   <xs:element ref="text"/>
  </xs:complexContent>
 </xs:complexType>
</xs:element>

</xs:schema>
```

Now, with this example you can see that most of the elements are contained in their own, standalone declarations. The parent element for the <article> is built by referencing the declarations.

The Salami Slice design is certainly more verbose than the Russian Doll design. The overall Schema itself is not self-contained, and instead is broken up into much smaller parcels of information. However, an advantageous side effect is that each component declaration is clearly visible, and easy to read. It's easy for us to locate and look at the structure of any one particular component, as opposed to the overall document structure.

This design also provides us with a great deal more flexibility with our elements. For example, because the elements are declared globally, we could take advantage of substitution groups if we wanted. And because the components are all declared globally, we could access them in other Schema as well.

For example, if we were building a <journal> Schema, we could include our article Schema:

```xml
<?xml version="1.0" encoding="UTF-8" ?>
<xs:schema xmlns:xs="http://www.w3.org/2001/XMLSchema"
xmlns="http://www.w3.org/2001/XMLSchema">

<include schemaLocation="http://www.myserver.com/article.xsd"/>

<xs:element name="journal">
 <xs:complexType>
  <xs:complexContent>
   <xs:element ref="article" maxOccurs="unbounded"/>
   <xs:element name="editorial" maxOccurs="unbounded">
    <xs:complexType>
     <xs:complexContent>
      <xs:element ref="headline"/>
      <xs:element ref="byline"/>
      <xs:element ref="text"/>
     </xs:complexContent>
    </xs:complexType>
   </xs:element>
  </xs:complexContent>
 </xs:complexType>
</xs:element>

</xs:schema>
```

In this example, we can use the <article> element from the included Schema, but we can also make use of the components which make up the <article> element, such as headline and byline, in order to create a new element, called <editorial>. This kind of flexibility in reuse is offered by the Salami Slice design.

There is one major drawback to this methodology, though, when it comes to namespace use. For example, if we had declared a targetNamespace for our article.xsd Schema

```
targetNamespace="http://www.myserver.com/article"
```

and we wanted to use the namespace qualified version in our instance document

```
xmlns:article="http://www.myserver.com/article"
```

the resulting instance would need to look like this:

```
<article:article>
 <article:headline>Mars Invades Earth</article:headline>
 <article:dateline>
  <article:submission>2001-04-01</article:submission>
  <article:publication>2001-04-01</article:publication>
 </article:dateline>
 <article:byline>Alan Smithee</article:byline>
 <article:text>Today the planet of Mars launched an invasion…</article:text>
</article:article>
```

The resulting namespace clutter can have an impact on readability, and can be an issue if the end users of your instance documents aren't familiar with namespaces and namespace issues. Of course, for automatically generated Schema, this is less of an issue.

VENETIAN BLIND DESIGN

The third style of XML Schema design addresses the issue of namespace localization similarly to the Russian Doll design, while still allowing the global declarations of components similar to the Salami Slice design.

This design is called the "Venetian Blind" design (so named because it is sliced like the Salami Design, but allows the toggling on/off of namespace qualification, like the Russian Doll design).

The Venetian Blind design is very similar to the Salami Slice design, in that each component is declared globally, for exposure and ease of reading and management. However, rather than being declared as elements, components are defined as types whenever possible, and then those types are used when declaring the elements within the content model of the parent component.

Let's take a look at the article.xsd Schema, redesigned using the Venetian Blind method:

```
<?xml version="1.0" encoding="UTF-8" ?>
<xs:schema xmlns:xs="http://www.w3.org/2001/XMLSchema">
<xs:simpleType name="headline">
 <xs:restriction base="xs:string">
  <maxLength value="50"/>
 </xs:restriction>
</xs:simpleType>

<xs:complexType name="dateline">
 <xs:complexContent>
  <xs:element name="submission" type="xs:date"/>
  <xs:element name="publication" type="xs:date"/>
 </xs:complexContent>
</xs:complexType>

<xs:simpleType name="byline">
 <xs:restriction base="string">
  <maxLength value="25"/>
 </xs:restriction>
</xs:simpleType>
```

```
<xs:complexType name="article">
 <xs:complexContent>
  <xs:element name="headline" type="headline"/>
  <xs:element name="dateline" type="dateline"/>
  <xs:element name="byline" type="byline" minOccurs="0"/>
  <xs:element name="text" type="xs:string"/>
 </xs:complexContent>
</xs:complexType>

<xs:element name="article" type="article"/>

</xs:schema>
```

As you can see, we now have a number of global types, such as `headline` and `byline` which we could `include` in another document. For example, our journal would look like this:

```
<?xml version="1.0" encoding="UTF-8" ?>
<xs:schema xmlns:xs="http://www.w3.org/2001/XMLSchema">

<include schemaLocation="http://www.myserver.com/article.xsd"/>

<xs:element name="journal">
 <xs:complexType>
  <xs:complexContent>
   <xs:element ref="article" maxOccurs="unbounded"/>
   <xs:element name="editorial" type="article" maxOccurs="unbounded"/>
  </xs:complexContent>
 </xs:complexType>
</xs:element>

</xs:schema>
```

By including the article Schema, we gain access to both the `<article>` element and the `article` type. This means we can use both, greatly simplifying our journal Schema by reusing those components.

We also have a much finer degree of control over namespaces, allowing you to "toggle" off and on namespace qualification in documents using the `elementFormDefault` attribute, which by default will hide the namespaces in your documents.

In general, the Venetian Blind schema design offers the best of both the Russian Doll design and the Salami Slice design, so it should be the design choice you examine first when considering design approaches. Of course, if limiting exposure of the components of your Schema is important, then the Russian Doll design is always an alternative.

There is no "right" or "wrong" approach to using any of these design models presented here; however, there are better choices than others, and by taking a look at how you intend to use your Schema, one of these design models will likely present itself as the best choice for you to use when authoring.

NAMESPACES

Quite possibly the most confusing aspect of XML Schema authoring is that of namespaces. While using namespaces themselves is trivial—it amounts to making use of a handful of tags and some prefixes—keeping track of how those namespace declarations impact your Schema and instance documents can be nightmarish.

There are three major issues that will confront most authors when it comes to dealing with namespaces and XML Schema:

- Expose or hide namespaces—This applies to namespaces in the instance documents the users of your Schema will be creating. Do you limit the users' exposure to namespaces? Or do you require full namespace disclosure through the use of prefixes?

- Default namespaces—What is the best approach for declaring default namespaces in your Schema, and what is the impact on using the Schema with other Schema and instance documents?

- Multiple Schema, multiple namespaces—What is the best namespace approach when you are creating multiple document Schema? Should they all share one namespace? No namespaces? Should each Schema have its own namespace?

Let's take a look at each one of these issues in greater detail and see what might constitute the best practices.

NAMESPACES AND INSTANCE DOCUMENTS

Many users of instance documents find the use of namespaces unappealing. The prefixes often make it difficult for them to read the instance documents, and there is often much confusion over what namespace applies where.

With designs such as the Russian Doll design and the Venetian Blind design, you have the ability to shield users by keeping namespaces localized to the Schema, or exposing them in the instance document, requiring the use of the namespace prefix.

This is another of the many grey areas in XML. There are advantages and disadvantages to both approaches. For example, let's say that you are building a specification for mobile phones, importing two Schema:

```
<?xml version="1.0" encoding="UTF-8" ?>
<xs:schema xmlns:xs="http://www.w3.org/2001/XMLSchema"
xmlns:nokia="http://www.nokia.com"
xmlns:motorola="http://www.motorola.com"
targetNamespace="http://www.mobilephone.com"
xmlns="http://www.mobilephone.com"
elementFormDefault="unqualified">

<import namespace="http://www.nokia.com" schemaLocation="nokia.xsd"/>
<import namespace="http://www.motorola.com" schemaLocation="motorola.xsd"/>

<xs:element name="phone">
 <xs:complexType>
```

```
    <xs:complexContent>
     <xs:element name="features" type="nokia:features"/>
     <xs:element name="description" type="motorola:description"/>
    </xs:complexContent>
   </xs:complexType>
  </xs:element>

 </xs:schema>
```

Now, we have an instance document which looks like this:

```
<?xml version="1.0" encoding="UTF-8" ?>
<phone xmlns="http://www.mobilephone.com"
       xmlns:xsi="http://www.3.org/2001/XMLSchema-Instance"
       xsi:schemaLocation="http://www.mobilephone.com
       http://www.mobilephone.com/phone.xsd">

<features>Silent Ringing</features>
<description>Sleek and small...</description>
</phone>
```

This is descriptive, and the user is unaware that the `<features>` element and the `<description>` element are both being imported from different namespaces. In many cases, that might not be important. But it also means that users will be unaware that if one of those imported Schema changes, they will need to change their instance documents. If we change the `elementFormDefault` to `"qualified"` we toggle on the namespaces, and the instance document looks like this:

```
<?xml version="1.0" encoding="UTF-8" ?>
<phone xmlns="http://www.mobilephone.com"
    xmlns:xsi="http://www.3.org/2001/XMLSchema-Instance"
    xsi:schemaLocation="http://www.mobilephone.com
    http://www.mobilephone.com/phone.xsd"
    xmlns:motorola="http://www.motorola.com"
    xmlns:nokia="http://www.nokia.com">

<nokia:features>Silent Ringing</nokia:features>
<motorola:description>Sleek and small...</motorola:description>
</phone>
```

Now it is clear to the user that these elements have been imported from another namespace. But neither approach is inherently better; it is simply a question of how much information about the structure of your Schema you want to provide to the end user of the instance documents your Schema is based on.

DEFAULT NAMESPACES

When you are declaring the namespaces for your Schema, you can declare a number of different namespaces for the Schema document. How the namespaces are declared for your document affects your ability to effectively `import` and `include` other Schema and their components.

If you recall from our chapter dealing with multiple document Schema, we created a number of Schema which had no `targetNamespace` declared, in order to make them easy to `import` into new Schema.

Schema which do not have a targetNamespace are called *Chameleon* schema, because when they are imported, they effectively become a part of your Schema. So what happens when we have a Schema that does not have a default namespace declaration?

```
<?xml version="1.0" encoding="UTF-8" ?>
<xs:schema xmlns:xs="http://www.w3.org/2001/XMLSchema"
    xmlns:my="http://www.myserver.com"
    targetNamespace="http://www.myserver.com">
</xs:schema>
```

In this case, we have two namespaces, the XML Schema namespace, and the "http://www.myserver.com" namespace, both of which have prefixes assigned. The problem with this design is that if we now try to import a Chameleon Schema, it will by nature become part of the default namespace, which in this case doesn't exist. And that will break things.

Another approach would be to declare the default namespace to be the XML Schema namespace:

```
<?xml version="1.0" encoding="UTF-8" ?>
<xs:schema xmlns:xs="http://www.w3.org/2001/XMLSchema"
    xmlns:my="http://www.myserver.com"
    targetNamespace="http://www.myserver.com"
    xmlns="http://www.w3.org/2001/XMLSchema">
</xs:schema>
```

Now we do have a default namespace, so when we import our Chameleon Schema, it will be treated as part of the default namespace, which in this case is the XML Schema namespace.

Of course, this would create errors as well, because now the imported components would be treated as part of the XML Schema namespace, but of course no declarations for them would exist in that namespace.

The correct approach to this issue, therefore, is to declare the targetNamespace as the default namespace:

```
<?xml version="1.0" encoding="UTF-8" ?>
<xs:schema xmlns:xs="http://www.w3.org/2001/XMLSchema"
    targetNamespace="http://www.myserver.com"
    xmlns="http://www.myserver.com">
</xs:schema>
```

This is the best practice, because this allows for all of your Schema declarations to be qualified (using the "xs" prefix) but imported Chameleon Schema are automatically considered a part of the targetNamespace you are in the process of defining. That way, you will not run into errors because of namespace conflicts or trying to reference components which are not defined.

NAMESPACES WITH MULTIPART SCHEMA

The final best practices area that we will discuss in this chapter relates to how to utilize namespaces when you are building multiple part Schema. We've seen one approach to this in Chapters 14, 15, "An Example Schema: Human Resources," and 16, "Building and Using the Schema." In those instances we used the Chameleon approach, by having the majority of our Schema documents have no targetNamespace specified so they could be easily imported.

However, this is not the only approach to the problem. The issue basically involves three choices:

- Many Namespaces
- One Namespace
- Zero Namespaces

So let's take a look at these approaches and their impacts.

MANY NAMESPACES

The first approach we might use would be to have a `targetNamespace` declared for each one of our multiple Schema:

```
<?xml version="1.0" encoding="UTF-8" ?>
<xs:schema xmlns:xs="http://www.w3.org/2001/XMLSchema"
    targetNamespace="http://www.myserver.com/Name"
    xmlns="http://www.myserver.com"/Name>
<xs:element name="name" type="xs:string"/>
<xs:schema>

<?xml version="1.0" encoding="UTF-8" ?>
<xs:schema xmlns:xs="http://www.w3.org/2001/XMLSchema"
    targetNamespace="http://www.myserver.com/Address"
    xmlns="http://www.myserver.com"/Address>
<xs:element name="address" type="xs:string"/>
<xs:schema>

<?xml version="1.0" encoding="UTF-8" ?>
<xs:schema xmlns:xs="http://www.w3.org/2001/XMLSchema"
    targetNamespace="http://www.myserver.com/Phone"
    xmlns="http://www.myserver.com"/Phone>
<xs:element name="phone" type="xs:string"/>
<xs:schema>
```

Here, we have three Schema, each representing a different namespace, and now we want to build a new Schema by including each of these Schema. The result would look like this:

```
<?xml version="1.0" encoding="UTF-8" ?>
<xs:schema xmlns:xs="http://www.w3.org/2001/XMLSchema"
    xmlns:name="http://www.myserver.com/Name"
    xmlns:address="http://www.myserver.com/Address"
    xmlns:phone="http://www.myserver.com/Phone"
    targetNamespace="http://www.myserver.com/Contact"
    xmlns="http://www.myserver.com"/Contact>

<xs:import namespace="http://www.myserver.com/Name" schemaLocation="Name.xsd"/>
<xs:import namespace="http://www.myserver.com/Address"
➥schemaLocation="Address.xsd"/>
<xs:import namespace="http://www.myserver.com/Phone" schemaLocation="Phone.xsd"/>

<xs:element name="contact">
 <xs:complexType>
  <xs:complexContent>
   <xs:element ref="name:name"/>
```

```
    <xs:element ref="address:address"/>
    <xs:element ref="phone:phone"/>
  </xs:complexContent>
 </xs:complexType>
</xs:element>

<xs:schema>
```

The biggest disadvantage to this approach is the clutter created in your Schema (and instance documents). There is a great deal of namespace information to keep track of in even our simple example, which only uses three declarations! As your Schema grow more complicated, this approach becomes more difficult to manage.

However, there is also a possible advantage: If you are using a number of elements and are worried about possible name conflicts, using multiple namespaces can be one way to keep all of the names in your various Schema straight without having to resort to long, complicated element names.

Another advantage is strict control over the namespace itself, which means that if you are publishing the namespace definition to a wide audience, this approach might be the best. By declaring namespace information for each Schema, you can ensure that users of your Schema will be bound to your namespace, and therefore, when you update your Schema, those changes will be enforced within the namespace. This is a good approach for rigid control and management of complex projects.

ONE NAMESPACE

Another alternative is to use a single, umbrella namespace, with each Schema belonging to that namespace:

```
<?xml version="1.0" encoding="UTF-8" ?>
<xs:schema xmlns:xs="http://www.w3.org/2001/XMLSchema"
    targetNamespace="http://www.myserver.com/Contact"
    xmlns="http://www.myserver.com/Contact">

<xs:element name="name" type="xs:string"/>
<xs:schema>

<?xml version="1.0" encoding="UTF-8" ?>
<xs:schema xmlns:xs="http://www.w3.org/2001/XMLSchema"
    targetNamespace="http://www.myserver.com/Contact"
    xmlns="http://www.myserver.com/Contact">

<xs:element name="address" type="xs:string"/>
<xs:schema>

<?xml version="1.0" encoding="UTF-8" ?>
<xs:schema xmlns:xs="http://www.w3.org/2001/XMLSchema"
    targetNamespace="http://www.myserver.com/Contact"
    xmlns="http://www.myserver.com/Contact">
<xs:element name="phone" type="xs:string"/>
<xs:schema>
```

The resulting "umbrella" Schema will look like this:

```
<?xml version="1.0" encoding="UTF-8" ?>
<xs:schema xmlns:xs="http://www.w3.org/2001/XMLSchema"
    targetNamespace="http://www.myserver.com/Contact"
    xmlns="http://www.myserver.com/Contact">

<xs:include schemaLocation="Name.xsd"/>
<xs:include schemaLocation="Address.xsd"/>
<xs:include schemaLocation="Phone.xsd"/>

<xs:element name="contact">
 <xs:complexType>
  <xs:complexContent>
   <xs:element ref="name"/>
   <xs:element ref="address"/>
   <xs:element ref="phone"/>
  </xs:complexContent>
 </xs:complexType>
</xs:element>
```

Since all of the Schema are part of the same namespace, we can include the Schema. And we also can eliminate much of the clutter from the multiple namespace approach.

However, one distinct disadvantage is that although our namespace is reflected in each of the documents, none of them is a complete definition of the components in the namespace. That means, if we publish these Schema, someone could reference one of our multiple parts, and only gain access to a portion of the namespace, but be under the impression they are accessing the whole namespace. That can lead to problems, which is why the "zero" namespaces, or Chameleon approach makes sense.

ZERO NAMESPACES

The Chameleon approach has the benefits of using the umbrella approach, in that it allows importing, and it also eliminates clutter. The multiple parts of the Schema do not have any namespace declaration:

```
<?xml version="1.0" encoding="UTF-8" ?>
<xs:schema xmlns:xs="http://www.w3.org/2001/XMLSchema">
 <xs:element name="name" type="xs:string"/>
<xs:schema>

<?xml version="1.0" encoding="UTF-8" ?>
<xs:schema xmlns:xs="http://www.w3.org/2001/XMLSchema">
 <xs:element name="address" type="xs:string"/>
<xs:schema>

<?xml version="1.0" encoding="UTF-8" ?>
<xs:schema xmlns:xs="http://www.w3.org/2001/XMLSchema">
 <xs:element name="phone" type="xs:string"/>
<xs:schema>
```

But then we can create another "umbrella" Schema as before:

```
<?xml version="1.0" encoding="UTF-8" ?>
<xs:schema xmlns:xs="http://www.w3.org/2001/XMLSchema"
```

```
        targetNamespace="http://www.myserver.com/Contact"
        xmlns="http://www.myserver.com/Contact">

<xs:include schemaLocation="Name.xsd"/>
<xs:include schemaLocation="Address.xsd"/>
<xs:include schemaLocation="Phone.xsd"/>

<xs:element name="contact">
 <xs:complexType>
  <xs:complexContent>
   <xs:element ref="name"/>
   <xs:element ref="address"/>
   <xs:element ref="phone"/>
  </xs:complexContent>
 </xs:complexType>
</xs:element>
```

Because Chameleon Schema take on the namespace characteristics of the document they are included in, this has a similar effect to the "one namespace" approach outlined in the previous section. However, now we have a set of Schema which can be used easily not just with this Schema, but with any others in our organization as well, without worrying about namespace restrictions. And we still have one single Schema that accurately describes the complete namespace we were describing. On the whole, this is a very effective, dynamic approach to segmenting Schema.

However, there is one big caveat with this technique, and that is that without using namespaces, the potential for namespace collisions increases dramatically. If Schema are being authored by multiple groups within your organization, for example, it would be possible for two groups to come up with a similar element that would conflict. For example, let's say a design group came up with an element called `<color>` for a product, which specified a precise part number for a paint manufacturer's color code, while a marketing group came up with a `<color>` element which specified the consumer-friendly, marketing names of colors for the product. With the chameleon approach, this situation would cause a namespace conflict, as both `<color>` elements would be incorporated into the final Schema. The best way to avoid potential conflicts such as this is to make use of namespaces; that is why they exist.

BEST PRACTICES RESOURCES

The best resource for the development of best practices as they relate to XML Schema comes from the discussions on the xml-dev mailing list. Those discussions are being turned into a constantly evolving document maintained by Roger Costello, which can be found at

`http://www.xfront.com/BestPracticesHomepage.html`

If you are interested in contributing to the development of XML Schema best practices, or would like to learn more about best practices as they are discussed, this is undoubtedly the best resource available.

Contributors to the discussions about best practices read like a who's who of XML: Rick Jelliffe, Robin Cover, Henry Thompson, Tim Bray, and a host of others have debated these issues and tried to reach some consensus about what constitutes best practices.

CONCLUSIONS

This chapter does not represent a comprehensive list of all the issues that will confront you when authoring your XML Schema, nor does it address all of the issues relating to the development of best practices when it comes to Schema authoring. To do that would really be beyond the scope of this book. Aside from that, it is simply not possible. XML Schema have not been a technology long enough for a set of best practices to be developed which could even come close to being considered comprehensive.

However, what we have tried to do is give you an overview of some of the more common best practice issues you will face in Schema authoring, and more importantly, give you an idea about some of the considerations that go into the development of best practices.

In any technology area, best practices are only developed through a combination of efforts: experience and dialog. The best practice you can engage in when authoring Schema is to consult with other developers about issues when you are confronted with a problem, and to discuss possible solutions, along with the implications of those solutions. That practice will lead to the best designed solutions possible.

IN THE REAL WORLD

Best practices are not designed by a committee at the W3C, but rather through the knowledge and discussion of experts in the field who are using the technology. The experience they develop as early adopters of a technology, such as XML Schema, can be valuable in helping to avoid making the same mistakes others have already made.

While we have outlined some of these issues in this chapter, the best approach to developing best practices in your own Schema authoring efforts would be to participate in the communities of developers dedicated to working with XML. You should be aware of resources, such as the XML-DEV mailing list, and use those resources for information and discussion as you confront issues with building your own Schema. Location of these resources, including where to subscribe to the XML-DEV, list are listed in Appendix A, "Schema Resources."

Of the best practice issues we've discussed in this chapter, the one you will face the most often, is whether to use namespaces, and how to use those namespaces. While there are some instances where not using a namespace can serve as a shortcut, and make your life easier, you should also be aware of the possible consequences. If you choose not to use namespaces in a multipart Schema, such as in a chameleon method, you should be aware that you are setting up the potential for namespace conflicts, should your namespace ever be used outside the organization, or if your Schema grows to become more complicated. Namespaces were developed to help keep complicated Schema and names in check, and more often than not, you should make use of them.

Similarly, the Russian Doll design, while not the most flexible Schema design, can be a useful tool when rapidly prototyping. Very often, you will find that it is quick and easy to generate a Russian Doll Schema, and then as you evaluate your needs more closely, shift that Schema to another paradigm, such as the Venetian blind design.

In the Real World, the best thing you can do to adopt the best practices for Schema authoring is plan carefully. By determining the needs for your Schema in advance, working closely with the users of your Schema, and keeping up with events in the Schema development community, you can be sure that your Schema designs will be the best they possibly can be.

CHAPTER 18

SCHEMA ALTERNATIVES AND FUTURE DIRECTIONS

In this chapter

With any new technology, such as XML Schema, there will be a number of questions which will arise as you begin to use the technology in practical, everyday situations. The point of the XML Schema Recommendation is not to set something in stone which will never evolve, but rather to establish a standard so that everyone begins communicating (in this case, through Schema grammars) in the same way, so that problem areas and issues can be identified and then addressed.

While it may seem like exposing a technology's limitations is stifling, exactly the opposite is true; by discovering how Schema are best applied, and where they fall short, organizations such as the W3C can start working on solutions to address those problems.

The XML Schema Recommendation cannot be everything to everybody, and there are certainly a number of developers who feel that the XML Schema Recommendation falls short of the idealism that motivated XML in the first place.

While the debate continues about how to address shortcomings in the Recommendation, or if indeed, there are shortcomings, some have taken matters into their own hands.

There are a number of alternative schema languages which have been written by various groups, such as OASIS. These "alternative" Schema are not insignificant, in that many address problems found in the current version of XML Schema. And it is possible to create Schema which incorporate some of the features of these languages into them as well.

Some of the more popular alternatives to the XML Schema Recommendation include

- TREX—A Schema alternative written by James Clark, which is now being merged with RELAX.
- RELAX—A Schema alternative written by Makoto Murata, which is being merged with TREX to form the new OASIS sponsored RELAX NG standard.
- Schematron—A Schema alternative and supplement written by Rick Jelliffe and now being continued as an open source project.

Let's take a look at each one of these alternatives and what they have to offer as well as their limitations.

To give you an idea how each one of the alternative Schema technologies compares to the XML Schema Recommendation, we'll look at each technology and how it can be used to describe a simple XML instance document for a business card, as shown in Listing 18.1.

LISTING 18.1 AN EXAMPLE OF A BUSINESS CARD XML INSTANCE DOCUMENT

```
<?xml version="1.0" encoding="UTF-8" ?>

<card xmlns="http://www.myserver.com/card"
      xmlns:xsi="http://www.3.org/2001/XMLSchema-Instance"
      xsi:schemaLocation="http://www.myserver.com/card
      http://www.myserver.com/card.xsd">
```

LISTING 18.1   CONTINUED

```
<name>John Doe</name>
<title>President</title>
<company>John Doe Inc.</company>
<phone>800-555-1212</phone>
<email>jdoe@hiscompany.com</email>
</card>
```

The XML Schema that can be used to describe this instance document is shown in Listing 18.2.

LISTING 18.2   AN EXAMPLE OF A BUSINESS CARD SCHEMA WRITTEN USING THE XML SCHEMA RECOMMENDATION

```
<?xml version="1.0" encoding="UTF-8" ?>
<xs:schema xmlns:xs="http://www.w3.org/2001/XMLSchema"
    xmlns:xsi="http://www.w3.org/2001/XMLSchema-Instance"
    targetNamespace="http://www.myserver.com/card"
    xmlns="http://www.myserver.com/card">

<!-- Define the card -->
<xs:element>
 <xs:complexContent>
  <xs:complexType name="card">
   <xs:element name="name" type="xs:string"/>
   <xs:element name="title" type="xs:string"/>
   <xs:element name="company" type="xs:string"/>
   <xs:element name="phone" type="phone_number"/>
   <xs:element name="email" type="xs:string"/>
  </xs:complexType>
 </xs:complexContent>
</xs:element>

<!-- Define the Phone Number type -->
<xs:simpleType name="phone_number">
 <xs:restriction base="xs:string">
  <xs:pattern value="[0-9]{3}\-[0-9]{3}\-[0-9]{4}"/>
 </xs:restriction>
</xs:simpleType>

</xs:schema>
```

As we present the alternative technologies, you might want to see how they compare to the XML Schema shown in Listing 18.2. You will probably notice that many of the alternatives look very similar to XML Schema, and that is because they are all based in XML, so there are bound to be some similarities. Also, because we are working with a simple example, many of the Schema alternatives will function similarly to XML Schema at this level. However, there are often some fundamental differences that might not be apparent, but we will be sure to point those out.

PART

IV

CH

18

TREX

The first alternative Schema we will look at is *Tree Regular Expressions for XML*, or *TREX*. TREX was developed by James Clark, a leading SGML and XML developer, and is supported in his Web site located at

```
http://www.thaiopensource.com/trex/
```

Like XML Schema, TREX is a grammar-based solution that allows you to describe patterns for XML instance documents using an XML-based syntax.

Caution

Although TREX is presented here as a Schema alternative, it is not wise to base your documents on the TREX standard. The current TREX standard is no longer being developed, but instead is being merged with the RELAX standard to form RELAX NG, which is covered later in this chapter. Because RELAX NG is a merger of TREX and RELAX, this section will aid you in understanding RELAX NG, but should be considered informational only.

The result is documents which look very similar to XML Schema; however, there are some differences.

The main features of TREX include

- An XML-based syntax
- Simple, easy to learn syntax
- Support for XML namespaces
- Datatype support based on the XML Schema Part II Recommendation
- Anonymous datatypes
- Nesting of TREX grammars
- The creation of name classes

You can use these features to create a Schema which will accomplish nearly everything that an XML Schema can accomplish. However, there are some features which are not supported by TREX at all. Features *not* included in TREX are

- No default values for attributes
- No entity support
- No notation support
- Whitespace is not significant

The most notable of the features not included in TREX are the lack of support for entities and notations. Both of these features are included in XML Schema to maintain backward compatibility with DTDs. However, these are very advanced features of XML which are frequently not used and are often the source of errors and confusion. Therefore, unless you explicitly need entity and/or notation support, the lack of these features is not really significant.

TREX Schema are called grammars, and an example of the grammar which would describe our business card XML instance document is shown in Listing 18.3.

LISTING 18.3   AN EXAMPLE OF A TREX SCHEMA, FOR A SIMPLE BUSINESS CARD

```
<?xml version="1.0" encoding="iso-8859-1"?>
<grammar xmlns="http://www.thaiopensource.com/trex"
xmlns:xs="http://www.w3.org/2001/XMLSchema"
ns="http://www.myserver.com/card">

 <element name="card">
  <sequence>
   <element name="name">
    <anyString/>
   </element>
   <element name="title">
    <anyString/>
   </element>
   <element name="company">
    <anyString/>
   </element>
   <element name="phone">
    <xs:restriction xmlns:trex="http://www.thaiopensource.com/trex"
➥base="xs:string" trex:role="datatype">
     <xs:pattern xmlns="" value="[0-9]{3}\-[0-9]{3}\-[0-9]{4}"/>
    </xs:restriction>
   </element>
   <element name="email">
    <anyString/>
   </element>
  </sequence>
 </element>
</grammar>
```

If you are interested in a more detailed explanation of the features and syntax of TREX, you can turn to Appendix B, "Schema Alternatives: TREX," which contains more detailed information about writing your own TREX grammars.

RELAX

The debate over the complexity of the XML Schema Recommendation also sparked activity from Makoto Murata, who authored *RELAX (Regular Language description for XML)*. RELAX has also been adopted by INSTAC XML SWF, which is a part of the Japanese Standard Association (JSA). In addition to this support, Murata has committed to supporting RELAX publicly for a number of years, and maintains a site dedicated to RELAX activity located at

```
http://www.xml.gr.jp/relax/
```

However, RELAX is also in a state of evolution, and the Organization for the Advancement of Structured Information Standards (OASIS) has formed a working committee to create a Schema alternative based on both TREX and RELAX called RELAX NG.

Caution

Although RELAX is presented here as a Schema alternative, it is not wise to base your documents on the RELAX standard. Although the RELAX author has pledged to support the RELAX Core for five years, RELAX is being merged with the TREX standard to form RELAX NG, which is covered later in this chapter. Because RELAX NG is a merger of RELAX and TREX, this section will aid you in understanding RELAX NG, but if you are considering using RELAX as an alternative to XML Schema, you should instead look at RELAX NG.

Despite the unfortunate name, RELAX NG does promise to be a widely supported information standard, and we discuss it later on in this chapter. However, since it is based on the RELAX standard, it's helpful to know a little about RELAX as well.

RELAX is broken up into two sections: RELAX Core and RELAX Namespaces. The RELAX Core only supports single namespace documents, while the RELAX Namespaces standard supports multiple namespace documents. Some features of both RELAX parts include

- Easy to learn, simple syntax
- XML-based syntax
- Support from standards organizations (JSA and ISO/IEC)
- Support for datatypes through XML Schema Part II
- Support for entities (unparsed external entities) and notations

RELAX does not offer support for multiple namespaces in the RELAX Core.

While RELAX does include support for some of the DTD features that are also supported in XML Schema, the authors of RELAX caution against using these features. Features such as entities and notations are included in RELAX through the inclusion of the XML Schema Recommendation, Part II. This makes using these features complicated and can lead to the introduction of errors in your RELAX documents. In general, if you need to use these features, it is best to stick to the XML Schema Recommendation.

RELAX Schema are called modules, and Listing 18.4 shows an example of the RELAX module that would describe our business card XML instance document. If you look closely, you will note many similarities to XML Schema.

LISTING 18.4   AN EXAMPLE OF A RELAX SCHEMA, FOR A SIMPLE BUSINESS CARD

```
<?xml version="1.0" encoding="UTF-8" ?>

<module
    moduleVersion="1.0"
    relaxCoreVersion="1.0"
    targetNamespace="http://www.myserver.com/card"
    xmlns="http://www.xml.gr.jp/xmlns/relaxCore">
```

LISTING 18.4   CONTINUED

```
<interface>
 <export label="card"/>
</interface>

<elementRule role="card">
 <tag name="card"/>
 <sequence>
  <ref label="name"/>
  <ref label="company"/>
  <ref label="title"/>
  <ref label="phone"/>
  <ref label="email"/>
 </sequence>
</elementRule>

<elementRule role="name" type="string"/>
<tag name="name"/>

<elementRule role="company" type="string"/>
<tag name="company"/>

<elementRule role="title" type="string"/>
<tag name="title"/>

<elementRule role="phone" type="string">
 <tag/>
 <pattern value="[0-9]{3}\-[0-9]{3}\-[0-9]{4}"/>
</elementRule>

<elementRule role="fax" type="string">
 <tag/>
 <pattern value="[0-9]{3}\-[0-9]{3}\-[0-9]{4}"/>
</elementRule>

<elementRule role="email" type="string" occurs="?"/>
<tag name="email"/>

</module>
```

If you are interested in learning more about the specific syntax and implementation of RELAX modules, RELAX is covered in greater detail in Appendix C, "Schema Alternatives: RELAX."

SCHEMATRON

While TREX and RELAX bear striking similarity to the XML Schema Recommendation, one alternative takes a very different approach: Schematron.

Schematron was developed by Rick Jelliffe, and is not so much an alternative to XML Schema as it is a supplemental technology. Jelliffe has described Schematron as a feather duster that reaches into the corners that the XML Schema vacuum cleaner can't reach. Schematron is supported via a Web site, located at

```
http://www.ascc.net/xml/schematron
```

What makes Schematron different from the other Schema alternatives is that Schematron is *not* grammar-based. Instead, it is rules-based, and therefore provides a level of validity checking simply not possible with XML Schema.

For example, Schematron allows you to check the content of elements and attributes, and then check for dependencies based on those results. Schematron also provides you with a mechanism for returning "plain English" error messages which are easily understood.

For example, let's say you had the following XML instance:

```
<employee SSN="331001234">Jane Doe</employee>
```

Schematron would allow you to check to make sure that the `<employee>` element had the SSN attribute, count the digits in the SSN attribute, and ensure that a name was included for the element content. And if there was a problem, using Schematron, you could specify an error message such as

```
"Social Security Numbers should be exactly 9 digits"
```

Schematron is very flexible, and in fact, it can be used not only with XML Schema, but also with RELAX modules and TREX grammars as well!

As if that weren't enough, Schematron is also very simple. There are only six basic elements in Schematron, and the technology is built using XSLT and XPath. So if you already know XPath and XSLT, Schematron can be learned *very* quickly.

Schematron works by using XPath to specify the location and conditions which are being checked, and it uses XSLT to perform the manipulation of the Schematron Schema and the application of the Schematron Schema to your instance documents.

Another advantage of Schematron is that because it is based on core XML technologies, Schematron Schema can actually be nested directly within XML Schema, using an `<annotation>` and the `<appinfo>` elements.

Because of the fundamentally different approach, Schematron Schema look very different from XML Schema and RELAX or TREX Schema, as can be seen in Listing 18.5.

LISTING 18.5   AN EXAMPLE OF A SCHEMATRON SCHEMA, FOR A SIMPLE BUSINESS CARD

```
<?xml version="1.0" encoding="UTF-8" ?>
<schema xmlns="http://www.ascc.net/xml/schematron">
<title>An Example Schematron Schema for Business Car</title>

<pattern name="Root Element">
 <rule context="/*">
  <assert test="name()='card'">Root element should be card.</assert>
 </rule>
</pattern>

<pattern name="Count Elements">
 <rule context="/*">
  <assert test="count(name) = 1">There should be 1 name element.</assert>
  <assert test="count(title) = 1">There should be 1 title element.</assert>
```

LISTING 18.5   CONTINUED

```
    <assert test="count(company) = 1">There should be 1 company element.</assert>
    <assert test="count(email) = 1">There should be 1 email element.</assert>
  </rule>
</pattern>

<pattern name="Check the Phone Number Element">
  <rule context="phone">
    <report test="string-length(phone) &lt; 10">Please check the phone number
➥and make sure it is at least 10 digits</report>
  </rule>
</pattern>

</schema>
```

However, if you are already familiar with XPath and XSLT, the Schematron syntax is incredibly simple and easy to learn.

Schematron is an excellent choice for a supplementary technology to provide a finer level of validation than possible with XML Schema. If you are interested in learning more about the specifics of the Schematron standard and implementation, it is covered in Appendix D, "Schema Alternatives: Schematron."

OASIS AND SCHEMA

Although XML is a Web-related technology, and the World Wide Web Consortium does work closely with Web-related technologies, the W3C is certainly not the only organization concerned with XML. XML is a technology that is not strictly related to the Web, but rather, because of its roots in SGML, XML is being watched by a number of organizations that deal with structured data and markup.

One of those organizations is the Organization for the Advancement of Structured Information Standards, or OASIS. The OASIS mission statement is

> "OASIS, the Organization for the Advancement of Structured Information Standards, is a non-profit, international consortium that creates interoperable industry specifications based on public standards such as XML and SGML, as well as others that are related to structured information processing."

So, how does OASIS relate to XML and XML Schema? Well, it is important to remember that while the W3C is seen as the authoritative body for Web standards, it is actually not a standards organization in the traditional sense. Recommendations are developed by committee, but adopted only when approved by Tim Berners-Lee, the W3C director. Other organizations, such as OASIS, also enjoy prowess in the development of standards, and those standards are just as likely to be adopted in industry or by true standards bodies, such as the ISO.

With a Recommendation as controversial as XML Schema, this is not insignificant. In fact, OASIS has formed a working committee to put forth an alternative Schema language, called

RELAX NG, which is a combination of the TREX and RELAX Schema languages. While the standard is still in its infancy, it is a turn of events which should be noticed. The W3C XML Schema Recommendation will certainly enjoy wide adoption; however, OASIS could provide a real, viable alternative with RELAX NG, which is something to consider when you are evaluating the technologies for your needs.

RELAX NG

The most promising Schema alternative currently being developed is the RELAX NG standard, which is being sponsored by OASIS. The RELAX NG standard is the result of a positive reception among developers to both TREX and RELAX, and the desire to see features of each incorporated into the other. Thus, RELAX NG, or RELAX "Next Generation," is a merger of TREX and RELAX.

OASIS has formed a working committee charged with the development of RELAX NG, and it maintains a site located at

`http://www.oasis-open.org/committees/relax-ng/`

which tracks development of the RELAX NG standard.

RELAX NG does combine the features of TREX and RELAX into one syntax, and it is also XML-based. The goal of RELAX NG is to provide a simple, easy to learn syntax for describing grammars which is not necessarily hampered by backward compatibility and complexity as is the case with XML Schema.

The result is a promising, although still nascent, Schema language which could prove a viable and worthy alternative to XML Schema. Let's take a look.

ELEMENTS IN RELAX NG

Elements are declared in RELAX NG using the `<element>` element, which accepts a `name` attribute to specify the element name. To denote that an element has text content, you can use the `<text/>` element. For example

```
<element name="title">
 <text/>
</element>
```

declares an element called `<title>` which can contain a `string`.

There are also some other elements which can be used as children of the `<element>` element to denote the occurrence of children, such as

- `<choice>`
- `<optional>`
- `<zeroOrMore>`
- `<oneOrMore>`

These elements control content depending on the nesting order. For example, to denote that an element is optional

```
<element name="phone">
 <optional>
  <element name="extension">
   <text/>
  </element>
 </optional>
</element>
```

This creates a `<phone>` element, with an optional child element of `<extension>`.

The `<choice>` element allows us to create an "or" similar to "|" in a DTD:

```
<element name="preferred_number">
 <choice>
  <element name="phone">
   <text/>
  </element>
  <element name="cell">
   <text/>
  </element>
 </choice>
</element>
```

This creates an element called `<preferred_number>` with a choice between `<phone>` and `<cell>` as the child element. Finally, to achieve the same results as the "*" and "+" symbols in a DTD, we have the `<zeroOrMore>` and the `<oneOrMore>` elements. These can be used to specify that a child element must occur either zero or more times, or one or more times:

```
<element name="name">
 <oneOrMore>
  <element name="phone">
   <text/>
  </element>
 </oneOrMore>
 <zeroOrMore>
  <element name="email">
   <text/>
  </element>
 </zeroOrMore>
</element>
```

This RELAX NG element declaration specifies that a `<name>` element must have at least one `<phone>` child, but could have many more, and that the `<email>` element is optional, but it may also contain multiple `<email>`s.

ATTRIBUTES IN RELAX NG

Attributes in RELAX NG are handled similarly to elements, and there is an `<attribute>` element which has a name attribute to specify the attribute name:

```
<element name="phone">
 <text/>
 <attribute name="ext">
  <text/>
```

```
</attribute>
</element>
```

The `<attribute>` declaration itself is nested within the `<element>` declaration for which the attribute is being defined. The attribute content is specified in the same manner as elements, with the `<text/>` element being used for text. (For datatypes, see the next section.)

In fact, you can also use the `<choice>` or `<optional>` elements with attributes as well:

```
<element name="phone">
 <text/>
 <optional>
  <attribute name="extension">
   <text/>
  </attribute>
 </optional>
</element>
```

This creates a `<phone>` element with an optional extension attribute.

DATATYPES IN RELAX NG

Datatype support in RELAX NG is fairly robust. RELAX NG uses *datatype libraries* which allow you to specify the namespace for your datatypes, giving you access to any other datatype definition set, such as the XML Schema Recommendation, Part II.

The datatype library can be specified for an individual element or attribute:

```
<element name="quantity">
<data type="integer"
➥datatypeLibrary="http://www.w3.org/2001/XMLSchema-datatypes"/>
</element>
```

Or it can be declared globally for your RELAX NG grammar:

```
<grammar xmlns="http://relaxng.org/ns/structure/0.9"
         ns="http://relaxng.org/ns/structure/0.9"
         datatypeLibrary="http://www.w3.org/2001/XMLSchema-datatypes">
```

To express constraining facets for datatypes, you can make use of the `<param>` element, which has a name attribute that can be used to express the name of the constraining facet, with the value of the facet contained in the `<param>` content:

```
<element name="quantity">
 <data type="integer"
➥datatypeLibrary="http://www.w3.org/2001/XMLSchema-datatypes">
  <param name="minInclusive">0</param>
  <param name="maxInclusive">12</param>
 </data>
</element>
```

This allows you to exploit the full range of datatypes from other standards and incorporate them into your RELAX NG documents. Datatypes can be used with both elements and attributes in RELAX NG.

RELAX NG grammars look very similar to both TREX grammars and RELAX modules, as can be seen in Listing 18.6, which shows the RELAX NG version of our business card example.

LISTING 18.6   AN ALTERNATIVE SCHEMA, WRITTEN IN RELAX NG

```xml
<?xml version="1.0" encoding="UTF-8" ?>

<grammar xmlns="http://relaxng.org/ns/structure/0.9"
         ns="http://relaxng.org/ns/structure/0.9"
         datatypeLibrary="http://www.w3.org/2001/XMLSchema-datatypes">

 <start>
  <element name="card"/>
   <ref name="card_info"/>
  </element>
 </start>

 <define name="card_info">

  <element name="name">
   <text/>
  </element>

  <element name="title">
   <text/>
  </element>

  <element name="company">
   <text/>
  </element>

 <element name="phone">
  <data type="string">
   <param name="pattern">[0-9]{3}\-[0-9]{3}\-[0-9]{4}</param>
  </data>
 </element>

  <element name="email">
   <text/>
  </element>

 </define>
</grammar>
```

Now that you have a basic understanding of how RELAX NG works, let's take a look at another example of a RELAX NG grammar.

Caution

The information presented here concerning RELAX NG is by no means intended to be comprehensive. As is the case with any beta standard, RELAX NG is in a constant state of evolution. Should you decide to pursue RELAX NG or any other Schema alternative for your projects, you should always consult the latest version of the standard directly from the source responsible for the standard's development.

PART

IV

CH

18

A RELAX NG EXAMPLE

The RELAX NG standard is still in a state of flux; however, let's take a look at an example using the current RELAX NG version and see how it compares to an XML Schema.

We'll start with the XML Schema for a contact instance document, as shown in Listing 18.7. This Schema describes an instance document that contains a root <contact> element, with its children being a <name> element, optional <company> and <department> elements, a required <phone> element, and optional elements for <fax>, <cell>, <pager>, and <email>.

LISTING 18.7   AN XML SCHEMA DESCRIBING A CONTACT XML INSTANCE DOCUMENT

```
<?xml version="1.0" encoding="UTF-8" ?>
<xs:schema xmlns:xs="http://www.w3.org/2001/XMLSchema"
    xmlns:xsi="http://www.w3.org/2001/XMLSchema-Instance"
    targetNamespace="http://www.myserver.com/Contact"
    xmlns="http://www.myserver.com/Contact">

<!-- Define the types for the Contact Schema -->

<!-- Define the Contact type -->
<xs:complexType name="contact">
 <xs:element name="name" type="xs:string"/>
 <xs:element name="company" type="xs:string" minOccurs="0"/>
 <xs:element name="department" type="xs:string" minOccurs="0"/>
 <xs:element name="phone" type="phone_number"/>
 <xs:element name="fax" type="phone_number" minOccurs="0"/>
 <xs:element name="cell" type="phone_number" minOccurs="0"/>
 <xs:element name="pager" type="phone_number" minOccurs="0"/>
 <xs:element name="email" type="xs:string" minOccurs="0"/>
</xs:complexType>

<!-- Define the Address type -->
<xs:complexType name="address">
 <xs:sequence>
  <xs:element name="address" type="xs:string"/>
  <xs:element name="address2" type="xs:string" minOccurs="0"/>
  <xs:element name="city" type="xs:string"/>
  <xs:element name="state" type="state"/>
  <xs:element name="zip" type="zip"/>
 </xs:sequence>
</xs:complexType>

<!-- Define the State type -->
<!-- Long winded enumeration restricts state abbreviation values to
➥valid states -->
<xs:simpleType name="state">
 <xs:restriction base="xs:string">
  <xs:enumeration value="AL"/>        <!--Alabama -->
  <xs:enumeration value="AK"/>        <!--Alaska -->
  <!-- ETC.. -->
  <xs:enumeration value="WI"/>        <!--Wisconsin -->
  <xs:enumeration value="WY"/>        <!--Wyoming -->
 </xs:restriction>
</xs:simpleType>
```

LISTING 18.7   CONTINUED

```
<!-- Define the ZIP type -->
<xs:simpleType name="zip">
 <xs:restriction base="xs:string">
  <xs:pattern value="[0-9]{5}(\-)?([0-9]{4})?"/>
 </xs:restriction>
</xs:simpleType>

<!-- Define the Phone Number type -->
<xs:simpleType name="phone_number">
 <xs:restriction base="xs:string">
  <xs:pattern value="[0-9]{3}\-[0-9]{3}\-[0-9]{4}"/>
 </xs:restriction>
</xs:simpleType>

</xs:schema>
```

Now, to begin the process of converting the XML Schema into a RELAX NG Schema, we first start out with a <grammar> element, which replaces the <schema> element:

```
<grammar xmlns="http://relaxng.org/ns/structure/0.9"
         ns="http://relaxng.org/ns/structure/0.9"
         datatypeLibrary="http://www.w3.org/2001/XMLSchema-datatypes">
```

Our <grammar> element contains similar information, such as an xmlns attribute which declares the namespace, as well as an ns namespace attribute for the RELAX NG namespace. There is also an attribute called datatypeLibrary, which is used by RELAX NG processors to determine where the datatypes used in the document are defined. In this case, we are importing the datatypes from the W3C XML Schema Part II Recommendation. However, you could in theory use this attribute to link to your own custom datatype libraries as well, which gives RELAX NG some added flexibility.

Next, we make use of the <start> element to define our instance document's root element:

```
<start>
 <element name="card">
  <ref name="personal_info"/>
  <ref name="us_address"/>
  <ref name="phone_info"/>
 </element>
</start>
```

The <start> element contains an element declaration for the root element, and then we use a series of references to define the content model for our root element. This helps keep the content model simple and easy to read, and in RELAX NG, it is legal to reference items which have not yet been defined. So we have broken the content up into three sections, "personal_info", "us_address", and "phone_info", which we will now define.

RELAX NG provides an element called <define> which allows you to group together a series of element declarations into a single definition which can be referenced in other content models, as we have done with our <start> element. So, now we're going to use <define> to create the "personal_info" section:

```
<define name="personal_info">
 <element name="name">
  <text/>
 </element>
 <optional>
  <element name="company">
   <text/>
  </element>
  <element name="department">
   <text/>
  </element>
 </optional>
</define>
```

As you can see, our element declarations are very simple, since they are just strings. We've also used the `<optional>` element to denote the elements which are not required in the instance document.

Next, we move on to define the `"us_address"` section:

```
<define name="us_address">
 <element name="address">
  <text/>
 </element>

 <optional>
  <element name="address2">
   <text/>
  </element>
 </optional>

 <element name="city">
  <text/>
 </element>

 <element name="state">
  <choice>
   <value>AL</value>      <!--Alabama -->
   <value>AK</value>      <!--Alaska -->
   <!--ETC… -->
   <value>WI</value>      <!--Wisconsin -->
   <value>WY</value>      <!--Wyoming -->
  </choice>
 </element>

 <element name="zip">
  <data type="string">
   <param name="pattern">[0-9]{5}(\-)?([0-9]{4})?</param>
  </data>
 </element>
</define>
```

Here, we have a number of straightforward element declarations, but then we have two slightly more advanced declarations for our `<state>` and `<zip>` elements.

For the `<state>` element, we make use of the `<choice>` attribute, which denotes an enumeration, and then allows us to specify the enumeration values with each value contained in a `<value>` element.

With the `<zip>` element, we are using a datatype. Recall that we specified our `datatypeLibrary` in the `<grammar>` element, which defines the namespace for our datatypes. So here, all we needed to do was to use the `<data>` element with the `type` attribute to specify our datatype, in this case a `string`. To use the constraining facets to apply a regular expression to our `string`, we use the `<param>` element, which through the `name` attribute allows you to specify the constraining facet you would like to apply for the datatype. The value of the constraining facet is then specified as the content of the `<param>` element.

We can make use of that same technique for datatypes in the `"phone_info"` section as well:

```
<define name="phone_info">
 <element name="phone">
  <data type="string">
   <param name="pattern">[0-9]{3}\-[0-9]{3}\-[0-9]{4}</param>
  </data>
 </element>
</define>
```

When we bring all of the elements together, we have a completed RELAX NG schema, as shown in Listing 18.8.

LISTING 18.8   THE SCHEMA FOR A CONTACT XML INSTANCE DOCUMENT, WRITTEN USING THE RELAX NG STANDARD

```
<?xml version="1.0" encoding="UTF-8" ?>

<grammar xmlns="http://relaxng.org/ns/structure/0.9"
         ns="http://relaxng.org/ns/structure/0.9"
         datatypeLibrary="http://www.w3.org/2001/XMLSchema-datatypes">

 <start>
  <element name="card">
   <ref name="personal_info"/>
   <ref name="us_address"/>
   <ref name="phone_info"/>
  </element>
 </start>

 <define name="personal_info">
  <element name="name">
   <text/>
  </element>

  <optional>
   <element name="company">
    <text/>
   </element>
   <element name="department">
    <text/>
   </element>
  </optional>
 </define>
```

LISTING 18.8 CONTINUED

```
<define name="us_address">
 <element name="address">
  <text/>
 </element>

 <optional>
  <element name="address2">
   <text/>
  </element>
 </optional>

 <element name="city">
  <text/>
 </element>

 <element name="state">
  <choice>
   <value>AL</value>        <!--Alabama -->
   <value>AK</value>        <!--Alaska -->
   <!--ETC... -->
   <value>WI</value>        <!--Wisconsin -->
   <value>WY</value>        <!--Wyoming -->
  </choice>
 </element>

 <element name="zip">
  <data type="string">
   <param name="pattern">[0-9]{5}(\-)?([0-9]{4})?</param>
  </data>
 </element>
</define>

<define name="phone_info">
 <element name="phone">
  <data type="string">
   <param name="pattern">[0-9]{3}\-[0-9]{3}\-[0-9]{4}</param>
  </data>
 </element>

 <element name="fax">
  <data type="string">
   <param name="pattern">[0-9]{3}\-[0-9]{3}\-[0-9]{4}</param>
  </data>
 </element>

 <element name="cell">
  <data type="string">
   <param name="pattern">[0-9]{3}\-[0-9]{3}\-[0-9]{4}</param>
  </data>
 </element>

 <element name="pager">
  <data type="string">
   <param name="pattern">[0-9]{3}\-[0-9]{3}\-[0-9]{4}</param>
  </data>
```

LISTING 18.8   CONTINUED

```
   </element>
  </define>

</grammar>
```

As you can see, RELAX NG looks similar to XML Schema, but still has some significant differences. Overall, RELAX NG is much simpler to implement, without being significantly less powerful. However, RELAX NG is still in the early stages of development, and there is potential for change. As RELAX NG continues to develop, it could become bogged down in debates over features and complexity, or it could mature into a very nice, robust technology. If you are seeking stability and long-term support for your projects, XML Schema are currently a better choice for your projects; however, RELAX NG is a technology to keep a close eye on for the future.

THE SEMANTIC WEB

As the standards and technologies change, the makeup of the Web itself also continues to change. And as the users of the Web develop more sophisticated information applications, there is a need for new and innovative models of information delivery and access: the Semantic Web.

From the W3C site (`http://www.w3.org/2001/sw/`), the goal of the Semantic Web is

> "The Semantic Web is a vision: the idea of having data on the Web defined and linked in a way that it can be used by machines not just for display purposes, but for automation, integration and reuse of data across various applications. In order to make this vision a reality for the Web, supporting standards, technologies and policies must be designed to enable machines to make more sense of the Web, with the result of making the Web more useful for humans. Facilities and technologies to put machine-understandable data on the Web are rapidly becoming a high priority for many communities. For the Web to scale, programs must be able to share and process data even when these programs have been designed totally independently. The Web can reach its full potential only if it becomes a place where data can be shared and processed by automated tools as well as by people."

Thus the goal of the W3C is clearly to move forward in the direction of facilitating standards that will lead toward the vision of the Semantic Web. Many of these standards are XML-related, and will have a direct impact on how XML-based information is processed and distributed on the Web. While the Semantic Web is still in the nascent stages of development, anyone serious about XML development should be keeping an eye on Semantic Web activity at the W3C, and how that activity may impact your own development projects.

CONCLUSION

The XML Schema Recommendation provides a flexible and robust framework for writing the grammars necessary to describe XML instance documents. XML Schema addresses some very complicated issues, such as backward compatibility with DTDs, and the integration of datatypes into XML. However, some of the features which are necessary also create a level of complexity that can keep many from adopting the technology.

As a result of dissatisfaction, alternatives such as RELAX NG and Schematron have come up to address the flaws or shortcomings of the XML Schema Recommendation. These technologies offer viable alternatives to XML Schema, or they can serve as supplemental technologies as well.

There are no easy answers as to what technology is right or wrong for your project. Only through a careful study of your options and careful planning will you be able to determine which technology best addresses your own organization's needs.

Keeping that in mind, XML Schema are not for everyone; however, they do provide a flexible, comprehensive, XML-based solution for specifying XML grammars. And with support from organizations like the W3C, and the wealth of information and resources about XML Schema usage, it is a powerful technology that can help you organize and distribute your XML documents.

IN THE REAL WORLD

Schema alternatives are being used by organizations in place of XML Schema, but with some reservations. RELAX is perhaps the most widely accepted of the alternatives, having been recognized by the ISO. However, because RELAX is being combined with TREX in the form of RELAX NG, it would probably be best to hold off on developing RELAX-only Schema.

In reality, the two alternatives to Schema that you should consider for your projects are RELAX NG and Schematron. However, because at the time of this writing, RELAX NG is not a complete standard, it would be hard to recommend the usage of this alternative to the XML Schema Recommendation. If you are looking for alternatives to XML Schema though, this is the standard to watch; OASIS is a pretty large force in the world of structured information, and while the W3C is seen as an important force in Web developments, the use of Schema extends well beyond the Web, so RELAX NG is likely to be an important development.

In the real world, we haven't encountered many applications using Schematron, even though we are impressed with its versatility and elegance. In reality, Schematron is not really a replacement for XML Schema, but rather a great tool for extending the functionality of a Schema, if you have specific demands and a great deal of control over the environment in which the Schema is used. If you have control over the parser, for example, then Schematron could be a great way to increase the functionality of your Schema. However, if you are exchanging Schema with outside organizations, you should probably shy away from a reliance on Schematron, since it is not widely supported.

Finally, in the real world, if you choose to use an alternative to the XML Schema Recommendation, then you should pay very special attention to the development of whatever you choose, and watch for its acceptance by a standards body. An unsanctioned standard is not likely to become common, and without common usage and widespread support, an alternative is not nearly as useful.

APPENDIXES

APPENDIX $\quad$ A

SCHEMA RESOURCES

In this Appendix:

XML AND XML SCHEMA RESOURCES

The resources contained in this appendix are meant to point you to online documentation and information available concerning XML and XML Schema. Keeping in mind that XML and XML Schema are both evolving technologies, you should use these resources to keep abreast of changes to the standards as they occur. Of course, from a standards point of view, the most important resources here will be those found at the World Wide Web Consortium (W3C); however, there are many other excellent resources on the Web which can help you keep on top of XML activity.

And as always, the Web itself is a dynamic, ever changing information space, so should some of these resources change their location, we've tried to provide you with enough information about the source so that you will be able to track down the intended information.

W3C OFFICIAL WEB SITES

The following sites comprise the pages found at the World Wide Web Consortium (W3C) that relate to XML and XML Schema. These pages should always be the first place you consult if you have a question regarding XML, XML Schema, or the implementation of XML-related technology. Recommendations and information on the W3C are updated all the time, so consulting the site on a weekly basis for the latest updates and news is a good idea.

Among these sites listed are the official published recommendations for XML and XML Schema. Although these documents are not easy to read, you should take the time to go over them and see how the languages you are using are officially defined:

- The World Wide Web Consortium Home Page
  `http://www.w3.org`
- Extensible Markup Language (XML) Activities
  `http://www.w3.org/XML/`
- Extensible Markup Language (XML) 1.0 (Second Edition)
  `http://www.w3.org/TR/REC-xml`
- XML Schema Activities
  `http://www.w3.org/XML/Schema`
- XML Schema Part 0: Primer
  `http://www.w3.org/TR/xmlschema-0/`
- XML Schema Part 1: Structures
  `http://www.w3.org/TR/xmlschema-1/`
- XML Schema Part 2: Datatypes
  `http://www.w3.org/TR/xmlschema-2/`
- Namespaces in XML
  `http://www.w3.org/TR/1999/REC-xml-names-19990114/`

- XML Path Language (XPath)
  `http://www.w3.org/TR/xpath`
- Semantic Web Activity
  `http://www.w3.org/2001/sw/`

XML RESOURCES

XML Schema are XML and therefore it makes sense that you should always consider XML resources as a starting point for learning more about XML Schema. There are a number of mailing lists, newsgroups, and Web sites which track information regarding XML. Here are a few of the more comprehensive and better maintained resources available.

- `comp.text.xml`

  The `comp.text.xml` Usenet newsgroup is the haunt of XML developers, XML users, and XML newbies alike. A community of people working with XML is readily available to provide you with some answers to XML questions, as well as some spirited debate regarding XML implementations and practices. As with most newsgroups, the signal to noise ratio at `comp.text.xml` could be better, but it is still a resource worthy of checking out.

- xml-dev

  One of the most active XML resources is the xml-dev e-mail list, which hosts thousands of subscribers who routinely post news and information regarding the progress of XML. The list serves as a source of dialogue among members of the XML development community, who often debate XML techniques, best practices, and the activities of the W3C. Any serious XML developer should consider a subscription to this list. To subscribe, send a message to `xml-dev@xml.org` with the word `"subscribe"` in the body of the message.

- xml-dev Archive (`http://lists.xml.org/archives/xml-dev/`)

  The xml-dev mailing list has been in existence for quite a few years, so there is a chance that if you have a question, someone else might have asked and answered it long ago. The archives of the mailing list can be an excellent place to search for information about your XML questions. It's also a place where you can follow the activity of the list without having a subscription filling up your inbox constantly.

- xml.org (`http://www.xml.org`)

  XML.org is a Web site sponsored by OASIS (see below) which contains many XML resources, including an XML catalog and a registry, and plays host to the xml-dev list and archives.

- XML Coverpages (`http://xml.coverpages.org`)

  Robin Cover has been writing about XML since the earliest days of the W3C's XML activity. Providing a broad range of coverage (pun intended) to all topics XML, the Cover Pages are an excellent source of news and information regarding XML.

- XML Hack (`http://www.xmlhack.com`)

  Another valuable site for information related to XML. This site is geared toward developers, and although they don't generate a lot of original content, they often serve as a great mechanism for highlighting the best content on other sites.

- James Clark's XML Resources (`http://www.jclark.com/xml/`)

  A founding father of many things SGML and XML, James Clark is an undisputed expert in the field of structured markup languages. He maintains this small resources page on his site, where you can find information about his many projects, including a number of XML parsers. This is a very valuable resource for XML developers.

- xml.com (`http://www.xml.com`)

  XML.com is a commercial site dedicated to tracking news and information regarding XML and XML-related standards. Hosted by O'Reilly, it can sometimes feel a bit like an online trade magazine, mostly because it is in fact an online trade magazine. Still, with excellent reporting and writing, you can glean a great deal of information about XML, XML Schema, and all other XML-related subjects here. It's also a great site to read about controversy and gossip regarding XML and the adoption of XML standards.

- XML FAQ (`http://www.ucc.ie/xml/`)

  Read the FAQ. If you haven't already familiarized yourself with the basics of XML, check out the Frequently Asked Questions. Posting a question to a newsgroup or mailing list which has already been addressed here is in bad form, and will likely result in the terse "Read the FAQ" response.

- OASIS (`http://www.oasis-open.org`)

  OASIS is the Organization for the Advancement of Structured Information Standards. A nonprofit, international trade organization, OASIS works to track and aid in the development of standards for structured markup and document delivery. Interoperability is the key word at OASIS, and they are a considerable lobbying power in the world of structured markup. They've also been around long before XML, with a heavy investment in SGML, so they are not lightweights, and their site can provide an incredible amount of standards-related information. Among the efforts they are involved with is ebXML, which is a set of XML standards designed to facilitate Electronic Business (the "eb") with XML.

- XML Conformance Test Suite (`http://www.oasis-open.org/committees/xmltest/testsuite.htm`)

  One of the resources hosted at the OASIS site is the XML Conformance Test Suite. You can use this test suite to check your applications to see how rigidly they adhere to the W3C Recommendation.

XML SCHEMA RESOURCES

There are a small number of resources on the Web which are dedicated to information about XML Schema. The limited number of Web resources for XML Schema simply reflects the youth of the Recommendation; however, as the prevalence of Schema grows, so will the number of resources available.

In the meantime, these are among the best Schema resources currently available, and they are also sites to watch for future XML Schema Resources as they become available.

- XML Schema Activities (`http://www.w3.org/XML/Schema`)

  The official W3C Schema Activities page. This is the place to watch for news that impacts the XML Schema Recommendation, such as updates to the published Recommendation or new proposals for related Recommendations.

- XML Schema Part 0: Primer (`http://www.w3.org/TR/xmlschema-0/`)

  An unusual site for the W3C, while not a defining recommendation, "Part 0" to the XML Schema Recommendation is an excellent tutorial on XML Schema and their usage.

- XML.com—Schemas (`http://www.xml.com/schemas/`)

  The XML.com site has a section dedicated entirely to tracking the evolution and usage of XML Schema. This is an excellent resource for news surrounding the Recommendation itself, other Schema alternatives, and tutorials and guides to implementing XML Schema.

- Using W3C XML Schema (`http://www.xml.com/pub/a/2000/11/29/schemas/part1.html`)

  Author Eric van der Vlist takes a look at the XML Schema Recommendation in a step-by-step tutorial on authoring Schema.

- XML Schema Specification in Context (`http://www.ascc.net/~ricko/XMLSchemaInContext.html`)

  This site examines how XML Schema relate to other types of schema which have come before (such as DTDs). Written by Rick Jelliffe, the developer of the Schematron language, it's a good site for helping get a grasp of XML Schema and where they fit into the structured markup grammar world.

- Schema Tutorials (`http://www.xml.com/pub/rg/Schema_Tutorials`)

  XML.com's guide to XML Schema tutorials on the Web.

- Schema Software (`http://www.xml.com/pub/rg/Schema_Software`)

  XML.com's guide to XML Schema-related software currently available. The pickings are slim, but sure to improve as XML Schema become more established.

SCHEMA DEBATES AND ALTERNATIVES

The XML Schema Recommendation was a long time coming, and during the process there was much heated debate about the features and directions that the Working Group should include in the final recommendation. The result is a recommendation that some people are happy with, some grudgingly accept, and some have flat-out rejected. Here are some resources concerning the politics behind the scenes, and more importantly, the major-player alternatives that have been developed:

- XML Ain't What It Used To Be

  (http://www.xml.com/pub/a/2001/02/07/politics.html)

  Author Simon St. Laurent takes on the topic of XML and the juggernaut of standards which XML has become. If you find yourself confused by all of the different recommendations, all with the letters "XML" in the title, this is an article worth your reading.

- The Politics of Schemas

  Part 1 (http://www.xml.com/pub/a/2001/01/31/politics.html)

  Part 2 (http://www.xml.com/pub/a/2001/02/07/politics.html)

  In this excellent two-part essay, author Kendall Grant Clark examines the nature of the "Semantic Web" and tackles the notion of a "universal data format." This is a fantastic article which addresses some of the issues surrounding organizational interests in Schema development and their impact on information as a whole.

- TREX—Tree Regular Expressions for XML (http://www.thaiopensource.com/trex/)

  One of the dissenting voices concerning XML Schema is none other than James Clark. To address his issues with the XML Schema direction, he developed TREX, Tree Regular Expressions for XML. This site explains the details of the TREX specification and implementation.

- RELAX—Regular Language description for XML (http://www.xml.gr.jp/relax/)

  A group of Japanese researchers has also developed an XML Schema competitor, RELAX (Regular Language description for XML), which has garnered a lot of attention and is explained in detail here.

- Relax NG (http://www.oasis-open.org/committees/relax-ng/index.shtml)

  In an effort to support the development of alternative Schema, OASIS has undertaken the project of combining the RELAX standard and the TREX standard into RELAX NG. As RELAX NG is developed and the standard written, this Web site will chart the activity of the OASIS Technical Committee for RELAX NG.

- Schematron (http://www.ascc.net/xml/resource/schematron/)

  Another prominent figure in structured markup, Rick Jelliffe, designed the Schematron language as a means for supplementing the validation of XML, using either DTDs or XML Schema. Schematron is not grammar-based, but instead lets you test for validity against tree patterns in a document. This removes some of the limitations of XML, especially when dealing with data-intense documents. More information about Schematron can be found here.

SCHEMA ALTERNATIVES: TREX

In this appendix

INTRODUCING TREX

In response to the debate surrounding the features and complexity of the XML Schema Recommendation, James Clark developed Tree Regular Expressions for XML, or TREX. Much like RELAX, TREX was designed to provide a simplified implementation for describing grammars for XML, and it has been quite a success. TREX was designed and maintained by James Clark, and more information can be found at the TREX Web site:

```
http://www.thaiopensource.com/trex/
```

However, because of the success and wide acceptance of Schema alternatives among the XML development community, OASIS has co-opted both TREX and RELAX, and is merging them into a common standard called RELAX NG. Information about RELAX NG can be found on the OASIS site at

```
http://www.oasis-open.org/committees/relax-ng/
```

As is stated on the TREX Web site, TREX is no longer being actively maintained, in favor of development on RELAX NG. Therefore, we will not present TREX in great detail here, but will provide you with an overview so that you can get an idea of where TREX is coming from. This overview, along with the RELAX overview presented in Appendix C, " Schema Alternatives: RELAX," should give you an idea of where RELAX NG is headed. If you are considering alternatives to the XML Schema Recommendation, you should not choose TREX, but rather look at the new RELAX NG standard.

STRUCTURE OF A TREX PATTERN

Like XML Schema and RELAX, TREX is based on XML, and TREX grammars are well-formed XML documents. As you might surmise from the "Tree Regular Expressions" name, TREX is based on building a tree that represents a pattern for describing your XML structures. That TREX tree is called a pattern, and a TREX pattern will look something like this:

```
<element name="contact">
 <zeroOrMore>
  <element name="name">
   <anyString/>
  </element>
  <element name="phone">
   <anyString/>
  </element>
 </zeroOrMore>
</element>
```

This TREX pattern describes an XML instance such as

```
<contact>
<name>John Doe</name>
<phone>555-1212</phone>
</contact>
```

As you can see from this example, TREX defines its grammar through the tree structure, using elements such as <zeroOrMore> to place constraints on the occurrence of elements in the instance> document.

ELEMENTS IN TREX

Elements are defined in TREX by using the <element> element, along with a name attribute that defines the name of the element type being declared. The constraints which are placed on element content are then contained inside the <element> element itself. Thus, content models for elements are self contained. For example, if we wanted to declare an element for the city in an address, we would use

```
<element name="city">
<anyString/>
</element>
```

The <anyString> element denotes that the content of our <city> element could be literally any string. If we wanted to build an element which had element content, such as an address, we could simply nest the element declarations:

```
<element name="address">
 <element name="street">
  <anyString/>
 </element>
 <element name="city">
  <anyString/>
 </element>
 <element name="city">
  <anyString/>
 </element>
 <element name="city">
  <anyString/>
 </element>
</element>
```

In this example, because we have not specified any restrictions on the occurrence of the child elements, they each must appear once, and in the order they are described in the tree.

There are a number of different restrictions you can place on elements, which include the following:

- <oneOrMore>
- <zeroOrMore>
- <optional>
- <mixed>
- <group>
- <choice>
- <interleave>

The `<oneOrMore>` and `<zeroOrMore>` elements restrict the number of occurrences of an element type in the content model. For example, we saw previously how we could specify the occurrence of just one element. However, we could also specify one or more, for example, for phone records (so we could enter multiple phone numbers, but still have at least one required):

```
<element name="contact">
 <element name="name">
  <anyString/>
 </element>
 <oneOrMore>
  <element name="phone">
   <anyString/>
  </element>
 </oneOrMore>
</element>
```

There is also another element called `<optional>` which can be used to denote an optional element, similar to specifying an occurrence of zero or one. For example

```
<element name="contact">
 <element name="name">
  <anyString/>
 </element>
 <oneOrMore>
  <element name="phone">
   <anyString/>
  </element>
 </oneOrMore>
 <optional>
  <element name="email">
   <anyString/>
  </element>
 </optional>
</element>
```

This would add an optional `<email>` element to our contact listing. We can also create a choice between two elements, similar to using a "|" in a DTD, by using the `<choice>` element.

For example, let's say we wanted to only have one phone number listed, but it could either be a work phone or home phone:

```
<element name="contact">
 <element name="name">
  <anyString/>
 </element>
 <choice>
  <element name="work_phone">
   <anyString/>
  </element>
 <element name="home_phone">
   <anyString/>
  </element>
 </choice>
</element>
```

This still limits the occurrence of a phone element to one, but allows the instance author to choose between a `<work_phone>` or a `<home_phone>` listing.

To facilitate building content models, we can also use a `<group>` element, to group elements together:

```
<element name="contact">
 <element name="name">
  <anyString/>
 </element>
 <choice>
  <element name="work_phone">
   <anyString/>
  </element>
  <group>
   <element name="home_phone">
    <anyString/>
   </element>
   <element name="cell">
    <anyString/>
   </element>
  </group>
 </choice>
</element>
```

In the TREX pattern above, we use the `<group>` element to create a grouping of `<home_phone>` and `<cell>` so that if we use the "choice" of a `<work_phone>` we can just use one number, but if we choose to use a `<home_phone>` we must also include a `<cell>`. So we could use either:

```
<contact>
<name>John Doe</name>
<work_phone>555-1212</work_phone>
</contact>
```

or

```
<contact>
<name>John Doe</name>
<home_phone>555-1212</home_phone>
<cell>555-1234</cell>
</contact>
```

Of course, not all element content breaks down into nice, neat, element-only content models. You can also create mixed content models with the use of `<mixed>` which allows you to specify a mixed content model. For example

```
<element name="letter">
 <mixed>
  <element name="title">
   <anyString/>
  </element>
  <element name="name">
   <anyString/>
  </element>
 </mixed>
</element>
```

PART

V

APP

B

Which would allow you to create something like this:

```
<letter>
Dear <title>Dr.</title><name>Smith</name>:
We are writing...
</letter>
```

which has mixed text and element content.

Finally, there are times when the order of your elements might not be important, or when elements may occur in any order. The best example of this is in HTML, when you can use elements anywhere in an HTML document. For these cases, TREX provides the `<interleave>` mechanism, which means that elements may be used in any order. For example

```
<element name="list">
 <interleave>
  <element name="store">
   <anyString/>
  </element>
  <element name="quantity">
   <anyString/>
  </element>
  <element name="item">
   <anyString/>
  </element>
 </interleave>
</element>
```

This would allow you to create any of the following XML instances:

```
<list>
<store>Five and Dime</store>
<quantity>3</quantity>
<item>shirt</item
</list>

<list>
<store>Five and Dime</store>
<item>shirt</item
<quantity>3</quantity>
</list>

<list>
<item>shirt</item
<quantity>3</quantity>
<store>Five and Dime</store>
</list>
```

All of which are equally valid instances with interleaved elements.

ATTRIBUTES IN TREX

Attributes in TREX are specified in a manner similar to the way elements are specified:

```
<attribute name="name"/>
```

The attribute declaration itself is nested within the element declaration that it is to be used for. For example, if we wanted to create a <name> element with a phone attribute:

```
<element name="name">
 <anyString/>
 <attribute name="phone">
  <anyString/>
 </attribute>
</element>
```

As you can see, we can use the <anyString> element to represent that the attribute may have any string as its content.

We can also use some of the same elements to restrict the occurrences of attributes as we can with elements. For example, to create an optional attribute, we use the <optional> element:

```
<element name="name">
 <anyString/>
 <optional>
  <attribute name="SSN">
   <anyString/>
  </attribute>
 </optional>
</element>
```

This creates an optional element type called SSN for a Social Security Number.

Just as with elements, we can create <group>s of attributes as well. And the order in which attributes appear is not significant, since XML does not distinguish between the order of attributes.

DATATYPES IN TREX

TREX does not directly include support for datatypes. Instead, datatypes are included in TREX patterns by incorporating the datatypes from the W3C XML Schema Recommendation. That means that any of the datatypes used in the XML Schema Recommendation, Part II, can also be used in a TREX pattern.

Up until now, we've been using <anyString> for the content of our elements and attributes, which is fine if we want them to be able to contain any string. But if you want to restrict element or attribute content to a particular datatype, you will need to use the XML Schema type.

This is accomplished by defining a namespace, and then referencing the appropriate datatype from the Schema Recommendation. For example, if we wanted to create an element that was an integer, say for an inventory count:

```
<element name="inventory" xmlns:xs="http://www.w3.org/2001/XMLSchema">
 <data type="xs:integer">
</element>
```

This would create an element called <inventory> which had an associated integer datatype. We can also use the datatypes to perform pattern matching with regular expressions, just as in XML Schema:

```
<element name="phone" xmlns:xs="http://www.w3.org/2001/XMLSchema">
 <xs:restriction base="xs:string" trex:role="datatype">
  <xs:pattern xmlns="" value="[0-9]{3}\-[0-9]{3}\-[0-9]{4}"/>
 </xs:restriction>
</element>
```

So while TREX does not have any native support for datatypes, by making use of the datatypes in XML Schema, you can use datatypes with TREX patterns.

MODULARITY AND REUSE

TREX does not really provide a mechanism for defining your own datatypes, like Schema do; however, it does provide some mechanisms for allowing you to reuse definitions within your TREX patterns.

First is the <grammar> element, which allows you to define TREX patterns as individual grammars, which can then be reused in other TREX patterns. In fact, all TREX patterns are enclosed in <grammar> elements, and they will have a <start> element which denotes the root element of an instance document.

Within the <grammar> structure, you can also use a <define> element, which enables you to build a content model which can then be referenced in other <define> elements, or within an <element> element itself.

For example, if we wanted to include a generic datatype for a phone number, based on the XML Schema datatype, we could use:

```
<define name="phone-number">
 <xs:restriction xmlns:trex="http://www.thaiopensource.com/trex" base="xs:string"
➥trex:role="datatype">
  <xs:pattern xmlns="" value="[0-9]{3}\-[0-9]{3}\-[0-9]{4}"/>
 </xs:restriction>
</define>
```

Now we have a phone-number defined, which we could then apply to other elements within our TREX documents:

```
<element name="fax">
 <ref name="phone-number"/>
</element>
```

This is essentially the same as if we had defined the content model within the element declaration itself. The ability to reference previously defined sets of grammar information provides a great deal of flexibility, similar to using <complexType> and <simpleType> in an XML Schema.

FEATURES NOT INCLUDED IN TREX

The goal of TREX is to provide a simplified mechanism for describing sets of XML documents, and therefore there are a number of features that were deliberately not included in the TREX feature set.

For example, TREX does not allow you to specify default attributes or to specify whether whitespace is preserved, because these features would alter the document's information set in the process of validation. TREX also does not make any provisions for the inclusion of Notations or entities. These are features that are used by only a small portion of advanced XML users, and therefore, to keep TREX simple, these features are not included either.

A TREX EXAMPLE

In order to provide you with an example of how TREX grammars differ from XML Schema we present here the Contact.xsd Schema used from the appendix on RELAX, as shown in Listing B.1. The TREX Representation of this Schema is then shown in Listing B.2. Also, comparing the two schema designs is a good idea, since the two techniques are being combined into the RELAX NG standard. Since TREX is no longer actively being developed, we won't step through the development of the TREX grammar, but looking at the differences between the two documents should give you an idea of how TREX relates to XML Schema.

LISTING B.1   AN EXAMPLE FOR A CONTACT SCHEMA, WRITTEN USING THE XML SCHEMA RECOMMENDATION

```
<?xml version="1.0" encoding="UTF-8" ?>
<xs:schema xmlns:xs="http://www.w3.org/2001/XMLSchema"
    xmlns:xsi="http://www.w3.org/2001/XMLSchema-Instance"
    targetNamespace="http://www.myserver.com/Contact"
    xmlns="http://www.myserver.com/Contact">

<!-- Define the types for the Contact Schema -->

<!-- Define the Contact type -->
<xs:complexType name="contact">
 <xs:element name="company" type="xs:string" minOccurs="0"/>
 <xs:element name="department" type="xs:string" minOccurs="0"/>
 <xs:element name="name" type="xs:string"/>
 <xs:element name="phone" type="phone_number"/>
 <xs:element name="fax" type="phone_number" minOccurs="0"/>
 <xs:element name="cell" type="phone_number" minOccurs="0"/>
 <xs:element name="pager" type="phone_number" minOccurs="0"/>
 <xs:element name="email" type="xs:string" minOccurs="0"/>
</xs:complexType>

<!-- Define the Address type -->
<xs:complexType name="address">
 <xs:sequence>
  <xs:element name="address" type="xs:string"/>
  <xs:element name="address2" type="xs:string" minOccurs="0"/>
  <xs:element name="city" type="xs:string"/>
  <xs:element name="state" type="state"/>
```

PART

V

APP

B

LISTING B.1   CONTINUED

```xml
  <xs:element name="zip" type="zip"/>
 </xs:sequence>
</xs:complexType>

<!-- Define the State type -->
<!-- Long winded enumeration restricts state abbreviation values to valid
➡states -->
<xs:simpleType name="state">
 <xs:restriction base="xs:string">
  <xs:enumeration value="AL"/>      <!--Alabama -->
  <xs:enumeration value="AK"/>      <!--Alaska -->
<!-- ETC -->
  <xs:enumeration value="WI"/>      <!--Wisconsin -->
  <xs:enumeration value="WY"/>      <!--Wyoming -->
 </xs:restriction>
</xs:simpleType>

<!-- Define the ZIP type -->
<xs:simpleType name="zip">
 <xs:restriction base="xs:string">
  <xs:pattern value="[0-9]{5}(\-)?([0-9]{4})?"/>
 </xs:restriction>
</xs:simpleType>

<!-- Define the Phone Number type -->
<xs:simpleType name="phone_number">
 <xs:restriction base="xs:string">
  <xs:pattern value="[0-9]{3}\-[0-9]{3}\-[0-9]{4}"/>
 </xs:restriction>
</xs:simpleType>

</xs:schema>
```

LISTING B.2   AN EXAMPLE FOR A CONTACT SCHEMA WRITTEN USING THE TREX IMPLEMENTATION

```xml
<?xml version="1.0" encoding="iso-8859-1"?>
<grammar xmlns="http://www.thaiopensource.com/trex"
xmlns:xs="http://www.w3.org/2001/XMLSchema"
ns="http://www.myserver.com/Contact">

 <element name="contact">
  <group>
   <element name="name">
    <anyString/>
   </element>

   <optional>
    <element name="company">
     <anyString/>
    </element>
    <element name="department">
     <anyString/>
    </element>
   </optional>
```

```
<define name="us_address">
 <group>
  <element name="address">
   <anyString/>
  </element>
  <optional>
   <element name="address2">
    <anyString/>
   </element>
  </optional>
  <element name="city">
   <anyString/>
  </element>
  <element name="state">
    <choice>
     <string>AL</string>
     <string>AK</string>
     <string>AZ</string>
     <string>AR</string>
     <string>CA</string>
     <string>CO</string>
     <string>CT</string>
     <string>DE</string>
     <string>FL</string>
     <string>GA</string>
     <string>HI</string>
     <string>ID</string>
     <string>IL</string>
     <string>IN</string>
     <string>IA</string>
     <string>KS</string>
     <string>KY</string>
     <string>LA</string>
     <string>ME</string>
     <string>MD</string>
     <string>MA</string>
     <string>MI</string>
     <string>MN</string>
     <string>MS</string>
     <string>MO</string>
     <string>MT</string>
     <string>NE</string>
     <string>NV</string>
     <string>NH</string>
     <string>NJ</string>
     <string>NM</string>
     <string>NY</string>
     <string>NC</string>
     <string>ND</string>
     <string>OH</string>
     <string>OK</string>
     <string>OR</string>
     <string>PA</string>
     <string>RI</string>
     <string>SC</string>
     <string>SD</string>
```

PART

V

APP

B

LISTING B.2   CONTINUED

```
        <string>TN</string>
        <string>TX</string>
        <string>UT</string>
        <string>VT</string>
        <string>VA</string>
        <string>WA</string>
        <string>DC</string>
        <string>WV</string>
        <string>WI</string>
        <string>WY</string>
      </choice>
    </element>
    <element name="zip">
      <xs:restriction xmlns:trex="http://www.thaiopensource.com/trex"
➥base="xs:string" trex:role="datatype">
        <xs:pattern xmlns="" value="[0-9]{5}(\-)?([0-9]{4})?"/>
      </xs:restriction>
    </element>
    </group>
  </define>

  <define name="phone.role">
    <xs:restriction xmlns:trex="http://www.thaiopensource.com/trex"
➥base="xs:string" trex:role="datatype">
      <xs:pattern xmlns="" value="[0-9]{3}\-[0-9]{3}\-[0-9]{4}"/>
    </xs:restriction>
  </define>

  <element name="phone">
    <ref name="phone.role"/>
  </element>
  <element name="fax">
    <ref name="phone.role"/>
  </element>
  <element name="cell">
    <ref name="phone.role"/>
  </element>
  <element name="pager">
    <ref name="phone.role"/>
  </element>
  </group>
 </element>
</grammar>
```

CONCLUSION

TREX is a viable alternative to XML Schema, and it does allow you to design grammars for XML which make sense from a pattern matching perspective. However, you should not consider TREX for your own projects, since development work on TREX has been merged into the work on RELAX NG, which is being supported by OASIS. If you are looking for an alternative to XML Schema, RELAX NG would be a better technology to examine than TREX.

APPENDIX C

Schema Alternatives: RELAX

In this appendix

Introducing RELAX

RELAX is the Regular Language description for XML, and was developed by a group of Japanese researchers in response to the XML Schema Recommendation. Many groups of developers have insisted that the XML Schema Recommendation is too complicated for the vast majority of potential XML users. RELAX is one proposed solution: a simplified means of expressing XML-based languages.

The Official RELAX page is maintained at

```
http://www.xml.gr.jp/relax/
```

In addition, RELAX is gaining in popularity with the XML community at large, so much so that OASIS has undertaken an initiative to create a new standard for Schema based on both TREX and RELAX, called RELAX NG. Information about RELAX NG can be found on the OASIS site at

```
http://www.oasis-open.org/committees/relax-ng/
```

While this flurry of activity can be somewhat intimidating, the important thing to know is that all organizations recognize the XML Schema Recommendation from the W3C, and these alternative technologies are being designed with co-existence in mind. In fact, RELAX is published as a note by the International Standards Organization (ISO) which is an official standards body. This is an important milestone for RELAX, and goes a long way toward establishing it as a viable alternative. XML Schema will likely be around for a long time, and while they might be appropriate for some, there is still room for simple alternatives.

RELAX is intended to provide similar functionality to XML Schema, but with a simplified and streamlined syntax. RELAX is divided into two sections: the RELAX Core and RELAX Namespaces. The RELAX Core covers documents using a single namespace, while the Namespaces section addresses multiple-namespace documents. In this appendix, we will be looking exclusively at the RELAX Core. The one caveat of working with RELAX is that much of the documentation is in Japanese. Although English translations are coming along, currently there isn't an English translation of the RELAX Namespaces section.

The RELAX Core

RELAX is built around a specification called the RELAX Core, which can be downloaded as a PDF from the RELAX site:

```
http://www.egroups.co.jp/files/reldeve/JISTRtranslation.pdf
```

Note

Due to the recent acquisition of eGroups by Yahoo, the above URL may change. Always consult the RELAX site (`http://www.xml.gr.jp/relax/`) for the latest documentation.

The Core also has an associated DTD, which can be found at

```
http://www.xml.gr.jp/relax/relaxCore.dtd
```

The RELAX Core specifies how RELAX works with elements, attributes, datatypes, and so on. In fact, the RELAX Core does borrow some from the W3C XML Schema Recommendation. RELAX Core includes datatypes from the Schema Recommendation, so you will be able to use the datatypes you are already familiar with from Schemas with RELAX documents.

So now, let's take a look at how RELAX documents are structured and written.

A RELAX DOCUMENT

RELAX grammars are expressed in "modules" which can be used individually, or combined. Modules are formed using the `<module>` element, which accepts a number of attributes:

- `moduleVersion`—The `moduleVersion` attribute provides a mechanism for keeping track of the version of your module.

- `relaxCoreVersion`—The `relaxCoreVersion` attribute allows you to specify the RELAX Core version for the module.

- `targetNamespace`—The `targetNamespace` attribute allows you to specify the target namespace for which this module describes components.

- `xmlns`—This attribute specifies the namespace for the module itself, and should be set to the official RELAX namespace, `"http://www.xml.gr.jp/xmlns/relaxCore"`.

A completed `<module>` component looks like this:

```
<module
    moduleVersion="1.0"
    relaxCoreVersion="1.0"
    targetNamespace="http://www.myserver.com/example"
    xmlns="http://www.xml.gr.jp/xmlns/relaxCore">

</module>
```

The module itself contains the specifications for the RELAX grammar that describes your XML Documents. The first step in that description is the `<interface>` element, which allows you to specify the root element for the document the current grammar describes:

```
<interface>
<export label="root-element"/>
</interface>
```

You can also include multiple `<export>` elements in the interface, which allows you to use a single RELAX grammar to describe multiple XML documents with different root elements. However, the `<module>` itself only has one `<interface>` element.

With the `<module>` and `<interface>` out of the way, it's time to look at how elements and attributes are specified using RELAX.

PART

V

APP

C

ELEMENTS IN RELAX

Element declarations in RELAX consist of an `<elementRule>` element, which has the same effect as an `<!ELEMENT` declaration in a DTD or an `<element>` component in XML Schema.

The `<elementRule>` element has a number of attributes, which include

- `role`—The `role` attribute defines the name for the element type, which can be used in an XML instance document.

- `label`—The `label` attribute defines a name for the `<elementRule>` itself, so that it can be referenced elsewhere in the RELAX module. The attribute is optional, and if no label is specified, the label for the `<elementRule>` is the same as the `role` attribute.

- `type`—The `type` attribute allows you to specify a datatype (from the XML Schema Recommendation Part II: Datatypes) for the element.

The content of the `<elementRule>` itself is called a *hedge model*, which is just another way to say "content model". An element is said to contain a "hedge" and therefore, the model that describes the hedge is the hedge model. Hedge models can be an element hedge model, a datatype reference, or a mixed hedge model.

Just as an element content model would be a content model which contained only other elements, an element hedge model defines element content. And just as a mixed content model defines mixed content, so does a mixed hedge model.

ELEMENT HEDGE MODEL

The hedge model for an element declaration can be one of several types (similar to content models): empty, none, ref, choice, or sequence. Each of these hedge models is governed by its own set of rules, so let's take a look at each of them now.

empty

The `<empty>` tag allows you to specify an element with empty content, similar to `EMPTY` in a DTD. For example, if you wanted to create an element called `page_break` that was empty, you could use the following:

```
<elementRule role="page_break">
<empty/>
</elementRule>
```

This would allow you to use

```
<page_break/>
```

in an XML instance document. In fact, `<page_break>` would not be allowed to contain any content.

The <none> element is unique to RELAX, and it is used to specify an element that may not match anything. While this might seem a little curious, the reasoning behind the <none> element is so that it can be used as a placeholder for creating an extensible hedgeRule model (more about hedge rules later).

ref

Just like XML Schema, RELAX allows you to take advantage of references, using the <ref> element, which can be used to reference another <elementRule> or <hedgeRule>. For example, if we have an element rule as follows:

```
<elementRule role="title" label=i"book_title" type="string"/>
```

we could then reference the element rule in another element rule:

```
<elementRule role="catalog">
 <ref label="book_title" occurs="*"/>
</elementRule>
```

The <ref> tag here results in the inclusion of the <title> element in the <catalog> element's content. You will also notice the use of the occurs attribute here, which is used to denote the number of times the child element may appear in the parent element's content. The occurs attribute may have three values:

- * Denotes the element may occur zero or more times.
- \+ Denotes the element may occur one or more times.
- ? Denotes the element may occur zero or one times.

The *, +, and ? symbols are used here similarly to how they are used in DTDs.

choice

The <choice> element functions as an "or" operator, similar to "|" in a DTD, giving authors a choice of element content. For example

```
<elementRule role="book_title" type="string"/>
<elementRule role="magazine_title" type="string"/>

<elementRule role="catalog">
 <choice occurs="+">
  <ref label="book_title"/>
  <ref label="magazine_title"/>
 </choice>
</elementRule>
```

Here we have two elements, <book_title> and <magazine_title>, either of which could occur one or more times as children of the <catalog> element.

PART

V

APP

C

sequence

The <sequence> allows you to specify a sequence of elements that should occur in the hedge model of your parent element. For example, if we had two elements

```
<elementRule role="title" type="string"/>
<elementRule role="author" type="string"/>
```

and we wanted them to occur in a sequence together, or not at all, we could use

```
<elementRule role="publication">
 <sequence occurs="?">
  <ref label="title"/>
  <ref label="magazine_title"/>
 </sequence>
</elementRule>
```

With this <elementRule> a <publication> would either be empty, or it would contain both a <title> and an <author>, because of our use of "?" as the value for the occurs attribute.

DATATYPE REFERENCE

An <elementRule> can also be used to declare an element which accepts values of a specific datatype; for example, we have already used the string type in previous examples. We could also use integer:

```
<elementRule role="quantity" type="integer"/>
```

This is similar to using datatypes in XML Schema. In fact, all of the built-in datatypes that are defined in the XML Schema Recommendation may be used with RELAX. For more information, see the section "Datatypes in RELAX," later in this chapter.

MIXED HEDGE MODELS

You can create mixed models for your element using the <mixed> element, which allows your element content to consist of both text data and element data.

For example, if you wanted to use elements within a chunk of text:

```
<letter>Dear Mr. <name>Smith<name></letter>
```

You could use the following:

```
<elementRule role="name" type="string"/>

<elementRule role="letter">
 <mixed>
  <ref label="name"/>
 </mixed>
</elementRule>
```

This would allow the <letter> element to contain both text and the <name> element in its content.

You can also use the other hedge elements, such as <sequence> and <choice>, with <mixed> content as well. For example

```
<elementRule role="title" type="string"/>
<elementRule role="name" type="string"/>

<elementRule role="letter">
 <mixed>
  <sequence>
   <ref label="title"/>
   <ref label="name"/>
  </sequence>
 </mixed>
</elementRule>
```

would require that the `<title>` element came before the `<name>` element:

```
<letter>Dear <title>Mr.</title> <name>Smith<name></letter>
```

This allows you to create a very flexible or a very rigid content model for your elements.

hedgeRule AND hedgeRef

Much like `<complexType>` and `<simpleType>` in XML Schema, RELAX does have a mechanism for abstraction. Although by no means as extensive as creating your own datatypes, the `<hedgeRule>` type does allow you to create a hedge rule which can then be referenced by label in `<elementRule>` elements.

In general, `<hedgeRule>` elements function similarly to `<elementRule>` elements, but there are some very important distinctions.

First, `<hedgeRule>` elements may *not* contain datatype references. Therefore, you may *not* have

```
<hedgeRule label="title" type="string"/>
```

The above is *not* a valid `<hedgeRule>`. Similarly, `<hedgeRule>` elements may not contain `<mixed>` content. The only acceptable models for `<hedgeRule>` are element hedge models: `<choice>`, `<sequence>`, `<empty>`, or `<none>`.

For example, let's look at a simple publication module:

```
<elementRule role="title" type="string"/>
<elementRule role="author" type="string"/>
<elementRule role="ISBN" type="string"/>

<hedgeRule role="book">
  <sequence>
   <ref label="title"/>
   <ref label="author"/>
   <ref label="ISBN"/>
  </sequence>
</hedgeRule>

<hedgeRule role="article">
  <sequence>
   <ref label="title"/>
   <ref label="author"/>
  </sequence>
</hedgeRule>
```

```
<elementRule role="publication">
 <choice occurs="+">
  <hedgeRef label="book"/>
  <hedgeRef label="article"/>
 </choice>
</elementRule>
```

Here, we have created three elements for describing publications: <title>, <author>, and <ISBN>. The <ISBN> will only apply to books, not articles, so we can create two <hedgeRules> which make use of these elements: one for books, which contains the <ISBN> element; and another for articles, which does not include the <ISBN> element.

Next, we can create an <elementRule> for a publication, which allows an instance author to choose between a <book> or an <article>, making use of our <hedgeRules>.

Now, with all of these names, labels, and references lying about, there are some guidelines to follow when working with hedgeRules and elementRules:

- A hedgeRule may *not* reference itself.
- Multiple hedgeRules may have the same label. When this is the case, the content model may match *either* of the specified rules and be considered valid.
- Multiple elementRules may have the same label. When this is the case, the content model may match *either* of the specified rules and be considered valid.
- hedgeRules and elementRules may *not* have the same label. This will result in an error, because there are different restrictions on the types of content which elementRules and hedgeRules may have.

If you keep those rules in mind, hedgeRules and elementRules can actually be combined to accomplish very complex content models.

ATTRIBUTES IN RELAX

Attributes in RELAX are handled through a <tag> element. In fact, all elements in RELAX have an associated <tag> element, whether they have attributes or not.

For example, if we have the following element type:

```
<elementRule role="title" type="string"/>
```

We declare the tag with

```
<tag name="title"/>
```

Note that the <tag> name attribute matches the role attribute of the <elementRule>. This is how the <tag> is matched to the appropriate element. This is important, since it is actually within the <tag> element that we specify attribute types for our element types.

Attributes are specified in RELAX using an <attribute> element, which may have a number of attributes:

- name—Specifies the name of the attribute type.
- role—Specifies the role of the attribute type.
- type—Specifies the datatype of the attribute.
- required—Specifies whether the attribute is required or is optional.

So, for example, let's say we wanted to create an element called `<feature>` with an attribute called enabled:

```
<elementRule role="feature" type="string"/>

<tag name="feature">
<attribute name="enabled" type="string" required="true"/>
</tag>
```

This creates our element and associated attribute:

```
<feature enabled="yeah"/>
```

However, the value of enabled can be any string. We can also apply constraining facets from the XML Schema Recommendation to attribute types by including them in the `<attribute>` tag:

```
<tag name="feature">
 <attribute name="enabled" type="string" required="true">
  <enumeration value="true"/>
  <enumeration value="false"/>
 </attribute>
</tag>
```

You can use the appropriate constraining facets for the datatype in this manner to restrict the content of attributes in your documents.

attPool

In order to maintain simplicity, RELAX does not provide any mechanism for parameter entities, as they are used in DTDs. However, one of the most common uses of parameter entities in DTDs is to describe a common group of attributes that can then be applied to an element. RELAX does have a mechanism for grouping attributes so they can be reused: attPool.

The `<attPool>` element takes a role attribute, which is used to specify the role the attPool plays, and which is how the attPool is referenced later. An `<attPool>` element is simply a grouping of attributes:

```
<attPool role="address">
<attribute name="city" type="string"/>
<attribute name="state" type="string"/>
<attribute name="zip" type="string"/>
</attPool>
```

Now, we could use that attPool group by reference in a `<tag>` element:

```
<tag name="contact">
<ref role="address"/>
</tag>
```

PART

V

APP

C

And that is all there is to it. It's a very simple mechanism which actually provides a great deal of power and flexibility. For example, we can also reference attPools from other attPools, to create complex structures:

```
<attPool role="address-ATTN">
<attribute name="name" type="string"/>
<attribute name="Department" type="string"/>
<attribute name="Company" type="string"/>
</attPool>

<attPool role="address-STREET">
<attribute name="street" type="string"/>
<attribute name="suite" type="string"/>
</attPool>

<attPool role="address-CITY">
<attribute name="city" type="string"/>
<attribute name="state" type="string"/>
<attribute name="zip" type="string"/>
</attPool>

<attPool role="address">
<ref role="address-ATTN"/>
<ref role="address-STREET"/>
<ref role="address-CITY"/>
</attPool>
```

All of the attributes defined in the address-ATTN, address-STREET, and address-CITY attribute pools are also referenced in the final address attribute pool. So if we could use the address attPool with a <tag> element to gain those attributes, we would be referencing *all* of the declared attributes from all of the attPools combined.

As you can see, that allows you to define a number of attributes which could then be reused in various parts of your RELAX module.

ADVANCED ROLES

The most innovative and flexible feature of RELAX is the ability to define multiple roles for an element or attribute, and then to have that role determined based on the context in which the element or the attribute is used.

For example, let's say that you had an element called <inventory> which you wanted to use to keep track of the quantity of a part in stock. But suppose that in addition to parts which can be represented by an integer, you also had parts (like oil) which might be represented by a volume, in the form of a decimal. In RELAX you could use the following:

```
<elementRule role="inventory" label="parts-integers" type="integer"/>
<elementRule role="inventory" label="parts-decimal" type="decimal"/>
<tag name="inventory"/>
```

While it might seem like this is a conflict because we have two elementRules with the same role, this is perfectly valid in RELAX. This simply creates a situation where the content of the `<inventory>` element could be a `decimal` or an `integer`. This type of multiple definition can be done for `elementRules`, attributes, or `hedgeRules`.

In fact, we could go one step further. Let's say we wanted to have the definition switch between three types of inventory:

- `count`—For items which can be counted
- `volume`—For items sold by volume
- `weight`—For items sold by weight

We could create three different element rules:

```
<elementRule role="inventory-count" label="count" type="integer"/>
<elementRule role="inventory-volume" label="volume" type="decimal"/>
<elementRule role="inventory-weight" label="weight" type="decimal"/>
```

We could then also add an attribute, called `inventory-type`, and define different tags which would allow us to choose the role based on the value of the attribute:

```
<tag name="inventory" role="inventory-count">
<attribute name="inventory-type" type="string" required="true">
<enumeration value="count"/>
</attribute>
</tag>

<tag name="inventory" role="inventory-volume">
<attribute name="inventory-type" type="string" required="true">
<enumeration value="volume"/>
</attribute>
</tag>

<tag name="inventory" role="inventory-weight">
<attribute name="inventory-type" type="string" required="true">
<enumeration value="weight"/>
</attribute>
</tag>
```

Now, this allows us to use any of the following in an instance document:

```
<inventory inventory-type="count">4</inventory>
<inventory inventory-type="volume">3.5</inventory>
<inventory inventory-type="weight">16.5</inventory>
```

Each of those instances is valid, because the role (and therefore the element datatype and constraints) is determined by the value specified in the `inventory-type` attribute.

As you can see, this gives you an incredible amount of power over your content, allowing you to accomplish context sensitivity not really possible with XML Schema.

Another advantage of the multiple definitions is that you will never invalidate a previously acceptable rule. For example, if you defined `inventory` earlier as being a `string`, you can simply add these new definitions, rather than writing over the old definition. Since multiple definitions are allowed in RELAX, the older definition will remain valid, so backward compatibility is easily achieved.

PART

V

APP

C

DATATYPES IN RELAX

Datatypes used in RELAX are actually borrowed from two locations. First, a number of types are borrowed directly from the XML 1.0 Recommendation:

- NMTOKEN, NMTOKENS
- ID
- IDREF, IDREFS
- ENTITY, ENTITIES
- NOTATION

In addition to these types, RELAX also incorporates the built-in datatypes which are defined in the XML Schema Recommendation, Part II.

Unlike XML Schema, however, there is no mechanism in RELAX for creating your own datatypes, although you can use the constraining facets associated with a datatype in order to restrict the value set of an element or attribute.

In addition to these "borrowed" datatypes, there are two new datatypes introduced by RELAX: none and emptyString.

none

The none datatype is an empty datatype, which contains no value whatsoever. The reason none is provided is to provide a mechanism for prohibiting the use of attributes. For example, let's say we have the following:

```
<tag name="phone">
<attribute name="number" type="none"/>
</tag>
```

In this example, it would now actually be *illegal* to use the number attribute with the <phone> tag. You might use this as a technique to prevent instance authors from accidentally using an attribute incorrectly in their documents.

emptyString

The emptyString type is similar to declaring an "EMPTY" element in a DTD, so that an element may be used, but with no content. For example, in HTML the paragraph tag <p> typically has no attributes. With RELAX, we can disallow any attributes in this tag:

```
<elementRule role="p" type="emptyString"/>
```

This would allow instance authors to use

```
<p/> or <p></p>
```

So long as their was no content (or whitespace) within the <p> element itself.

Other RELAX Features

RELAX does support a few other features that are worth mentioning here. The first are annotations. Much like the XML Schema Recommendation, RELAX supports an <annotation> element which may contain a <documentation> element and a <appinfo> element. This mechanism can be used to document your RELAX modules.

Additionally, RELAX allows you to use a <div> tag, to denote a collection of <elementRule> or <hedgeRule> elements to be documented:

```
<div>
<elementRule name="title" type="string"/>
<elementRule name="author" type="string"/>
<elementRule name="publisher" type="string"/>
</div>
```

The <div> tag is only used for grouping, and shouldn't have any impact on the structure of your document.

Another feature of RELAX is that modules can be divided into smaller parts, and then included, using an <include> tag. The <include> tag has a moduleLocation attribute that allows you to specify the location of the .rlx module to include:

```
<include moduleLocation="another-module.rlx"/>
```

That allows you to build multiple-part RELAX modules, similar to multiple part XML Schema.

Missing Features

Experienced users of XML will notice that there are some features missing from RELAX, such as Notations and unparsed entities. (You can get around this because RELAX allows the importing of XML Schema datatypes, but there is no native support for these features in RELAX.) There is also no mechanism for describing default values. These features were considered by the RELAX authors, but they are in conflict with the primary goal of RELAX: simplicity.

So those features simply aren't included in RELAX. If you have the need for entities or Notations in your documents, then you will need to rely on a DTD or an XML Schema, as your document requirements are too complex for RELAX to handle. On the other hand, those features are often unnecessary for general XML users, and only confuse many XML novices, so by eliminating them, RELAX does make life a little simpler.

A Sample RELAX Document

Now let's take a look at a completed RELAX module. Let's start with an XML Schema based on the XML Schema Recommendation. This is a simple contact.xsd document, with a few datatypes to help keep our data formatted correctly. The entire Schema is shown in Listing C.1.

```
<?xml version="1.0" encoding="UTF-8" ?>
<xs:schema xmlns:xs="http://www.w3.org/2001/XMLSchema"
    xmlns:xsi="http://www.w3.org/2001/XMLSchema-Instance"
    targetNamespace="http://www.myserver.com/Contact"
    xmlns="http://www.myserver.com/Contact">

<!-- Define the types for the Contact Schema -->

<!-- Define the Contact type -->
<xs:complexType name="contact">
 <xs:element name="company" type="xs:string" minOccurs="0"/>
 <xs:element name="department" type="xs:string" minOccurs="0"/>
 <xs:element name="name" type="xs:string"/>
 <xs:element name="phone" type="phone_number"/>
 <xs:element name="fax" type="phone_number" minOccurs="0"/>
 <xs:element name="cell" type="phone_number" minOccurs="0"/>
 <xs:element name="pager" type="phone_number" minOccurs="0"/>
 <xs:element name="email" type="xs:string" minOccurs="0"/>
</xs:complexType>

<!-- Define the Address type -->
<xs:complexType name="address">
 <xs:sequence>
  <xs:element name="address" type="xs:string"/>
  <xs:element name="address2" type="xs:string" minOccurs="0"/>
  <xs:element name="city" type="xs:string"/>
  <xs:element name="state" type="state"/>
  <xs:element name="zip" type="zip"/>
 </xs:sequence>
</xs:complexType>

<!-- Define the State type -->
<!-- Long winded enumeration restricts state abbreviation values to valid
➥states -->
<xs:simpleType name="state">
 <xs:restriction base="xs:string">
  <xs:enumeration value="AL"/>      <!--Alabama -->
  <xs:enumeration value="AK"/>      <!--Alaska -->
  <xs:enumeration value="AZ"/>      <!--Arizona -->
  <xs:enumeration value="AR"/>      <!--Arkansas -->
  <xs:enumeration value="CA"/>      <!--California -->
  <xs:enumeration value="CO"/>      <!--Colorado -->
  <xs:enumeration value="CT"/>      <!--Connecticut -->
  <xs:enumeration value="DE"/>      <!--Delaware -->
  <xs:enumeration value="FL"/>      <!--Florida -->
  <xs:enumeration value="GA"/>      <!--Georgia -->
  <xs:enumeration value="HI"/>      <!--Hawaii -->
  <xs:enumeration value="ID"/>      <!--Idaho -->
  <xs:enumeration value="IL"/>      <!--Illinois -->
  <xs:enumeration value="IN"/>      <!--Indiana -->
  <xs:enumeration value="IA"/>      <!--Iowa -->
  <xs:enumeration value="KS"/>      <!--Kansas -->
  <xs:enumeration value="KY"/>      <!--Kentucky -->
```

LISTING C.1   CONTINUED

```xml
      <xs:enumeration value="LA"/>     <!--Louisiana -->
      <xs:enumeration value="ME"/>     <!--Maine -->
      <xs:enumeration value="MD"/>     <!--Maryland -->
      <xs:enumeration value="MA"/>     <!--Massachusetts -->
      <xs:enumeration value="MI"/>     <!--Michigan -->
      <xs:enumeration value="MN"/>     <!--Minnesota -->
      <xs:enumeration value="MS"/>     <!--Mississippi -->
      <xs:enumeration value="MO"/>     <!--Missouri -->
      <xs:enumeration value="MT"/>     <!--Montana -->
      <xs:enumeration value="NE"/>     <!--Nebraska -->
      <xs:enumeration value="NV"/>     <!--Nevada -->
      <xs:enumeration value="NH"/>     <!--New Hampshire -->
      <xs:enumeration value="NJ"/>     <!--New Jersey -->
      <xs:enumeration value="NM"/>     <!--New Mexico -->
      <xs:enumeration value="NY"/>     <!--New York -->
      <xs:enumeration value="NC"/>     <!--North Carolina -->
      <xs:enumeration value="ND"/>     <!--North Dakota -->
      <xs:enumeration value="OH"/>     <!--Ohio -->
      <xs:enumeration value="OK"/>     <!--Oklahoma -->
      <xs:enumeration value="OR"/>     <!--Oregon -->
      <xs:enumeration value="PA"/>     <!--Pennsylvania -->
      <xs:enumeration value="RI"/>     <!--Rhode Island -->
      <xs:enumeration value="SC"/>     <!--South Carolina -->
      <xs:enumeration value="SD"/>     <!--South Dakota -->
      <xs:enumeration value="TN"/>     <!--Tennessee -->
      <xs:enumeration value="TX"/>     <!--Texas -->
      <xs:enumeration value="UT"/>     <!--Utah -->
      <xs:enumeration value="VT"/>     <!--Vermont -->
      <xs:enumeration value="VA"/>     <!--Virginia -->
      <xs:enumeration value="WA"/>     <!--Washington -->
      <xs:enumeration value="DC"/>     <!--Washington,D.C. -->
      <xs:enumeration value="WV"/>     <!--West Virginia -->
      <xs:enumeration value="WI"/>     <!--Wisconsin -->
      <xs:enumeration value="WY"/>     <!--Wyoming -->
    </xs:restriction>
  </xs:simpleType>

  <!-- Define the ZIP type -->
  <xs:simpleType name="zip">
   <xs:restriction base="xs:string">
    <xs:pattern value="[0-9]{5}(\-)?([0-9]{4})?"/>
   </xs:restriction>
  </xs:simpleType>

  <!-- Define the Phone Number type -->
  <xs:simpleType name="phone_number">
   <xs:restriction base="xs:string">
    <xs:pattern value="[0-9]{3}\-[0-9]{3}\-[0-9]{4}"/>
   </xs:restriction>
  </xs:simpleType>

</xs:schema>
```

PART

V

APP

C

So let's see how we build the RELAX module. First, we start off with the XML declaration, followed by the `<module>` tag, which contains our information about the module itself and the version of RELAX we're using:

```
<?xml version="1.0" encoding="UTF-8" ?>

<module
    moduleVersion="1.0"
    relaxCoreVersion="1.0"
    targetNamespace="http://www.myserver.com/Contact"
    xmlns="http://www.xml.gr.jp/xmlns/relaxCore">
</module>
```

Next, we need to use the `<interface>` element, to declare our root element:

```
<interface>
 <export label="contact"/>
</interface>
```

Now we're ready to declare elements. Remember that RELAX uses an `<elementRule>` element, along with a `<tag>` element to declare an element type, and specify the appropriate tag:

```
<elementRule name="name" type="string"/>
<tag name="name"/>

<elementRule role="company" type="string" occurs="?"/>
<tag name="company"/>

<elementRule role="department" type="string" occurs="?"/>
<tag name="department"/>

<elementRule role="email" type="string" occurs="?"/>
 <tag name="email"/>
```

We can also embed the `<tag>` element within our `<elementRule>` just to keep things looking a little nicer. We can also use the constraining facets of datatypes in order to restrict element values as well. So, for our `<phone>`, `<fax>`, `<pager>`, and `<cell>` elements, our RELAX code looks like this:

```
<elementRule role="phone" type="string">
 <tag/>
 <pattern value="[0-9]{3}\-[0-9]{3}\-[0-9]{4}"/>
</elementRule>

<elementRule role="fax" type="string">
 <tag/>
 <pattern value="[0-9]{3}\-[0-9]{3}\-[0-9]{4}"/>
</elementRule>

<elementRule role="cell" type="string">
 <tag/>
 <pattern value="[0-9]{3}\-[0-9]{3}\-[0-9]{4}"/>
</elementRule>

<elementRule role="pager" type="string">
 <tag/>
 <pattern value="[0-9]{3}\-[0-9]{3}\-[0-9]{4}"/>
</elementRule>
```

The most complicated section of our RELAX module will make use of a hedgeRule, so that we can define the role of us_address and then use that to create an address element. Remember that hedgeRules may contain elementRules as their content:

```
<hedgeRule label="us_address">
 <sequence>
  <elementRule role="address" type="string"/>
  <tag name="address"/>

  <elementRule role="address2" type="string" occurs="?"/>
  <tag name="address2"/>

  <elementRule role="city" type="string"/>
  <tag name="city"/>

  <elementRule role="state" type="string">
   <tag/>
   <enumeration value="AL"/>     <!--Alabama -->
   <enumeration value="AK"/>     <!--Alaska -->
   <enumeration value="AZ"/>     <!--Arizona -->
   <!--ETC -->
  </elementRule>

  <elementRule role="zip" type="string">
   <tag/>
   <pattern value="[0-9]{5}(\-)?([0-9]{4})?"/>
  </elementRule>

 </sequence>
</hedgeRule>
```

Now we can create an element type based on the hedgeRule by referencing it:

```
<elementRule role="address">
 <tag/>
 <hedgeRef label="us_address"/>
</elementRule>
```

Finally, we're ready to define the root element itself, which we do by including all of our document elements as references:

```
<elementRule role="contact">
 <tag name="contact"/>
 <sequence>
  <ref label="name"/>
  <ref label="company"/>
  <ref label="department"/>
  <ref label="address"/>
  <ref label="phone"/>
  <ref label="fax"/>
  <ref label="cell"/>
  <ref label="pager"/>
  <ref label="email"/>
 </sequence>
</elementRule>
```

PART

V

APP

C

Just as is the case with XML Schema, RELAX modules do not require specific ordering of components. Therefore, items may be referenced in the document before they are actually defined. When we bring all of the pieces together, we have a finished RELAX module describing a contact XML instance document, as shown in Listing C.2.

LISTING C.2   A RELAX MODULE FOR CONTACTS, CONTAINING THE SAME DATA AS THE XML SCHEMA, WRITTEN USING THE RELAX STANDARD

```
<?xml version="1.0" encoding="UTF-8" ?>

<module
    moduleVersion="1.0"
    relaxCoreVersion="1.0"
    targetNamespace="http://www.myserver.com/Contact"
    xmlns="http://www.xml.gr.jp/xmlns/relaxCore">

 <interface>
  <export label="contact"/>
 </interface>

 <elementRule role="contact">
  <tag name="contact"/>
  <sequence>
   <ref label="name"/>
   <ref label="company"/>
   <ref label="department"/>
   <ref label="address"/>
   <ref label="phone"/>
   <ref label="fax"/>
   <ref label="cell"/>
   <ref label="pager"/>
   <ref label="email"/>
  </sequence>
 </elementRule>

 <elementRule name="name" type="string"/>
 <tag name="name"/>

 <elementRule role="company" type="string" occurs="?"/>
 <tag name="company"/>

 <elementRule role="department" type="string" occurs="?"/>
 <tag name="department"/>

 <elementRule role="address">
  <tag/>
  <hedgeRef label="us_address"/>
 </elementRule>

 <elementRule role="phone" type="string">
  <tag/>
  <pattern value="[0-9]{3}\-[0-9]{3}\-[0-9]{4}"/>
 </elementRule>
```

LISTING C.2   CONTINUED

```
<elementRule role="fax" type="string">
 <tag/>
 <pattern value="[0-9]{3}\-[0-9]{3}\-[0-9]{4}"/>
</elementRule>

<elementRule role="cell" type="string">
 <tag/>
 <pattern value="[0-9]{3}\-[0-9]{3}\-[0-9]{4}"/>
</elementRule>

<elementRule role="pager" type="string">
 <tag/>
 <pattern value="[0-9]{3}\-[0-9]{3}\-[0-9]{4}"/>
</elementRule>

<elementRule role="email" type="string" occurs="?"/>
<tag name="email"/>

<hedgeRule label="us_address">
 <sequence>
  <elementRule role="address" type="string"/>
  <tag name="address"/>

  <elementRule role="address2" type="string" occurs="?"/>
  <tag name="address2"/>

  <elementRule role="city" type="string"/>
  <tag name="city"/>

  <elementRule role="state" type="string">
   <tag/>
   <enumeration value="AL"/>        <!--Alabama -->
   <enumeration value="AK"/>        <!--Alaska -->
   <enumeration value="AZ"/>        <!--Arizona -->
   <enumeration value="AR"/>        <!--Arkansas -->
   <enumeration value="CA"/>        <!--California -->
   <enumeration value="CO"/>        <!--Colorado -->
   <enumeration value="CT"/>        <!--Connecticut -->
   <enumeration value="DE"/>        <!--Delaware -->
   <enumeration value="FL"/>        <!--Florida -->
   <enumeration value="GA"/>        <!--Georgia -->
   <enumeration value="HI"/>        <!--Hawaii -->
   <enumeration value="ID"/>        <!--Idaho -->
   <enumeration value="IL"/>        <!--Illinois -->
   <enumeration value="IN"/>        <!--Indiana -->
   <enumeration value="IA"/>        <!--Iowa -->
   <enumeration value="KS"/>        <!--Kansas -->
   <enumeration value="KY"/>        <!--Kentucky -->
   <enumeration value="LA"/>        <!--Louisiana -->
   <enumeration value="ME"/>        <!--Maine -->
   <enumeration value="MD"/>        <!--Maryland -->
   <enumeration value="MA"/>        <!--Massachusetts -->
   <enumeration value="MI"/>        <!--Michigan -->
   <enumeration value="MN"/>        <!--Minnesota -->
   <enumeration value="MS"/>        <!--Mississippi -->
```

LISTING C.2 CONTINUED

```
      <enumeration value="MO"/>        <!--Missouri -->
      <enumeration value="MT"/>        <!--Montana -->
      <enumeration value="NE"/>        <!--Nebraska -->
      <enumeration value="NV"/>        <!--Nevada -->
      <enumeration value="NH"/>        <!--New Hampshire -->
      <enumeration value="NJ"/>        <!--New Jersey -->
      <enumeration value="NM"/>        <!--New Mexico -->
      <enumeration value="NY"/>        <!--New York -->
      <enumeration value="NC"/>        <!--North Carolina -->
      <enumeration value="ND"/>        <!--North Dakota -->
      <enumeration value="OH"/>        <!--Ohio -->
      <enumeration value="OK"/>        <!--Oklahoma -->
      <enumeration value="OR"/>        <!--Oregon -->
      <enumeration value="PA"/>        <!--Pennsylvania -->
      <enumeration value="RI"/>        <!--Rhode Island -->
      <enumeration value="SC"/>        <!--South Carolina -->
      <enumeration value="SD"/>        <!--South Dakota -->
      <enumeration value="TN"/>        <!--Tennessee -->
      <enumeration value="TX"/>        <!--Texas -->
      <enumeration value="UT"/>        <!--Utah -->
      <enumeration value="VT"/>        <!--Vermont -->
      <enumeration value="VA"/>        <!--Virginia -->
      <enumeration value="WA"/>        <!--Washington -->
      <enumeration value="DC"/>        <!--Washington,D.C. -->
      <enumeration value="WV"/>        <!--West Virginia -->
      <enumeration value="WI"/>        <!--Wisconsin -->
      <enumeration value="WY"/>        <!--Wyoming -->
    </elementRule>

    <elementRule role="zip" type="string">
     <tag/>
     <pattern value="[0-9]{5}(\-)?([0-9]{4})?"/>
    </elementRule>

   </sequence>
  </hedgeRule>

 </module>
```

CONCLUSION

RELAX is a viable alternative to XML Schema, especially if you are authoring simple documents which do not require the ability to create your own customized datatypes. And with an organization such as OASIS providing support for RELAX, it is a standard that is likely to become commonly used, even if not all applications support it.

The best recommendation about RELAX which can be made is to keep it in mind for your projects and watch as it continues to develop. OASIS recently announced a project to merge RELAX and TREX into a single standard called RELAX NG. As the technologies continue to evolve, RELAX NG will probably be the best alternative schema technology to consider.

SCHEMA ALTERNATIVES: SCHEMATRON

In this appendix

INTRODUCTION TO SCHEMATRON

Of all the "alternate" schema languages developed to address shortcomings in the XML Schema Recommendation, perhaps the most unique and innovative is Schematron.

The goal behind Schematron is not really to replace Schema, or to create an alternative schema language, but rather to provide a supplemental method for checking the validity of XML documents based on patterns, as opposed to grammars. The difference can be tremendously powerful, and allow for checking simply not possible with DTDs or XML Schema.

Lets say you had a system for number parts, and when a part was in stock, the part number started with "ST" but when an item was out of stock, the part number was listed as "XO". Something like this:

```
<item>
<stock>4</stock>
<part>ST4522</part>
</item>

<item>
<stock>0</stock>
<part>XO4588</part>
</item>
```

Now, using pattern matching with datatypes, you could create an XML Schema that would check to make sure that all part numbers began with either "ST" or "XO". But what you could not do would be to check to ensure that *if the* `<stock>` *element had a value of zero, then the* `<part>` *element had to start with* "XO". Schematron lets you do just that. It allows you to check an XML instance document for a pattern, and then validate the pattern based on some other condition.

Schematron was developed by Rick Jelliffe, and he maintains a site dedicated to the development of Schematron, located at

```
http://www.ascc.net/xml/resource/schematron/schematron.html
```

Schematron is also in the process of becoming an Open Source initiative, so there should be widespread support for Schematron for a long time to come.

XSLT AND XPATH

Schematron is built around the XSLT and XPath technologies, and the fact that Schematron is almost entirely based on the XML family of technologies is one of its strengths. In order to learn Schematron, you don't need to learn complicated new syntaxes, but instead you can apply XML core technologies that you will likely already be using in other aspects of XML development.

Let's look at how XSLT and XPath are used by Schematron. First, Schematron is really a set of XSLT meta-stylesheets. The process for using Schematron first involves authoring a

Schematron Schema. That Schema is then transformed using one of the Schematron XSLT Stylesheets. Then, the resulting stylesheet (the Schematron-transformed version of your original stylesheet) is applied to your XML document for validation.

On the Schematron site there are four XSLT Stylesheets that map out the functionality of Schematron:

- schematron-report
- schematron-basic
- schematron-message
- schematron-conformance

These four sheets implement the core of Schematron, and in fact, you can even modify them (if you are comfortable with XSLT and XPath) to customize your implementation of Schematron. All this makes it a very flexible and powerful Schema solution.

SCHEMATRON BASICS

Schematron is deceptively simple; the syntax is very straightforward and easy to learn, but that does not stop Schematron from being a very powerful alternative to XML Schema. There are only six core elements in Schematron:

- `<schema>`—This element denotes the Schematron Schema that is contained in the document, and also defines the namespace for the Schematron Schema.
- `<title>`—This element is optional, and is used to give your Schematron Schema a title.
- `<ns>`—This element is used to define namespaces, necessary for the XPath components, and for including other namespaces in your Schematron Schema.
- `<pattern>`—This element is used to establish a pattern, which will in turn contain the rules for validation.
- `<rule>`—A specific rule that is being applied to the XML instance in question.
- `<assert>`—A statement which is being asserted in relation to the selected context.
- `<report>`—A statement which is being reported in relation to the selected context.

Let's take a look at these elements in greater detail and see how they work in a Schematron Schema.

assert AND report

At the heart of Schematron are the `<assert>` and `<report>` elements. These are used to define assertions and reports, as they relate to a specific context in an XML instance document.

`<assert>`

First, let's take a look at assertions. Using `<assert>` we can apply a test to a selected node, and then if the test fails, we can return an error message. Basically the `assert` is a traditional boolean. For example, let's say that we wanted to check an element called `<employee>` for the presence of an `SSN` attribute for the employee's Social Security Number. We could use the following assertion:

`<assert test="@SSN">This employee's Social Security Number is missing!</assert>`

Now, within the proper rule and pattern (with the "employee" node selected), this assertion would check to see whether the `SSN` attribute was present. If the attribute was present, the assertion would be true, and therefore no action would be taken. However, if there was no `SSN` attribute then Schematron would generate the error "This employee's Social Security Number is missing!"

As you can see, this represents a great improvement over the error reporting of many XML processors. Rather than an "Attribute Expected" error, we can make use of the assertion to specify a plain-English error message that is very user-friendly.

`<report>`

At the other end of the spectrum is `<report>`. While `<assert>` checks a condition, and then issues an error if the condition is not met, `<report>` checks a condition, and issues an error if the condition is true. For example, we could check to see if the `SSN` attribute was *not* present:

`<report test="!@SSN">This employee's Social Security Number is Missing!</report>`

While we might use an `assert` to warn us if the e-mail address did not contain an "@" symbol, we can use `<report>` as a confirmation device, letting us know when the string is present.

Both elements take a similar form:

```
<assert test="Condition being tested">The message to report if false.</assert>
<report test="Condition being tested">The message to report if true.</report>
```

Those are the building blocks of Schematron, and the only two elements used for creating the rules of validation. The remaining elements deal with selecting the elements to be validated, and grouping. But already you can see how simple the most fundamental building blocks of Schematron are.

rule AND pattern

The basis of Schematron is to select a component in an XML document (an XPath node) and then to apply some rules to see whether the component matches them. Therefore, Schematron needs some mechanisms to group similar rules together, and those mechanisms are `<rule>` and `<pattern>`.

`<rule>`

`<rule>` is used to group together `<assert>` and `<report>` elements which are being applied to a single selected node. The `<rule>` element takes one attribute, context, which is used to select the context (as an XPath expression) for the assertion or report.

For example, let's look at our Social Security example. The element context we want to check is employee, because that is the element we want to test for the SSN attribute. So we can create a `<rule>` that looks like this:

```
<rule context="/employee">
 <assert test="@SSN">This employee's Social Security Number is missing!</assert>
</rule>
```

This defines a rule that is applied to the employee element. We can also create abstract rules which can then be referenced in other rules, using the abstract attribute and the `<extends>` element. For example, say we wanted to check many entries to make sure they did not contain an invalid symbol, such as the "@" sign. We could first define an abstract rule:

```
<rule abstract="true" id="symbolCheck">
 <report test="contains(.,'@')">Invalid symbol @ detected.</report>
</rule>
```

This creates an abstract rule, with an id of "symbolCheck", which we could then use in another rule:

```
<rule context="name">
 <extends rule="symbolCheck"/>
</rule>
```

Here we have included our previously defined rule by referencing its id. This allows you to create sets of common rules which can be easily reused throughout your Schematron Schema.

`<pattern>`

Now, we also need a mechanism for grouping together rules that are all part of the same pattern, which is where the `<pattern>` element comes in. For example, let's say we had the following instance document:

```
<name email="jdoe@myserver.com">John Doe</name>
```

And we want to test an e-mail address to make sure that it contained both an "@" symbol, and the letters ".gov" for a mailing list only going out to government employees.

We can create a pattern for testing the record for a name and e-mail address, and then also checking the e-mail address for validity. Here's what our pattern would look like:

```
<pattern name="EmailCheck">

 <rule context="name">
  <assert test="@email">This record does not have an associated email
➥address!</assert>
 </rule>

 <rule context="@email">
```

```
    <assert test="contains(.,'.gov')">Address does not contain .gov</assert>
  </rule>

</pattern>
```

Of course this is a simplified example, but it does illustrate how rules can be combined in patterns in order to create a more complex set of checks on XML instances. You do need to be careful about the order in which you apply rules within a `<pattern>`; rules are processed linearly, so order is important, as is the context of your XPath selections.

Integrating Schematron with XML Schema

Schematron Schema are contained in a `<schema>` element and may also contain an optional `<title>` element. However, there is one feature of Schematron's that is unique, and not possible with other Schema alternatives: the ability to include the Schematron Schema within the XML Schema.

This procedure involves nesting the Schematron Schema within the `<appinfo>` inside an `<annotation>` element. This allows Schematron-aware applications to easily access the Schematron Schema, because it is based on XSL Stylesheets, and therefore, is easily extracted by the parser when nested in the `<appinfo>` element.

A Schematron Example

Now let's take a look at some very basic Schematron examples. First, we are going to build a Schematron Schema that can be used in conjunction with an existing XML Schema, as outlined previously. So first we start with the `contact.xsd` schema shown in Listing D.1.

Listing D.1   The `contact.xsd` XML Schema Which Cannot Express Certain Validity Constraints

```xml
<?xml version="1.0" encoding="UTF-8" ?>
<xs:schema xmlns:xs="http://www.w3.org/2001/XMLSchema"
    xmlns:xsi="http://www.w3.org/2001/XMLSchema-Instance"
    targetNamespace="http://www.myserver.com/Contact"
    xmlns="http://www.myserver.com/Contact">

<!-- Define the types for the Contact Schema -->

<!-- Define the Contact type -->
<xs:complexType name="contact">
 <xs:element name="company" type="xs:string" minOccurs="0"/>
 <xs:element name="department" type="xs:string" minOccurs="0"/>
 <xs:element name="name" type="xs:string"/>
 <xs:element name="phone" type="phone_number"/>
 <xs:element name="fax" type="phone_number" minOccurs="0"/>
 <xs:element name="cell" type="phone_number" minOccurs="0"/>
 <xs:element name="pager" type="phone_number" minOccurs="0"/>
 <xs:element name="email" type="xs:string" minOccurs="0"/>
</xs:complexType>

<!-- Define the Address type -->
```

```
<xs:complexType name="address">
 <xs:sequence>
  <xs:element name="address" type="xs:string"/>
  <xs:element name="address2" type="xs:string" minOccurs="0"/>
  <xs:element name="city" type="xs:string"/>
  <xs:element name="state" type="state"/>
  <xs:element name="zip" type="zip"/>
 </xs:sequence>
</xs:complexType>

<!-- Define the State type -->
<!-- Long winded enumeration restricts state abbreviation values to valid
➥states -->
<xs:simpleType name="state">
 <xs:restriction base="xs:string">
  <xs:enumeration value="AL"/>       <!--Alabama -->
  <xs:enumeration value="AK"/>       <!--Alaska -->
  <!-- ETC -->
  <xs:enumeration value="WI"/>       <!--Wisconsin -->
  <xs:enumeration value="WY"/>       <!--Wyoming -->
 </xs:restriction>
</xs:simpleType>

<!-- Define the ZIP type -->
<xs:simpleType name="zip">
 <xs:restriction base="xs:string">
  <xs:pattern value="[0-9]{5}(\-)?([0-9]{4})?"/>
 </xs:restriction>
</xs:simpleType>

<!-- Define the Phone Number type -->
<xs:simpleType name="phone_number">
 <xs:restriction base="xs:string">
  <xs:pattern value="[0-9]{3}\-[0-9]{3}\-[0-9]{4}"/>
 </xs:restriction>
</xs:simpleType>

</xs:schema>
```

In order to make the existing Schema a little more robust, we are going to create a Schematron Schema that will check some of the data in our instance document to ensure that our document contains good data in our XML file. We will create rules to check

- <name> must not be empty.
- If a <company> is present, there must be a <department> listed.
- If there is no <phone>, there must be an <email> address.
- <email> must contain an @ symbol.
- If there is an <address2> there must be an <address>.

So, let's take a look at the patterns and rules we will use to build the Schematron Schema. First, we start with the <schema> element and the <title> element. In the <schema> element, we include the namespace declaration for the Schematron namespace:

```
<?xml version="1.0" encoding="UTF-8" ?>
<schema xmlns="http://www.ascc.net/xml/schematron">
<title>An Example Schematron Schema for a contact schema</title>
</schema>
```

Next, we are ready to move on to the pattern and rule in which we will check to see whether the <name> element is empty:

```
<pattern name="emptyCheck">
<rule context="contact">
 <assert test = "normalize-space(.)">The name element is empty!</assert>
</rule>
</pattern>
```

Here we use an assertion to check the element, and the error message will only be returned if the test is evaluated and turns up false.

Next, we make use of another assertion to check and make sure that our e-mail address contains an "@" symbol:

```
<pattern name="emailCheck">
 <rule context="email">
  <assert test="contains(.,'@')">Email address does not contain @.</assert>
 </rule>
</pattern>
```

Again, the error will be returned only if the e-mail address does not contain an @ symbol.

Finally, we create a pattern to check the relationships between the elements in an instance document, essentially creating some dependencies:

```
<pattern name="elementRelationships">
 <rule context="contact">
 </rule>
</pattern>
```

First, we use an assertion to test that the number of <company> and <department> elements are equal. This is because if there is a company listed, we must also have a departmental listing as well:

```
  <assert test="count(company) = count(department)">If a company is listed there
➥must also be a department.</assert>
```

Next, we test to make sure that for every <address2> element, we also have an <address> element. We do this by checking to make sure the number of <address2> elements does not exceed the count of <address> elements:

```
  <report test="address2/preceding-sibling::address">You must have a first address
➥line for each second.</report>
```

And finally, we test to make sure that there is either a <phone> element or an <email> element present, since we know we must have one or the other listed in our contact:

```
  <report test="count(phone) = 0 and count(email) = 0">The contact must have
➥either a phone or an email listed.</report>
```

When we bring all of these components together, we have a completed Schematron Schema. The final version of our Schematron Schema is shown in Listing D.2.

LISTING D.2   AN EXAMPLE OF A SCHEMATRON SCHEMA TO CHECK A CONTACT XML INSTANCE DOCUMENT, BASED ON THE contact.xsd **SCHEMA**

```xml
<?xml version="1.0" encoding="UTF-8" ?>
<schema xmlns="http://www.ascc.net/xml/schematron">
<title>An Example Schematron Schema for a contact schema</title>

<!-- The name element must not be empty -->
<pattern name="emptyCheck">
<rule context="contact">
 <assert test = "normalize-space(.)">The name element is empty!</assert>
</rule>
</pattern>

<!-- The email must contain an @ symbol -->
<pattern name="emailCheck">
 <rule context="email">
  <assert test="contains(.,'@')">Email address does not contain @.</assert>
 </rule>
</pattern>

<pattern name="elementRelationships">
 <rule context="contact">

  <!-- If a company is listed, there must also be a department -->
  <assert test="count(company) = count(department)">If a company is listed there
➥must also be a department.</assert>

  <!-- If there is a second address line, there must be a first -->
  <report test="address2/preceding-sibling::address">You must have a first
➥address line for each second.</report>

  <!-- If there is no phone listed, there must be an email -->
  <report test="count(phone) = 0 and count(email) = 0">The contact must have
➥either a phone or an email listed.</report>

 </rule>
</pattern>

</schema>
```

Finally, if we want to incorporate our new Schematron Schema into our existing contact.xsd, we can do this by nesting the Schematron Schema within the XML Schema.

As mentioned earlier, this is accomplished by using the <annotation> and the <appinfo> elements. Since we are now incorporating elements from the Schematron namespace, we will need to declare a prefix and use it within the document.

The results are shown in Listing D.3, which shows the fully integrated XML Schema contact.xsd complete with the Schematron Schema as well.

LISTING D.3 AN EXAMPLE OF A SCHEMATRON SCHEMA NESTED WITHIN THE `contact.xsd` **SCHEMA, USING THE** `<appinfo>` **ELEMENT IN AN ANNOTATION**

```xml
<?xml version="1.0" encoding="UTF-8" ?>
<xs:schema xmlns:xs="http://www.w3.org/2001/XMLSchema"
    xmlns:xsi="http://www.w3.org/2001/XMLSchema-Instance"
    xmlns:sch="http://www.ascc.net/xml/schematron">
    targetNamespace="http://www.myserver.com/Contact"
    xmlns="http://www.myserver.com/Contact">


<xs:annotation>
 <xs:appinfo>
  <?xml version="1.0" encoding="UTF-8" ?>
  <sch:schema xmlns:sch="http://www.ascc.net/xml/schematron">
   <sch:title>An Example Schematron Schema for a contact schema</sch:title>

   <!-- The name element must not be empty -->
   <sch:pattern name="emptyCheck">
    <sch:rule context="contact">
     <sch:assert test = "normalize-space(.)">The name element is
➥empty!</sch:assert>
    </sch:rule>
   </sch:pattern>

   <!-- The email must contain an @ symbol -->
   <sch:pattern name="emailCheck">
    <sch:rule context="email">
     <sch:assert test="contains(.,'@')">Email address does not
➥contain @.</sch:assert>
    </sch:rule>
   </sch:pattern>

   <sch:pattern name="elementRelationships">
    <sch:rule context="contact">

     <!-- If a company is listed, there must also be a department -->
     <sch:assert test="count(company) = count(department)">If a company is
➥listed there must also be a department.</sch:assert>

     <!-- If there is a second address line, there must be a first -->
     <sch:report test="address2/preceding-sibling::address">You must have a first
➥address line for each second.</sch:report>

     <!-- If there is no phone listed, there must be an email -->
     <sch:report test="count(phone) = 0 and count(email) = 0">The contact must
➥have either a phone or an email listed.</sch:report>

    </sch:rule>
   </sch:pattern>
  </sch:schema>
 </xs:appinfo>
</xs:annotation>

<!-- Define the types for the Contact Schema -->
```

LISTING D.3   CONTINUED

```
<!-- Define the Contact type -->
<xs:complexType name="contact">
 <xs:element name="company" type="xs:string" minOccurs="0"/>
 <xs:element name="department" type="xs:string" minOccurs="0"/>
 <xs:element name="name" type="xs:string"/>
 <xs:element name="phone" type="phone_number"/>
 <xs:element name="fax" type="phone_number" minOccurs="0"/>
 <xs:element name="cell" type="phone_number" minOccurs="0"/>
 <xs:element name="pager" type="phone_number" minOccurs="0"/>
 <xs:element name="email" type="xs:string" minOccurs="0"/>
</xs:complexType>

<!-- Define the Address type -->
<xs:complexType name="address">
 <xs:sequence>
  <xs:element name="address" type="xs:string"/>
  <xs:element name="address2" type="xs:string" minOccurs="0"/>
  <xs:element name="city" type="xs:string"/>
  <xs:element name="state" type="state"/>
  <xs:element name="zip" type="zip"/>
 </xs:sequence>
</xs:complexType>

<!-- Define the State type -->
<!-- Long winded enumeration restricts state abbreviation values to valid
➥states -->
<xs:simpleType name="state">
 <xs:restriction base="xs:string">
  <xs:enumeration value="AL"/>        <!--Alabama -->
  <xs:enumeration value="AK"/>        <!--Alaska -->
  <xs:enumeration value="AZ"/>        <!--Arizona -->
  <xs:enumeration value="AR"/>        <!--Arkansas -->
  <xs:enumeration value="CA"/>        <!--California -->
  <xs:enumeration value="CO"/>        <!--Colorado -->
  <xs:enumeration value="CT"/>        <!--Connecticut -->
  <xs:enumeration value="DE"/>        <!--Delaware -->
  <xs:enumeration value="FL"/>        <!--Florida -->
  <xs:enumeration value="GA"/>        <!--Georgia -->
  <xs:enumeration value="HI"/>        <!--Hawaii -->
  <xs:enumeration value="ID"/>        <!--Idaho -->
  <xs:enumeration value="IL"/>        <!--Illinois -->
  <xs:enumeration value="IN"/>        <!--Indiana -->
  <xs:enumeration value="IA"/>        <!--Iowa -->
  <xs:enumeration value="KS"/>        <!--Kansas -->
  <xs:enumeration value="KY"/>        <!--Kentucky -->
  <xs:enumeration value="LA"/>        <!--Louisiana -->
  <xs:enumeration value="ME"/>        <!--Maine -->
  <xs:enumeration value="MD"/>        <!--Maryland -->
  <xs:enumeration value="MA"/>        <!--Massachusetts -->
  <xs:enumeration value="MI"/>        <!--Michigan -->
  <xs:enumeration value="MN"/>        <!--Minnesota -->
  <xs:enumeration value="MS"/>        <!--Mississippi -->
  <xs:enumeration value="MO"/>        <!--Missouri -->
  <xs:enumeration value="MT"/>        <!--Montana -->
  <xs:enumeration value="NE"/>        <!--Nebraska -->
```

LISTING D.3   CONTINUED

```
<xs:enumeration value="NV"/>    <!--Nevada -->
<xs:enumeration value="NH"/>    <!--New Hampshire -->
<xs:enumeration value="NJ"/>    <!--New Jersey -->
<xs:enumeration value="NM"/>    <!--New Mexico -->
<xs:enumeration value="NY"/>    <!--New York -->
<xs:enumeration value="NC"/>    <!--North Carolina -->
<xs:enumeration value="ND"/>    <!--North Dakota -->
<xs:enumeration value="OH"/>    <!--Ohio -->
<xs:enumeration value="OK"/>    <!--Oklahoma -->
<xs:enumeration value="OR"/>    <!--Oregon -->
<xs:enumeration value="PA"/>    <!--Pennsylvania -->
<xs:enumeration value="RI"/>    <!--Rhode Island -->
<xs:enumeration value="SC"/>    <!--South Carolina -->
<xs:enumeration value="SD"/>    <!--South Dakota -->
<xs:enumeration value="TN"/>    <!--Tennessee -->
<xs:enumeration value="TX"/>    <!--Texas -->
<xs:enumeration value="UT"/>    <!--Utah -->
<xs:enumeration value="VT"/>    <!--Vermont -->
<xs:enumeration value="VA"/>    <!--Virginia -->
<xs:enumeration value="WA"/>    <!--Washington -->
<xs:enumeration value="DC"/>    <!--Washington,D.C. -->
<xs:enumeration value="WV"/>    <!--West Virginia -->
<xs:enumeration value="WI"/>    <!--Wisconsin -->
<xs:enumeration value="WY"/>    <!--Wyoming -->
 </xs:restriction>
</xs:simpleType>

<!-- Define the ZIP type -->
<xs:simpleType name="zip">
 <xs:restriction base="xs:string">
  <xs:pattern value="[0-9]{5}(\-)?([0-9]{4})?"/>
 </xs:restriction>
</xs:simpleType>

<!-- Define the Phone Number type -->
<xs:simpleType name="phone_number">
 <xs:restriction base="xs:string">
  <xs:pattern value="[0-9]{3}\-[0-9]{3}\-[0-9]{4}"/>
 </xs:restriction>
</xs:simpleType>

</xs:schema>
```

CONCLUSION

Schematron is unique in comparison to other Schema alternatives, because it can also easily be used to supplement the validation of existing XML Schema. When you take into account the power of Schematron, simple implementation, the ease of integration with existing XML Schema, and the fact that it is an Open Source initiative, it quickly becomes obvious that Schematron is a winning technology. However, Schematron is not for all applications, and many users will not need the extra validation capabilities Schematron provides. However, if you do, Schematron is an excellent choice.

INDEX

E

Z

Hey, you've got enough worries.

Don't let IT training be one of them.

InformIT

Get on the fast track to IT training at InformIT,
your total Information Technology training network.

InformIT | **www.informit.com** | **QUE**®

■ Hundreds of timely articles on dozens of topics ■ Discounts on IT books
from all our publishing partners, including Que Publishing ■ Free, unabridged
books from the InformIT Free Library ■ "Expert Q&A"—our live, online chat
with IT experts ■ Faster, easier certification and training from our Web- or
classroom-based training programs ■ Current IT news ■ Software downloads
■ Career-enhancing resources